Viking Age
Denmark

Viking Age Denmark

Else Roesdahl

translated by
Susan Margeson
and
Kirsten Williams

A Colonnade Book

Published by British Museum Publications Ltd

Colonnade books
are published by British Museum Publications Ltd
and are offered as contributions to the enjoyment,
study and understanding of art,
archaeology and history.
The same publishers also produce the official
publications of the British Museum.

British Library Cataloguing in Publication Data
  Roesdahl, Else
    Viking age Denmark.—(A Colonnade book)
    1. Vikings 2. Denmark—Social life and customs
    I. Title II. Danmarks Vikingetid. *English*
    948.9′01   DL133
ISBN 0 7141 8027 0
Published by British Museum Publications Limited,
46 Bloomsbury Street, London WC1B 3QQ
Designed by Brian Paine
Set in 10 on 12pt Monophoto Plantin 110 by
Northumberland Press Ltd,
Gateshead, Tyne and Wear
and printed in Great Britain by
Fletcher and Son Ltd, Norwich

Contents

To my parents

Foreword

I should like to offer my warmest thanks to the many who have helped with this book—many more than are named here. Above all I thank David Wilson who encouraged me to write it and furthermore read the whole manuscript and suggested a great many improvements. In addition I should like to thank Sue Margeson and Kirsten Williams warmly for the very careful translation and their many useful comments, and Peter Foote for kind help in many ways. I am also grateful to Orla Svendsen for his drawings, and to Celia Clear for all her co-operation in the book's production. Many have let me use as yet unpublished material and have assisted with illustrations or with other specific problems, as will be clear from the notes. Special thanks to Mogens Bencard, Torben Grøngård Jeppesen, Steen Hvass, Niels Lund, Kurt Schietzel, Mogens Schou Jørgensen and Stine Wiell. Nor would the book have come into being without many years of discussions with, and inspiration from, Erik Moltke and Olaf Olsen. Sigrid Fallingborg, Lene Larsen and Jytte Olsson have assisted me with the typing. The Danish Research Council for the Humanities and the Ministry of Culture gave financial help for travelling. Little 'Styrbjørn' played rather a special role. He kept me company during the writing of much of the book, and put off his arrival until it was almost finished.

Århus, June 1980   E.R.

Fig. 1 *Map of Denmark.*

1 Introduction: Denmark's Viking Age

The Viking Age can be seen today in a clearer light than ever before, not only because much new information has emerged but also because interest in this dramatic period has increased phenomenally in recent years.

This interest is at present giving rise to a stream of books treating in different ways various aspects of the period in a single country, in Scandinavia or in the whole great Viking world. The purpose of this book is to define important features and developments of the Viking Age in Denmark and to put them in their context: to describe the domestic background to the great adventures in foreign lands and to investigate what actually happened at home and abroad. The people of the Viking Age were evidently far more than their conventional portrayal as mere pillagers. They laid the foundations of the society we know today and they had a deeply original culture.

My account is based on sources relating particularly to Denmark or the Danes. Further information about the material on which the book is based can be obtained from the notes and from the list of sources. Material from the rest of Scandinavia is only discussed briefly since it has more bearing on its place of origin than on Denmark. For although a Scandinavian could make himself understood throughout the whole of the mighty Northern World during the Viking Age, and although the separate countries had strong cultural similarities, there were nevertheless great differences between them. These were determined in part by widely differing natural conditions which (to some extent) resulted in different occupations, and in part by the varying foreign contacts the countries owed to their geographical positions. Sweden looks east and south, Norway looks west, and Denmark in the south has always had connections—and problems—with its southern neighbours.

Denmark here means Viking Age Denmark (fig. 1), with the ramparts of the Danevirke and the river Eider in the north of modern Germany as its southern border. To the east the country included Skåne and Halland, now in Sweden. In these regions of Germany and Sweden once in Denmark, emphasis will be placed for the most part on the towns of Hedeby and Lund and on the Danevirke. Apart from these, I will concentrate on what is now Denmark, but ignore the Faeroes and Greenland because their chief links were with Norway and Iceland during the

Viking Age and the Middle Ages. Outside Scandinavia only those regions will be discussed with which Danish Vikings had particular contact and in which they settled, and the most important results of the research in progress there will be summarised. I have kept the nomenclature 'Vikings' and 'Viking Age', by now generally accepted, even though they give a somewhat one-sided view both of the Scandinavians and of the period. For the word Viking really means 'one who fights at sea', or 'pirate' (Old Norse *vikingr*) or 'war foray by sea' or 'harrying' (Old Norse *viking*).

It is traditional to regard the Viking Age as spanning *c.* 800–1050. To be precise its inception is usually taken to be the year 793 when, to the great consternation of the Christian world, the Vikings sacked the famous monastery on Lindisfarne. This is a gross over-simplification however, for several of the works of engineering and the institutions characteristic of the Viking Age were already in existence by the mid eighth century. They appeared in Denmark by the end of the later Germanic Iron Age, *c.* 550–800, about which next to nothing is known. The oldest phase of the Danevirke was constructed in the year 737 or shortly after, and Ribe, Denmark's oldest town, can be traced back to the eighth century, as can several other settlements that flourished in the Viking Age. Agriculture seems to have expanded, and there were well-established contacts with Western Europe. Evidently there were events of decisive importance in Denmark in the eighth century.

The end of the Viking Age in Denmark has long been accepted as being about 1050, and with good reason. Elsewhere, the Viking Age lasted longer, in Ireland for instance into the following century, but the death of King Harthacnut in 1042 (after drinking at a wedding-feast) meant the end of a succession of Danish kings in England, the end of their North Sea empire, and the end of Denmark's dominating position in Scandinavia and the Baltic. A lengthy struggle with Norwegian contenders for the Danish crown followed, and at the same time aggressive Slav tribes from the south Baltic shores also created problems for Denmark. At this time many of the institutions and ideas characteristic of the Middle Ages were either well established or in process of vigorous development. The monarchy was engaged in increasing its areas of power, the Christian system of administration through bishoprics was expanding greatly, coinage was issued, and there were several towns. At the same time, and by way of contrast, Scandinavian art and several types of objects characteristic of the Viking Age were rapidly becoming outdated. European Romanesque styles became the main inspiration in art, and European culture in general played an ever-increasing role in the country, partly because of the international role and connections of churchmen. Cultural features once distinctively Scandinavian gradually became variants of a common European stock.

This book is based to a great extent on archaeological material. Other sources and the results achieved by other disciplines have, however, also been used. In the Viking Age, there appear for the first time in Denmark's history written sources that can contribute to an understanding of the developments and help to fill in the bare bones with flesh and blood.

They are few, however. As a rule they are also brief, often biased, difficult to understand and mostly foreign. Indigenous sources are largely confined to terse messages on rune stones and the quantity of written sources hardly increases at all, in contrast to the archaeological evidence, which has, of course, grown enormously and continues to do so. Written sources have, however, been reinterpreted many times and today the tendency is to interpret them if possible in the light of the archaeological sources. Seen in the right context, these can reveal much more than purely material aspects of Viking Age culture.

It used to be the other way round: the archaeologist's view of the Viking Age was largely dependent on that of the historians, and their view was, essentially, that Denmark (like the rest of Scandinavia) was a wild, vast, barbaric region which received all benefits and progress from the south. Its society was considered primitive and remote in comparison with the rest of Europe; its trade was thought to have been conducted by the diligent Frisians, its art slavishly subject to foreign impulses, its architecture not worth considering, its kings always weak, and Denmark generally in the shadow of the German kingdom. However, the many foreign accounts of successful Viking expeditions led to a rather grudging admission that the Vikings had a certain talent for war. Because of the existence of scaldic and eddaic verse, it was also necessary to ascribe to them a certain talent for poetry (not discussed in this book). Some degree of imagination and creativity had to be allowed them, and they were good sailors. Otherwise there was nothing much either positive or interesting to say about them.

In the light of recent archaeological finds and of more broadly based studies, this picture has been totally altered. In Denmark, the turning-point came with the excavation of Trelleborg in the 1930s and 1940s. The discovery of this immense fortress and the three similar ones in other parts of the country was staggering. For they clearly demonstrated a superior organisational ability and a high technical achievement quite incompatible with the notion of a primitive and barbarian Denmark. This made people rethink their old ideas, and since then more impressive pieces of engineering work have been demonstrated. Similarly, well-known structures like the Danevirke and the royal monuments at Jelling have been subjected to fresh investigation and revaluation. Viking Age art, buildings, hoards, graves, and many other features have been reconsidered with new vigour.

The Viking Age now becomes a period in which Denmark and the rest of Scandinavia, internally and externally, were marked by exceptional activity. The Northern peoples are seen to have been fertile in artistic, commercial and technical ideas, forceful in their impact on the outside world. The period left behind innumerable fascinating monuments in architecture, ornamental art, poetry and ships, as well as great deeds of exploration and adventure, some of which have made their effects felt to this day. We need only think of the vast numbers of Scandinavian loan-words in modern English or the many place-names that signify Nordic settlements in the British Isles and Normandy.

Though it took a long time, it has now been accepted that medieval historians' and writers' accounts of Viking Age heroes and their great deeds are to be regarded as fiction, examples of narrative art (sometimes of the highest standard), rather than historical records of events which took place several centuries earlier. 'Reality', so far as it appears in archaeological finds, sometimes illustrated by contemporary written sources and in a few cases by scaldic verse, may in fact seem no less exciting for all its substantiality. Who can fail to be stirred by the remains of the bridge across Ravning Enge near Jelling, a kilometre long and a thousand years old, by a perfectly executed ornament, by a grave whose occupant lies fully equipped for the journey to the Other World, or by the remains of a whole farm revealed under the soil? Seen in a wider context, such finds can also throw light on social matters, such as the division of society into classes, features of royal power, pagan religious beliefs, the transition to Christianity, the development of transport, trade associations and technology.

The most recent survey of all the archaeology of Denmark's Viking Age can be found in the second edition (1960) of Johannes Brøndsted's book *Danmarks Oldtid*, III. Since then, the archaeological evidence has greatly increased, as mentioned above, including many types of structures and objects hitherto unknown. The many new results are due in part to increased research based on traditional and well-established archaeological methods, but even more to new excavation techniques and new scientific dating methods. The most significant new method in excavation is the use of machines to uncover large areas quickly and cheaply. Clearing large areas is, after all, a prerequisite for obtaining information about the layout of farms and villages, for when the shovel was the chief tool, it was rarely possible to examine more than a couple of houses on a given site. At other sites very detailed and time-consuming methods have provided new information about the construction of houses, female burial-customs and much else. Underwater archaeology is also a relatively new technique. Wrecks can be examined in the water by divers, and wrecks in shallow water can be excavated in almost traditional fashion, once sheet piling has been erected and the water has been pumped out. This was done in Denmark for the first time in 1962 in Roskilde fjord—the reward was the five Skuldelev ships.

Dendrochronology is the most important new dating method. It entails measuring the widths of the year rings in a piece of timber and comparing them with those in another piece of known age. Given suitable conditions, this allows the precise year the first piece of timber was felled to be determined, and that means that the foundation of a structure can be reliably dated. By this method, for example, the oldest phase of the Danevirke has been dated to 737, the large bridge across Ravning Enge to about 979, and Trelleborg to the autumn of 980 or the spring of 981. Seen in a wider perspective, it is possible in the right circumstances to assign structures to the reign of a particular king and perhaps also to place them in a specific political context.

In C-14 dating, which has now been used for many years, the amount of radioactive carbon in the remains of plants and animals is measured. Such carbon is absorbed in organisms while alive but breaks down after

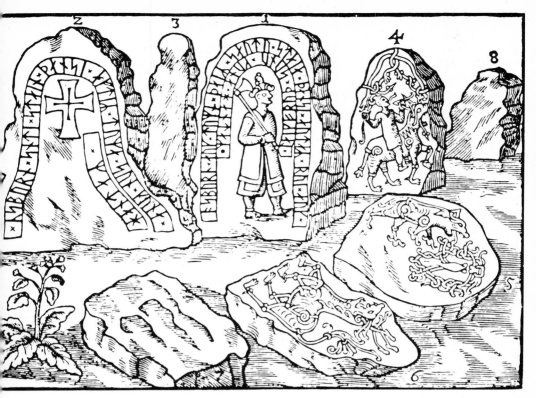

Fig. 2 *The Hunnestad monument in Skåne, as illustrated in Ole Worm's* Danicorum Monumentorum libri sex *of 1643. Only stones 1, 2 and 4 survive today.*

death. Dating arrived at by this method has a margin of uncertainty—in the case of the Viking Age usually ± 50 to 100 years—but in spite of this, the method is of great value in that it can be used in assessing the age of problematic objects or structures.

Recent co-operation between archaeologists, conservators, environmentalists, philologists and historians has also resulted in innovations. Finds are now usually conserved in such a way as to allow subsequent technical and scientific examination, for example to see what technique was involved in making an axe, or what type of wood was used in a knife-handle. Analysis of bones and plant and seed remains from excavations has supplied information on animal husbandry, cereal cultivation and diet, and sometimes on contacts with distant regions as well. Philological studies of place-names and personal names are still throwing light on such topics as the development of the settlement in Denmark and on Viking settlement abroad. Valuable and often tantalising information has been culled from runic inscriptions and scaldic verse, and, as mentioned above, historians now usually view their documentary and literary sources with due regard to the results of research in other disciplines.

This inter-disciplinary co-operation has introduced both Viking Age archaeologists and other scholars in the field to quite new approaches, and has contributed to the understanding of a number of structures and other finds which were previously merely recorded. Specialist historians and popular 'sociological' interests have prompted archaeologists to branch out into new areas such as systematic settlement archaeology and to ask new questions of their material, sometimes with astonishing answers. It should also be mentioned that reconstructions of ships, buildings and technical processes—as drawings, or as working replicas—have certainly contributed both to the increase of general interest in the technology of the age and also to a deepening of understanding. Indeed, one can say that the reconstructions are themselves an expression of this new interest and understanding. Finally, co-operation and exchange of ideas between countries has in recent years provided stimulation and new viewpoints, and an even broader background against which to evaluate the material.

However, we should not have got far in our new Viking Age studies without public interest in the past, evidenced by the popularity of radio and television programmes, lecture series, periodicals and books. An important reason for this interest in Scandinavia must, it seems, be a search for 'roots' and preferably roots capable of instilling pride and fostering imagination. In many ways, the Viking Age can do just this.

Finally it must be emphasised that, although much more about the Viking Age is known in 1980 even than in 1970, an immense number of problems remain, both unsolved and insoluble. Since a millennium has intervened, only a fraction of what the period left has actually survived (fig. 2), and much of it still lies underground or underwater. Yet no one knows what the future will bring in the way of new methods, new epoch-making archaeological finds, new investigations which may revolutionise our interpretation of particular aspects of the period. It is one of the most fascinating things about archaeology that we can always embark on new 'voyages of discovery' and find fresh fields of learning to conquer. It also means that it will not be many years before at least some parts of every book on the Viking Age will be outdated.

2 The Country and the People

COUNTRY AND PEOPLE

Scattered references in written sources of the ninth century—in particular the Frankish annals, the *Life* of the missionary Ansgar, and the supplement by King Alfred of Wessex to his translation of Orosius' *History of the World*—give us to understand that Denmark was then already united under one king and that its boundaries were more or less those it was to keep right down to 1658, the year when Skåne and the other provinces east of Øresund were ceded to Sweden. Much later again, in 1864, the old southern border was moved north, when South Jutland was lost to Prussia, and only the most northerly part of this region was restored to Denmark by the border adjustment of 1920. Present-day Denmark is thus considerably smaller than the Denmark of the Viking Age (fig. 1).

Viking Age Denmark comprised the Jutland peninsula north of the river Eider, with Saxons, Frisians and various Slav tribes (fig. 39) as neighbours to the south; and the islands of Fyn, Sjælland (Zealand) and about five hundred more of varying size, as well as Skåne and Halland (now South Sweden). The island of Bornholm had a king of its own *c*. 890, and the present Swedish province of Blekinge (east of Skåne) belonged to the *Svear*, although about the middle of the eleventh century, when a border-treaty was made between Denmark and Sweden, it was regarded as Danish. Great local variations undoubtedly existed and at times conflict between the various regions and between the pretenders to the throne. From time to time this led to a division of Denmark into several kingdoms, just as it did in the twelfth century for example. But there is no doubt that almost all of what we know as medieval Denmark was already considered one realm at the beginning of the Viking Age— we also know the names of some of the kings. But it is uncertain when the country was first united.[1]

The 'Danes' as the name of a people is first mentioned in Jordanes' *Getica*, written in Constantinople around the year 550. People with this name have lived on Danish territory ever since, but their origins are lost in the mists of time. We do not know whether the Danes were new conquerors when Jordanes wrote or whether they had long lived in Jutland and the islands. In any case, by the beginning of the Viking Age, their claim to the lands they lived in was certainly long established.[2]

The realm with its many islands is the key to the Baltic (fig. 51). The waters connecting these islands—Kattegat, Øresund, the Great Belt (Store Bælt), the Little Belt (Lille Bælt), and the Baltic Sea itself—are comparatively sheltered and the ships of the period could sail comfortably in them in most weathers. One could also sail almost anywhere in the kingdom without losing sight of land, and a passage across open sea—between Århus in Jutland and North Sjælland for example—was no great venture. In addition, rivers, fjords and bays cut deep into the country on all sides, giving access to the interior, and in good weather one could run ships in to the shore nearly everywhere. There are also many well-protected natural harbours. Land transport did not present great difficulties either, for Denmark is a flat country; its highest point at present is a mere 173 m above sea-level. From ancient times the Army Road (Hærvej) or Ox Road ran up through the middle of Jutland, and there were, of course, many other roads. Communication within and between the various regions was thus comparatively easy. This was a vital precondition for this early formation of the kingdom.

The land-surface of Denmark is almost entirely shaped by glaciation. During the last Ice Age only the eastern part of the country—roughly to a line from Bulbjerg (north of Limfjord) across Viborg and down through the centre of Jutland—was covered by ice, and essentially it is the varied circumstances of its melting which are responsible for the present forms of the Danish landscape and for its surface deposits. East Jutland and the rest of eastern Denmark is primarily covered by fertile clay- (and in small areas sand-) moraines, but West Jutland consists largely of poor gravel and sandy heath-land, surrounding the higher moraines of the earlier Ice Ages, the 'hill islands'.[3]

Pl. 1 *Detail of br brooch with male head.*

The country lies in the temperate zone and today has a comparatively mild climate. It is in a border area between Atlantic and Continental climates, so that the winters are usually fairly mild, while the summers can be hot. Between 1931 and 1960 the average temperature in the coldest month of the year, February, was $-0.4°C$ and in the hottest month, July, $+16.6°C$. The lowest recorded temperature is $-31°C$ in January 1942, while the highest recorded is 36.4 °C in August 1975. The country also lies in the temperate deciduous forest belt but close to the border of the coniferous belt. In 1965, 70.2 per cent of present-day Denmark was utilised for agriculture and market-gardening.[4]

The relationship of the natural environment and climate of Viking Age Denmark with today's is, however, unclear. The coast-lines are not quite the same, mainly because the sea-level varies and also because the country tilts on an axis running south-east/north-west, which means that the south-western part of the country is sinking while the eastern part is slowly rising. Sea-erosion, the activities of tides and currents, sand-drift and so on have also affected the appearance of the coasts. There are further man-made alterations, especially by reclamation of land. We have only sparse information about the situation in the Viking Age, but the changes may be considerable. In Langballigau, north of Hedeby, the present coast-line apparently lies about 80 cm higher than it did a thousand years ago. The west of Jutland, north of Limfjord, was in all probability a series of islands in the Viking Age, and the coast-line was certainly much more indented than it is now. Recent investigations in the harbour area at Hedeby will soon give more precise information about conditions there. The water-level has risen considerably.[5]

The alterations in the interior of the country since the Viking Age are due to human activity in particular. Vast areas of meadow and bog have been drained and there has been widespread cultivation for centuries, so the actual appearance of the realm in the Viking Age is not known. The archaeological material is too scattered and too incidental to show which areas were inhabited or cultivated, and which were covered by forest or unused for other reasons.[6] Nor have there been many scientific studies of these problems,[7] and the early descriptions by foreign travellers are not always quite reliable. This is also true of the oft-quoted description of the Nordic and Baltic regions, written about 1070 by the German cleric Adam of Bremen. Part of it is clearly far removed from reality. But as one of Adam's informants was the Danish king Svein Estridsson (1047–74), one can presumably trust some of it.[8] It is, however, impossible to believe him when he says that in Jutland 'hardly a cultivated spot is to be found anywhere, scarcely a place fit for human habitation', for much of Jutland, especially the eastern part, is just as fertile as the islands, while in central and West Jutland—for example around the waterways—there are large areas of good meadow land eminently suitable for pasture. Besides, archaeology shows that there were many Viking Age settlements in Jutland and a large number of place-names there originated in this period and earlier. Adam does continue, however, 'but wherever there is an arm of the sea it has very large cities'. Fyn is described in much more positive terms and 'small islands encircle it, all abounding in crops'. Even better is Sjælland, 'which is very celebrated as much for the bravery of its men as for the abundance of its crops', and here lies Roskilde, 'the seat of Danish royalty'. But Skåne 'is the province of Denmark fairest to look upon . . . opulent of crops, rich in merchandise, and now full of churches'.[9] It may be the last point which endeared Skåne in particular to Adam, the cleric. We are probably best informed about Viking Age settlement by the many place-names originating in this period and earlier (even though a settlement with such a name will not necessarily have remained on exactly the same site ever since). Various archaeological finds and some scientific investigations correspondingly seem to indicate that a large part of the country—in Jutland too—was broken for cultivation in the Viking Age and that this process continued through the early Middle Ages. This opening-up of the country in the Viking Age took place after a period of increased growth in forest and vegetation in the later Germanic Iron Age, which had meant a reduction of the cultivated area.

These points are discussed in more detail later (ch. 4) and here mention need only be made of some studies on forestation and the use of timber. Analysis of timbers and pieces of wood, especially from Hedeby (founded in the eighth century) and from Lund (founded c. AD 1000) show that the demand for wood in these towns helped to open up the landscape around them and to alter its vegetation.[10] In both places there was an enormous consumption of oak. About half the numerous samples of wood so far examined are oak, and in other settlements, too, where the species of wood have been examined, we find a great preponderance of oak, though the number of samples analysed is in general fairly small.[11] In the eleventh century the timber in Lund came both from free-standing oaks, which must have been growing on park-like commons, and from forest trees. But in the period from about 1150 to 1350, all the oak found in Lund and elsewhere in south-west Skåne apparently came from free-standing trees or smaller groves. This suggests that Skåne's open, unforested landscape was created in this period. Many medieval wood-samples from Svendborg on Fyn have also been examined, and these show that use of oak was greatly diminished compared with its use in Viking Age Lund and Hedeby.[12] The probable explanation is that the old natural forests of oak, ash, lime and so on largely disappeared during the Viking Age and early Middle Ages—at least in the neighbourhood of towns. Oak forests were felled for buildings, ships and so on; foliage and twigs were used for animal fodder, and grazing animals prevented new growth. Added to this there was deliberate clearing to provide more arable land. In less severely exploited areas, however, it was possible for beech forest to spread, as beech needs slightly different growing conditions from oak. The advance of beech at the expense of oak is thus primarily due to human interference, and the ruthless exploitation of oak in Viking times goes some way to explain why beech forest is the typical woodland of Denmark today.[13]

Sources on climatic conditions of the Viking Age are scarce and often difficult to interpret. Quite simply, very little is known about possible variations in comparison with today's. Investigations of Danish raised bogs do, however, indicate that during recent millennia the climate has changed in cycles of about 260 years. Thus, changes of climate to colder and/or wetter conditions have been recorded around c. AD 500, AD 1000, AD 1300 and so on. But at the beginning of the Viking Age, around the year 750, no such changes have been observed. It is, however, difficult at present to judge the extent of these changes and their consequences for the Viking Age.[14] But there can be no doubt that agriculture was then the all-predominant occupation, just as it remained until quite recently.

The size of the population in the Viking Age is difficult to determine. The population in the thirteenth century is cautiously estimated at about one million. Reckoning on an increase in population in the intervening centuries comparable to that in Western Europe, it is further estimated that at the end of the Viking Age there were over 700,000 inhabitants.[15] One may at any rate guess that the figure was between half a million and a million.

Skeletal remains indicate that the people of the Viking Age were comparatively tall. The average height in Hedeby (on the basis of thirty-one skeletons) was 165.6 cm or 169.1 cm for men, and 157.6 cm or 154.5 cm for women (the variant figures are due to different methods of measurement). A similar quantity of other Danish remains has yielded slightly higher figures: about 170 cm for men and about 160 cm for women.

Pl. 2 *Gold gamin piece. May originally have be fixed to a base. Ha and garments indicate that it represents a woma Height 1.95 cm.*

These correspond well with those derived from skeletons from Viking Age Lund (men 171.0 cm and women 160.2 cm), and with other material from Hedeby, where fourteen or fifteen male skeletons gave an average 168.4 cm or 171.2 cm, and four female skeletons an average 165 cm or 168 cm, which is no mean height![16]

We may compare the average height (168.5 cm) of 28,000 twenty to twenty-two year old conscripts in Schleswig-Holstein measured in 1876–80. The average Danish male was about the same height at that time,[17] but in 1977 the average height of Danish conscripts was 179.3 cm.[18] It must be remembered, however, that relatively few measurable skeletons are known from the Viking Age in Denmark, that methods of calculation vary, and finally that a person's height depends, among other things, on diet and thus on social circumstances. The average height of the upper class was doubtless something over that of poor agricultural workers and slaves. We may also note that some people were very tall even by today's standards. A man of about twenty-five buried in a chamber-grave in the Stengade II cemetery on Langeland was about 193 cm tall; a slave of thirty to thirty-five was killed to keep him company and his height was about 174 cm.[19]

Dental decay is among the few diseases which may be recognised in skeletons, but is rather rarely seen. However, teeth are often badly worn because of tough and gravelly food.[20] Causes of death can rarely be determined, but occasionally unhealed injuries from weapons have been identified and in some cases these wounds may have been mortal.[21] No average life-span can be calculated because infant mortality must have been great, though graves of infants rarely occur in the cemeteries of the period. Investigations (though not based on a particularly large sample) indicate, however, that a little over half of those who reached the age of fourteen or fifteen would be dead before their fortieth birthday. Most of these would be women, undoubtedly because of the hazards of childbirth. Most others would be dead before they were sixty, but some men and women did survive much longer.[22]

We know little about the treatment of disease and medicinal cures, but some people undoubtedly possessed great knowledge of healing and many more or less efficacious medicinal herbs must have been known.[23] Henbane in moderate doses has pain-killing effects and the oldest finds of this plant in Denmark are from a woman's grave at the fortress of Fyrkat. But the plant also has euphoric effects and can be used as a poison.[24] The death-cap mushroom may also have been eaten by the so-called berserks to induce a state of frenzy which gave them enormous strength; they became insensible to pain and behaved like wild animals. Several other plants with euphoric effects were known and were presumably used—also by people wishing to establish contact with the supernatural.[25]

The personal names and naming customs of the age are quite well documented, for more than two hundred different names are known from Danish inscriptions (on rune stones and other objects). In addition we have information from foreign sources and from the many Viking Age place-names which are compounded with personal names, both in

Denmark and in the Danish colonies in England and Normandy.

It was thus common to call children after dead kinsmen, for example a maternal or paternal grandfather, and names compounded with the name of the god Thor were very common (in contrast to pre-Viking times). About a quarter of the people in Danish Viking Age inscriptions had such names, and names of the same type occur frequently in the widespread place-names compounded with -*torp*. There are also examples of nicknames of various kinds derived from appearance, intellectual or physical skills, features of character, place of origin and so on, and there are many pet-names or abbreviated names. A selection of masculine and feminine names still in common Danish use is (in modern orthography) Thorkild, Thorsten, Troels, Bjørn, Erik, Gunnar, Arne, Karl, Gorm, Harald, Svend, Knud; Thora, Thyra, Tove, Gunhild, Ragnhild, Åse. Foreign contacts, especially with England, are reflected to some extent in the surviving names, and after the conversion to Christianity many biblical and saints' names were gradually introduced. But these belong chiefly to the Middle Ages.[26]

WRITING

The art of writing was known in the North by about AD 200 and perhaps even earlier. But it was probably not until the Viking Age that it became widespread. The letters—runes—were originally modelled on one or more Mediterranean alphabets. They were chiefly designed to be cut in wood, not to be written with pen and ink on parchment. For this reason most runes are formed by vertical or diagonal lines, while horizontal strokes do not occur—these might easily coincide with the grain of the wood and make letters difficult to read.

When and where runes were invented we do not know. Originally there were twenty-four characters and they were used over the entire Germanic area. Around the beginning of the Viking Age, however, a simplification of the runic alphabet (the *Futhark*, after the first six characters) took place in Scandinavia which reduced it to sixteen characters and provided a distinct Scandinavian script. This occurs in two main

Fig. 3 *The Futhark (runic alphabet) with 'normal' or 'Danish' runes.*

types: 'normal' or 'Danish' runes (fig. 3), and 'short-branch' or 'Swedish–Norwegian' runes. The latter are characterised by fewer and mostly shorter 'branches' on the vertical staves—sometimes produced by a deep stab with the knife-point—and some letters only consist of half a stave (i.e. in comparison with the 'normal' runes). Some scholars think that the two types of the sixteen-symbol series are the result of different local developments. But the 'Danish' runes also occur outside Denmark and the 'Swedish–Norwegian' outside Sweden and Norway (for example in Hedeby and in other international trade centres), and there are also differences in writing techniques between the types. These factors have led other scholars to think that the two types were known and used side by side over large areas, so that the 'normal' or 'Danish' runes were primarily used epigraphically for inscriptions on stones while the 'short-branch' or 'Swedish–Norwegian' runes were used particularly for everyday notes. They were quicker to write and so possibly also the ones preferred by traders.[27]

Runic inscriptions can occur on all kinds of objects wherever such characters can be cut, scratched, or chiselled, and they appear on many materials: wood, bone, antler, metal, stone—even on a piece of human skull. As metal and stone normally survive better than wood, bone or antler, there are many more examples of inscriptions on these materials. First and foremost there are the rune stones: stones raised by one or more persons as a memorial to one or more other persons, or perhaps (very rarely in Denmark) to the raiser of the stone himself.

Some 182 rune stones are known from Viking Age Denmark, including the ones which have disappeared but about which information is extant (cf. fig. 2).[28] An immense number must have been destroyed without leaving any trace. Churches, roads, embankments and other building works have taken their toll throughout the ages. Rune stones were presumably erected all through the Viking Age, but most of the Danish ones are from the middle and second half of the tenth century and the beginning of the eleventh. Thereafter the custom largely died out in Denmark (apart from Bornholm), but it continued vigorously in Sweden, where by far the greatest number of rune stones date from the eleventh century. In spite of their brevity, the inscriptions give much important information about the culture of the age. We learn most about names and language from them, but quite frequently they also record the position in society of the dead man or characterise him, and perhaps also the stone-raiser, in some other way. They tell of great deeds, for example, or of the place where the dead man lost his life, or of his kin. King Harald Bluetooth's great rune stone at Jelling—the grandest runic monument anywhere (pls. 35 and 42)—also uniquely conveys a political message. Although only a few rune stones remain on their original site today, most must in their time have been raised by the public highway or in other places where there were many passers-by. For they were commemorative stones, meant to be seen and read by many—and they presuppose that quite a lot of people were able to read, at least among the well-to-do who had the rune stones erected.

However, the art of writing and reading must, it seems, have been fairly widespread in the Viking Age, even outside these more affluent circles—at any rate in towns and trading-centres. As mentioned above, runes may appear on any kind of object, and there is a fair number of runic inscriptions on stray objects from the Viking Age towns. Such an inscription may give the name of the owner, for example, or of the person who manufactured the object, or both. It may also have a magical function, or the inscription may be an obvious enough label, as when *kąbr* (= comb) is written on a comb. The *Futhark* itself appears quite frequently too. Then there are large numbers of inscriptions which cannot be interpreted, partly because of bad preservation, partly because our knowledge of the language of the times is imperfect, partly because the rune-carvers sometimes miswrote, and partly because a runic alphabet of only sixteen characters means ambiguity, when a single rune has several possible phonemic values (e.g. the u-rune may stand for all the vowels conventionally written u, o, ö, y, and the semivowel v). Finally, some inscriptions that seem to have had a magical purpose are today quite incomprehensible. Other inscriptions simply consist of casually scratched runes which were never intended to mean anything.

In recent years a completely new and very important group of runic inscriptions has come to light: runic correspondence. Extensive excavations in Bergen in Norway have uncovered a large number of medieval rune sticks, of varying dimensions and cut to various shapes, some of them with messages and even long letters on them. They include trade documents, military and political plans, personal messages. In West Norse such a rune stick was called a *rúnakefli*. A few years ago a couple more were found in Hedeby, both from the ninth century and written in 'short-branch' runes. One contains a *Futhark* but the rest of it cannot be

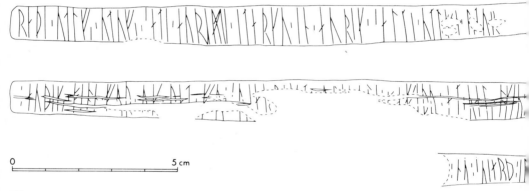

Fig. 4 *Runic letter inscribed on a stick found at Hedeby. These runes are the 'short-branch' or 'Swedish–Norwegian' runes.*

interpreted. The other (fig. 4) is apparently a real letter or document which concerns a transaction by barter between two named men. The runes are however badly preserved and the inscription is not fully understood. The stick itself, cut square and inscribed on three sides, is 16.2 cm long and about 1.4 cm across. When one considers the insignificant size of such a stick, and how many bits of wood turn up in the Hedeby excavations, and elsewhere where wood has survived, it is not surprising that rune sticks were only found in Hedeby when experience from Bergen had taught the excavators what to look for.[29]

The second Hedeby rune stick shows in particular that runes already had their function in everyday life at the beginning of the Viking Age— and that quite a number of people must have been able to use them. There is also a foreign ninth-century source which refers to a written message, no doubt a rune stick. In his account of the missionary Ansgar, Rimbert tells that, when Ansgar left the great Swedish town of Birka in 831, he brought for Emperor Louis the Pious evidence of the accomplishment of his mission written by King Björn 'by his own hand with letters formed according to their custom' (*cum litteris regia manu more ipsorum deformatis*).[30]

The Norwegian runologist Aslak Liestøl, who has worked on the rune sticks from both Bergen and Hedeby, expresses the following opinion of the art of reading and writing amongst the Vikings:

> I am not trying to conjure up a picture of the literate Viking as a bookworm—a kind of library Viking, complete with desk and files. The advantage of runes was that one was independent of desk, ink and pen, nor was there any need for special protection of the writing materials or the finished documents from frost and rain. The Viking skilled in runes had at his disposal a means of communication with people far away and a means of documentation. Runes enabled him to jot down whatever notes he needed should his memory fail him— in fact, he could write whatever circumstances might require him to. All he needed was a knife to cut a twig from the nearest tree. And surely this is how he must have used his accomplishments: he wrote messages, he made notes of agreements and arrangements, and he wrote down any verse which appealed to him so much that he did not want to risk forgetting it.[31]

Runes were widely known until well into the Middle Ages, but exactly how extensive their use was in Denmark in that period is uncertain. With the introduction of Christianity *c*. 960 and increasing influence from Western Europe, official Denmark apparently went over fairly quickly to the Latin alphabet, and documents and official inscriptions were generally composed in Latin. The oldest coin legends (from the 990s) thus use Latin letters and it is quite exceptional to find among the coinage of Svein Estridsson (ruled 1047–74) a series with the legend in runes. Denmark's oldest known document, St Cnut's deed of gift in 1085 to St Lawrence's in Lund, was written in Latin and in Latin script, with the new materials of pen and ink on parchment, and its legality was guaranteed by the royal seal—all according to European custom.[32]

SOCIETY

In older accounts of Viking Age history, society is sometimes described as a democracy where free farmers met at the assembly and made democratic decisions on public affairs, and where the king was *primus inter pares* ('first among peers'), in the words of a Frankish source. The king may have had this status on expeditions abroad, and theoretically perhaps at home too, for policy decisions and laws had to be accepted at the assemblies until well into the Middle Ages. But Viking Age society certainly did not consist wholly of *pares*, equals, and important decisions were doubtless made in reality by a relatively small upper class, members of particular kinship groups. Their power was based on large land-holdings and their primary loyalty was to their own kindred.

Both written and archaeological sources can throw some light on the social structure of the Viking Age. There are foreign sources—annals, chronicles, travel descriptions, the lives of famous men, charters and

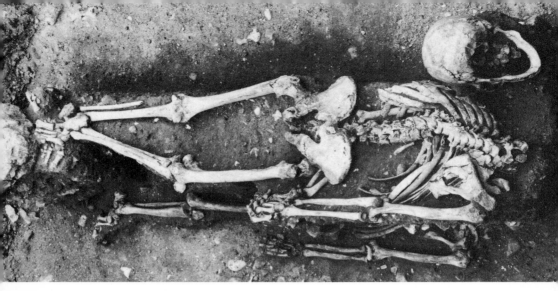

Pl. 3 *Double grave from Lejre. The uppermost body was beheaded; it was most likely that of a slave who had to accompany his master in death.*

decrees—and scanty native sources, particularly the rune stones. There are also sources written after the Viking Age was over, but these must be used with great caution since in many cases it is quite uncertain how society developed in the intervening period. Among archaeological sources are cemeteries and graves, their arrangement and furnishings, and memorials to the dead, along with farms, villages, fortresses and hoards, jewellery and much else. For it is obvious that not just anybody was able to build the great fortresses (fig. 40) or own the silver ornament from Nonnebakken (pl. 41) or the sword from Bustorf (fig. 49), to cite just a few examples. The sources do not, however, allow us to draw a very clear picture of society, and what follows is no more than a rough sketch, largely based on information from rune stones. More details will emerge in the following chapters and further information about the evidence of written sources can be obtained from specialist literature.[33]

The peak of society was represented by the king and his family and by other great landowners—undoubtedly proud, well-nourished, well-dressed people with a certain fixed set of moral standards and rules for good behaviour. At the bottom were the slaves, and the born slaves were probably often marked by deficiency diseases and bad living conditions generally, and their attitudes and behaviour were naturally rather different from those of the great men.

Slaves have been much written about in recent years, but really there is not much factual information about them from the Danish Viking Age. Archaeological evidence is confined to a few graves containing skeletons of two people, one of whom, no doubt a slave, had been killed in order to accompany the other in the grave (pl. 3).[34] In addition we know a single rune stone which a freed slave raised in memory of his former master.[35] There are also scattered references in foreign sources, including mention of slaves in Hedeby. But, as slaves cannot be expected to leave particularly marked traces in the extant sources, the sparse information tells us no more than that slaves existed in Denmark. It tells us nothing about their number, which may well have been large. Foreign sources show clearly that Vikings took many captives on their expeditions and that slaves were a valuable and sought-after commodity on the European markets. Around 1070, Adam of Bremen also relates that the people of Sjælland paid tax to the Danish king in return for permission to plunder other Baltic peoples, but that instead they often captured compatriots and sold them. Perhaps a large number of captives in fact ended up in Denmark, and greatly augmented the existing stock of slaves. Many of the small sunken-featured buildings of the period (fig. 20) may have been inhabited by slaves, and possibly it was slave labour that built the massive fortresses and other great works of Viking Age engineering, and cleared land for the plough. However, it is not known for certain, and there was undoubtedly also a large number of landless people who lived by occasional work and who were free in principle but whose daily lives were not markedly different from those of the slaves.[36]

The other end of the social scale was, as mentioned above, represented by the king, and naturally both kings and queens appear on rune stones. The king was probably usually chosen from a particular family but any male in that line could be considered for election—unless he was a conqueror who established his rule by force of arms. Scholars seem to agree that he functioned as a military leader and had certain sacred duties. He must also have been responsible to some extent for the maintenance of law and order and in return have been entitled to certain dues and fines. Large royal structures, such as the Jelling monuments, also show that he had very considerable resources at his disposal, and until very recently the possibilities open to Danish Viking Age kings for exerting authority have certainly been underestimated. But there can hardly be any doubt that a king's actual power was also dependent on his personal qualities and on the political conditions of his reign. Kings reigned within a framework determined in part by the customary and formal nature of the office—which presumably underwent some development during the three centuries of the Viking Age—in part by their own position of power within and outside the family, and in part by international and economic conditions. But not least, a circle of proud nobles —sometimes with a will of their own—also set bounds to the effective power of the king.

When the nobles of the realm are encountered in written sources they often appear as jointly responsible for important negotiations, peace-treaties and border edicts, as well as in wars. Some of them—the *þegn* and *dreng* of the rune stones—were most likely allied to the king by a personal bond of fealty or dependence, as they were or had been the king's *hempægar*, 'home-receivers' or retainers.[37]

Other nobles, however, could have *hempægar* too, and such a noble was presumably the Alli in whose honour his widow Ragnhild and his sons raised one of the most splendid memorials in the country, probably around AD 900. It stood as the prow-stone of a ship-setting *c.* 60 m long

Pl. 4 *The Glavendrup monument raised around* AD *900 in memory of Alli. The large rune stone in the background has Denmark's longest runic inscription. The text is given below. It is likely that the stone originally stood in the west prow of the ship-setting, about 60 m long and now incomplete, projecting at its eastern end from a Bronze Age mound. Today the stone stands on a small mound made in 1864 near the west end of the ship-setting.*

(pl. 4). The inscription runs:

> Ragnhild set this stone after Alli *goði* (priest of the Sölvi, honourable *þegn* (leader) of the *via líþ* (*via*-troop). Alli's sons made this memorial after their father, and his wife after her husband; and Suti carved these runes after his *dróttinn* (lord). May Thór hallow these runes. May he become a *ræte* (outcast) who harms this stone or drags it away [as a memorial] after someone else.

The usual meaning of *líþ* is band of men, supporting troop, levy-force but what *via* means is disputed. Alli was thus both priest (*goði*) and leader (*þegn*) of a war-band. He was also the rune-carver's lord (*dróttinn*) and his title of *þegn* presumably means he was or had been associated with the king's military retinue.[38]

Not all the personal descriptions on rune stones, however, have or imply a military significance (on military organisation see ch. 8). Some stones mention stewards (*bryti*) and overseers (Old Danish *landhirþir*) who managed the estates of the king or other nobles. There are also possible royal officials (Old Danish *landmannr*) and a single *bomannr*; both were probably large landowners as were undoubtedly most of those with the title *þegn* and *dreng*. Other men are referred to as owners of villages. There are further men who owned ships jointly, possibly as trading partners, and there are stones raised by X to his companion Y. One of them is usually called *dreng* and the two were thus presumably companions in, again, a war-band or levy troop.

The two last-mentioned groups step beyond family relationships, but most rune stones were raised to commemorate close relatives and in themselves added to the honour of whoever paid to put them up: the name of the man or woman who had the stone erected is virtually always given in the inscription. The virtues which are praised are loyalty to comrade and lord, bravery in war, and generosity with food (i.e. being a good lord); exceptional achievements and, not least, high birth are also recorded. In a few cases, however, human feelings of a more general nature are expressed. The inscription on the Randbøl stone, which is still standing in its original site on a small burial-mound, says: 'Tufi the steward (*bryti*) raised this stone to the steward's spouse (*leika*). May these staves live very long for Þorgunna'.

Most stones were raised by men and in memory of men—always adults. Evidently no rune stones were set up for children. But it is remarkable how many women are commemorated on rune stones, especially when we think of the church-influenced derogatory attitudes to women in later ages. They are especially mothers and wives, but one sister is also commemorated, and more than twenty of the known rune stones were raised by women. One (pl. 46) was even raised by a woman in memory of a woman. The rune stones thus demonstrate—as graves also do—that women might be highly respected, have much power and be active in many fields, and that good women made their contribution to the fame of the family.[39] The formal legal status of women is virtually unknown. But an Arab from Spain who visited Hedeby in the second half of the tenth century records that women had the right of divorce, and this independence is confirmed by another Arab writer, also from Spain, who around 850 is said to have been an emissary to a Viking king and to have become a close friend of the queen.[40]

Bearing in mind all the reservations that must cast doubt on the accuracy of such descriptions of foreign people and their customs, based as they are on comparatively short visits or secondhand information, and further complicated and perverted by difficulties of translation and transmission, we may nevertheless read with interest a couple of passages from the work of two foreign authors of the tenth and eleventh centuries respectively. The first is ascribed to at-Tartuschi, the first of the Arab writers mentioned above. The second is by Adam of Bremen.

Schleswig is a very large town by the coast of the ocean. Inside it are springs with fresh water. The people there are worshippers of Sirius, apart from a small number, who are Christians and have a church there.... They have a feast, when they all gather in order to honour the god and in order to eat and drink. He who slaughters a sacrificial animal erects a wooden scaffolding by the door of his house and places the animal upon it, be it an ox or a ram or a he-goat or a pig. Then people know that he has sacrificed it to honour his god. The town is poor in goods and wealth [lit. blessing]. Their chief food is fish; it is plentiful there. If a child is born to any of them, they throw it in the sea, so they shall have fewer expenses. He [at-Tartuschi] tells further that the right to divorce among them belongs to the women; the wife divorces when she wants. There is also an artificially produced eye-paint. When one paints oneself with that, it never disappears, and the beauty increases both in men and women. And he says: I have heard no song more ugly than the song of the people in Schleswig. It is a growl, which emerges from their throats, like the barking of dogs and even more like a wild animal than that.[41]

In many other respects, indeed, both in their laws and in their customs, do the Danes run contrary to what is fair and good. None of these points appears to me worth discussing, unless it be that they immediately sell women who have been violated and that men who have been caught betraying his royal majesty or in some other crime would rather be beheaded than flogged. No kind of punishment exists among them other than the ax and servitude, and then it is glorious for a man who is convicted to take his punishment joyfully. Tears and plaints and other forms of compunction, by us regarded as wholesome, are by the Danes so much abominated that one may weep neither over his sins nor over his beloved dead.[42]

A long way from these ethnographical descriptions is the Nordic poem *Hávamál*, with its practical rules of conduct and its down-to-earth wisdom. It may be as old as the ninth century. One of the stanzas is:

Byrði betri	Burden better
berrat maðr brautu at	bears none abroad with him
en sé mannvit mikit;	than a cool discretion;
vegnest verra	picnic poorer
vegra hann velli at	packs no departing one
en sé ofdrykkja ǫls.	than a big load of beer.[43]

3 Transport and Communications

Good transportation was crucial to the internal development of Denmark and of Scandinavia generally during the Viking Age, as well as to the external events which characterise the period. Without sailing ships, both the military expeditions abroad and the widespread trading associations are inconceivable. Furthermore, in an area like Denmark with many islands, fast, reliable ships were fundamental to the establishment of a kingdom and to the maintenance of power within it. But an efficient road system and reasonable means of transporting people and goods on land are equally necessary for the unity of a kingdom, its defence and its trade. It is precisely in the realm of transport that we find a notable expansion in the period leading up to the Viking Age and presumably also in that age itself. The level of achievement here remained essentially the same for the next two to three hundred years.

The well-preserved ships from the burial-mounds at Oseberg and Gokstad in Norway are among the corner-stones of Norse marine archaeology, and the same applies to the sledges and wagon from Oseberg in the case of land transport.[1] In recent years, however, much important evidence has also come to light about Viking Age transport in Denmark. The development of underwater archaeology, for example, has revolutionised ship archaeology. In the past, evidence of ships was based almost entirely on the graves of well-to-do persons (and ship burials were never common in Denmark), but now not only can submerged wrecks be examined but also lifted and conserved. In Denmark the turning-point came when the five Viking ships in Roskilde fjord were salvaged in 1962.[2] New advances in the study of land transport have resulted above all from the use of scientific dating methods, C-14 and dendrochronology for example, which have made it possible to ascribe a number of causeways and bridge-systems to the Viking period. Further information about vehicles has been obtained in the last few years from both recent and old grave-finds of the bodies of wagons and their fittings.

To understand the transport of that age and its variations, however, it is also important to be aware of the natural conditions in which this transport had to function. Apart from the North Sea, Danish waters are relatively sheltered, in contrast to Norwegian waters, and this must have affected the design of ships. It must presumably also have been of significance for the use of wagons that Denmark (again unlike Norway) is a flat country and that in normal conditions its rivers are not particularly wide or deep.

SHIPS AND BOATS

The Viking ships of Scandinavia are among the most impressive products of the period; they have fascinated us as well as their contemporaries. They were depicted on rune stones and coins (fig. 22). Outline sketches of them occur on many objects (fig. 48). Memorials and ornaments took their form from them (pls. 4 and 39). They were sung about by scalds, and spoken of with dread, but often also with admiration, by foreign writers. About 1040, for example, a monk of St Omer in his *Encomium Emmae* described the fleet with which Cnut the Great set sail from Denmark in 1015 to conquer England:

> So great, also was the ornamentation of the ships, that the eyes of the beholders were dazzled, and to those looking from afar they seemed of flame rather than of wood. For if at any time the sun cast the splendour of its rays among them, the flashing of arms shone in one place, in another the flame of suspended shields. Gold shone on the prows, silver also flashed on the variously shaped ships. So great, in fact, was the magnificence of the fleet, that if its lord had desired to conquer any people, the ships alone would have terrified the enemy, before the warriors whom they carried joined battle at all. For who could look upon the lions of the foe, terrible with the brightness of gold, who upon the man of metal, menacing with golden face, who upon the dragons burning with pure gold, who upon the bulls on the ship threatening death, their horns shining with gold, without feeling any fear for the king of such a force?[3]

Such a description is fascinating though not necessarily very realistic. More reliable (if more fragmentary) information can be found in the scaldic verse of the Northern world,[4] but a number of finds in Scandinavia have already given much concrete information about the appearance of ships in the Viking period. The ships were of several specialised types with different functions, all of which had, in the words of O. Crumlin-Pedersen, the following structural features and hull-shape in common: 'a clinker-built, double-pointed hull with keel and almost identical under-run prow and stern. The shell of the hull is stiffened inside with a number of naturally curved frames which cross the keel and the bottom strakes to reach the same height on both sides. Above each frame sits a cross-beam or *bite* with a knee on each side for stiffening the ship's side. The cross-beams often serve to support the deck planking as well. The frames divide the hull crossways into a number of rooms, and the construction of Scandinavian Viking ships seems to be arranged on a room-module system'.[5]

Picture stones from Gotland, graffiti from the Oseberg ship and elsewhere, and pictures on the earliest Hedeby coins and on some Danish rune stones, however, also show a ship with a triangular or pointed infilling beneath the prow, or beneath both prow and stern.[6] The type must have existed and the infilling could have served to keep the boat on course, reducing leeway. But such ships or boats have not as yet been found, and the pictures help to emphasise that, despite a fair number of finds, relatively little is known about the range of ship types in the Viking period. This applies not least to regional variations and to developments within the period.

Another feature common to the larger ships throughout the whole period,[7] both in archaeological finds and in pictures, is that they are steered by a large steering-oar. Known already from the Nydam boat of about AD 400, this is usually located on the right of the ship looking forward: starboard (OE *stēor*, 'steering'). All the larger ships of the period known archaeologically, though not all the depictions of such ships,[8] apparently had masts: they were propelled by means of a square sail (suspended from a yard), most of them also having oars. From pictures it is also evident that the sail could be reefed, that is to say that the sail area could be reduced to match the strength of the wind. This was accomplished by a method still in use today whereby a greater or lesser lateral area at the top of the sail is bunched to the yard with the help of pieces of rope sewn into the sail in horizontal rows. Probably another reefing system was also used by which the lower part of the sail was folded up and lashed. The yard itself could be raised and lowered.[9]

The earliest Scandinavian ship known definitely to have carried sails is the Oseberg ship from the beginning of the ninth century, but the Kvalsund boat, also Norwegian, from about the year 700, has a type of keel and hull-construction which would allow it to carry sails; the boat is, however, too badly preserved to establish whether it actually had a mast. In the eighth century, sailing ships were depicted on the Gotlandic picture stones, so by this century at the latest Scandinavian ships must have been equipped in some way to carry sails, a practice known elsewhere in Europe for many hundreds of years. It is scarcely a coincidence that Scandinavian expansion across the Atlantic began in the eighth century and that towns such as Ribe and Hedeby also had their beginnings in this century. In subsequent centuries Scandinavian ships developed into sailing vessels which were outstanding for their time.

No ships are yet known from the early Viking period in Denmark. Besides fragments of wrecks, which are difficult to date, and some boat fragments and badly preserved remains in graves,[10] the finds consist of the following:

1 Fragments of iron and the impression of a ship in the earth from the burial of a wealthy man at Ladby, Fyn, of the mid tenth century.[11]
2 Iron from the ship of the so-called boat chamber-grave at Hedeby from the end of the ninth or beginning of the tenth century.[12]
3 The wreck from the harbour at Hedeby known so far only from minor investigations but now (1979) being excavated. The ship is most likely to date from the tenth or eleventh century.[13]
4 The wrecks of the five Skuldelev ships sunk in the early eleventh century to block the channel in the fjord leading to Roskilde. The

Pl. 5 *Reconstruction of warship (or ship for personal transport) Skuldelev 5. Built in 1969 by scouts for sailing in Danish waters and called* Sebbe Als.

ships are numbered 1, 2, 3, 5 and 6 (wreck no. 4 turned out to be part of wreck no. 2).[14]

Remains of a ferry-barge 7 m long from about 1100 found at the ferry-stage Egernsund in South Jutland may also be mentioned.[15] There is furthermore a well-preserved steering-oar fished up out of the sea off Vorså in North Jutland,[16] an anchor from the Ladby ship and another from Ribe (the latter from about the year 750),[17] as well as a gilt-bronze horse from a weather-vane, probably found on Lolland.[18] Through wrecks found at Eltang, Lynæs and Ellingå, the development of ships can be traced into the early Middle Ages.[19]

Viking Age ships from Denmark are mostly made of oak, so far as the wood has been identified, though other wood is used too. This does not apply, however, to wrecks 1 and 6 from Skuldelev, where the strakes, for example, are of pine; given the sturdy dimensions of these planks, the ships must have been built abroad (perhaps in Norway or Gotland) since pine trees of such proportions did not grow in Denmark at this time. Thorough investigation of the Skuldelev ships has shown that the selection and cutting of the wood were undertaken with great care and with great craftsmanship and technical knowledge. As far as possible they looked for wood where the grain followed the shape of the finished pieces in order to get elements which were strong and flexible yet at the same time slender and light. For the same reason, all the shaped pieces were made from heartwood. The oak strakes were shaped from logs which had been quarter-hewn (split radially), while pine and ash strakes were formed from flat-split logs (in which the strake's cross-section is orientated tangentially to the log's growth-rings).[20]

As mentioned above, the ships had specialised functions. They can be divided into two main groups: warships or ships for travelling on the one hand, and trading or cargo vessels on the other. The warship (or ship for personal transport) is represented in Denmark by the Ladby ship, the two Hedeby ships and Skuldelev 2 and 5 (pl. 5). They are long, narrow and of shallow draught, presumably with decks that ran the whole length of the ship and with oar-holes evenly distributed over the entire length with two to each 'room'. By means of a specially constructed mast-fish (supporting the mast at deck level) and a mast-step of distinctive form in the keelson, the mast could be lowered without much trouble, a feature which would have been extremely useful in case of portage, navigation under bridges, and military emergencies and deck-operations. The combination of sail and oar made for particularly good manœuvrability: the ships could be employed both at sea and on rivers, and over short distances were not dependent on wind conditions. These features are already known from the older Norwegian ships from Oseberg, Gokstad and Tune, but it must be emphasised that the state of preservation of the Danish ships does not always allow conclusions to be drawn about decks, oar-holes and the mast arrangements.

Trading or cargo ships are represented by Skuldelev 1 and 3 (figs. 5–6) and these are the first ships of this type to be identified. Here we

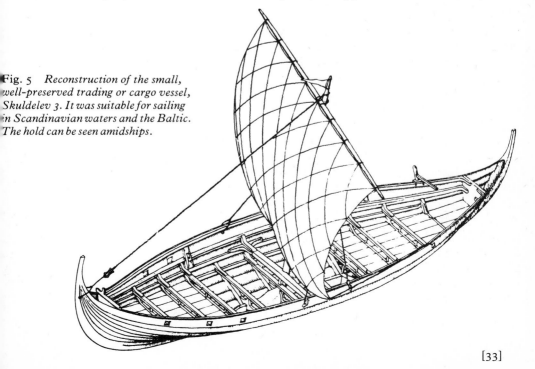

Fig. 5 *Reconstruction of the small, well-preserved trading or cargo vessel, Skuldelev 3. It was suitable for sailing in Scandinavian waters and the Baltic. The hold can be seen amidships.*

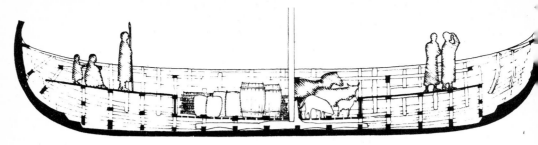

Fig. 6 *Reconstructed longitudinal section of the large seagoing trading or cargo ship, Skuldelev 1.*

are dealing with short, broad ships with a high freeboard and with half-decks fore and aft to leave room for a hold amidships. The mast is fixed in the mast-step and could not easily be lowered or raised. There are only a few oar-holes located above the half-decks, presumably mostly for use in narrow waters and for manœuvring in harbour as well as for extra momentum when under sail, especially when going about. These ships are regular sailing ships. This specialised division into war or transport vessels on the one hand, and trading or cargo ships on the other, may have begun with the Viking period or before; the construction amidships on the Äskekär ship from the Götaälv may be an indication of this.[21]

The last vessel falls outside both groups mentioned above: Skuldelev 6 may have been a ferry or a fishing-boat. It was 11.6 m in length and carried sail; if a ferry, it must have had oars as well.

Among the war or transport vessels, the Ladby ship, the Hedeby ships and Skuldelev 5 form a group in contrast to the considerably larger Skuldelev 2. The Ladby ship was about 20.6 m in length and 3.2 m in beam, and according to recent investigations it is presumed to have had eight strakes on each side of a 12 cm-high keel. The frames divided the ship into 'rooms' and there appears to have been space for sixteen pairs of oars. Roughly level with the gunwale, just aft of midships, four solid iron rings were found on each side; these were probably rings for fastening the mast's supporting ropes: the shrouds. Iron ornaments were found at both prow and stern. The spiral iron bands on the prow were presumably the neck-curls from a dragon-head as seen on a mould from Birka; iron ornaments are also known from the prow of the Viking ship on the Île de Groix in Brittany.[22] The iron anchor, 136 cm long, was fastened to an iron chain about 10 m long which was itself attached to a three-stranded bast-rope. This lay where an anchor ought to lie, forward in the prow.

The ship from the Hedeby boat chamber-grave was probably between 17 and 20 m in length. The beam cannot be determined exactly but there were probably eight strakes on each side. The ship from the harbour at Hedeby was at least 16 m long and had at least seven strakes on each side. It survives in a comparatively poor state but is of unusually beautiful workmanship. As already mentioned, further information about this will soon be available.

Skuldelev 5 was about 17.4 m long and about 2.7 m in the beam. There were seven strakes on each side and it was about 0.6 m in draught. The keel was between 10 and 12 cm in height and both this and the lowest strakes were very worn. The ship had sixteen frames over which lay the cross-beams which supported the deck. Above twelve of the frames, and 30 cm above deck-level, there were fixed thwarts with corresponding oar-holes in the top strake on each side. The ship was thus rowed by twenty-four men but the keelson shows that it also had mast and sail. Incidentally, the uppermost strakes came from another ship and it was therefore necessary to close a number of the original oar-holes and to cut new ones suitable for this ship. On the outside of the uppermost strake there was a batten for shields. Such a batten is known from the Oseberg and the Gokstad ships,[23] and both literature and pictures (in Denmark: pictures on coins and rune stones and a ship-shaped brooch[24]) indicate that shields were positioned along the sides of the war or travelling ship. Carved on one strake is a Ringerike-style tendril, a style which corresponds well with the C-14 datings of the ship.

Trials with life-size reconstructions of the Ladby and Skuldelev 5 ships have shown that they were speedy under sail, seaworthy and manœuvrable, and with their shallow draught were able to run almost right up on the shore of the flat Danish coastline and could easily be drawn up on to land and possibly even transported over land for short distances. Indeed, signs of wear on Skuldelev 5 show that the bottom of the ship had often come into contact with beach and sea-bed. These ships are greatly reminiscent of the ships shown on the Bayeux tapestry of c. 1070, transporting William the Conqueror's invasion force to England. The Danish ships were suitable for navigation in Danish waters and we may assume they were used for travelling by the wealthy or as regular Viking ships carrying twenty-five to thirty men. This also accords with the fact that the Ladby ship and one of the Hedeby ships come from the graves of rich men. That the ships are both shallower and narrower than the Norwegian ones can probably be explained by the completely different physical conditions of the two countries.

Skuldelev 2 is the least well preserved of the ships from Roskilde fjord. The length has been estimated at about 28 or 29 m, the beam about 4.5 m. There were more than seven strakes on each side. The keel was about 13 cm in height but is very worn as are the lowest strakes. The keelson (13.3 m in length) shows that the ship carried mast and sail but the upper strakes are missing so it cannot be proved that it had oars too. If it had, as is likely, there was space for between twenty and twenty-five pairs of oars. The ship has been classified as the longship of the sagas; it is a regular Viking ship which was capable of transporting a large number of people, probably between fifty and sixty men, over the sea to England, for example. Its dating fits well, incidentally, with Svein Forkbeard's raids at the end of the tenth and very beginning of the eleventh century.

Trading or cargo ships had a completely different character, illustrated by Skuldelev ships 1 and 3. The latter is the best preserved of all the Skuldelev ships in that, in all, three-quarters of the ship survives: the entire fore part as well as the hold amidships. The prow is the only complete prow to have survived from the entire Viking period (proudly excavated by the author in 1962). It is 3.7 m long, a maximum of 0.55 m wide and carved from a single piece of oak. On each side there is an elegant continuation of the lines of the ship's side strakes converging towards the tip of the prow.

The ship was small and roomy (fig. 5): about 13.8 m long, 3.3 m in the beam and with eight strakes on each side of the keel which was originally 12 cm in height but is badly worn. The height from the underside of the keel to the gunwale was about 1.6 m and the ship's loaded draught was at most 1 m. The keelson has a deep mast-step and various arrangements in the planks of the gunwale were for the mast's shrouds and stay, and for the sheets. There are only a few oar-holes. The ship is thought to have had a sail area of 40–45 m², and to have had a cargo-carrying capacity of about 5 tons, with a crew of five or six. It has so many details in common with the war or transport ship Skuldelev 5 that they might have had the same boat-builder, and judging by the wear on the bottom both had often been in contact with the sea-bed and beach. Skuldelev 3 was presumably a local type; it was suited for trading activities in Scandinavia and the Baltic.

The large ship Skuldelev 1 (fig. 6) may have been constructed in Norway or Gotland, as mentioned above. It was about 16.3 m long, about 4.5 m in the beam and with twelve strakes on each side of the keel, which was roughly 16 cm in height. The height amidships from bottom to gunwale was about 1.9 m and the maximum loaded draught was about 1.5 m; the hold amidships was 5.5 m long and the cargo capacity between 15 and 20 tons. The keelson has a deep mast-step, the sail area is thought to have been about 100 m², and there was a small number of oar-holes where the ship was decked fore and aft. The ship was solidly built with fourteen frames and many extra internal reinforcements. It has been characterised as a cargo vessel suited to the transport of large loads over open seas, but too large and heavy to be often beached and quite unsuitable for overland portage. The ship is possibly a so-called *knǫrr*—the type of ship which according to literary sources was used in sailing the Atlantic, for example to Iceland and Greenland.

The sailing capabilities of Viking ships have been the subject of lively discussion, and opinions vary because only a few, small and often dubious fragments of masts, sail and other rigging have survived, because the literary and pictorial sources can be difficult to interpret, and because the flexible hulls have properties whose positive effects on the ships' sailing capabilities are difficult to assess.[25] That their sailing efficiency was outstanding for the period is, however, evident enough from the many Scandinavian loan-words which were adopted into nautical vocabulary in the countries around the North Sea and the English Channel,[26] and not least from the fact that the Scandinavians of the Viking period actually got so far afield.

The Viking Ship Museum at Roskilde has carried out a number of sea-trials using life-size reconstructions of Viking ships (pl. 5), and also a Nordland boat (a Norwegian type of boat with square sail in normal use until about 1900), in order to investigate the sailing characteristics of the ships in actual conditions at sea. Analyses of these seem to show that, with an experienced crew, ships of the Viking period could sail close-hauled (with the wind before the beam) and could therefore also tack forward into the wind, though probably not making much headway if they did. But, with a fresh wind from the right quarter, Viking ships are thought to have been capable of sailing at up to 10 or 12 knots (18–22 km per hour).[27] In that case a journey from the western outlet of Limfjord to Tynemouth, for example, could have been made in just about twenty-four hours in optimum conditions. In normal conditions and with an average speed of about 5 knots this journey could have been done in between two and two and a half days, and, with the same average speed, the journey from north-west Denmark across Skagerrak to the southern tip of Norway in about twelve hours.

Further information about navigation can be gleaned from the Norwegian Ohthere, who in about the year 890 told Alfred the Great, King of England, that one could sail from his home in Halogaland in northern Norway (now Nordland) to *Sciringes heal* (presumably Kaupang in Tjölling on the west side of Oslo fjord) in southern Norway in a month, if one camped by night and had fair winds by day. He sailed the whole way along the coast, i.e. in sheltered waters. And from *Sciringes heal* he took five days to sail to Hedeby. For the first three days he had Denmark (now Sweden) to port and open sea to starboard; for the last two, he sailed between the Danish islands (see fig. 51).[28]

It was probably customary to navigate shallow and difficult waters camping by night and sailing by day, as Ohthere did, so it was possible to find directions by distinctive landmarks. In more open waters such as the Baltic, one could sail right across, as did Wulfstan, Ohthere's contemporary, who told King Alfred that he sailed from Hedeby to Truso (in the Gulf of Danzig, probably Elbing) in seven days and nights.[29] Across the open sea, for instance sailing direct from Denmark to England, or from Norway to Iceland, one had to steer by means of a no doubt highly precise feeling for time and speed, by sea-birds which stay near land, and by wave formation. One could also navigate by means of the celestial bodies—the sun and stars—and in fair weather maintain accurate latitude sailing for days on end. Viking navigation, like the sailing capabilities of the ships, is, however, a hotly debated subject. Navigational instruments of the period are unknown, and contemporary literary sources few and far between, but numerous theoretical suggestions have been made as to how Norsemen may have solved their navigational problems.[30]

HARBOURS AND CANALS

There is relatively sparse evidence of Viking-period harbours, both in Denmark and in Scandinavia as a whole. Semicircular rows of piles bordered a harbour basin at Hedeby, and current excavations in connection with the ship mentioned above have discovered, in addition, a series of pile constructions in Hedeby harbour, some of which were

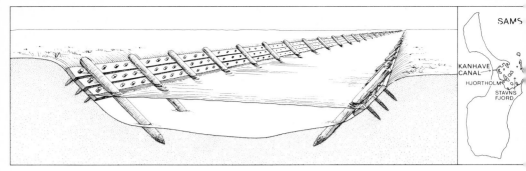

Fig. 7 *Schematic reconstruction of the partly timber-sided Kanhave canal on Samsø, c. 1 km long.*

jetties.[31] Similar jetties, but partly stone-built, are also known at Birka in Sweden and Kaupang in Norway.[32] Jetties and other harbour installations were not necessary everywhere, however. Because of their shallow draught and low keel, the ships were able to run directly on to flat beaches or to go alongside river banks.

Boat-houses (*naust*), where ships and their equipment could be kept during winter and while they were made ready in spring, would not have been essential in Denmark either. Archaeological evidence here is consequently also sparse: a couple of earth banks about 25 m long and almost ellipsoid, with openings towards the beach at Harrevig, in Limfjord, have been interpreted as boat-houses and attributed to the Viking period or to the early Middle Ages. Likewise some features on the small island of Sejrø have been interpreted as Viking or medieval boat-houses.[33]

There is no archaeological evidence for places over which boats could be dragged, perhaps on rollers, for short distances between one stretch of water and the next: when portage is mentioned in literature, the reference is to small vessels and to the lightly built warships, and in the latter case there was some compelling military reason for portage. One no doubt normally preferred to sail if it was at all possible, unless a great deal of time and uncomfortable sailing could be saved by the use of 'slipways', or where the portage was a regular activity and not done by the crew. Thus one may imagine that in the Hedeby area there was an organised 'slipway' service across the most southerly part of Jutland from the bottom of the Schlei fjord to the Rheide or Eider rivers, and that here one could pay for portage to avoid the long journey round Jutland. But for the present this is nothing more than speculation. There is neither archaeological nor literary evidence from the period to support the idea.[34]

Where land blocked the passage of ships, the problem could also be solved by a canal. Such a ship-canal of the Viking period has been found in Samsø, the island in the centre of the kingdom.[35] Kanhave canal (fig. 7) links the deeply indented Stavnsfjord (an exceptionally good natural harbour) with the sea to the west of the island. The canal was about 1 km long and 11 m wide, and was able to accommodate ships with a draught of up to 1.25 m, quite adequate for ships of the Viking period. Where the bottom was of sand, the sides were prevented from caving in by an inclining timber construction consisting of three horizontal planks laid one above the other. These were fixed to the side of the canal by sloping piles positioned at intervals of three metres and by means of large wooden pegs hammered through square holes cut in the planks and into the sides of the canal. The canal demanded constant maintenance while in use, but that does not seem to have been for long. Dating is based on a C-14 test of part of the canal's timbers (result: AD 800 ± 100 years),[36] as well as by inference from the shallowness of the canal. It is hoped to get a precise dating in the near future from dendrochronology.

The canal's intended function must essentially have been military; it cannot have made much difference to the trading ships and fishing-boats lying in Stavnsfjord to sail round the island's northern tip in order to proceed to the south-west. Samsø, however, lies in the middle of the Kattegat, and from the island Hjortholm in Stavnsfjord one has a splendid view over the sea and can keep an eye on traffic to and from both Denmark's main straits: the two Belts. A fleet in Stavnsfjord would be able to sail out rapidly towards the east, but the canal was essential for controlling the sea towards the west; thus the entire central area of Danish waters could be covered. Needless to say, this might be as advantageous for a band of pirates as for the upholder of law and order, namely the king, and until the canal is dated precisely we cannot with certainty attribute it to one or the other. However, except for the last couple of centuries, Samsø has belonged to the king as far back as the island can be traced in written records. The canal may perhaps indicate that, as early as the Viking period, the king saw it as his duty to uphold peace and order at sea. Otherwise, the proliferation of pirates could very easily destroy trade and other communications in a land such as Denmark. Adam of Bremen, for instance, expressed an undisguised fear of pirates in Danish waters.[37]

The Kanhave canal represents a completely new type of construction among the many great works of engineering of the Viking period and it is highly likely that there were also canals in other places of strategic importance in the country.

WINTER TRANSPORT

Apart from skates, or more correctly 'ice-legs' there are only a few traces of the means of transport used over ice and snow, and skates were most likely used to a large extent for sport and pleasure. Many of those found are so short that they must have been for children. They are usually made from the metatarsals of horses which have been ground flat on the underside and smoothed on the top. There may be a hole at the front for a thong which fastened the skate to the foot, and a hole at the back for a small peg which likewise served to fasten a thong. But skates can also function perfectly well without thong-fasteners, because one normally propelled oneself over the ice by means of a spiked stick (the pointed iron ferrules of such sticks have been found), without needing to lift the feet at all.[38] In the mid sixteenth century, Olaus Magnus published woodcuts of people using skates,[39] and modern trials have demonstrated that they function remarkably well.[40]

In order to stand firmly on frozen surfaces, both men and animals could be equipped with crampons, iron mounts with short spikes which were fastened under the feet or footgear.[41] Skis were probably known, but there is no archaeological evidence of this from the Viking period in Denmark.[42]

Sledges like the famous Oseberg sledges[43] presumably existed in Denmark also, but the only sledge fragments so far identified are a fragment of a wooden runner from Trelleborg and possibly another of bone from Lund.[44] They are probably from simple work sledges, but not necessarily only for winter transport. Right up to our own times, sledges have been used in the country for the transport of such things as hay in the fields,[45] and the stone sledge from Risby discussed below should also be considered.

HORSE EQUIPMENT. WAGONS AND OTHER TRANSPORT AIDS

People moved overland by foot, on horseback or in wagons. They may also have used litters, but no examples are known. Riding animals were horses, while draught-animals could be either horses or oxen (see ch. 4).

Horse and riding equipment in Denmark is best known from the tenth-century graves of rich men. These grave-finds illustrate what was used by the upper classes in society (ch. 9). Besides the harness itself, of which only single fragments remain, along with associated strap-buckles, strap-distributors, and decorative mounts, the equipment consists of the following: bit, saddle (almost exclusively very small, often doubtful fragments and fittings), stirrups and spurs.[46] While bit, saddle and spurs have ancestors in Scandinavia, stirrups which assist mounting and give better balance while riding, not least in battle, were probably introduced to Scandinavia roughly at the beginning of the Viking period.[47] They were not, however, necessarily associated with the introduction of cavalry (see ch. 8). On these oldest Scandinavian stirrups, the loops for leathers lie at right-angles to the more or less rounded bows, and the loop is usually separated from the stirrup by a twisted bar. Most Scandinavian stirrups of this sort have been found in Norway;[48] probably only one stirrup with a transverse loop has been found in Denmark (at Trelleborg), but we know few Danish graves of the eighth and ninth centuries.[49] In this case, however, the loop for the leathers is not twisted away from the bow, and the shape of the stirrup approaches the elongated triangular form with straight tread which became the norm in the tenth century, where loops lie in the same plane as the bows. Such stirrups are known from a large number of horsemen's graves in Denmark (pl. 6).[50] Stirrups are scarce, however, among finds from settlements of the period.[51]

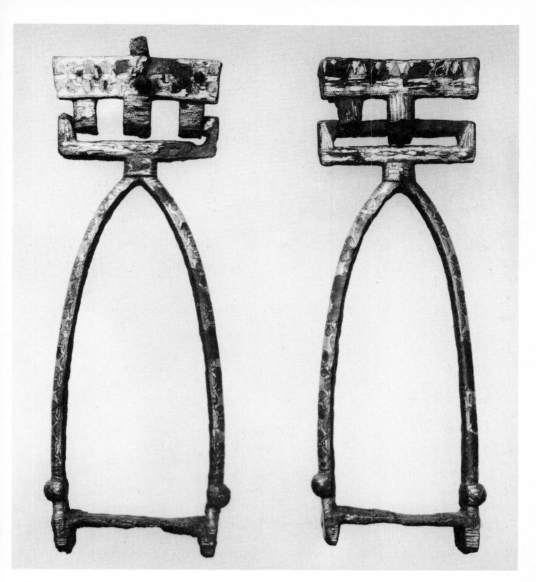

6   Iron stirrups
~th silver and
~pper inlay from the
~rseman's grave at
~rre Longelse on
~ngeland.

Horseshoes were possibly introduced in the late Viking period, as may be indicated by some finds from Hedeby and Lund, for example. However, they are not found among the contents of the tenth-century horsemen's graves or settlement sites.[52] Horse-hobbles are not known from graves but have been found at Trelleborg, for instance.[53]

The horse equipment of the horsemen's graves is comparatively uniform and has southern prototypes.[54] But much is still of native manufacture, such as the beautifully worked spurs and stirrups inlaid with silver and copper wire, and bits decorated with silver or tin plates. Examples are known from Stengade and Nørre Longelse on Langeland (pl. 6), from Brandstrup near Århus and from Thumby-Bienebek near

Pl. 7 *Wooden harness-bows with gilt-bronze mounts from draught-horses in the Søllested grave on Fyn. One is shown in use in fig. 9.*

Hedeby,[55] and elsewhere. The horse equipment from Velds in North Jutland is an example of foreign import; the ornament suggests it was made in the south of England in about AD 1000.[56]

It must be emphasised, however, that the horse equipment in these graves does not give a realistic picture of everyday tackle as used by ordinary people. For this we must turn to the settlements, where there are more modest forms and materials such as coarsely produced bits made of antler (now fragmentary) and very simple snaffle-bits of iron.[57] People must often have managed with even less.

Horsemen's graves are always male graves and riding was probably the normal form of transport for men who had the means. Women of the same class usually seem to have travelled by wagon, at any rate on journeys and for ceremonial occasions. This is indicated by a series of richly equipped female graves containing portions of wagons and driving gear (ch. 9), and the idea is supported by medieval pictures and literature.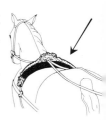

The only surviving cart from the Viking period is from the Oseberg burial (fig. 8),[58] but fragments of wagons and their appurtenances from Denmark show that similar four-wheeled vehicles were common there. Wheels are known from the road at Risby (see below) and from the settle-

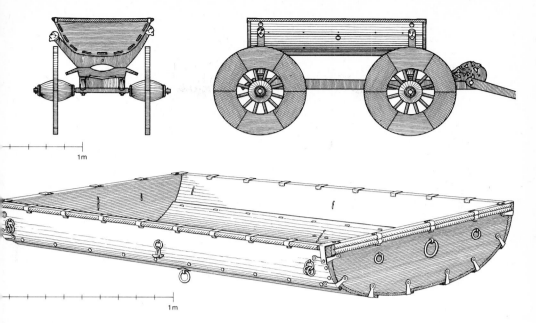

Fig. 8 *Top: schematic drawing of the wagon from the Oseberg burial in South Norway. Bottom: reconstruction of a wagon-body used as a coffin at Thumby-Bienebek near Hedeby. Rings hang on the sides and end, and there are also Thor's hammers (symbols of the pagan god Thor) on the sides.*

g. 9   Splendid
rness-bows (see
, 7) were part of the
uipment used by
e wealthy for their
aught horses.
heir practical
nction was to keep
e reins together.

ments at Omgård and Lindholm Høje,[59] and axles from Risby and Omgård.[60] There are also cart or wagon fragments from the fill of the South Mound at Jelling.[61] In a number of cases, wagon bodies of about 2×1 m, like the Oseberg wagon's removable body, were used as coffins in rich female graves of the tenth century, as in the fortress at Fyrkat and in Thumby-Bienebek near Hedeby, which have been reconstructed with many fine details (fig. 8).[62] There were also iron traces connecting the ends of the front axles to the harness of the draught-horse; examples have been found, together with two bits, in each of the following graves: Søllested on Fyn, Møllemosegård on Fyn, Gryderup on Sjælland and Süderbrarup in South Schleswig. Two more fragmentary traces are known, possibly from the grave or hoard at Mammen in central Jutland[63] which, like the graves at Søllested and Møllemosegård, contained harness-bows for draught-horses with richly decorated bronze-gilt fittings (fig. 9). Yet another harness-bow is known from Elstrup on Als.[64] Draught-harness was presumably breast-harness, as on the horses represented on the Oseberg tapestry.[65] The bodies of wagons were probably often covered with a tight-drawn cloth when in use, as grave-finds seem to show, and as indicated by some of the carts on the Oseberg tapestry, as well as by medieval literature and pictures.[66] Wheel-tracks also provide evidence about wagons; examples have been found at different places in the country, e.g. at Risby, at Ravning Enge bridge, at Fyrkat and at Lindholm Høje (pl. 12).[67] Finally it may be mentioned that, according

Pl. 8 *Hand-barrow for turf used in construction of the South Mound at Jelling. Found during excavation of the mound.*

to Frankish annals, there was only one gateway in the Danevirke of King Godfred through which carts and horsemen could go in and out.[68]

Grave-finds give evidence of the magnificent vehicles used to carry people, but many of the wooden fragments mentioned above must belong to broken down work-carts or wagons, as is clearly shown by the Jelling and Risby finds. With all this evidence there can be no doubt that carts and wagons were well known and in common use in Denmark during the Viking period for carrying both people and goods.[69]

Some goods were undoubtedly carried by pack-animals, but of this there is no firm evidence. For moving extremely heavy objects such as large stones (for rune stones, ship-settings, fords or bridges), stone sledges could be used. There is an example of one from Risby. Hand-barrows could be used for moving goods or building materials, such as turf, over small distances. The barrows, carried by two people, consisted of a number of boards tied to each other and to two carrying-poles. A complete hand-barrow was found in the South Mound at Jelling (pl. 8) and fragments in the ramparts of the Danevirke and at Hedeby.[70] Block and tackle was probably used for lifting, sinking or dragging cumbersome material such as bridge-piles or large stones. A block about 23 cm long (fig. 10) and various fragments of blocks of similar size have been found at Hedeby.[71] Each of these could have been used for pulling in the sheets of a sail. But is it not possible that larger blocks were also known and might they not have been used for pulleys?

Finally it should be mentioned that a number of staffs or crutches are known. Some are made entirely of wood; others consisted of a wooden staff with an antler top. The most beautiful walking-stick comes from Lund; it terminates in an animal head with a mane of tendrils (fig. 50) and the shaft bears the owner's name: Ulfkil.[72]

Fig. 10 *Wooden block from Hedeby Length 23.2 cm.*

Roads have wound their way across the Danish landscape right from Neolithic times when the wagon was first introduced. In general their routes have followed the dryshod rule, keeping to areas with the fewest possible streams and marshes to cross. Until well after the Middle Ages, the roadway consisted merely of wheel-tracks worn into the natural surface of the earth, or of broad bands of parallel ruts; such ruts can still be seen on preserved sections of the Army Road or Ox Road, the chief line of communication through Jutland in prehistoric and medieval times.

Where streams, rivers and marshy areas had to be crossed, however, roads and causeways were of great benefit to traffic, and such constructions are known right back to Neolithic times. A number of investigations in different parts of the country have revealed roads laid with branches and brushwood, and, from the Iron Age onwards, roads laid with stone and timber too. It is notable that the road system in southern Sjælland expanded in the late Roman Iron Age at the same time as the area grew greatly in prosperity.[73]

In the Viking period, the road system seems to have once more undergone a major expansion in order to make it easier to cross streams and marshes. It was especially important for the wheeled traffic, and it is striking that the oldest datable bridges in Denmark are from this period. Among the fords and causeways of that period so far investigated are Sjellebro in North Jutland, and Risby and Elverhøj in southern Sjælland.[74] There are bridges at Varpelev and Risby in southern Sjælland, and at Ravning Enge in central Jutland, and there is most likely a bridge at Falgård near Ry, also in central Jutland.[75] It is worth noting that these four structures can all be dated to the late Viking period, as can so many other large structures in Denmark (ch. 12); the same applies to the short bridges over the ditches at Trelleborg.[76] It is possible that the inspiration for the building of bridges came from Slav regions which had close contacts with Denmark and where impressive bridge-building was taking place.[77]

The structures at Risby, Varpelev and Falgård may represent local roads and bridges of the Viking period. Risby can serve as an example.[78] Investigations have been made of a small area around an old river bed, where numerous roads from widely different periods have been built, sometimes on top of each other, sometimes a short distance apart. Two of the roads laid with branches and brushwood have been dated by C-14 to the eighth century and the ninth/tenth century respectively; stratigraphically these are older than the wooden bridge mentioned above. There are also five stone-paved roads, one of which C-14 datings put to about AD 1000 or to the first half of the eleventh century. The bridge lay partly underneath this road, and so far only part of it has been examined.

The supporting sections of the bridge have turned out to consist of two vertical squared piles set 2.5 m apart, each with an angled buttress. There was about 3.4 m between each section, and the length of the bridge

Pl. 10   *Aerial photograph of Ravning Enge in the valley of the river Vejle about 10 km south-west of Jelling. The course of the bridge, almost 1 km long, is indicated by the broken line; the arrow points to an excavation area. An older river-bed is just discernible. The present road is the light band curving across the picture.*

was probably about 70 m. The stone-lined road from about the year 1000 (or slightly later) has been thoroughly investigated (pl. 9). It was about 70 m long, 2.5 m wide, and edged along both sides with close-set kerb stones, each about 1 m in height. The road surface consisted of a packing up to 40 cm deep of between three and five layers of hand-sized, water-worn stones covered with a layer of sand up to 15 cm deep, all founded on a bed of branches, logs and discarded timber; there were distinct wheel-tracks in the roadway. Where the road had to pass the half-overgrown river, it was supported on the side closest to the river by a bulwark of tree-trunks laid crossways, and a roadway constructed of worked beams was carried over the river on a frame 4.5 × 2.6 m. Similar constructions to this 'sleeper-track' are known at Sjellebro for example, and on streets in the towns and fortresses of the period. Here at Risby it rested on a large stone which in turn lay on a heap of discarded wood: off-cuts, branches, logs, broken wheels and cart-axles; a primitive stone sledge lay directly beneath the large stone.[79]

This roadway over the Risby river-valley demanded a considerable effort, but that is nothing to the effort needed in the years just around 979 to construct the bridge over Ravning Enge near Jelling,[80] which was just under 1 km long and a good 5.5 m wide (pls. 10 and 11, fig. 11). The number of supporting sections here has been estimated at around 400 (not all of which have been excavated). There was about 2.4 m between each section, and each consisted of four vertical piles with an angled post at each side. The distance between the piles of one section was about 1.5 m. The piles are square in section, with a side of about 29.5 cm (one Roman foot), and their lowest portions now survive to a height of 2–4 m (pl. 11). Judging by the bridge's estimated length, there would have been about seventeen hundred supporting piles, with eight hundred angled posts and other timbers for the superstructure,

9   *The stone-ed road at Risby, ith Sjælland, seen n the present r-bed. In the kground, the ?per-road' which sed the Viking river.*

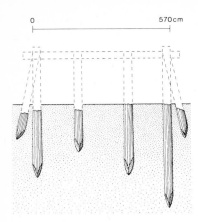

Fig. 11   *One section of the great bridge at Ravning Enge. Only the lower parts of the posts survive. A possible superstructure is indicated by the dotted lines. See pls. 10–11.*

whose exact character is as yet unknown—a prodigious outlay in labour and materials. Added to this is the construction of the land approaches to the bridge: roadways of faggots and cobbles led up to the north end of the bridge and sunken roads were dug down into the steep hill to the north so that the descent would not be too violent for wheeled (and possibly heavy) vehicles. The weight the piles could take is estimated at 5 tons.

The Ravning Enge bridge is the largest and perhaps one of the first of the Viking Age bridges in Denmark. It is one of the great engineering works of Viking Denmark and was built with a precision that parallels what is known from the contemporary Trelleborg-type fortresses (Trelleborg was begun in 980/81, see ch. 8). However, like these fortresses and the Kanhave canal, the bridge only functioned for a short time; it does not appear to have been repaired. The scale of the construction indicates that it was built by the king, and the dating points to the end of Harald Bluetooth's reign (died *c.* 986). It must have been he who was responsible for this bridge so close to Jelling.

At this time, kings in Western Europe could command people to build and maintain bridges[81] but it is not known whether the same applied in Denmark.[82] At any rate, with this bridge the king improved conditions for road traffic. The bridge lies near the route which the Army Road/Ox Road is known to have followed after the Middle Ages, but it is uncertain precisely where the route or routes were in the Viking period; routes of roads have never been completely stable. It can, however, be safely reckoned that the strong, convenient bridge over the almost impassable Vejle river-valley attracted traffic to it—even if it meant that people had to alter their usual routes.[83] The king may have charged a toll for crossing the bridge to recompense him for his efforts, and a good bridge was in any case a convenient control-point, like the single gate in King Godfred's Danevirke of 808. From the king's point of view, the expansion of the road system had other advantages too. A good road system facilitates the movement of troops and thereby control over the kingdom. A good road system also improves normal communications together with trade, and thus markets and towns which presumably paid taxes to the king.[84]

Pl. 11 *The remains one of the piles of th great bridge over Ravning Enge bein drawn up out of th marsh. Length abo 3.5 m.*

In addition to this, it was prestigious to build bridges and causeways. This is clear from some rune stones whose inscriptions emphasise that the private individuals who raised them were bridge-builders. These stones most likely date from the late Viking period and the early Middle Ages[85] but other rune stones from the tenth century or from about AD 1000, found *in situ* beside disused causeways or bridges (like the stone at Sjellebro in North Jutland),[86] show that such places were already sought after by stone-raisers, just as the important main roads were.[87] It is an obvious conclusion that the people who put up these stones also saw to it that the bridges and roadways they had made were kept in order for a time. There are eleventh-century rune stones in Sweden and Norway too which tell of the building of bridges and causeways.[88]

The speed and comfort of journeys were totally dependent on the weather and on the condition of roads, causeways, bridges, and whether one walked, rode or drove. The information we have about the duration of particular journeys must be at an average speed in reasonable weather. Around 1070, Adam of Bremen wrote that it took from five to seven days to travel the direct route from Schleswig to Ålborg, and about a hundred years later an Icelandic guide-book for pilgrims records that the journey from Ålborg to Viborg took two days and from there to Schleswig took seven days. This gives an average day's journey of about 40 km or 25 miles—clearly a walking pace by road. Adam also says that Sjælland is two days' journey in length and nearly the same in breadth.[89] However, there is no indication as to which means of transport Adam thought of for these journeys, and there is no evidence as to how journeys were organised with regard to inns, hiring animals, vehicles and so on.

A bookish foreigner like Adam of Bremen devotes much of his description of the North to recording the dangers and discomforts of travelling. I wonder, however, whether the habitual travellers of the period might not have described it differently. The speed and convenience of journeys achieved by the technology of the Viking period were in any case not really surpassed until after the Middle Ages.

4 Settlement and Survival

SETTLEMENT PATTERNS

Villages and farms were the economic backbone of society, but until recently only very few Viking Age settlements were known (in contrast to many from the early Roman Iron Age for example). It is thought that many of the village names -*toft*, -*torp* and -*by* were formed during the Viking Age (partly because such names also occur in Normandy and in English regions conquered by Vikings in the ninth century)[1] and the reason for the sparse archaeological evidence for Danish settlements of this period once appeared to be simply that they lay concealed under existing villages. The place-names guaranteed continuity and showed that there had indeed been many settlements in the country during the Viking Age.[2]

It did not pass unnoticed, however, that a discrepancy existed between the dating of the place-names and the archaeological dating of the earliest phases of those few villages which had been investigated.[3] This discrepancy has been confirmed by recent excavations. A new theory may be advanced giving quite a different picture of the settlement pattern in Viking Age Denmark.[4] The excavations on which this is based can be roughly divided into five groups:

1 Excavations of varying numbers of farm sites in existing or deserted villages in order to trace them back to their foundation (in particular at Hejninge, Pebringe, Borup Ris and Store Valby, all in Sjælland).[5]
2 Systematic trial excavations of small areas in villages of different name types in order to determine the actual time of their foundation (thirteen existing and one deserted village on Fyn).[6]
3 Major systematic excavations of Viking Age settlements in order to determine as far as possible their extent and plan (in particular Sædding, Vorbasse and Omgård, all in central or West Jutland). These settlements were discovered in the course of major engineering work or by current excavation of other complexes. Extensive use has been made of mechanical excavators to remove the topsoil on these sites.[7]
4 Excavations of parts of Viking Age settlements discovered in the same manner as the above, settlements like Lindholm Høje and Aggersborg which were in fact by-products of excavations of (respectively) the burial-ground and the fortress. There have also been a number of

rescue excavations and minor investigations. Traces of settlements examined in this manner are now known from many parts of the country, though only a few from Sjælland.[8]

5 Systematic field-walking to find evidence of Viking Age settlement. Until recently, however, it has not been possible to recognise settlements in Denmark by this method. The reason is that the ordinary pottery of the period was so inferior that it disintegrates very quickly once it comes to the surface. However, concentrations occur of pot-boilers that are functionally associated with poorly fired pottery and are known in Viking Age contexts. Their dating can be checked by small trial excavations. It is also useful to employ aerial photography in the search for Viking Age settlements, since sunken-featured buildings in particular often show up well in the fields.[9]

As yet only a few of these numerous investigations have been published and many of the settlements traced cannot for the present be dated to any particular time in the period from about AD 700 to 1100, because the chronology of the pottery, which is the predominant basis for dating, has not yet been fully established. Some settlements have therefore been attributed to the popular Viking period on flimsy and sometimes doubtful grounds. Nevertheless a pattern is now emerging.

In existing villages and in villages deserted in the High Middle Ages (such as Borup Ris) or later (such as Store Valby), it is only rarely possible to trace the settlement, as in the case of Lejre, further back than to the end of the Viking Age or the early Middle Ages.[10] Similarly, there have been a great many excavations in churches in various parts of the country, but only exceptionally have they revealed earlier churches, graves or even objects datable to before c. 1100.[11] The Viking Age settlements known today (fig. 12) were also in general deserted in that period or in the early Middle Ages. They were situated, however, close to the later villages, often between 400 and 500 m from the church, but the distance may vary.[12] It is also a common feature that burial-grounds of the Viking Age are relatively small and were in use for a comparatively short period.[13] Finally, only a few Viking Age settlements in present-day Denmark can be traced back to the Germanic Iron Age, and those that can only to its latest stage.[14]

It must be concluded that the villages of the Viking Age were often mobile. After a certain time, perhaps a couple of centuries or so, they were moved to a new site, not necessarily very far from the previous site, within the settlement area.[15] This also applies to early Iron Age settlements,[16] and almost without exception to the trading centres and towns, both in Denmark and in the rest of Scandinavia. Hedeby, for example, was abandoned in favour of Schleswig, Ribe was apparently moved across the river, Kaupang in Norway was deserted and Birka in Sweden left in favour of Sigtuna. Arhus may be an exception.[17] It thus looks as if a stabilisation of settlements took place during the late Viking Age and early Middle Ages, quite a novelty for the settlement pattern in Denmark.

Returning to place-names, the traditional sources of settlement

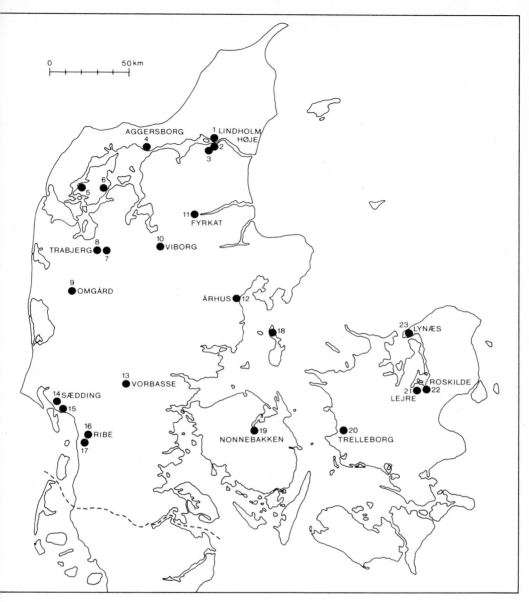

Fig. 12 *Viking Age settlements in present-day Denmark traced archaeologically (cf. Appendix, Finds List 1, p. 249).*

history, there is no reason why a settlement which got a new and stable site in the late Viking/early medieval period should not take its earlier name with it, though in some cases it may have acquired a new name.[18]

Many of the features mentioned above are excellently illustrated in the case of Vorbasse.[19] Since 1974, extensive and as yet incomplete excavations have revealed traces of a mobile settlement here in existence from around the birth of Christ to about 1100. So far, however, evidence of the period from about AD 500 to about 800 is absent. This village, as it undoubtedly was between about AD 200 and 500 and again in the Viking Age, moved its site and that of its burial ground more than once, though never far at a time and always in the vicinity of the present village of Vorbasse. Both the moves themselves and the large-scale alterations in the layout of the settlement in the fourth and fifth centuries, when the village remained on one site for a long time, show that the settlement was then subject to some form of organisation. The village of Vorbasse is mentioned first in written sources between 1330 and 1348, but since it has a Romanesque church of granite ashlar it must have been on its present site probably in the twelfth and certainly in the thirteenth century.[20]

There must be some reason why settlements of the late Germanic Iron Age (c. 550–750) are virtually unknown in Denmark despite fairly large numbers of settlements from both earlier and later periods.[21] As mentioned above, the later settlements begin to crop up during the eighth century and around 800, that is, roughly contemporary with the beginning of the Viking Age and the first Viking raids abroad. This is the date of both agricultural settlements and centres of trade and industry like Ribe and Hedeby. The Danevirke had already been established in the first half of the eighth century, and in 808 the ramparts were extended on the orders of the proud King Godfred.[22] Economic expansion must lie behind all this activity after a long period of apparent stagnation characterised by a scarcity of finds; and that expansion most likely depended on changed agricultural conditions, which, after a period of decline, may have allowed an increase of the land under cultivation. This explanation is supported in part by the many place-names dated to the Viking Age and in part by scientific analyses of Danish raised bogs. These suggest that in the late Germanic Iron Age a drastic reduction in land under cultivation was taking place and that this was gradually reclaimed during the Viking and early medieval periods.[23] In that case a steady increase of agricultural production must have occurred and is doubtless an important reason for the general economic expansion in the Viking Age. It must also have been fundamental to the foundation of the towns.

In the Viking Age it was evidently normal to move after a certain length of time. This explains the many deserted Viking Age settlements,[24] which are therefore not to be regarded as out of the ordinary or failures. The causes for such movement have been much discussed. It appears to have taken place over short distances, so it was not an attempt to find new land in place of impoverished soil. A current explanation is that frequent moves occurred to allow cultivation of areas previously settled, well-manured by many years of use and thus fertile.[25] This may have been a common cause. In the case of Lindholm Høje, one vital reason seems to have been massive drifting of sand,[26] and at Trelleborg and Aggersborg (though perhaps only partially at Aggersborg) the civilian settlements were shouldered out by the large fortresses.[27] Perhaps the reasons for movement were manifold, and once the need arose it may have been a straightforward matter to transplant an entire settlement, given the comparatively light buildings and certain conditions of landownership and use.

I.12 *Field at Lindholm Høje under excavation. It was preserved beneath a thick layer of drift sand. Wheel tracks cross the ridges.*

For the time being, reasons as to why the sites of villages became permanent can only be hypothetical. The cause is above all thought to lie in an improved agricultural technique: the introduction of the mould-board plough (replacing the ard or the simple plough), and in connection with that a fixed distribution of land as part of an organised system of communal cultivation. This last feature is characteristic of village organisation in the Middle Ages and right up to the end of strip-farming around 1800.[28] Up to now, the oldest known marks of the mould-board plough in Danish soil are in fact from the late tenth or eleventh century (at Viborg and probably at Aggersborg)[29] but ard-marks from Viking times[30] have also been found, and the oldest dated fragment of a plough in Denmark remains the beam from Navndrup with a C-14 date of 1220 ± 100 years.[31] However, in the marshes round Bremen the mould-board plough was already in use in the first century AD;[32] if it did not come into general use in Denmark until the late Viking or early medieval periods, this might show that organised cultivation on a communal basis—or a new form of it—was introduced at this time.

The old familiar ard was comparatively light to handle but did little more than loosen and stir the soil. The wheeled mould-board plough was a great technical advance in many ways: it turned the soil and could plough in manure, and weeds, and it was well adapted for breaking new ground. But it was heavy and required as many as six or eight, or even more, draught animals—doubtless more than most individuals could provide. Turning a cumbersome mould-board plough was difficult, so long fields, convenient for the ard, must have been almost a prerequisite for the plough.[33]

We have very little knowledge of the fields and field-systems of the Viking Age and the early Middle Ages, and conclusions can only be provisional. The long ridges, 75 and 125 cm wide and about 25 cm high, on the late Viking Age fields of Lindholm Høje (pl. 12) are now seen by some as beds for the cultivation of crops that needed hoeing.[34] There are similar ridges beneath Grydehøj at Lejre, but they may be as much as five to six hundred years older.[35] The ard may have been used in both places.[36] The long, flat, relatively narrow early medieval fields at Borup Ris in Sjælland may not be quite typical—they too may have been ploughed by the ard.[37] Some other traces of the same type of fields are known.[38]

For the present, however, it may be a fruitful working hypothesis to think that a new form of village and agricultural organisation based on the mould-board plough was the cause of a general stabilising of habitation sites in the eleventh and twelfth centuries, one of the most significant developments ever in the pattern of Danish settlement. The wish for more effective methods of working the land may lie behind this development, and such a wish may have been caused by an increase in population during the late Viking and early medieval periods, for which there were no longer sufficient outlets in emigration or in new clearings at home.[39]

It may also be fruitful to be aware of the possible role in this process of those in power. Stable settlements with fixed, regular codes of ownership were an advantage when it came to the collection of taxes, rents, military contributions and tithes, and were in general advantageous for the expanding power of the monarchy. The advantages were even greater if stable settlements were based on a new agricultural method that gave bigger yields than before.[40]

Finally, however, some reservations must be expressed. Mention should first be made of the traditional Danish interpretation of these problems, which has stood for half a century and more. This sees the introduction of the mould-board plough as the prime reason for the first *foundation* of the settlements[41] in contrast to the explanation outlined above, which makes it a reason for their *stabilisation*. Secondly, there is little concrete evidence to show exactly when the plough came into general use in Denmark. Thirdly, we have no truly precise dating of the earliest phases of permanent village sites—so that theories about a

vej
3,7
Sønderris Bæk

3,3

grusgrav
9,4

7,3

7,7

minkfarm

9,4

0   50   100 m

ig. 13 *Village of*
ædding near
bjerg. Plan of the
cavated part
owing buildings
d contours in
tres. The open
uare can be seen in
centre. The
eam runs top
ht. North to the
.

superior political influence behind their formation become all the more speculative. Fourthly, we must remember that many of the villages that came into existence between about 400 BC and AD 600 must have been organised on communal lines in some way; and the public square at Sædding shows clearly that the same was true of Viking Age villages as well.

VILLAGES AND FARMS

The excavations mentioned above have also provided quite new information about the appearance of villages, farmsteads and houses of the Viking Age. It is often impossible to decide whether traces of settlements represent part of a village, or only one or more single farms. Sædding, near Esbjerg, however, is undoubtedly a village (fig. 13): a fairly large

[57]

number of farms joined together in a community subject to certain fixed rules.

From 1974 to 1976 an area of about 35,000 m² was examined, comprising the central, most densely populated area.[42] This is presumed to represent approximately one-third of the total area; trial trenches indicate that up to 100,000 m² (10 ha) were inhabited. It is dated to the tenth and eleventh centuries and there is no doubt as to continuity within this period. It is uncertain where the village moved to subsequently.

Its centre was a large open square of about 120 × 25 m, which must have been a public area. The square was not encroached on by any building during the entire lifetime of the village and, since all the houses are orientated towards it, the village must have been planned around it. The finds consist of the typical Jutland pottery of the period, spindle-whorls, loom-weights, soapstone vessels and many other objects, as well as sunken-featured buildings and houses of familiar form and construction. There were good grazing areas along a nearby stream, and also good arable land. The inhabitants must have lived chiefly by farming. There is admittedly only inconclusive evidence of byres but, since between 40 and 50 cm of topsoil had to be removed before the post-holes of the buildings appeared distinctly, traces of stall partitions may easily have been lost. Of agricultural implements only a scythe and a couple of hoes have been found, but there are blacksmiths' tools and a smithy, as well as tools of the woodworker and weaver.

A total of 115 buildings has been investigated as well as about 75 sunken-featured buildings, many other pits of different sorts (among them some cooking pits/earth-ovens), and seven wells, four of them with wooden linings. Many houses had been rebuilt several times, and both orientation and siting were sometimes altered. No fences were discovered —traces of these have probably been destroyed like those of the stall partitions—and some presumed boundary ditches cannot be proved to be associated with the houses. It is therefore impossible to decide which of the many buildings existed contemporaneously, or to define the buildings belonging to individual farms. If the buildings are divided into groups according to size, however, and the presence or absence of fire-places and the distribution of the groups over the whole area taken into account, a pattern emerges of large buildings (between 23 and 56 m long) surrounded by smaller buildings. This matches exactly the layout of the better preserved farms in Vorbasse.

The large buildings, in which as a rule cross-partitions and one or more fireplaces have been detected, were dwelling-houses, most likely often with a byre at one end. The smaller buildings must have been chiefly storehouses, tool-sheds, workshops, dwellings for servants or slaves, and so on. Some small buildings, appearing as four posts set in a square, have been interpreted as hay stores, but the function of smaller buildings can rarely be determined individually, here or elsewhere.

Except in some small buildings, the long walls of the houses were curved and the gable ends straight. The walls can be identified by a regular line of post-holes, and as only very little daub has been found it is probable that the walls too were of wood. With few exceptions the roof was supported by two inner rows of posts, the end pairs of which were in the gables. There was thus a very fixed style of building in the village, though with a few notable exceptions. Thus a house 15 m long had no inner posts, but a wall ditch, and its roof was evidently supported by the walls. Two other houses seem to have had both inner posts for roof support and sloping external posts. The plan of another house corresponded to that of houses in the Viking fortresses (figs. 40 and 42), though not of the same dimensions, but their sloping external posts have not come to light. Finally it should be mentioned that one of the houses seems to have had a cellar near one gable, while another, unique here, had a clay floor. In this latter building there seem to be traces of wall-benches as well.

The sunken-featured buildings are concentrated in groups of varying numbers all over the excavated area, but it has been impossible to demonstrate any connection between them and the other buildings. They exhibit the usual features of such huts. Here they are between 2.5 and 5.5 m long, and from 2 to 4.75 m wide; they have been partly dug into the earth so that the earth wall combined with the soil thrown out formed a wall or at least a partial wall; they are rectangular, oval or almost circular in shape. They have two roof-bearing posts placed opposite each other, one on each of their short sides; some have been shown to have had an interior wall-cladding of planks, turf or similar material. Elsewhere (in Århus for example, fig. 20)[43] ovens, fireplaces, wall-benches and entrances have also been detected in buildings of this sort. When their useful life was over, such buildings usually ended up as rubbish pits. This happened at Sædding too. Many of the artefacts found here in fact came out of these pits.

Sunken-featured buildings are characteristic of the settlements in large parts of northern Europe from about AD 400 until the late Viking or early medieval periods. Then they disappear or become very rare. Many interpretations of their function are possible: dwellings for slaves or for the poor, workshops (especially for weaving—they often contain loom-weights), winter or seasonal dwellings, and so forth,[44] and some were undoubtedly cellars.[45] They were presumably used for a great variety of purposes. They were quick to make, but the essential reason for their existence must have been their capacity to maintain a steady temperature. As they were both small and sunken, and their walls above ground level were presumably well protected by the earth dug out to form the pit and by the roof, they must have been easy to heat in winter (by a fire, oven or just by brazier or human warmth) because of the heat retained by the earth.[46] The other types of houses were of comparatively light construction and much more vulnerable to cold. Storehouses dug down like this may also have been frost-proof. On the other hand they must have been correspondingly cool in summer. Perhaps they went out of fashion because people began to build houses with better insulation.

The Viking Age settlement at Trabjerg in West Jutland most likely represents a village too.[47] From 1972 to 1976 an area of about 25,000 m² was uncovered, containing both houses and sunken-featured buildings situated near a stream and good pasture. An uninhabited part may have

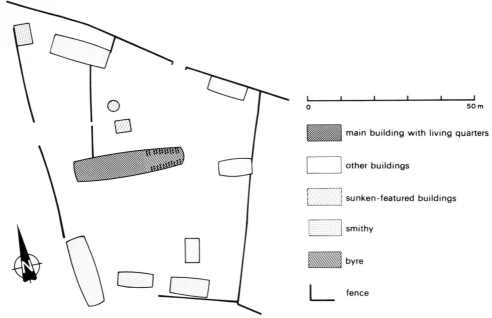

Fig. 14   *Plan of Viking Age farm at Vorbasse. These buildings were probably contemporary.*

been the public area of the village, but as it is low-lying it may simply have been unsuitable for habitation. Not many artefacts have been found, but they are typical of the Viking Age and very reminiscent of those from Sædding. The village was in existence from about AD 725 to 1050. There is greater variation of building style than at Sædding. Besides the sunken-featured buildings there were, for example, houses both with curved and with straight long walls; some had sloping external posts while others had two rows of inner posts supporting the roof, the latter also apparently sloping towards each other. The walls were revealed either as post-holes or as ditches. No traces of byres or of fences have been found, so we cannot tell how the individual buildings made up farm complexes. The explanation of that is presumably the same as at Sædding.

New finds at Vorbasse (figs. 14–15)[48] show what a Viking Age farm might have looked like, and the model seems to fit other sites where the buildings are less well preserved. The only two Viking Age farms to be examined up to now were found in 1977 and 1978, and the excavations are continuing. Each farm had a main building of about 32 m long containing both dwelling and byres. They were both located in the centre of a fenced yard about 80 × 80 m, surrounded by a number of smaller buildings, some situated along the fence. One of these was a smithy. In addition there were some sunken-featured buildings. The long walls of the main buildings were curved, as were those of several of the smaller ones, and in both cases the byre was at the eastern end; traces of stall partitions showed that there had been room for about twenty-two large animals in the byres of both farms. They were probably mostly cattle.

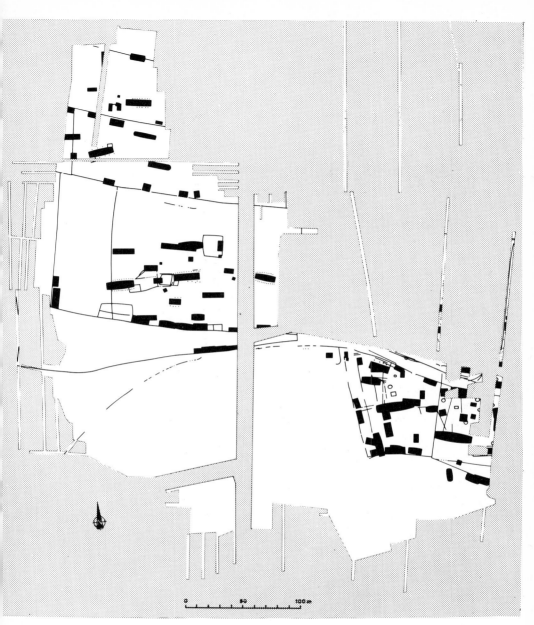

The two farms adjoined each other on the south side of an area which produced no finds, between 8 and 10 m wide, probably a road, and trial trenches have shown that there was a number of other farms in the area. The objects found correspond to those found on other Viking Age settlements. In particular there were nine small horse-shaped mounts of sheet bronze and two silver coins. One is a coin of the type thought to have been minted at Hedeby *c.* AD 975–80 and the other a German coin from Stade minted between 1038 and 1040.

At some time the settlement was enlarged or shifted towards the north-west (fig. 15). On the north-western side of the road mentioned above, a large fenced farm evolved (about 215 × 160 m) and to the north of this two smaller farms, also fenced, each half the width of the large farm to the south. These three farms have been discussed in a number of publications. The number of finds is small, but they show that the farms date at the earliest to the very end of the Viking period, and more likely belong to the early Middle Ages—that is, from the second half of the eleventh or twelfth century. Characteristic Viking Age objects are absent, and it is notable that there were no sunken-featured buildings on these farms either. Another characteristic feature is that dwelling and byre are separate. The dwelling-houses, built on modified versions of the plan known from Viking fortresses, are still located in the centre of the yard, but the byres often lie along the fence. In addition there are workshops, as a rule also in separate buildings, and a number of buildings of indeterminate function. All three farms have been altered considerably and it cannot be decided precisely which buildings were in simultaneous use. If all the byres of the southern farm functioned at the same time, there would have been space for about a hundred animals. Certainly the farm must be designated a rich man's farm, where the keeping of livestock played a considerable role; the region is also highly suitable for this purpose. As at Trabjerg, several different types of buildings and methods of construction are present.

In 1974–6, investigations were made of large areas (33,000 m²) of a Viking Age settlement at Omgård in West Jutland.[49] Some C-14 dates indicate activity during the tenth century, but there are several phases and it is difficult as yet to put dates to the origin and end of the settlement, but it may have continued into the eleventh century. All the sunken-featured buildings probably belong to an older phase. In a more recent phase, buildings (some used as workshops) occur which are closely related to the houses of the Viking fortresses (figs. 40 and 42), and found in association with fences and palisades. There are also byres. The settlement is located by the crossing-place of a stream and there are good pastures nearby. A fair amount of wood, from the fence for example, has been preserved in the damp ground near the stream, and fragments of wheels and of wagon axles and other wooden objects have been found in the old stream bed. The water-mill that existed there may be as old as the Viking Age, but at the moment its date is uncertain.

Finally a group of farms in the most southerly part of the old kingdom of Denmark deserve mention. From 1954 to 1964 major excavations were carried out on the northern bank of the Eider in Elisenhof, near Tønning.[50] The excavations were on a *værft* (a farm mound) which turned out to date back to the eighth century. In the lower levels, wood from buildings and fences was well preserved up to a height of 2 m, and many wells were also found. The main buildings were divided into a living area and a byre with stall partitions. The larger houses were rectangular, and several had sloping external posts to support the weight of the roof. It was clear from the excavated material that many cattle were kept and were of decisive significance in the settlement's economy.

Surplus production must have been exported by way of the Eider, which could be reached by road. The inhabitants were presumably Frisians.

Apart from the most recent constructions at Vorbasse and Omgård, the villages and farms discussed above, all in central and West Jutland, in general correspond well to what is known of other rural settlements in Jutland, such as Aggersborg where many sunken-featured buildings and at least seven houses with curved walls have been excavated.[51] The longest was about 41 m long and apparently had a byre at the western end.[52]

Only minor investigations of Viking Age settlements on the Danish islands have been carried out, but a house at Lejre[53] and a couple of others from the civilian settlement beneath Trelleborg[54] show that, like the houses of this fortress, buildings with curved long walls also existed on the islands, and sunken-featured buildings have been discovered on Samsø, Fyn and Sjælland.[55] It should also be mentioned that both at Sædding and at Omgård there appear to be constructions with three irregular wings (or three houses joined together at an angle).[56] Some buildings at Lindholm Høje were interpreted as courtyard houses when they were excavated, but so far remain unparalleled.[57] Only in the Viking fortresses are there structures reminiscent of them.

In general terms, the building style in Denmark in the Viking Age can be described as north-west European,[58] but an overall analysis of the now very substantial material is badly needed. Some chronological levels may be isolated and it is likely that there were regional differences. This may be indicated, for example, by the houses at Sædding and by the wall constructions in the houses of the Viking fortresses.[59] Villages and farms may have differed in other respects too from region to region. Thus in Skåne quite a number of settlements with sunken-featured buildings are known from the Viking period and earlier,[60] but no houses have been found apart from a few of the first half of the eleventh century at Lund, one of them with curved walls and sloping external posts, divided into rooms rather like the Trelleborg houses.[61] Since posts of houses were frequently dug down deep, one would expect some traces to remain. It may be that it is often seasonal settlements that have so far been found. Löddeköpinge, for example, has been explained in this way.[62] The explanation may also be that another building method was employed which did not sink house-posts into the ground. But it is hardly likely that people in Skåne in the Viking Age rested their posts on stone sills. The oldest evidence of this method in Denmark is in the third church at Jelling (eleventh century), but long after this posts of ordinary buildings in the country continued to be dug into the earth. However, there may have been log houses in Skåne, that is houses constructed of horizontal timbers as in the Slav regions south of the Baltic and in the pine forests of Scandinavia.[63]

Seasonally inhabited sites, such as markets, may often have had sunken-featured buildings or even less permanent structures; men must have lived in tents too. Löddeköpinge, where there were sunken-featured buildings, and Lynæs, where only lighter structures have been found, have both been interpreted in this way.[64] There is a distinct difference, however, between all the settlements mentioned above and Hedeby, where the houses inside the Semicircular Wall were almost exclusively small and rectangular. The difference between this town on the one hand and villages and farms on the other must be chiefly functional and perhaps also social. As far as one can see, there was not much agriculture at Hedeby, and the trade and industry carried on there did not require much space. Not much is known about Viking Age buildings in other Danish towns, but the situation in eleventh-century Viborg and Lund resembles that at Hedeby; so far only sunken-featured buildings have been found in Ribe and Århus.[65]

With regard to actual well-to-do farms of the Viking Age it must be said that very little is known about their appearance and possible functions, other than their purely agricultural ones. People like Alli, who is remembered on the tenth-century Glavendrup rune stone, and his wife Ragnhild, who had the stone raised (pl. 4),[66] may have resided in a long main building with a byre at one end, like the house 56 m long at Sædding or the house 41 m long in the civilian settlement at Aggersborg. A large gold arm-ring, fragments of glass beakers and other rare objects from this Aggersborg house demonstrate the wealth of its owner. As at Vorbasse, several small buildings of various functions were probably situated around Alli's and Ragnhild's main house. During the eleventh century the upper classes presumably often resided in farms like those of the later phases at Vorbasse and Omgård, where the dwelling was separate from the byre. This separation may go further back, for in the second half of the tenth century the top ranks of society could meet in the halls of the Viking fortresses, and these perhaps set the fashion. Throughout the Viking period, at least abroad, noble halls existed without integral byres.[67] They might easily have been the pattern, perhaps even for some ordinary farms, although these are more likely generally to have resembled the older farms at Vorbasse.

AGRICULTURE AND FISHING

Stock breeding undoubtedly played a large role in Danish agriculture of the Viking Age. The number of beasts housed on each of the two farms at Vorbasse was about twenty-two, and in the later phases at Vorbasse and Omgård the numbers were greater. Domestic animals can be identified from bones found in many places; at Ribe, through deep layers of manure too.

Horses, oxen, pigs and sheep were common, and goats were also known; in addition, hens and geese were kept, as well as dogs and cats.[68] The animals were generally smaller than nowadays. Skeletal measurements show that many horses were about the size of the Icelandic horse of today, but larger horses of up to 15 hands (i.e. a shoulder-height of about 150 cm) are also known from some richly equipped graves. One of these horses, from a grave containing driving equipment at Gryderup on Sjælland, has been described as a well-proportioned horse of medium height, which presumably was very similar to modern Scandinavian

Fig. 16 *Shov. the Danevirke (upper part of s missing) and sp. from Jelling, le. 95 cm.*

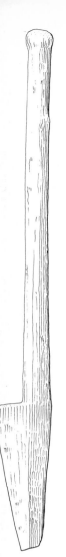

breeds such as the *Dølehest* and the North Swedish and Finnish horses.[69] Horses were used for riding and as draught animals, and some were also eaten.[70] The metatarsal bone was sometimes used for skates, and other bones for needles, pins and bodkins.[71] The hides were undoubtedly utilised as well. Pigs yielded meat and some of their bones were used for needles.[72] Oxen and cows could be used for meat and milk, and harnessed as draught animals. Their hides were made into such things as shoes, scabbards and straps.[73] Calf-skins, too, were in demand for making books in the monasteries and centres of learning of Europe.[74] Ox-bones were used for skates and spindle-whorls, and other things.[75] Sheep yielded meat, warm sheepskins, leather for shoes and so on, as well as wool for textiles. From their bones one could make handles and whistles,[76] and other objects. Goats were also eaten, their skins often used for shoes and their horns worked.[77] Both sheep and goats were presumably milked. Fowl were eaten, and their feathers no doubt widely used for pillows and eiderdowns. The significance of castration for the quality of meat and the general effect of the operation on living creatures was probably well known.[78]

Cats were useful domestic animals, attractive then as now because they could catch mice. A number of different breeds of dog occur, from heavy, coarse-jawed animals to slight, long-legged ones and small dogs with a shoulder-height of only about 25 cm, as well as everything in between. There must have been a certain amount of breeding out to produce hunting-dogs, sheep-dogs, guard-dogs, lap-dogs and so forth.[79]

The most important agricultural implements were the ard and the mould-board plough discussed above, but no Danish examples can be dated to the Viking Age, though an iron ard-blade was found at Trelleborg.[80] Fields and plough- and ard-marks were also discussed above. The marks of harrows have been found in the soil at Lindholm Høje.[81] Other types of tools for working the soil include wooden shovels and spades (fig. 16),[82] and iron blades doubtless from hoes or digging-sticks.[83] Harvesting tools were scythes (the so-called short scythes) as well as sickles and leaf knives (fig. 17).[84]

Cultivated cereal crops were chiefly barley, rye and oats, but wheat was also known. The cultivated plants of the Viking Age have not been thoroughly investigated, but rye seems to have been greatly on the increase during this period. From the fortress of Fyrkat came a large find of particularly good quality rye thought to have originated in Poland or some more distant part of Eastern Europe.[85] Among other cultivated plants we find peas and beans, and flax was probably grown.[86] Fruit, berries and nuts are discussed below (ch. 7). Large hayfields were necessary for winter feed, and indeed the settlements are often situated close to good meadows.[87]

Game was evidently not of significance in the diet,[88] but fishing was carried out in those settlements which lay near the sea or other good fishing waters, for example Hedeby, Lund, Århus and Aggersborg. Fishing implements and fish-bones both testify to this. Such finds have not been made in Sædding, however, though only about 1.5 km from the Vadehav (tidal flats on the coast of South Jutland), but at any rate mussels

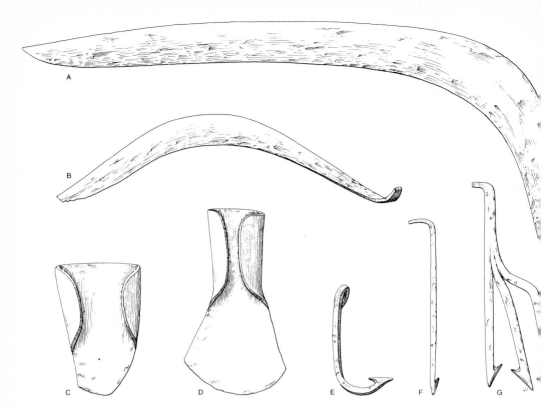

Fig. 17 *Agricultural and fishing tools, all iron. A scythe blade from Trelleborg; B sickle or scythe blade from Tjele; C ard blade from Trelleborg; D head of hoe or digging-stick from Aggersborg; E fish-hook from Aggersborg; F–G fishing-spear tines from Århus and Trelleborg. Scale about 1 : 3.*

were gathered here and elsewhere—obviously a favourite food—as well as oysters and snails.[89]

Fishing implements like hooks and barbed fishing-spears (fig. 17) occur in a number of places. Fishing-nets were also used. A net fragment from Lund has been interpreted as from a fishing-net, but usually the only evidence for nets is in the shape of sinkers and floats, and perhaps the net-sticks used for gathering up the net after fishing.[90] Some fragments of nets have also been interpreted as hunting or carrying nets.[91] The most common fish were the same as those caught today, i.e. various flat fish, cod and herring, but the last have such small bones that they are unlikely to survive excavation under normal conditions. Garfish, eel, sturgeon, salmon and trout, and many other sorts of fish were known.[92] Finds at Hedeby indicate that a certain amount of trade in fish took place, for example herrings.[93]

Though fishing thus played an important role in some places, people in the country must have lived basically on agriculture. There is only a little evidence of industry in these settlements, apart from tools and waste products from smithies, carpenters' tools, and implements used in textile manufacture. All of this was indispensable in a village community as well. But objects that came from outside, whether brought by trade or other means, have also been found in nearly all settlements, and testify to the extent to which agriculture flourished during the period. There are, for example, soapstone vessels and whetstones from Norway, quernstones from the Rhineland, glass beads and other professionally manufactured ornaments and imported pottery (ch. 6).

These finds reflect solid prosperity and a sense of good quality, as well as appreciation of the rare and picturesque. In Sædding, Trabjerg and Vorbasse, for example, the prosperity must have resulted from the sale of agricultural surplus, perhaps in processed form, and the locations of the civilian settlements at Aggersborg and at Lindholm Høje beside crossing-points over the busy Limfjord may explain why the finds from these sites show particularly close connections with the world outside. Markets may have been held here, even though the economy was based on agriculture. In the vicinity of some of these centrally situated settlements (such as Lindholm Høje), towns developed (in this case Ålborg). But at Aggersborg the village had already been entirely or partly deserted in the tenth century to make way for the great fortress, and throughout the Middle Ages the king continued to own a fortress or royal estate here.[94]

5 The First Towns

The Viking Age saw the first growth of towns in Denmark and the rest of Scandinavia, a new style of settlement: large, quite densely packed and permanent, with various centralised services for the surrounding regions. The chief service was the provision of regular markets, but a town could also function as a religious centre, be the site of a regular legal assembly— a *Thing*—and headquarters for a regional administration. The occupations of townspeople were industry and trade for the most part, rather than agriculture and fishing. Many of the goods produced and sold in towns were those which could not be manufactured at home on the farms, either because the raw materials were not available or because specialist work was required. Some towns also functioned as entrepôts in a larger network of long-distance trade, centres for the distribution of goods.[1]

The first essential for settlements with such centralised functions and specialist work is a good transport system, allowing easy and regular communication between the town and its surrounding area in order to facilitate trade as well as the exchange of daily necessities. As seen in ch. 3, such conditions did indeed exist in the Viking Age and they were developed further during the period. A second essential is the availability of an agricultural surplus to feed the inhabitants of a town, and a significant expansion in agriculture apparently did occur during the Viking Age and perhaps continued in the succeeding centuries when towns went on being founded (see ch. 4). A third essential is good international trading conditions to further the general exchange of goods. In the Viking Age, towns and trading-centres did indeed spring up all over northern Europe. In Norway, Kaupang in Vestfold (on the west side of Oslo fjord) and later Oslo, Trondheim and others belong to this period. In Sweden, Birka on an island in Lake Mälaren emerges as an important centre at the beginning of the Viking Age, followed by the townships Sigtuna, Skara and others.[2]

Between the towns proper and ordinary countryside villages there was a kind of intermediate stage. Such was the civilian settlement at Aggersborg where people presumably lived mostly by farming, but where the population was evidently also very busy in other ways (partly reflected in the large numbers of artefacts) and had many connections with the outside world. Aggersborg was a permanent settlement, centrally placed with regard to traffic, where trade or the exchange of

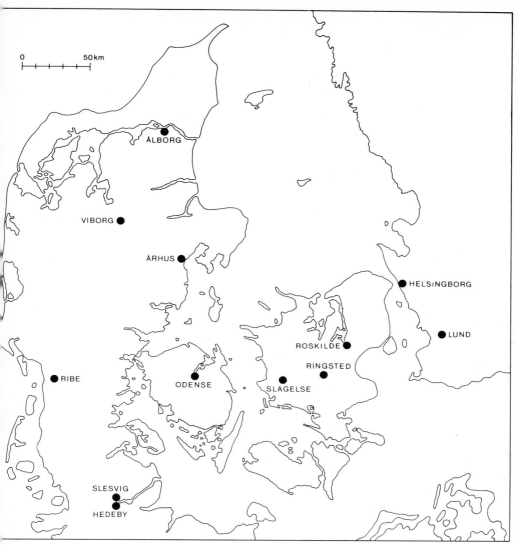

Fig. 18 *Settlements which were towns by the end of the Viking Age or later developed into towns.*

goods would certainly have taken place; but the wares, apart from agricultural products, were probably not often produced on the spot, judging by the very few traces of industries. Other settlements, like Lynæs in North Sjælland and Löddeköpinge in Skåne, are thought to have been largely seasonal and dependent on markets (cf. ch. 4) and, all in all, markets of various kinds were probably of great importance both for the sale of goods and for general communications. There may also have been other types of settlement where trade was of significance.[3]

Sustained archaeological effort has produced much new information about Danish Viking Age towns (fig. 18)—when they were founded, how they developed in topographical terms, what occupations their inhabitants followed, and much else. This is particularly true of Hedeby, Ribe,

Århus, Viborg and Lund. A large-scale archaeological and historical investigation is under way which will in the course of time shed more light on the emergence and earliest development of Danish towns.[4] Written sources also give illuminating glimpses of the early towns, and coins come to play an ever-increasing role in our knowledge of towns because, from the beginning of the eleventh century onwards, the mint is usually included in their legends.[5] It must be emphasised, however, that the word 'town' is used in a wide sense in this book.

HEDEBY

Hedeby and Birka were the most important towns in the North during the Viking Age. Hedeby is mentioned in a number of written sources and is also archaeologically the best known.[6] It was the furthest south of all Scandinavian towns, on the neck of the Jutland peninsula near to the old Danish–German–Slav border, and was closely associated with the border fortifications, the Danevirke (ch. 8). The location of the town at the head of the Schlei fjord, on the edge of the inlet Haddeby Nor, made the land passage across Jutland a short one and the journey was further eased by the proximity of the rivers Rheide and Treene; they met at Hollingstedt and from there ran into the river Eider, which connected with the North Sea. Furthermore, the main north–south traffic artery in Jutland, the Army Road or Ox Road, passed close to Hedeby. Thus there were good geographical conditions for a main trading centre.

Written sources—the *Life* of the missionary Ansgar, the travel accounts of the merchants Ohthere and Wulfstan, and the description of the North by Adam of Bremen—give a concrete impression of the town's trading connections. An Arab source probably also refers to the town (ch. 2). In these Hedeby appears as an international town, linked with Norway to the north, with Sweden to the east, with the Slav and other peoples south and east of the Baltic coast, and with Russia and the Byzantine world via the large rivers. There are also references to southward contacts with the Saxons and with the town of Dorestad in Frisia to the south-west. In England, Hedeby was known as a large town. All such connections are reflected in the archaeological finds of objects manufactured in these areas. Naturally, there were also contacts with the rest of Denmark.

Hedeby was identified in 1897, and since then large excavations, particularly in the 1930s and again in the 1950s and 1960s, have produced a wealth of archaeological material. In recent years dendrochronology has provided precise datings, and excavations in Schleswig, Hedeby's successor, have illustrated the development. Though the Hedeby excavations have been extensive, only about 5 per cent of the total area enclosed within the semicircular ramparts of the tenth century has been examined (pl. 13). In addition, a minor area in the so-called *Südsiedlung* and part of a large cemetery south of the ramparts have been investigated, and various trial trenches and sections dug, along with some other cemetery and grave sites. Only minor investigations have been made of the fort, *Hochburg*, which lies immediately north of the ramparts and

Pl 13 *Aerial photograph of Hedeby with the Semicircular Wall and the Connecting Wall, see fig. 39. The areas excavated in 1963–9 and 1979 are marked. North is to the top.*

whose age is unknown. It may have been a refuge fortress for Hedeby before the ramparts were built. Major excavations are currently (1979–80) being carried out in the harbour area of the town, where the early shore-lines have been established, lying more than a metre below the present levels. All in all, the history of the habitation of the Hedeby area is very complex and much remains unclear.

The earliest settlement so far found is the *Südsiedlung* of Hedeby, in existence for a century from *c.* 750 onwards. Thirty-three sunken-featured buildings, one house 13 m in length, various pits and a cemetery have been excavated here. The sunken-featured buildings often have fireplaces and were consequently used for human habitation, and in many of the earliest of them there were traces of industry in the shape of raw

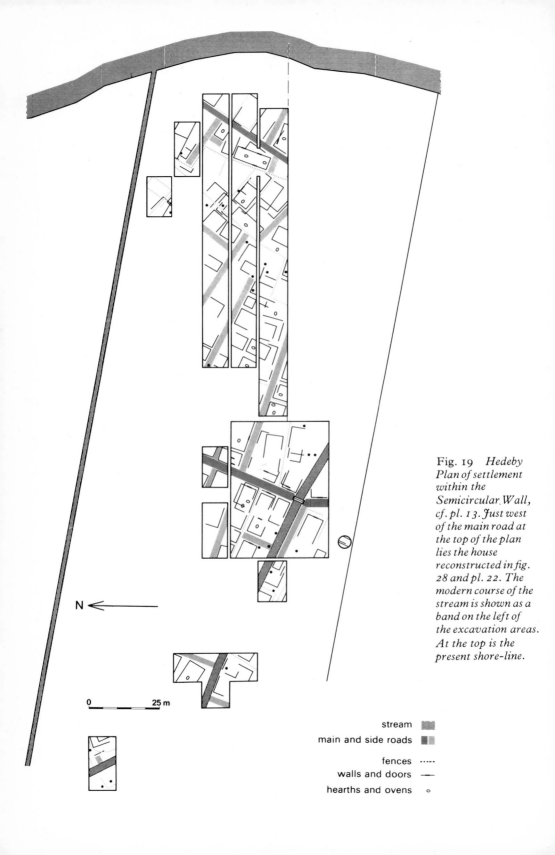

N ←

0   25 m

Fig. 19   *Hedeby*
Plan of settlement
within the
Semicircular Wall,
cf. pl. 13. Just west
of the main road at
the top of the plan
lies the house
reconstructed in fig.
28 and pl. 22. The
modern course of the
stream is shown as a
band on the left of
the excavation areas.
At the top is the
present shore-line.

stream ▦

main and side roads ▦

fences ·····

walls and doors ——

hearths and ovens ○

materials, half-finished objects and refuse. In its later phase, the *Südsiedlung* co-existed with the settlement within the area later enclosed by the semicircular ramparts, and during the ninth century there may have been a third settlement area north of the ramparts, near the fort of *Hochburg*, though only a few traces suggesting this have been found.

Hedeby is first documented in written history around AD 800. The Frankish annals relate that in 804 King Godfred came to 'the place which is called Sliesthorp in the borderland between his realm and Saxony'. The same annals relate that, four years later, Godfred conducted a military expedition against the Abodrites, Slav allies of Charlemagne, and they continue:

> But before his return Godfred ordered the destruction of one trading station, situated on the shore of the sea, which in the language of the Danes was called Reric, and which gave his realm great benefit by the collection of taxes. He carried the merchants from here away with him and then went with his entire army by sea to Sliesthorp. Here he stayed for several days and decided to protect the border of his realm towards Saxony with a wall ...[7]

The precise location of Reric is not known—there have been several suggestions[8]—but presumably Sliesthorp is identical with Sliaswich, mentioned in the *Life* of Ansgar, with the *æt Hæthum* of Ohthere and Wulfstan, and with the Haithabu of Danish rune stones. The situation and character of the settlement certainly correspond to Hedeby's, up to now there have been no finds in Schleswig which go back as far, and in the *Chronicle* of the Anglo-Saxon Æthelweard of about 970 it is said that the main town in the district of Angeln is called *Slesvic* in Saxon, *Haitha by* in Danish.[9]

It appears from the passage in the annals mentioned above that Reric paid taxes and that Godfred pursued his own commercial and trading policy by destroying its trading station and removing its merchants. Strictly speaking, the annals do not record that he deposited these merchants in Hedeby, but it is an obvious conclusion from the passage, and the assumption is to some extent supported by archaeological finds. The settlement evidence from within the semicircular ramparts is quite different in character from that of the *Südsiedlung*, and further shows that it began as a planned settlement at the beginning of the ninth century. So it appears that Godfred deliberately founded the Hedeby which was to become the entrepôt for much Viking Age trade between the Baltic and Western Europe. Presumably it was also a reloading place for many of the goods sold in Denmark and for many Danish exports. It is also an obvious conclusion that many of Hedeby's local products were sold inside Denmark, though it is difficult to substantiate this archaeologically.

The older levels of this settlement are well preserved, thanks to the high water-level; it had a stream running right through the centre from west to east (fig. 19). This stream was very soon channelled, and the wood-paved streets of the settlement were for the most part laid either at right-angles to the stream or parallel with it. Along the streets there were relatively small rectangular houses on small, fenced plots—the house of about 5 × 12 m discussed below (ch. 7) was one of the larger ones. There were small outhouses on some plots, and many had their own wells. It is important to observe that almost all the plots retained their original size.

With the help of dendrochronology the settlement can at present be traced back to the year 811 without a break; a few stray pieces of wood have been shown, however, to date from the end of the eighth century. The latest dendrochronological dating so far is 1020 and comes from a well-lining (no wood from the latest phase has survived except from wells), but the town can be traced through artefacts to the middle of the eleventh century. Then it must have been moved to the place where Schleswig now lies. The earliest dendrochronological dating so far obtained in Schleswig is 1087, from a quay. According to written sources, Hedeby was destroyed by fire around the middle of the eleventh century, but probably the decision to move the town was in part dictated by the general sinking of the land-level, which made the area damp and unpleasant to live in (some of the Hedeby settlement is today under water) and in part by the development of ships with greater draught, which made Schleswig a more practical harbour. The large eleventh-century quay-constructions of this town show that this latter was important.

Ninth-century Hedeby lay close to the water. Later, the settlement was extended towards the west—sunken-featured buildings, for example, have been found here—and in the mid tenth century it was surrounded by the large Semicircular Wall (ch. 8) enclosing an area of 24 ha. However, this area was probably never inhabited in its entirety; we know that a burial-ground lay within the ramparts, for example, probably during the whole lifetime of the settlement. As already mentioned, Hedeby had several cemeteries. Some have fairly simple inhumation graves; one has richly furnished chamber-graves, and most splendid of all is a boat chamber-grave, richly equipped and with a ship placed on top, covered by a mound (chs. 3 and 9). The very varied character of the burial-grounds indicates that there were large social and economic distinctions among the people associated with Hedeby.

The number of people in the known cemeteries (so far only partly examined) has been calculated to far in excess of 10,000. So, many people lived in Hedeby, and this is confirmed by the dense building in the area examined within the Semicircular Wall and by the great quantities of artefacts found. As remarked in ch. 4, the traces of settlement alone show that occupations—at least within the ramparts—were quite different from those of the villages: the houses and plots in this Hedeby were relatively small, and only a single byre has been recorded among them; there would also have been very little space for animals in the buildings which have been found. The inhabitants must have lived by trade, crafts, fishing and casual or other work rather than by farming. Large numbers of objects from other parts of the world do indeed testify to trade or other exchange of goods, chiefly coins, but also soapstone and whetstones from Norway, quernstones, pottery and wine-barrels from the Rhine, pottery from the Baltic, articles of adornment from the British Isles and

Pl. 14 *Bell found by diving in the harbour area at Hedeby. Height 51.3 cm.*

the Frankish kingdom, and much else. There is extensive evidence of manufacturing: smithying, bronze-casting, comb-making, amber-working, shoe-making, carpentry and so on.

In accord with this, the written sources refer to Hedeby as the place where merchants put in—this is the case with Ohthere and Wulfstan, for example (ch. 3)—and Hedeby was the place where about AD 850 the missionary Ansgar was permitted by King Horik the Older to build the first church in Denmark. Under the succeeding king, Horik the Younger, Ansgar gained permission to place a bell in the church, even though the pagans did not care for bell-ringing. At the same time, a 'Count' of Hedeby is mentioned,[10] probably the king's representative. It is also thought that the first Scandinavian coins were minted in Hedeby around 800 or at the beginning of the ninth century and as the king, according to the written sources, seems to have been playing an important role in the town, it is quite likely that he was also the master of the mint, corresponding to the custom in Western Europe, whence the idea of a monetary system was derived (ch. 6). The archaeological finds confirm the picture of a town with a firm organisation, and four of the five rune stones from the vicinity of Hedeby mention kings. Two stones (pl. 15) were raised in memory of King Sigtrygg, who is thought to have held power in Denmark or in a part of Denmark some time in the first half of the tenth century. The other two stones mention a Svein who must be King Svein Forkbeard (died 1014).[11]

RIBE, ÅRHUS, VIBORG AND LUND

Ribe

Ribe [12] is situated on the west coast of Jutland, on the banks of the river Ribe, which cuts deep into the land and is navigable out to sea through the tidal flats called the Vadehav. The Vadehav today lies about 6 km from the town. The river Ribe thus gave access to a wide hinterland, and the sea-route south to the big West European rivers (the Elbe, Weser, Rhine and Mosel) was protected by a long series of islands which gave shelter from the North Sea. Around 1070 Adam of Bremen wrote that Ribe was surrounded by a 'waterway that flows in from the ocean and over which one sails for Frisia, of a fact, for England or for our own Saxony'.

Ribe is presumed to be Denmark's oldest town. It is first mentioned in written sources in the *Life* of Ansgar by Rimbert, where it is related that Ansgar obtained permission from King Horik to build a church there around 860. This was the third church known in Scandinavia, the first two being in Birka and Hedeby. In 948, and again in 965 and 988, Ribe is mentioned as a bishopric along with Schleswig, Hedeby and Århus, and in the eleventh century and from then on we hear of the town in an ever-increasing number of written sources. It was not until 1970, however, that archaeologists came upon the Viking Age town. It turns out that the settlements of that period lay north of the river, on the outskirts of the present town centre.

Pl. 15 *Rune stone found near Hedeby. Height 214 cm. The inscription reads: 'Ásfrid made this memorial (kuml) after Sigtrygg, her and Gnupa's son'. Another Hedeby stone refers to the same Sigtrygg as king, and Gnupa may be the Danish king who was defeated in 934 by the German king Henry the Fowler. Partly on the basis of the rune-forms here, it is thought that Gnupa and Sigtrygg were of Swedish extraction.*

An area of about 600 m² has been excavated here, revealing deep habitation levels and very rich finds which chiefly reflect trade and manufacturing. Metalworking and bronze-casting were carried out, elaborate glass beads and amber beads were produced too, as well as combs, shoes, textiles and many other things. There are also finds of pottery and animal bones, and a thick layer of animal manure. This last is conclusive evidence of stabled animals, either ordinary domestic animals or cattle intended for export, or both. Only two sunken-featured buildings have been found; a double row of sticks with wattle may be either from the wall of a house or from a fence. In addition there are some wells. Thirty-two tiny silver coins (Frisian *sceattas*) have turned up on the site, and these are decisive for a more precise dating. It has been assigned to around the mid eighth century.

The traces of industries give evidence of specialisation as well as of large-scale production of standardised goods (ch. 6) and this implies a larger market than just a single settlement. The products reflect Scandinavian taste: oval brooches, for example, belonged specifically to Nordic female dress (fig. 35). The links with other countries were primarily with the South and they were strong. The traders of Ribe must have been the middlemen in the export of Danish goods to Western Europe and these goods can hardly have been anything but agricultural produce.

The excavated material has not yet been fully investigated and there has been discussion as to whether the finds represent a permanent or a seasonal settlement. Recently, however, convincing arguments have been put forward for the former.[13] In relation to the size of the excavated area there is a remarkable number of spindle-whorls (about thirty) and loom-weights (about a hundred complete, and some fragments), and this is a strong indication that there were many women here with time for spinning and weaving as in the permanent settlements of the period. Furthermore, the sheep-bones are almost exclusively from older animals, and this must mean that they were kept for wool rather than for meat. Collectively these finds seem to show that all the processes involved in the manufacture of textiles were done on the spot, and since this is a lengthy business it is difficult to associate it with anything but a permanent settlement.

There is thus quite a clear picture of Ribe around 750, but little archaeological evidence for the succeeding 350 years or so. There are only a few stray finds. The medieval town developed south of the river around the cathedral and here there are no Viking Age finds at all. The settlement in Ribe, too, appears to have moved, either as the result of a slow process or because of orders from on high. Finally it must be mentioned that, despite Ribe's importance in trade, it was probably of minor importance as a mint during the Viking Age, and actual evidence of the king's presence in Ribe in this period is limited to the passage in the *Life* of Ansgar mentioned above.

Pl. 16   *The earthworks around Århus under excavation. The sloping lines of several phases of construction can be seen in the vertical section of the earth wall. In the foreground, the timber road bordering the inside of the rampart in phase 2.*

Århus

Århus is situated roughly midway along the east coast of Jutland by the mouth of the river Århus; the original name of the town, Aros, means the mouth of the river.[14] Århus is first mentioned in 948, when it is referred to as a bishopric, and similarly in 965 and 988. During the reign of King Harthacnut, around 1040, coins were struck in the town, and around 1070 Adam of Bremen wrote that from there one sailed to Fyn, Sjælland and Skåne—indeed all the way to Norway.

Six rune stones have been found in various parts of the town, and the excavations in 1963 and 1964 showed definitively that the Viking Age town lay in the present town centre. It was protected by a rampart, presumably semicircular, which enclosed 4–5 ha, and had a wood-paved street along the inner side (pl. 16). The settlement can be traced back to the tenth century, and the earliest phase of the investigated area seems to have been contemporary with the rampart. Seven or eight sunken-featured buildings (fig. 20) used as dwellings and workshops have been found near the inner side of the rampart, and others in a further excavation near the shore. So far no definite evidence of other house-types has appeared. Other finds give some indication of industry, such as comb-making and wood-carving, or reflect trade, for example scales and weights, quernstones from the Rhineland, soapstone pots from Norway or south-west Sweden, whetstones from Norway and pottery from the Baltic.

Finds from the eleventh century are best represented immediately west of the rampart around the present Church of Our Lady (formerly St Nicholas's) which was the cathedral until the beginning of the thirteenth century. The oldest part of the Church of Our Lady is a crypt built of calcareous tufa stone dating from the second half of the eleventh century. This is Denmark's oldest church interior. Town life presumably also continued within the ramparts and in 1203 the building of the present cathedral, St Clement's, was started in this area.

The Viking Age town may thus have been established—perhaps quite suddenly—as a major fortified settlement with trade and industry. If this was so, an organisation must have been behind it and it is obvious to think of the king as instigator. He had an interest in the growth of towns and, as already mentioned, he appears in the written sources in connection with both Hedeby and Ribe. The first actual evidence of a royal connection with Århus (apart from the minting of coins by Harthacnut) is its identification as royal property (*knogelev*) in the thirteenth century.

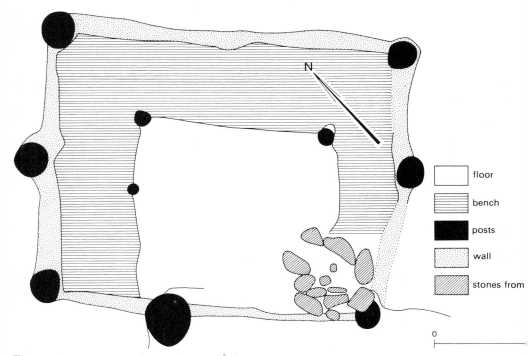

floor

bench

posts

wall

stones from

0

Fig. 20 *Sunken-featured building from Århus.*

Viborg

Viborg is situated in central Jutland and the Army Road or Ox Road, the main thoroughfare of the peninsula, went through it.[15] In the early Middle Ages the place was known as the seat of the Jutland regional assembly, where communal decisions were made and kings elected. The midwinter assembly in particular gave rise to the holding of large markets, and the numerous sites of medieval churches bear witness to the ecclesiastical importance of the town.

The name of the town, originally *wé-biærg* or 'the sanctuary hill(s)', makes it likely that the status of Viborg as a sanctified meeting-place had a long ancestry. The special significance of the assembly-place in the period which saw the establishment of the earliest ecclesiastical administration may perhaps be glimpsed in a local rune-stone inscription (from Asmild) and some coin legends from the time of Cnut the Great. Our first record of the name of Viborg is on coins minted in his reign, and soon afterwards (in 1049) the powerful 'Vale of Viborg bishop of the Danes' (*Wale Iburgensis Danorum episcopus*) was co-signatory on a German document concerning the settlement of an archiepiscopal dispute. Viborg may thus already have been a bishopric before the great division into dioceses around AD 1060 (ch. 9). The most recent archaeological work in the town must be seen against this background.

In 1966 and 1967, remains of a tenth-century farm-like settlement were uncovered on what was originally an elevated stretch of ground in the southern part of the town centre, and a few traces of a related settlement were later found on the cathedral mound to the east. A single eighth-century brooch suggests that the former settlement may possibly go back beyond the tenth century, but of greater interest are the slightly later adjustments made along the settlement's north side revealed by excavations from 1974 to 1978. Initially a new stone-paved road was made, the present Store Sct Pedersstræde, with plots laid out alongside it. These plots seem to have remained more or less unaltered in size through the ages. A fence was constructed along the edge of the road and the dwelling-houses were built parallel to the road, while other buildings lay at the back of the plots. The oldest dwelling on the most thoroughly examined plot was about 10 × 5.5 m. It had slightly curved long walls and was divided into three rooms: an entrance room and a small room at the east end, and at the west end a living-room reminiscent of a hall, measuring 5 × 7 m, with wall-benches and a fireplace in the centre. A craftsman specialising in fine metalwork lived here.

This extensive reorganisation is for the present dated to the reign of Cnut the Great or a little later, perhaps about 1050—a handle with incised decoration in the Ringerike style (fig. 48) is important dating evidence. If these theories hold good (the result of many years' work but only a limited number of excavations), Viborg was changed in this way from a number of large scattered farms to a town. We might guess that it happened at the command of Cnut the Great.

Lund

Lund[16] is situated a few kilometres from the west coast of Skåne, the region described by Adam of Bremen as 'the province of Denmark fairest to look upon ... opulent of crops, rich in merchandise, and now full of churches'. Two rune stones from the first half of the eleventh century have been found in the town; quantities of coins were minted there in the reigns of Cnut the Great and Harthacnut; and around 1060 the town became a bishopric and in 1103 or 1104 the first archiepiscopal see in Scandinavia. Important markets were held near Lund; and during the Middle Ages, and perhaps earlier, the Skåne assembly met nearby.

Excavations have been undertaken in the town ever since the 1890s, and for a long time it has been generally accepted that Lund was founded by Cnut the Great around AD 1020. However, investigation over a large area in the 1970s revealed part of a cemetery which was in use from about 1000 at the latest to about 1050, dated by dendrochronological analysis of the coffins. The buildings beside the cemetery have been dated by dendrochronology to around 1020, and they survived as long as the burial-ground, that is to around 1050 when the area was subject to extensive flooding, either as the result of an accident or perhaps as a planned measure to assist in the levelling of it. In any case it was reorganised immediately after the flooding. A large stave church (fig. 47) was built on the vacant site, and the secular buildings there were laid out in a more compact and regular way. The new fences, however, largely followed the courses of the earlier ones.

The burial-ground of the first half of the eleventh century was large— about 250 graves have been found in the area investigated. Neither buildings of the earliest phase nor a church have been found. The earliest house (of c. 1020) measured about 21 × 5.5 m, had curved long walls and sloping external posts, and was divided into three rooms: a large central room with a fireplace in the middle of the floor, and a smaller gable-room at each end. In principle this house thus corresponds to those known from the Viking fortresses (fig. 40) and from the large farms of the latest phase of Vorbasse (ch. 4). After the house was burnt down, others were built on top of it. In as far as the size of these houses can be determined, they were relatively small. Some had corner-ovens and several were the dwellings of metalworkers. On the neighbouring plot (the Thule site) fenced buildings dating from 1020–50 have been found, and probably a water-mill.

There are numerous traces of industry and trade in this earliest known phase of Lund's settlement. There is also some concrete evidence of the king's influence on early Danish towns: the oldest official document known in Denmark, St Cnut's deed of gift to the church of Lund in 1085, records that the town (and other towns) paid a land-tax called *arnegæld* (hearth-duty) to the king in his capacity as the town's overlord.

Odense, Roskilde and other towns

Very little is known about the character and appearance of other Danish towns during the Viking Age. Odense,[17] then as now the intersection of Fyn's major roads, is situated where the Odense river runs into Odense fjord. The town is first mentioned in 988, as the fourth bishopric in Denmark. Cnut the Great had coins struck here, and Adam of Bremen mentions Odense as the major town on Fyn. Excavations in the present town centre, near the cathedral, have shown that a settlement existed there from at least some time in the eleventh century and that various kinds of industry were carried on. So far, the only finds from Odense that are as early as its first mention in written sources come from the east of the town north of the river Odense (a splendid ring brooch), and from the area of Nonnebakken, south of the river. In all probability one of the large circular fortresses of the Trelleborg type was built here about 980 (ch. 8). If that is so, we may assume that the king already had close connections with the town by its first mention. The name Odense was originally *Óðins vé*, 'Odin's sanctuary', and in the Middle Ages, and perhaps earlier, the town was the site of the Fyn assembly.

Roskilde,[18] at the head of the long Roskilde fjord, became a bishopric *c.* 1020, in the reign of Cnut the Great, and Adam of Bremen relates that the town was the seat of the Danish kings and that Harald Bluetooth (died *c.* 986) was buried there, in a church which he himself had had built in honour of the Holy Trinity. This was probably the first predecessor of Roskilde Cathedral, which was in fact originally dedicated to the Holy Trinity. Around 1026, Cnut the Great had Earl Ulf killed in the Trinity Church at Roskilde, and after Ulf's funeral his widow Estrid, sister of King Cnut and mother of Svein Estridsson (reigned 1047–74), had the wooden church replaced by a stone one, the oldest known stone church in Scandinavia. Another stone church was built in the town about 1040. This was the first predecessor of St Jørgensbjerg church (originally St Clement's); it is dated by means of a coin-hoard discovered in the foundation trench. The Church was thus strongly developed in Roskilde in the first half of the eleventh century, in close connection with the royal family. In the reign of Cnut the Great and throughout the following three centuries the town was also an important mint. About AD 1000 the sea-route to Roskilde was protected by barring the narrow Peberrende channel (with the Skuldelev ships, see ch. 3). Otherwise only a few Viking Age objects have been found so far; the most important are a trefoil brooch found in St Hans' cemetery, a small disc brooch found in the Greyfriars' cemetery, a tenth-century German coin and other coins from the first half of the eleventh century, and a couple of fragments of soapstone. Current excavations will no doubt soon produce more. It already appears, however, that the town was surprisingly extensive in the eleventh century.

Excavations in Ålborg, situated on one of the most important crossings of the Limfjord, have not yet produced any Viking Age evidence,[19] perhaps because the settlement of that period was situated on Lindholm Høje and Bejsebakken (ch. 4); nor have the archaeologists yet found Viking Age levels in Ringsted and Slagelse, important places on the road-routes of Sjælland. So far, the only evidence to show that these three places existed in the Viking Age consists of coins with their names on minted in the first half of the eleventh century. Around 1070, Ålborg is mentioned by Adam of Bremen, who also says that there are large towns in Jutland 'wherever there is an arm of the sea', but gives no names. Helsingborg, in Skåne, is also mentioned by Adam as a crossing-place from Sjælland.[20] Around 1080, the bishop of Roskilde had stone churches built in Slagelse and Ringsted, demonstrating their importance in the eleventh century. It may also be added that Slagelse is only 5 km from Trelleborg and that Ringsted was the site of the Sjælland assembly in the Middle Ages and perhaps earlier.[21]

SUMMARY

We are thus presented with a somewhat uneven picture of the oldest Danish towns, not least because the archaeological evidence is in many respects different in character and of very varied scope. But it is by no means certain, either, that the towns were particularly similar. They came into existence at widely different times and in vastly different circumstances. Some, like Hedeby and Ribe, had more of an international character than the other towns. Some perhaps changed their character in the course of the period as well, but trade and manufacturing were important occupations, and large markets must have been held in all of them.

As the Viking Age progressed, the number of towns grew. At the close of the period their number was not inconsiderable (fig. 18) and in several cases it appears that a sudden development took place which transformed a community of village type into one of town-like character, in the shape either of a new, planned settlement close to an older one or of a re-organisation of an existing settlement. The growth of the inland towns during the late Viking Age is presumably related to increased internal trade and to technical innovations in land transport; many new bridges were built at this time (ch. 3), for example.

In the oldest towns, Ribe and Hedeby, the settlements can be traced back to the middle and second half of the eighth century. So far, Århus has been traced back to the first half of the tenth century, and Odense and Roskilde to the second half. In Viborg the traces of settlement do not take on a town-like character until the eleventh century, but there are older finds. The oldest finds from Lund are from c. AD 1000, and in the first half of the eleventh century Ålborg, Slagelse and Ringsted emerge as towns too, if one dares assume that all the sites where coins were struck at this time were towns and not just royal estates, for example. Minting also took place in Toftum (probably the present village of Gamtofte on Fyn) and in Ørbæk (probably in northern Jutland) as well as in Gori (presumably in Skåne) in the first half of the eleventh century.[22] It should also be mentioned that not all the country's Viking Age towns are necessarily known today. Some may have disappeared or been reduced to villages, and as the Viking Age towns may not have been in the centre of the present towns of the same name, or even close by, thorough investigation is required before the age of a town can be convincingly determined. Other towns as well as Ribe may be able to find their Viking Age predecessor 'on the other side of the river'.

The occupational structure in the towns is reflected in the artefacts left behind, especially traces of regular industries, and in the evidence of settlement clearly different in character from what is now known of villages and farms—such as planned street systems, and plots and houses with a town character. Sunken-featured buildings, however, apparently occur in all forms of settlement. Defensive structures have been demonstrated in several towns. Hedeby and Århus had ramparts, in both cases of the tenth century, and near these two towns a number of rune stones has been found, several of which mention kings and actual hostilities. About AD 1000 Roskilde was protected on its seaward side by ships sunk in the fjord, and if Nonnebakken in Odense was a circular fortress of the Trelleborg type, this may also have protected a civilian settlement for a time. It is worth noticing that major defensive works do not seem to have been necessary before the tenth century. This, however, is not unique to Denmark.[23]

The oldest churches in the country apparently belonged to towns or, like the church at Jelling, were connected with important royal estates. Others may have belonged to the farms of the well-to-do. In the towns, churches first appeared in Hedeby and Ribe around 850, then in Århus, and thereafter in Odense and Roskilde in the course of the tenth century. It is not, however, certain that real townships existed so early in the last two places mentioned; the settlements may instead have been mainly royal estates. Later, there is information about other churches. It is striking—and maybe not just a coincidence— that the earliest references to a church or, more precisely, the seat of a bishop in several cases coincide chronologically with the oldest archaeological evidence of a settlement at that place, and that nearly all the settlements mentioned above, or their successors, became bishoprics in the eleventh century at the latest. It may be noted that in this period the king had much say in Church affairs and co-operated closely with the clergy. It may also be repeated that Viborg and Odense were ancient pagan cult-places, and that Viborg, Odense, Ringsted and Lund (or nearby) were central assembly-places in the Middle Ages and perhaps earlier. Coins were also struck in all these towns in the Viking Age, though in widely different quantities, and minting was probably a royal prerogative.

When it came to building churches in the townships, constructing ramparts and issuing coins, the king was no doubt the prime mover, because much authority lay with him. The king's influence in this sphere is emphasised by the passage in the Frankish annals under the year 808 about Reric and Hedeby (see p. 73), and by the archaeological evidence which demonstrates the virtually contemporary foundation of a planned Hedeby. As mentioned before, there was a 'count' in Hedeby, almost certainly a royal officer, and the oldest surviving Danish document, the deed of gift of 1085, gives clear evidence of the relationship of the king with the towns. The king's manifest interest in trade can be illustrated by trade agreements[24] and his interest in improving communication in the country is shown by the huge bridge across Ravning Enge (ch. 3). Many European towns appear to have grown in close conjunction with the consolidation of central power[25] and the same seems to have been the case in Denmark. It is not certain, however, that the king had equal power in all the towns.

Most scholars now agree that the role apparently played by the king is to be explained in terms of his function as a protector: trade needed armed power to guarantee peaceful conditions both on land and sea. In return the protector received appropriate rewards, customs revenue, gifts, and first options on purchase.[26] This in turn explains the king's interest in the presence of churches in the towns. In the pagan period a church, and presumably also its priests with their knowledge of language, were an attraction to foreign Christian merchants, as is shown clearly in the *Life* of Ansgar.[27] Later it became natural to strengthen the towns with the most important centralised institutions, as the churches were, and with the associated clerics. Major church services and feastdays could also be accompanied by markets, preferably held conveniently close to the church.

The organisation and administration of individual towns may have had many sources of inspiration. As we saw at the beginning of the chapter, it was in the Viking Age that towns expanded and flourished throughout northern Europe, though at the end of the ninth and beginning of the tenth centuries this was probably most pronounced in England.[28] It is obvious to seek English models, at least for those towns thought to have been founded, or to have undergone vigorous development, in the reign of Cnut the Great. A strong English influence can be seen at this time in so many other fields, such as coinage and Church customs, that it would be strange if Cnut the Great, that powerful, energetic and modern-minded Anglo-Scandinavian monarch, had not strengthened Danish towns on the basis of his knowledge of English towns and their functions.[29] In any case, at the end of the Viking Age, towns were an integral part of Danish society and no doubt most people had at some time or another been 'up to town'.

6 Trade, Industries and Crafts

TRADE, MERCHANDISE AND MEANS OF PAYMENT

It used to be thought that the Frisians were the principal merchants of north-western Europe, but today it is generally agreed that the Scandinavians played a decisive role in trade at home and an important role in many of those foreign areas where they took political control. The Scandinavian contribution was also seen for a long time as a trade in luxury goods. Hides and furs from Norway and Sweden, walrus tusks from Norway, slaves, wax and amber are frequently mentioned as the chief goods they sold abroad. Trade in the North has also been seen chiefly as transit-trade, with Scandinavia flourishing in the Viking Age as the result of its role as intermediary between East and West after the Muslim incursion in the Mediterranean in the eighth century. This latter event was thought to have caused the closure of the traditional trade-routes and the opening of new ones by way of the Baltic and the great Russian rivers. More recently, however, it has become apparent that, although the Scandinavians undoubtedly acted as middlemen in the transfer of large quantities of goods from the Baltic and Russia, and had contacts with the East along the Russian rivers, Western Europe retained its own more southerly links with the Orient despite the Arab expansion.[1]

Today many are of the opinion that Scandinavian acquisition from plunder, ransom and Danegeld in a way stimulated demand and consequently trade in the North and Western Europe where economic expansion was already taking place. The accumulated wealth was dispersed and redistributed through the hands of the Vikings, and was subsequently largely converted into merchandise and property. Simultaneously the Scandinavians came to have political domination over a large area extending beyond their own countries and the North Atlantic islands. For a time they also played an important role on the south and east coasts of the Baltic, in Russia, and in parts of the British Isles and coastal areas of Western Europe. This vast area was thus controlled by people with more or less the same language, trading policy, faith and culture. Within this area a wide variety of goods could be exchanged, and it could also produce a large quantity of the goods for which there was demand in the rest of Western Europe, including the luxury goods

Pl. 17 *Soapstone pots from Norway or south-west Sweden found in the water at Hals Barre; quernstone of Rhenish lava found at Trelleborg.*

mentioned above, hides, furs, walrus tusks and slaves, all of which are mentioned in written sources. It seems likely that skins were also among the commodities traded, for they were in great demand for parchment to make the many books written in Christian centres of learning (after all, one skin would furnish no more than two good leaves in a large-sized book). Apart from luxury goods, however, quite ordinary commodities were also traded, even heavy, bulky and unwieldy goods.[2] The Skuldelev ships demonstrate that there were regular trading ships with holds (ch. 3), at least in the later part of the Viking Age.

To return to trading matters of specifically Danish character, it must be emphasised that, in the course of the Viking Age (which after all covers some three hundred years), there were doubtless changes in the nature of trade, in commodities and routes, handling equipment and means of transport. The situation around AD 800 cannot provide an immediate analogy to the situation around AD 1000; at present it is still difficult to trace the main lines of development.

A large number of imports can, however, be demonstrated archaeologically. Some are obviously the result of raids and of the large Danegeld payments, for example the masses of Anglo-Saxon coins of the late tenth and early eleventh centuries. Others may be cheap souvenirs,[3] and some may have entered the country as gifts or taxes. Some must also have been ordinary trade goods, among them pots and other objects of fireproof soapstone, which in Norway and south-western Sweden could be quarried directly from the rock. These pots are known from virtually

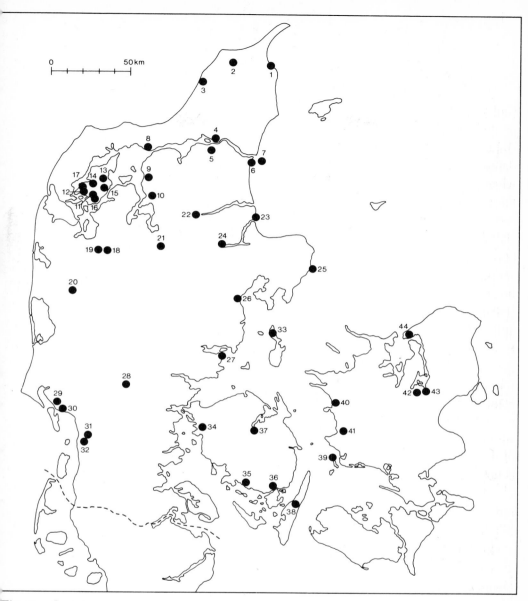

Fig. 21 *Soapstone*
in present-day
Denmark (cf.
Appendix, Finds
List 2, p. 250).

all the excavated Viking Age settlements in Denmark (fig. 21 and pl. 17). Their large-scale importation probably started at some time in the ninth century and continued throughout the Viking Age. It then seems to have diminished considerably or to have ceased altogether (ch. 7). An ordinary soapstone pot with a diameter of 26–35 cm weighs 5–6 kg. Pots such as these were thus heavy and fairly awkward to transport, but their distribution shows that the retail price was not astronomical.[4] Though most people managed with their own clay pots, nevertheless soapstone pots cannot be classified purely as luxury goods. They must have been transported by ship wherever possible; the many pots found on beaches or under water probably represent the soapstone cargoes of wrecked ships. These findings are more likely to provide evidence of waters dangerous to shipping than of soapstone trade-routes, however, at a time when there were no lighthouses and few other man-made navigational markers. (For further information on soapstone pots, see ch. 7.)

Another important commodity was whetstones, or perhaps rather the slates from which they were made. These have been found in Denmark both on land and under water, and those in the remains of a ship from southern Norway show they could form part of a cargo. There is probably no excavated settlement from the period which does not provide specimens, and they are also common in graves. The raw material is almost exclusively slate of certain types which in turn must have come from specific 'whetstone' regions. (If the stones had originated on or near the Danish sites where they occur, one would expect more stone-types to be represented.) Geological analysis shows that some of the more common whetstones—of light-coloured, rather coarse-grained slate—come from the Eidsborg area in Telemark, Norway, which also had substantial exports of whetstone in more recent times. The provenance of the other common type, of a fine-grained dark slate, has not yet been conclusively identified but no doubt soon will be. It is probably also Norwegian. Since the distribution of whetstones is so large, the price must have been fairly low and they can be classed as another mass import.[5]

Quernstones (pl. 17) must also have been common imports, probably at a reasonable price. Several of Rhenish lava have been found in Denmark; others are possibly from Norway and some may be native products. Reindeer antlers were sometimes used for comb-manufacture, as a substitute for the indigenous red deer antler, even though it had to be got from afar and is a rather bulky cargo. Again the price must have been reasonable.[6] Finally, all metal other than bog-iron—that is, gold, silver, copper, tin, lead and so on—was imported. Some iron was also imported, probably from Norway and perhaps also from Sweden. It has not yet been possible to determine the provenance of the iron bars found at Hedeby,[7] but near the shore at Gjerrild, in Djursland, twelve axe-heads have been found fixed on a single spruce pole, presumably a consignment of tools from Norway (pl. 18 and ch. 8). The attribution to Norway is likely as it was rich in iron in the Viking Age.

Luxury goods were of course also imported. Materials for the manufacture of glass beads came in the shape of raw glass, pieces of broken glass, and *tesserae*.[8] Finished articles of adornment were also imported from a number of countries: dress accessories and jewellery, silk and probably also other textiles, ornaments for the house and for the table such as glass drinking-vessels, jugs and cups of the fine Pingsdorf and Tating wares, glazed pottery, magnificent buckets with ornamented fittings, as well as wine and other things to brighten one's life, such as handsome swords and precious horse equipment, not forgetting the rather more mundane but vital salt. All these goods and others besides are discussed in more detail in later chapters.

Pl. 18 *A dozen axes on a spruce pole found near the beach on Djursland.*

The many ordinary trading commodities cannot all have been paid for by stolen silver or other spoils, by income from profitable transit-trade or by income received as taxes. Denmark must have had some articles for export to pay for the imports, chief amongst them agricultural produce. Right up to recent times, this has been the country's most important marketable commodity.[9]

However, it is almost impossible to demonstrate this archaeologically, since not only does the produce of necessity leave the country, but also skins, leather, meat, wool, livestock and so on leave little trace and in any case their provenance can only be determined in exceptional circumstances. No stock of any such products has been found by excavation in Denmark. But about twenty-two large animals stabled at each of the two farms at Vorbasse is quite a considerable number (though fewer than there were later at the same place, see ch. 4). The layer of cattle manure in Viking Age Ribe mentioned in ch. 5 may have been deposited by animals intended for export, and, as noted earlier, skins for parchment may also have been sent abroad. Wax, honey and oak (as raw timber or in finished form) may also have been exported (see chs. 2 and 7). The same may apply to textiles, which are after all a kind of refined agricultural product. It is thus difficult to be very specific about Denmark's exports in the Viking Age. There cannot be much doubt, however, that the export trade was essentially in agricultural produce, as it had probably also been in the late Roman Iron Age.

There must have been a fair amount of transit-trade through Denmark as well as direct import and export. Obviously there was also a great deal of internal or local trade. Imported goods had to be distributed to farms and villages, goods for export had to be dispersed abroad or to foreign buyers; furthermore, the towns had to have a supply of native raw materials for manufacturing—hides before or after tanning for shoes, sheaths and harness, deer antler for combs and other implements, amber for beads, and wool for textiles. Hedeby probably had foodstuffs brought in as well. In return, townspeople could offer specialist production of jewellery, combs, shoes, beads and much else. For instance, it looks as though oval brooches produced by a Ribe craftsman were distributed all over the country. At the same time, large numbers of imported

Pl. 19 *Silver hoard from Terslev on Sjælland. It consists of complete, chopped up and clipped objects: jewellery, ingots, bowls and coins. Of the 1751 coins 1708 were Cufic, 3 French, 11 German, 1 Italian, 10 English and 18 Danish. The lastest coin (a Viking coin from the north of England) was struck between 941 and 952 and the hoard was probably buried a short time afterwards, c. 960.*

commodities occur in Ribe: pottery, glass, metal, coins and so on. The situation seems to presuppose that many Danish exports were shipped to the south through Ribe. Nor can there be any doubt that the role of local trade became increasingly important in the course of the Viking Age. This is illustrated by the growing number of towns and by the fact that some of the latest towns founded in the Viking Age lie in the heart of the countryside (ch. 5). In addition, the Danish minting of coins increased greatly in the later Viking Age.

A large part of Viking Age trade was in all probability conducted by barter. An early Viking Age rune stick from Hedeby (fig. 4) seems to refer to such a transaction, and must be the oldest trade document in Scandinavia.[10] But silver was also used as a means of payment, probably increasingly so during the period. Up to the beginning of the eleventh century, payment was made in silver according to weight, whatever its form as jewellery, ingots or coins. This can be seen in the numerous hoards of hack-silver (pl. 19). These are cash reserves of precious metal, generally silver, concealed in the ground. Many of them were undoubtedly hidden away during times of unrest; others may have been 'bank deposits' which the owners were unable to retrieve for some reason or other; some may have been intended as votive offerings to the gods.[11]

Silver was weighed on collapsible pairs of scales, remains of which have been found with their accompanying weights in several settlements, in graves and among craftsmen's tools. They were necessary for buying and selling, according to the system of weights which possibly originated in the Islamic world.[12] Much silver jewellery, especially arm-rings, also seems to have been made according to certain weights systems.[13] There are particularly many hoards known from c. 950 to 1020, and in these the proportion of fragmented silver is notably larger than before, a fact which indicates that silver was now commonly used for small-scale purchases too. From the beginning of the eleventh century, hack-silver and ingots become less common in Danish hoards in comparison with the number of coins. This must be due to increased confidence in coins as a means of payment, as the result of the extensive coinage of Cnut the Great and his successors, and the stream of foreign coins pouring into Denmark, and, quite simply, the greater number of coins available.[14]

Coins had, however, been known in the country long before the Viking Age, and already in the eighth century large numbers of the tiny Frisian silver *sceattas* were used in Ribe.[15] The first coins to be issued in Denmark were struck at the beginning of the ninth century, doubtless at Hedeby, and obviously modelled on Carolingian coinage. A distorted and abbreviated form of Carolus (= Charlemagne) and Dorestad (the Frisian town where the prototypes were minted) appear on many of the Danish coins. Other coins are stamped with ships, animals and other devices (fig. 22). As elsewhere, the master of the mint was presumably the king; we may assume that the first Danish coins were the responsibility of the active King Godfred.

Fig. 22   Danish Viking Age coins. a–b belong to the earliest group, probably struck in Hedeby around 800; c struck in the reign of Harald Bluetooth; d struck in the 990s in the reign of Svein Forkbeard, whose name appears in the legend; e, according to the legend, struck in the reign of Cnut the Great at Lund; f struck in the reign of Harthacnut in Århus. Scale 1:1.

These early coins were hardly of great significance: not many were minted. Furthermore, minting seems to have ceased for a time in the second half of the ninth and beginning of the tenth century. From then until about 990, Danish coins were very much as before, though from about 975 to 995 we also find coins that are thought to be of Byzantine inspiration and to have been minted somewhere other than Hedeby (fig. 22c). Many of these coins must have been struck during the reign of Harald Bluetooth. Svein Forkbeard (reigned c. 986–1014) was the first Danish king to have his name and title struck on coins, along with the moneyer's name, but these are extremely rare. From then on and for the rest of the Viking Age, the coins are as a rule clearly inspired by Anglo-Saxon coins (fig. 22d–e) because of the immense Danegeld payments around AD 1000 and Denmark's close contacts with England, especially when Cnut and Harthacnut were kings of both countries 1018–35 and 1040–42. Many of these coins were actually struck by English moneyers. From the time of Cnut the Great onwards, the place of minting is also marked on most coins. Danish coins from the second half of the tenth century and later are also well represented in Baltic finds and give evidence of Danish relations with this region.

There were also large numbers of foreign coins in circulation in the country in the Viking Age. It is not until around the reign of Harald Hen (1074–80) that foreign coins disappear. It is likely that their use was prohibited—as was the case in Western Europe—as part of a major reform of coinage, reflected also in a more regulated Danish coinage. Henceforth the king as master of the mint could rake in even greater profits from his monopoly on coin issue, for example by levying a duty on the exchange of foreign coins.

Of foreign coins in circulation, Cufic (Arab) coins were most common up to around 970. Many of them were struck in Samarkand and Tashkent. Around 3,500 Cufic coins have been found in present-day Denmark (in comparison with about 80,000 in what is now Sweden, including affluent Gotland, and about 400 in Norway). From around the year 970, the numbers of West European and Danish coins increased in hoards. The large silver mines in the Harz mountains were opened around 960, and many German coins ended up in Denmark. Anglo-Saxon coins gain ground from around 990, even though the German coins are still predominant in the finds. About 15,000 Anglo-Saxon coins are known in Denmark and of these most (about 9,500) come from Skåne. Nearly all date from the end of the tenth century and the first half of the eleventh, which is not surprising given the political situation described above.[16]

Not a great deal is known about actual trade-routes during the Viking Age. Foreign coins and other commodities help to indicate trading connections and one must assume that the routes between source and destination were the most practical at any given time, taking political conditions and means of transport into account. Thus there can be little doubt that the Limfjord was much used, providing as it did a comfortable passage between the Baltic and the North Sea.[17] The accounts of Ohthere and Wulfstan from about 890 may well record current contemporary sailing routes.[18] More routes are mentioned in other written sources (ch. 5). Finally it is worth noting that the significance of overland trade-routes has probably been underestimated. Written sources do, in fact, mention overland journeys and the technology of land transport was quite well developed (ch. 3).

Neither can much be said about the characteristics of Scandinavian merchants or their organisation in the Viking Age. In all probability there were both fully professional merchants and those who, like Ohthere from Norway, went on a trading voyage when they had the merchandise to sell, but who otherwise lived chiefly at home by farming and fishing.[19] The commercial role of the king is considered in ch. 5, along with towns and markets where most trade took place.

INDUSTRIES AND CRAFTS

A number of archaeological finds illustrate the industry and technology of the period; the written sources are not much help in this respect. Large quantities of tools, raw materials, workshop waste and half-finished artefacts from Viking Age towns show that many craftsmen lived in them producing a wide variety of goods.[20] Few finds of this nature occur on village and farm sites: hardly anything but textile implements, tools for carpentry and wood-carving, and blacksmith's refuse. They sometimes also indicate that the bones of domestic animals were made into skates, spindle-whorls, pins and so on.[21] Here it was obviously a matter of producing basic daily necessities: textiles, wooden buildings or building elements, and other wooden objects, nails and various iron tools as well as simple bone implements. All these were also manufactured in towns, but they did not require any high degree of specialisation. Most women could spin and weave, and many people could carve simple objects in wood or bone and undertake straightforward carpentry and iron-working. On the other hand, it is also possible that in some villages and large farms so much weaving, iron-working and carpentry was needed that they could support one or two specialists. Such village industry may also have contributed a secondary income.

There are also traces of industrial activity in the Trelleborg and Fyrkat fortresses: blacksmiths, goldsmiths and comb-makers in the former; blacksmiths and goldsmiths in the latter. Comb-makers may have lived at Fyrkat too, but the conditions of survival make their presence impossible to trace. For the same reason we cannot demonstrate the presence of shoemakers in these fortresses, but they may have existed.[22]

It is often difficult to decide whether traces of industry (such as bronze-working on the large farm from the late phase in Vorbasse) represent the work of a resident or an itinerant craftsman.[23] But we assume that craftsmen were resident in the royal fortresses since actual workshops were incorporated in their overall plan and much manufacturing debris has been found in them.[24] Nor is it surprising that the king employed craftsmen. The Jelling monuments and finds, for example, show that he surrounded himself with choice artistic objects and commissioned much work. Craftsmen at a fortress or on a large farm had to satisfy the demands of their employer and perhaps meet the needs of the entire household. It is easy to imagine, for instance, that the smiths of the Viking Age fortresses produced weapons, but they may also have manufactured objects intended for general sale or as gifts: the great kings of scaldic poetry gave rich gifts to their men. Detailed analysis of riding equipment and other artefacts from the rich tenth-century graves may make it possible to attribute many products to one or more workshops and to establish their association with the king.[25]

Apart from craftsmen attached to towns, villages, fortresses and large farms, there were doubtless itinerant craftsmen too.[26] Such men may have owned the tool-chests found near Tjele in Jutland and the Halleby river in Sjælland, and also the famous, better preserved and altogether richer tool-chest from Mästermyr in Gotland.[27]

Among the craftsmen, the blacksmiths—or rather some of them, good weapon-smiths in particular—might enjoy comparatively high social status. Smiths are mentioned on three Danish rune stones[28] (but the word 'smith' may also refer to other craftsmen at this time).[29] A blacksmith has also been found buried with his tools[30] and in the village of Sædding the blacksmith's house seems to have been one of the largest.[31] This picture corresponds well with the impression gained from the archaeological material of the other Scandinavian countries (not least the Norwegian smiths' graves),[32] and from the written sources.[33] No doubt other craftsmen—some shipbuilders, house-builders, picture-carvers in wood or stone, for example—also enjoyed high esteem simply because of their supreme proficiency. However, a number of written sources and the rune stone from Nørre Hørning in Jutland indicate that craftsmen were sometimes bondsmen. The inscription on the rune stone reads: 'Tuki the smith raised this stone in memory of Þorgils, son of Guðmund, who gave him gold [?] and freedom'.[34] But generalisations about the status of craftsmen are impossible on the basis of extant sources.

Finally, it is worth mentioning that both workshops and collections of tools are rare and it is often a matter of subjective judgement as to whether one classifies an artefact as the product of specialised craftsmanship. Some artefacts, though, are of such technical and artistic quality that they are clearly the work of specialists. Others exist in characteristic series or in large numbers made from foreign raw materials and these cannot have been isolated one-off jobs. The Ribe finds, above all, show a surprising degree of specialisation already in the eighth century.[35] This does not mean, however, that the same degree of specialisation existed in all crafts.

What follows is a survey of various industries and domestic crafts, but it must be emphasised that the classification is rough and that it does not attempt to illustrate a firm division of professional skills.

Fig. 23 *Spinning with spindle. Here the spun yarn is wound round the spindle so only the spindle-whorl and little of the spindle can be seen.*

Textiles

Wool was the chief material used, but in recent years many fragments of linen (which does not survive very well in the ground) have been found, so flax was presumably cultivated and worked in Denmark. Some of the wooden clubs found in various places may have been used for crushing flax, and other implements have been interpreted as hackles.[36] There are also combs for combing wool prior to spinning.[37]

Spindle-whorls and loom-weights are known from virtually all Viking Age settlements and the contexts of the finds show that much spinning and weaving took place in sunken-featured buildings.[38] Spindle-whorls (placed on the end of a spindle to act as a fly-wheel for spinning, fig. 23) were mostly of fired clay and conical. They were in all probability home-made. Spindle-whorls were also made of soapstone (usually sherds from broken pots), sandstone and slate, limestone, bone (usually the head of an ox femur), antler, glass, lead and amber. The wooden spindle belonging to the spindle-whorl has rarely survived.[39] Some artefacts from the Norwegian Oseberg burial are thought to have been for holding the bundle of wool during spinning, and the same site also yielded special implements for winding up the finished yarn.[40] Finally, small bone thread-makers (lucets) are known which helped to wind thread into thicker strands.[41]

Loom-weights, used for weighting the warp (the vertical threads) in upright looms (fig. 24), were made of fired or unfired clay, and were roughly circular with a hole through which the warp threads were tied.[42] Nothing has survived of the looms themselves but the type has been

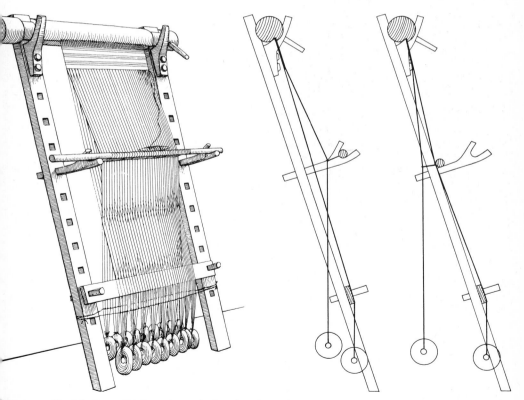

Fig. 24 Upright loom. Right: schematic drawing showing the heddle-rod with the warp threads in two different positions. The loom-weights hang below.

reconstructed on the basis of looms used in Norway and the Faeroes, and elsewhere, to the present day. In a few instances, warp-weights have been found disposed in such a way that they must have fallen from a burnt loom.[43] Loom-weights disappeared in Denmark in the eleventh or twelfth century, when upright looms were replaced by horizontal looms.[44] The conical spindle-whorls of clay also went out of use at roughly the same time, but other types seem to have continued for a while.[45]

Iron or bone weaving battens for beating in the weft or woof (the transverse threads in a weave) are known from many Norwegian graves, and there are thought to be fragments of an iron one in Denmark.[46] Small pointed pins of bone, antler or wood may have been used for keeping the weft straight (pin-beaters) or for picking out the warp threads when weaving a pattern.[47] Identification of these, however, is sometimes uncertain; some of them may have been toothpicks or nail-cleaners instead. A small bone object with a shaft and short teeth, a weaving-comb, is thought to have been used for beating the threads together in tapestries.[48]

Many garments had borders of woven bands made by means of small, flat, roughly square tablets, usually of wood, bone or antler, with a number of perforations through which the warp of the band passed.[49] These bands could be of silk worked with gold and silver threads, but it is uncertain whether such bands were actually manufactured in Denmark.[50] Other borders were plaited[51] and there are thought to be fragments of a special band-loom in the Oseberg burial.[52]

Knitting was unknown in Denmark until the late Middle Ages. The technique of looped needle-netting (by which loops of yarn are sewn together as they are being formed) was, however, current in the Viking Age. Runic inscriptions on a couple of bone needles indicate that they were used for this technique.[53] It is likely that spranging (a kind of plaiting done with the fingers with thread stretched over a frame) was known, because a frame of this sort has been identified among the Oseberg finds.[54]

Scissors were commonly of iron but also occur in tinned bronze. Their shape is reminiscent of modern sheep-shears and some have been found in their cases. Scissors with crossed blades (like modern ones) are known from Hedeby and graves at Birka, but they are rare. Many of the scissors found in women's graves must have been textile implements. Others may have been for personal use, and still others for sheep-shearing and mane-trimming—one would be inclined to associate shears found in men's graves with such purposes.[55]

Sewing needles could be of metal and very small. Some were kept in cylindrical needle-cases of metal or bone.[56] The precise function of all the very common bone pins can rarely be determined, but some of them were for netting work as mentioned above, others presumably for sewing, and yet others were probably dress pins.[57] A few dome-shaped linen-smoothers of dark glass have been found,[58] and some objects from Norwegian graves are thought to be 'smoothing-irons' while others have been interpreted as 'ironing-boards'.[59]

Dyeing of textiles was known long before the Viking Age and there is also contemporary evidence of it. (For this and for finished textiles and costume, see ch. 7.) It must be emphasised, however, that at present there are no very firm criteria for establishing which textiles were manufactured at home and which were imported, and where imported cloth came from.[60] So many textile implements have been found that we may wonder whether textiles were not manufactured in some parts of Denmark for sale, possibly even for export.[61] Most households, though, probably had enough to do in producing clothes for their own use. Both the grave-finds and the Norse written sources give us to understand that it was the women who worked on the textiles;[62] this work was carried out both in urban and rural contexts.

Wood

Wood was much used then as now. It was used for buildings, well-linings, boats, roads, bridges and wagons. These were almost exclusively in oak, while various other suitable kinds were used for furniture and domestic utensils.[63] The finds show great familiarity with the properties of different woods[64] as well as great technical mastery. Because of conditions of preservation, this is most clearly seen in the art of ship-building;[65] with regard to buildings, the most splendid surviving piece in Denmark is probably the carved and painted wall-plate from the church at Hørning in North Jutland (pl. 38).[66]

The technique of Viking Age woodworking can be glimpsed by examining tool-marks on surviving wood (e.g. the Skuldelev ships) as well as by examining contemporary tools and pictures (though the latter are all foreign).[67] Evidence of woodworking and the application of particular tools may nevertheless be difficult to identify, because Danish woodworking tools occur almost without exception as stray finds in various settlements. Most axes in graves are doubtless weapons rather than tools. However, the find from Mästermyr in Sweden mentioned above, consisting of both carpenter's and smith's tools in a single chest,[68] and Norwegian grave-finds[69] provide some help in determining tool-function, though woodworking tools were not necessarily alike all over Scandinavia. In addition there is a smaller group of wood-carving tools from a burnt-out, sunken-featured building in Århus: a wedge, a spoon-bit, a single-edged and a double-edged gouge, a spoke-shave (perhaps for wheel-making) and a scraper, as well as five whetstones of different sizes, perhaps a type series.[70] Incidentally, it seems to have been customary to use newly felled wood, unlike today when it is usually seasoned.

The most important woodworking tool was the axe and there were different types for different kinds of work. A heavy straight axe was used for felling and for rough dressing of timber.[71] If an axe had a flat back to the head it could be used, as could wedges, for splitting logs into planks.[72] The flat head of an axe could also function as a hammer or mallet. Axes were used, too, for trimming planks and for much else. Axe marks can be seen on a lot of Viking Age timber and it has been observed that the oak logs of the Skuldelev ships were split radially (quarter-hewn) into as many as thirty-two planks.[73] Some form of axe may also have been used for the rebating seen in many timber constructions[74]—at least, no other tool for this purpose has been identified. Straight axes for woodworking can, of course, be difficult to distinguish from weapons.

Sawn planks of the period have not been identified with any certainty. Long saws are not known either, but saw-marks on the roof-timbers of Romanesque churches suggest that such saws may already have existed in the Viking Age.[75] Short saws for trimming planks have been found in several places.[76] The broad axe and the adze were used for dressing planks and other timber. The broad axe is a side-axe (the smoothing side is flat and the axe consequently asymmetrical, with the cutting edge off-centre). There are a couple of these from Hedeby.[77] The beautifully decorated axe from the grave at Hadbjerg in North Jutland is also shaped like a broad axe, but the ornamentation shows it was not intended to be functional.[78] Perhaps it is the badge of honour of a master carpenter, as has also been suggested in the case of the large T-shaped axe inlaid with silver from a grave at Trelleborg, though this is not a side-axe.[79] Adzes (one or two-handed axes with transverse edge and slightly curved blade) occur in the Mästermyr hoard and in Norway, but have not so far been found in Denmark.[80] No marks of this tool have been found on the Skuldelev ships, but that does not preclude the use of this practical tool in Denmark as well.

Draw-knives of different sizes, gouges and flat planes could all be used for smoothing wood. Several examples of knives and gouges are known. Gouges were also used for a number of hollowing out jobs. Augers for boring holes have been found in Norway.[81] Viking Age flat planes have not survived, but planes such as these are known from the much older Vimose find, from an earlier Anglo-Saxon find, and others.[82] Moulding irons have left clear marks on surviving wood, for example the Skuldelev ships and the Hørning table (fig. 29), and some wood from the Jelling burial-chamber.[83] A spoke-shave and a scraper from Århus have already been mentioned.[84]

Chisels occur in different sizes, as do mandrels.[85] Spoon-bits are well known; they were used for making small holes like those for the trenails on the Skuldelev ships.[86] Gimlets have survived in Norway.[87] It is possible that a couple of fly-wheels are the remains of drills.[88] Some of the small axes mentioned elsewhere may have been used for small-scale woodwork such as coopering.[89] Turner's debris and turned wooden objects[90] have been found in quantity, though no cooper's tools have been found or identified. Awls, too, must have been used extensively for working wood as well as other materials such as leather,[91] and one of the most commonly used woodworking tools must have been the omnipresent and multi-purpose knife.[92]

Ropes and nets
Pieces of rope and net of various sizes have survived here and there. On analysis, the material always proves to be bast, and of 291 pieces from Hedeby 85 per cent were from oak, 13 per cent from lime, 1 per

cent from willow and 1 per cent other trees. The account of the Norwegian Ohthere around 890 tells us that ship's ropes were made of walrus-hide and seal-hide too. Bast ropes are always laid, never plaited. The commonest rope is double- or triple-laid, but rope of four, six and twelve strands also occurs. The finished rope was presumably treated with grease. Finer cord could be knotted in various ways to produce nets (for fishing, hunting, transport and so on),[93] using a bone needle or something similar. Some perforated and pointed implements of antler are most likely marline-spikes for splicing ropes.[94]

Leather

Leather was used for such necessities as shoes, scabbards, straps and harness besides much else, and in favourable conditions large quantities of discarded leather (especially shoes) have survived in settlements of the period. Analysis has identified leather from cattle, goats, horses and sheep. Cow-hide is the most common, but goat-skin was preferred for footwear.[95] Leather off-cuts from Ribe and Hedeby show that leather-working was carried out there; and there are also shoe-lasts from Hedeby. A fair degree of uniformity in the manufacture of footwear seems to indicate that this work was largely undertaken by professional shoe-makers. Furthermore, given their comparatively brief life, soft leather shoes must have been in such great demand that a professional industry can be presupposed, as probably in contemporary towns outside Denmark.[96] Elaborately ornamented scabbards must also have been produced by professional craftsmen, but examples are rare in Denmark[97] so it is uncertain whether these were in fact made there. Knives, scissors, awls and needles must have been among leather-working tools. A knife that may have been used in shoemaking has been found in Lund.[98]

Bone, horn and antler

The bones of domestic animals were used for a great many artefacts— pins, bodkins, handles, spindle-whorls, skates and so on. Naturally, the sort of bone used depended on the type of object, and the material was readily available in all kinds of settlement.[99] As bone is easy to work, it is reasonable to suppose that individual households carved their own bone implements. Evidence of this is, for example, the considerable amount of worked bone off-cuts from the Aggersborg civilian settlement.[100]

Worked goats' horns have been identified at Ribe, though their use is uncertain.[101] Ox-horns, however, were sometimes made into drinking-horns.[102]

Large quantities of red deer antler was used for combs as well as for handles, needles and bodkins, gaming-pieces, dice and so on. The same use was made of reindeer antler, of which the odd example turns up, and of the still rarer elk-horn and roe-deer antler.[103] Off-cuts and rough-outs of antler are commonly found in Viking Age towns in Denmark and elsewhere, and also in quantity at Trelleborg.[104] In the countryside in general, however, these finds are rare; only a very few pieces occur in the civilian settlement at Aggersborg, for instance.[105]

Antler-working was presumably carried out for the most part in the towns and apparently at times among the upper classes as well.

Supplies of raw material must often have been difficult to get. Red deer, roe-deer and possibly elk lived in Denmark, but reindeer antlers came from northern Scandinavia and even red deer antlers had to be bought, or bartered. Antlers shed in the course of nature and no doubt picked up in forests and in fields provided some raw materials, but others came from animals killed by hunting. However, while large quantities of antler-working debris occur in the towns, the bones of the animals themselves are almost entirely non-existent both in town and country, which must mean that red deer were not normally consumed in ordinary Danish settlements.[106] This may have been because hunting rights were preserved for the upper classes.[107] The supply of raw materials must have been organised in some way in Denmark, as it was elsewhere.[108]

It is likely that combs, and other objects of antler, were produced by professional craftsmen,[109] an assumption based not only on the circumstances described above but also on the way in which evidence of manufacture is concentrated in the towns (and one fortress). The theory is further supported by the uniformity of shape and ornament in each type of comb, by the good workmanship of many of the combs[110] despite the difficult material, and by the similarities in techniques used to work the antler. However, the opposite has been argued too, that most people produced their own combs.[111]

Antler workshops as such are unknown. Only a few vices have been found in the nature of tools, while finished artefacts and off-cuts variously show marks of saw, draw-knife, axe, chisel, a rough incising implement, knife, rasp, file, abrasive material, polishing agent, drill, hammer and fine implements for drilling and incising ornament. Some gaming-pieces were turned. There is no indication that antler was softened before working, though some softening would not have been particularly complicated in technical terms.[112] The individual stages in comb-manufacture can be seen in fig. 25.

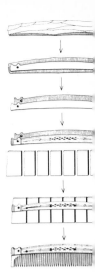

Fig. 25 *Diagram showing process of comb manufacture. Scale 1:5.*

Amber and glass

In Denmark, amber is most readily available on the west coast of Jutland, especially after a storm, but it can be gathered in other places on the Danish coast and occurs in large quantities in Poland and elsewhere in the South Baltic. It was used for beads, gaming-pieces and other decorative artefacts. In the Ribe excavations large numbers of amber fragments were found (about 2 kg), among them half-finished beads. One of the many in the country who cut amber evidently worked here.[113] A few amber fragments were found at Aggersborg, some of them worked.[114]

Glass objects are chiefly beads, but drinking-vessels and a number of other artefacts were also made of glass. While the vessels are still considered imports, it has now been demonstrated that glass beads were actually produced both in Denmark and elsewhere in Scandinavia.[115] A glass furnace with many glass fragments scattered around it was apparently excavated in Hedeby in 1913, but the find has not been published in detail.[116] The Ribe excavations in the 1970s, however, produced two beadmaker's workshops with raw materials, off-cuts and finished products that doubtless got mislaid. The workshops, which succeeded each other, were evidently fairly basic. There is no indication of roofed or even walled buildings, nothing but a sand floor with a fireplace on a clay slab, surrounded by various tools, as well as much of the glass debris mentioned above. There was a stone object, probably a mortar for crushing glass before smelting, a clay bellows-shield, a shallow metal pan in which the smelted glass may have been rolled into a cylinder, and a long iron rod probably used to produce perforated beads by rolling a little of the soft glass around it. Tongs for drawing out the glass have left marks on discarded ends of glass bars and threads. The raw material (*tesserae*, raw glass and broken vessels) was imported from Western Europe or via Western Europe. In Ribe this was made into simple monochrome beads, or monochrome beads with applied decoration in other colours, reticella beads (of multicoloured twisted rods) and mosaic beads; there may have been more types still. There is no doubt that this beadmaker (or these beadmakers) worked professionally. Fig. 26 shows the stages of manufacture of a mosaic bead.[117]

Bronze, silver and gold

Bronze and other copper alloys were used for keys, ornamental fittings, tableware and so on, as well as for buckles and jewellery. Most notable here are the oval brooches (pl. 26) which until some time in the second half of the tenth century were a fixed component of the characteristic female dress in the North (ch. 7).

Bronze-working was well known in Scandinavia, and traces of bronze-casting are known in several places. In Denmark the evidence is chiefly in Ribe, where there are tools, waste-products and probably a workshop site as well.[118] The extensive excavations in Hedeby have provided evidence of the casting of many different bronze artefacts.[119] A fragment of a mould for an oval brooch was found at Lindholm Høje,[120] while various workshops excavated in Lund include one with the so-called Urnes brooches among its products.[121] Moulds have been found at Århus[122] and Fyrkat[123] but we do not know what was made in them. It is probably no accident that most traces of casting occur in towns.

Tools such as crucibles, ingot moulds, tongs, draw-plates, hammers, metal shears and so on[124] have been found on a number of sites elsewhere, though we cannot always be sure what metals they were meant for. Traces of workshops with bronze fragments occur in various other places, such as Vorbasse,[125] and may have been used both in casting and in wire- and sheet-work. The large smithy find from Tjele includes both bronze off-cuts and bronze wire.[126] This smith worked chiefly with iron, but turned his hand to bronze as well.

Some surprising information about Viking Age bronze-working is provided by the numerous and thoroughly examined finds from Ribe. Most finds are concentrated in a small area, in all probability the craftsman's place of work. But, just as in the beadmaker's workshop, there were

26 The manufacture of a mosaic glass bead.

only faint signs of integral fittings and no indication of a building. A small hollow in the ground containing slag, with a collapsed bellows-shield above it, seems to have been the fireplace or the furnace where the bronze was smelted. That is all.

The bronze was smelted in small crucibles, of which there were several types, and bellows were used to produce the high temperatures needed. These have left traces in the form of small clay shields (furnace stones or forge-stones) which protected the bellows from the fire. There were about two thousand fragments of clay moulds, virtually all from double moulds. About two hundred fragments of moulds with visible impressions were connected with the workshop itself. Among them was a mould for a brooch in the form of a horse in motion, one for another brooch and two for keys. All the others were for oval brooches of the so-called Berdal type. The bronze-worker was apparently a specialist in this type of brooch, and his products (or at least those based on his prototypes) have been identified in several places in Denmark and elsewhere in Scandinavia.

Moulds thus cast an interesting light on craft specialisation in the Viking Age. The degree of specialisation could obviously be considerable, but it is equally clear that it was supported by a demand for high-quality oval brooches. In all, these finds from Ribe have provoked a positive revaluation of Viking Age bronze-casting.[127]

Close examination of the many fragments has also made possible a detailed reconstruction of the process by which these brooches were manufactured. First, a model of the desired brooch and its ornament was made, and then from this the upper and lower halves of a clay mould. The mould could only be used for a single casting.[128] The production of a pair of oval brooches thus took some time. However, other evidence shows that simple items of tin or bronze could be mass-produced from one mould made of stone or antler, or by the use of many identical clay moulds produced by pressing a model into soft clay to form a clear impression.[129] Casts often had to be filed down and polished to remove irregularities and then possibly engraved in order to delineate the details of the ornament. Some were then gilded.

Silver and gold were used for decorative objects, chiefly jewellery; but silver tableware of native manufacture, such as cups, is also known (pls. 19 and 36). Tableware was doubtless made in gold too though we have no surviving examples. A small gold gaming-piece (pl. 2) and remains of textiles with gold embroidery and borders worked with gold thread, along with gold jewellery and a few ingots, are tangible evidence of that delight in gold which finds enthusiastic expression in scaldic verse and runic inscriptions. As mentioned earlier in this chapter, silver was also used for coins and as a general standard. (The other objects referred to in this paragraph are discussed further in ch. 7.)

More or less the same tools and techniques were used for working gold and silver. The tools included crucibles for smelting, bellows and bellows-shields, tongs, moulds for ingots, heating trays (perhaps used for filigree and granulation work or maybe for purifying metals), hammers, anvils, metal shears, drawing tools for wire work, dies, pincers for filigree

20 *Gold brooch*
m Hornelund near
·rde. Width 8.5 cm.

work, engraving and chasing tools.[130] Quite outstanding technical and
artistic work was produced.

There are examples of cast objects, among them the Jelling cup, but
most artefacts were hammered. In addition there are chains of drawn
wire, plaited in various ways or made of many links, and twisted or plaited
rings for neck, arm and finger.[131] Silver objects (such as the Jelling cup)
might be partially gilded and the ornament delineated by black niello
inlay, or by gilding.[132] Apart from inset coloured stones,[133] gold jewellery
is rarely decorated with any other material. Hammered objects might
have stamped or engraved ornament. But the most splendid gold and
silver work (such as the brooches from Hornelund and Nonnebakken,
and the pendants from Hiddensee, pls. 20, 41 and 45) was produced as
follows: the front plate—gold or silver sheet hammered thin—was cut to
shape and the relief decoration impressed on it by a bronze die. A plain
back-plate was fixed to the front-plate, and filigree and granules soldered
to the front-plate's raised features. Lug and catch-plate were soldered on
to the back of the brooches and a pin attached.

Such jewellery was particularly fashionable in the middle and second
half of the tenth century and had a wide geographical distribution, from
England to East Germany and Poland. But the general distribution and
various finds of dies (such as one from Trelleborg and a group of about
forty found recently in a pouch in the harbour at Hedeby) seem to
indicate that Denmark was the centre of production. There is no doubt
that they were also manufactured elsewhere, as may be seen from a lead
object found in York (pl. 50). Its form is precisely that of a die for a

pendant with a bird's-head-shaped loop and it must have had some function in the manufacture of this kind of jewellery.[134]

There were also goldsmiths and silversmiths in the Fyrkat fortress in Jutland. One or more buildings were used as workshops and they may have made jewellery of the kind just mentioned. Nor is it surprising that these craftsmen and their expensive metals were to be found around the king (and no doubt in the vicinity of other affluent men) and in the large towns. Here lay safety as well as customers.[135]

Iron

Iron was everyday material, used for tools, domestic utensils, weapons, horse equipment, nails and rivets. Forging was presumably carried out in all settlements of a certain size, for tools always had to be made and repaired. Iron slag is also commonly found in town and country. There are occasional traces of workshops, as in the Fyrkat fortress, several of the Vorbasse farms (fig. 14), the village of Sædding and possibly at Lindholm Høje. Both in Denmark and abroad, the fire-risk led to the sensible location of smithies on the outskirts of settlements or perhaps at the edge of a farmyard, or out on their own.[136]

The smith's equipment is illustrated by two sets of tools, one from Tjele in Jutland and one from the river Halleby in Sjælland, by material from one burial and a number of single finds, along with the tools found outside Denmark, and early pictures. The two sets of tools were in all probability in boxes or chests. The Tjele find (fig. 27) is tenth century and by far the most comprehensive; as mentioned above, this smith worked with both iron and bronze, and possibly with other metals too. He had tools (tongs, hammers, anvils, nail-iron, chisel, file, drawing tool, ladles, metal shears, burnishing stone and so on), various raw materials (bronze and lead), a pair of scales and weights, and finally some finished products (an axe-head, sickle blades and an arrow-head). The hasps and hinges in the find no doubt come from a box or chest which has otherwise disappeared and to which the key may also have belonged. In addition there are various small fittings, a small bell and other minor items, as well as some indeterminate fragments. The Halleby find comprises an anvil, a pair of tongs, metal shears, a whetstone, a fly-wheel (perhaps for a drill), spoon-bit, a spear-head, a bronze box-mount, a piece that looks like the beginnings of a similar fitting, and an iron ingot or a rough-out. The box-mount dates the collection to sometime between 975 and 1050, and it seems as if this craftsman worked with wood, iron and bronze. The smith's grave is from Lejre and is tenth century. It contained a hammer, a pair of tongs and a file.[137]

The workshops have not left many traces. They can be identified by concentrations of smithying debris in pits which often seem to have constituted the furnaces. Thus there is evidence of fire pits and of working areas, along with lots of rubbish in two of the Fyrkat buildings.[138] Frequently there are also remains of large clay bellows-shields;[139] some shields were made of imported fireproof soapstone (pl. 21).[140] Iron bars are quite common, too.[141]

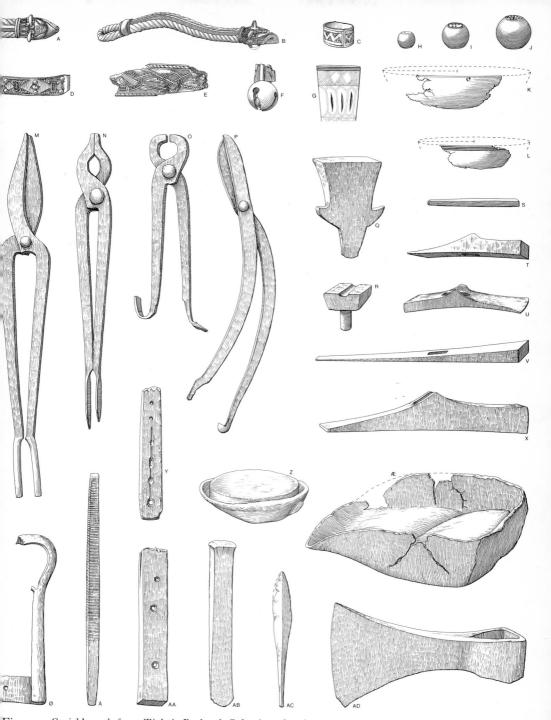

Fig. 27   *Smith's tools from Tjele in Jutland. Selection of tools, raw material and finished products etc. The hasps and perhaps the key may come from a box or chest which contained the rest. A–B two hasps of iron and bronze; C bronze ring; D–E bronze mount with silver and bone mount; F–G bronze bell and mount; H–J weights and K–L scale pans; M–O three iron tangs; P metal shears; Q–R two anvils; S whetstone or polishing stone; T–X four hammers; Y nail-iron; Z iron foundry ladle with lump of lead; Æ iron foundry ladle with lump of whitish, non-precious metal; ø iron key; Å, AA and AB file, drawing-plate and chisel; AC–AD arrow-head and axe-head. A sickle or scythe blade is illustrated in fig. 17B. Scale 1 : 3.*

Pl. 21 *Soapstone bellows-shield found in the water at Snaptun on Horsens fjord. Height 20 cm.*

The proficient smiths of the Viking Age were masters of their craft and saw to it that the iron in each object had precisely the qualities necessary for its function: that the springs in a lock (fig. 31) were flexible, that the cutting edge of axe, knife or sword was hard without being brittle, that arrow-heads were rigid and so on. To give an example: it is usual for the cutting edge of an axe to be of hard steel, while the material forming the body of the blade is of soft iron. The blades of knives were similar to those of today, that is, welded together with a central part forming the cutting edge and softer side pieces to give body to the blade and protect the core.[142]

Recent analysis of iron bars and finished objects has yielded much new information about techniques employed, and several practical experiments have been undertaken: welding of iron, case-hardening of iron to produce hard steel, complicated pattern-welding, tempering and much besides. Sometimes, of course, it is impossible to decide whether a particular object was manufactured at home or abroad and not every example can be taken to illustrate native techniques.[143]

Some smiths were also able to decorate their products with motifs and patterns in different coloured metals. This is seen in particular on stirrups, spurs, sword-hilts and occasionally on axe-blades. Thus the blade of the Mammen axe (pl. 28) was inlaid with silver wire,[144] while the hilt of the Bustorf sword (fig. 49) and the stirrups from Nørre Longelse (pl. 6) show another much commoner technique: encrustation. Here the whole surface is hatched and then covered with silver and copper wire pressed and hammered in to form both the pattern itself and its background.[145] It has been estimated that encrusting a particular pair of stirrups took about three hundred hours, or between four and six weeks' work.[146] Other iron objects which were to look decorative, such as box-fittings, might be covered with foil (*pressblech*), often tin, which was glued in place.[147]

It is not certain where this kind of smith's work was done, but we may guess that some of it came from the workshops of the large fortresses.[148] It is certain, in any case, that these splendid products were reserved for the wealthy and often accompanied them into their graves.

Water-mills
It may have been in the Viking Age that the Scandinavians learnt to use water-power in mills.[149]

Remains of a water-mill at the Viking Age settlement of Omgård were mentioned above, but this mill may be of later date. Mention has also been made of a structure at Lund, from the first half of the eleventh century, now interpreted as a water-mill. In addition there are the quite well-preserved remains of a mill at Ljørring in West Jutland. Two C-14 datings date the mill to the tenth century. The mills at Omgård and Ljørring had small horizontal wheels: similar mills could be seen in use in Norway and Sweden, the Faeroes, Ireland and other places right up to the present day. It is difficult to be certain whether the mill from Lund was of the same kind, or whether it may have had a large, vertical water-wheel.[150]

It may seem surprising that such constructions existed as early as the Viking Age. But water-mills from the period have also been found in England, for example (and in the late eleventh-century Domesday Book a total of 5624 mills were recorded).[151] Many people still had to grind their corn on hand-querns, but apparently some now got their flour from the mill. We can say that in many respects the level of technical achievement in Viking Age Denmark corresponds to that found in rural areas right up to the Industrial Revolution.

7 Daily Life

In the Viking Age—as in all ages—the life of the individual was much determined by his position in society: the daily life of the large landowner was quite different from that of slaves and the lower classes. Many of the latter probably lived at subsistence level, and much of what is discussed below was of course unknown in their surroundings.

HOUSES AND FURNISHINGS

Individual plots were often fenced, both in towns and on farms in the countryside too. As well as the main house, the enclosure might contain other buildings with specific functions. However, the functions of additional buildings can rarely be determined by excavation. At Hedeby individual plots often had wells, and some of the pits which occur there and on other settlement sites were probably latrines.

Hedeby provides the best information on a dwelling-house. Here the conditions for wood preservation are excellent, and many ground-plans and lower portions of buildings survive. In one case, moreover, walls of a building survive in a collapsed state, and they provide information about such things as the height of the walls and the slope of the roof; they had also protected other integral features. Dendrochronology indicates that the house was erected in AD 870 and the reconstruction (fig. 28 and pl. 22) gives a good impression of a Viking Age town house.

The house was rectangular, about 5 × 12 m, with walls of wattle and daub on timber frames. The weight of the roof was carried by sloping external posts which also supported the walls. The house was divided by cross walls into three rooms, the middle one with a central hearth and broad wall-benches. Access was through doors from each of the end rooms. One of these had one outer door, and in the gable there was a small window opening. The other had two outer doors and a dome-shaped baking-oven of clay. The central room must have been a combined kitchen and living-room with cooking done on the hearth. The other end room may have been a workshop. In 882, twelve years after its erection, the building was slightly altered: amongst other things, the oven was removed and a wooden trough placed in the room.[1]

Many features of this building can be found elsewhere too, and a number of scattered finds yields further information on the appearance

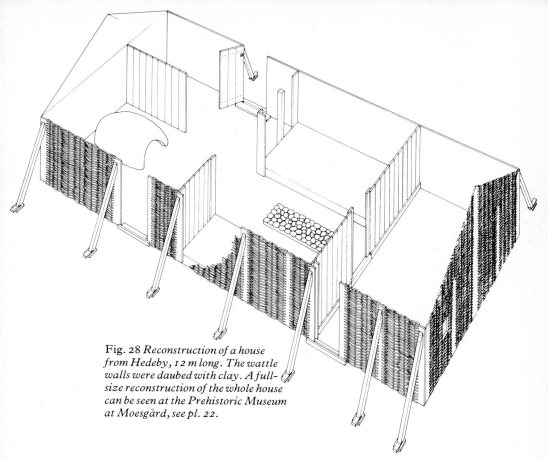

Fig. 28 *Reconstruction of a house from Hedeby, 12 m long. The wattle walls were daubed with clay. A full-size reconstruction of the whole house can be seen at the Prehistoric Museum at Moesgård, see pl. 22.*

and arrangement of buildings. There are quite well-preserved remains of late Viking Age buildings in Viborg[2] and Lund,[3] but there is no comprehensive survey of them or of the many that survive as post-holes on village and farm sites. These latter buildings are discussed in ch. 4, as are sunken-featured buildings, some of which were dwellings; buildings from Hedeby, Viborg and Lund have been further discussed in ch. 5.

Buildings were constructed of wood, either of oak planks joined in different ways, or wattle and daub on timber frames.[4] The roofs might be shingled over planks,[5] but various kinds of straw and reeds must have been by far the commonest roofing material.[6] We know very little about details of roof-construction.[7] The floor-level of buildings has often been destroyed, but simple earth floors seem to have been the norm, though a few floors of clay, pebbles or limestone have been found.[8] The lower parts of many door-frames, including the doorsteps, have survived at Hedeby and show that doors were in general between 80 and 90 cm wide.[9] A well-preserved door and remains of a hatch from the same site show how many doors must have looked: vertical planks were joined by a couple of horizontal battens to form the door itself, with the opening mechanism consisting of a peg at the top and bottom of one side plank, which turned in corresponding peg-holes in the door-casing.[10] Separate iron hinges and hinge pivots are also known, though, and show that

Pl. 22 *Central room in the Hedeby house, fig. 28, as reconstructed at Moesgård.*

hung doors existed.[11] Several iron and wood keys are of such size that they must have been for doors rather than for chests; similarly there were wooden and iron door-locks.[12]

The carved and painted plank, part of the wall-plate, from the first church at Nørre Hørning in Jutland of *c.* 1100 (pl. 38) suggests that the houses of the upper classes were splendidly decorated. There cannot be much doubt that this was in fact the case, given the universal delight in splendour, and given the virtuosity of the wood-carvings seen in the ninth-century Oseberg burial and the eleventh-century Urnes church in Norway.[13]

Traces of wall-benches are thought to have been found in some of the Fyrkat halls, in the Hedeby house mentioned above, at Viborg and at Sædding.[14] These wall-benches must often have been constructed of wood or of earth faced with wood. They were about 1.5 m wide at Fyrkat and in the Hedeby house, narrower at Viborg and Sædding. We do not know the height of the benches but better preserved wall-benches in Icelandic houses were about 40 to 50 cm high.[15] Reconstructions of them at Trelleborg (where no traces survive) and in the Hedeby house are not quite as high as that. Wall-benches of earth faced with wood sometimes occur in sunken-featured buildings. In some of the Århus houses their height was between about 15 and 30 cm, their width between about 50 and 90 cm.[16] Wall-benches were no doubt common in houses of the period. Narrow benches were practical for sitting or sleeping on, and the broader benches made functional living areas, avoiding draughts, cold and dirt.[17] In houses with benches such as these, the floor was chiefly an area for walking. In the fortresses, small porches in front of the outer doors of the halls were also intended to diminish draughts, and screen walls just inside the doors of the halls presumably served the same purpose.[18]

The hearth was traditionally located in the centre of the room, giving light and heat as well as fire for cooking. Hearths were generally oblong— probably often rectangular—and consisted of a layer of stone covered by a clay shield and sometimes with a frame of wood or of other material, for example lime or chalk kerbs. Some buildings, particularly those with sunken features, were equipped with an oven instead of a hearth (fig. 20) and the Hedeby house had both an oven and a hearth.[19]

Very little is known about windows; the small window opening in the Hedeby house was mentioned above. The most important source of light apart from the hearth must have been the louver or louvers through which the smoke from hearths and ovens escaped. There were other artificial sources of light, however. A number of small clay lamps on pedestals occur from the later Viking Age. These are about 8 to 10 cm high and have a shallow dish, containing the fuel.[20] Other small vessels may also have been lamps, but sometimes these are indistinguishable from other containers. We know of iron lamps from Norway with a spike of up to about 90 cm which could be stuck into the floor,[21] but these are so far unknown in Denmark. A wax candle 58 cm in height was found in the Mammen grave and pieces of another in the Jelling burial-mound,[22] so we may assume that wax (and tallow) candles were used in daily life too.

Pictures, wills and inventories show that household textiles (tapestries, cushions, pillows, rugs, eiderdowns, tablecloths, towels and so on) played a great role in the Middle Ages.[23] Such textiles were no doubt of equal importance in the Viking Age, but nothing has survived in Denmark apart from remains of eiderdowns and pillows stuffed with down or feathers in rich graves. At Mammen the finds also included a pillow-case.[24] The Oseberg tapestry and some early medieval tapestries from Norway and Sweden illustrate how on festive occasions the halls were decorated with polychrome textiles. They apparently acted as ornamental friezes against a background of plainer textiles which may normally have covered the entire wall, shielding against damp and draughts.[25] Decorated wooden panels such as the Flatatunga panels in Iceland[26] were in the same way both ornamental and functional, but nothing similar is known in Denmark.

Only a small amount of furniture survives and no doubt it was rare in the Viking Age itself—though much wood has been excavated at Hedeby, it is significant that hardly any of it can be identified as remains of furniture.[27] There are a couple of fragments from Lund, and the rest (where it can be reconstructed) is from graves. In addition there are individual objects such as chest-keys and a few fittings.[28]

Remains of chests, used as furniture or for travelling (and with a secondary use as coffins), are known from Lejre,[29] Fyrkat[30] and Forlev.[31] On all three chests the lids were originally fastened to the back by iron hinges and all the chests could be locked. The Lejre chest (fig. 29) was further decorated or strengthened with iron bands. The wood of the chests has not survived, however, so they have been reconstructed on the basis of the iron-work and its position, and from traces of wood in the earth. The three chests were about the same size: the Lejre chest 147 cm long, 37 cm wide and about 28 cm high; the Fyrkat chest probably about 130 to 135 cm long, about 50 cm wide, and between 25 and 35 cm high; the Forlev chest estimated at 140 cm long and 50 cm wide. None of them was thus long enough to contain an adult corpse, but one end of the Lejre chest (and probably of the Fyrkat chest too) had been broken in order to give more space, and the body in the Forlev chest had to lie with knees bent.

These chests were larger than the Oseberg chests and the tool-chest from Mästermyr on Gotland, which are less than a metre long. The wood of these chests has survived and it is characteristic that their end panels extend downwards to form feet to keep the base of the chest off the ground.[32] This feature is common in early medieval chests too,[33] and it is therefore reasonable to assume that many Danish Viking Age chests also had feet, even though none have survived. It is also likely that the end panels were rebated to hold the front and back panels which were nailed fast, and that the bottom was held in place by tongues as on the chests mentioned above.

Another chest is said to have been found in the burial-chamber in the North Mound at Jelling, but it was destroyed when the chamber was opened in 1820. Only two iron rings and some rivets have survived. A plait of hair, and a wooden board (in two pieces) about 135 cm long, about 11.5 cm wide and about 0.75 cm thick, may be from the same chest. One

Fig. 29 *Chest from Lejre, chair and stool from Lund and table from Hørning. Reconstructions. Drawn to the same scale.*

side of the board is covered with hide, with a row of nail or rivet holes about 12 cm apart along each edge. A description of the chest from 1820 refers to '. . . the casket, which is almost rotted away, looking like a small trunk, $3\frac{1}{4}$ ells [*c.* 2 m] long; the bottom was caulked with plaits of hair and held together with rivets. In its side were two iron rings which have been sent to Copenhagen. The lid consisted of two convex boards, with shanks of hair between them. There were traces of canvas on the outside of the casket as well as a very small piece of a narrow strip which looked like thin silver'.[34] It has been suggested that the object described here was the body of a cart rather than a chest.[35] But as it is expressly mentioned that it had a lid, and as lids have never been found in association with

Pl. 23   *The magnificent casket from the Cathedral Treasury at Bamberg in West Germany. Length 26 cm.*

bodies of carts, and since iron rings occur on early medieval chests and not just on cart bodies,[36] there is hardly any reason to doubt the old identification, made, after all, by people who actually saw the chest. The thickness of the board fits most satisfactorily with a chest, and a chest in a large chamber-grave is not surprising. However, this one was larger than any other chest from the Viking Age and the construction was different.

Finally, the Halleby river tools, and presumably also those from Tjele (ch. 6), were found in a wooden box or chest, like the Mästermyr find, but these chests have also disappeared.[37]

Chests were the storage furniture of the Viking Age (cupboards did not become common until the late Middle Ages), and the locks indicated that the contents of the chests were private property, just as door-locks marked the right of ownership to buildings and their furnishings. During the Middle Ages, theft of something kept under lock and key was considered a more serious crime than any other theft. Similarly, being a key-bearer was prestigious because it implied responsibility.[38] The numerous Viking Age locks and keys reflect people's awareness of such things.

Box-fittings, keys and padlocks occur in many settlements[39] but complete boxes have also survived, such as the two splendid caskets which were made, or ended up, as reliquaries: the Cammin casket, destroyed in the Second World War but of which descriptions, casts and many pictures exist, and the Bamberg casket (pl. 23), now in the Bayerisches Nationalmuseum in Munich. This was formerly part of Bamberg Cathedral treasure and by tradition is said to have belonged to Kunigunde, a daughter of Cnut the Great, who was married in 1036 to

Henry, later to be Henry III, emperor of Germany. The two caskets were made in the second half of the tenth century, or the beginning of the eleventh, and may well be of Danish workmanship. Both consist of a wooden shell, covered with decorated sheets of ivory or elk-horn and with decorated gilt-bronze bands. From these projected three-dimensional gilt-bronze animals and birds. Both caskets could be locked.[40]

Otherwise, the best examples of box-fittings (hinges, hasps, locks, keys) come from well-appointed female graves of the tenth century. The grandest remains of a box from a Danish grave (though in a poor state) come from Jelling and probably belonged to Queen Thyre.[41] Some of these boxes have been reconstructed,[42] as have some of the locks (fig. 31).[43] Graves also give us information about the everyday contents of boxes: needlework implements and other personal property.[44]

The back and back legs of a chair from Lund[45] is all that survives of Viking Age chairs in Denmark. It dates from the first half of the eleventh century and can be satisfactorily reconstructed (fig. 29). The seat must have been plaitwork, about 40 cm high, similar to the seat height of the only other surviving Viking Age chair in Scandinavia, the Oseberg chair (38 cm)[46] and a few centimetres lower than most modern dining-chairs. Chairs were most likely status symbols, but it is hardly justifiable to see the rather roughly made chair from Lund as a bishop's throne from a church, as has been done.[47] It may well have been the seat of honour of the master of a large household.[48]

The existence of another type of chair, a log-chair, cut from a single log of wood, can be deduced from a number of small pendants in the form of miniature chairs. Four such pendants exist in Denmark (fig. 30), as well as some Swedish ones, while the chairs which acted as models for such pendants are depicted in use on Gotlandic picture stones.[49] Finally, there are a couple of seats from three-legged stools from Lund (fig. 29), of the same shape as more recent milking-stools, and a similar four-legged stool is known from Hedeby.[50]

Large dining-tables from Viking Age Scandinavia are unknown, but they are shown in use in foreign pictures, and they were no doubt also used in Denmark on festive occasions, at any rate among the upper classes. They were no doubt accompanied by wooden benches, though none survive. The tables are thought to have had removable tops which were hung by rings on the wall when they were not in use.[51] In the woman's grave at Nørre Hørning, however, there are remains of another sort of table: a low, square table with projecting, finely bevelled edges. The legs were 20 cm high and the table-top about 50 cm square (fig. 29). A wash-basin was standing on it. Perhaps small, easily movable tables such as this were common in rich households.[52]

Free-standing beds were no doubt also only used by the upper classes. These occur in the Oseberg and Gokstad graves in Norway[53] but are so far unknown in Denmark. It is most likely that people usually managed with beds fixed to the walls (and thus destroyed along with the house), or that they simply unrolled bedding on top of the broad wall-benches. The few traces of Viking Age bedclothes from Denmark have been mentioned above. A shelf is known at Hedeby, of the simplest form

Silver chair-pendant from . Scale 1:1.

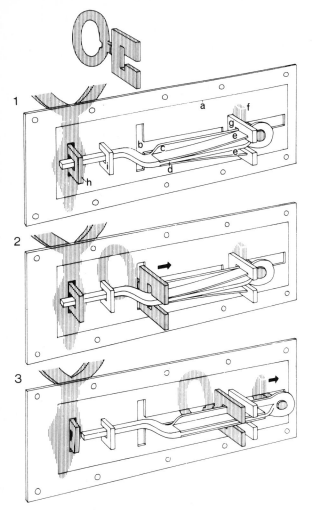

Fig. 31　*Box lock from Fyrkat.*
Reconstruction seen from inside the
box. (1) in locked position, (2) with
the key inserted and (3) unlocked.
a the edge of the lock casing; b keyhole
and slit for key; c guide plate for
key; d bolt; e bolt springs; f slide in
its slit; g stop; h loop of hasp and
i the guide plate of bolt. Scale 3 : 5.

imaginable, consisting of a board with two pegs at each end to hold strings for suspension.[54]

Finally it must be mentioned that some pieces of wood from the Jelling burial-chamber may well be fragments of furniture, particularly those openwork pieces which are painted on both sides (they include the figure of a man), and a couple of oak planks bevelled on all four edges. Several of the painted pieces are tongued so as to be fitted into a frame. But as they were clearly intended to be seen from both sides, they cannot have been part of a box as has been suggested. They may be from a bed or a chair: a high-seat perhaps.[55] The large bed and the chair in the Oseberg grave, for example, show that Viking Age furniture was indeed sometimes painted.[56]

In short, house-furnishings consisted first and foremost of built-in features such as wall-benches and hearths. Then there were textile hangings and coverings. In many homes a large, upright loom would be found, probably a lockable chest and perhaps also a stool, and a couple of boxes. Apart from this, furniture was undoubtedly scanty and chiefly reserved for the upper classes in their more spacious houses. Elsewhere, people presumably managed well enough by sitting on a chest or on a rug—either on the floor or, even better, on the wall-benches. This is after all how things are in many parts of the world today. Free-standing tables, benches, chairs and beds were both unnecessary and impractical in small houses.

FOOD AND DRINK. DOMESTIC UTENSILS AND PERSONAL HYGIENE

Agricultural products provided the main diet: meat (especially beef, pork, lamb and poultry), eggs, dairy products and cereals (especially barley, rye and oats). In coastal settlements, and presumably elsewhere, there was a fair amount of fish, for example cod, flat-fish and herring (see ch. 4). A couple of richly furnished graves containing bones of ox, calf, pigs, suckling pig, sheep, lamb and a gosling[57] give some idea of the constituents of meals.

Vegetables (such as peas and beans), fruit, berries and nuts (for example apples, plums, blackberries, raspberries, wild strawberries and hazelnuts) were an important supplement. Walnuts were known too, but they were probably often imported. Flax seeds have also been found and linseed was certainly used for cooking earlier in the Iron Age. And since herbs such as cress are known from the Norwegian Oseberg grave, it is reasonable to suppose that they were used in Denmark too, where people certainly made use of sloes and hops. It is also likely that elderberry, juniper, bog-myrtle and other edible plants were used in cooking, since they were and are, after all, indigenous in Denmark. And given that unworked branches of elder exceed by far the number of worked pieces in Hedeby, it follows that there were quite a lot of elder trees and bushes in and around that settlement. On the other hand, there are only a few unworked bits of fruit-tree wood here compared with the number of worked pieces, which may indicate that apples, plums and the like, as well as most berries, were usually gathered farther afield. Correspondingly, the apples of the Oseberg find were wild apples, but an apple-core from Lund may be from a cultivated apple, though it could have been imported.[58]

However, little attention has been paid to the cultivated plants of Denmark, or of the Viking Age in general. Similarly, virtually nothing is known about vegetable cultivation, and we are not sure whether gardens as such ever existed, or even how fruit, berries and nuts were gathered. Icelandic sagas, though frequently used for such purposes, are dubious sources of information on Danish conditions in the Viking Age. Was it, for example, common to have a kitchen-garden and a hazel thicket? Were there often a couple of elder-trees and perhaps an apple- or a plum-tree just outside the house? Was cultivated fruit very rare, in fact? Whatever the answer, there is hardly any doubt that a not insignificant part of people's supplementary diet was gathered in fields and forests, and that far more plants than those mentioned contributed in various ways to make food and drink.

Hunting played only a very small part in the food supply. Occasionally the bones of hares, ducks and the like occur, but it is remarkable that there are usually only a few bones of game animals and birds, and that bones of wild animals such as boar, roe and red deer are hardly ever found.[59] Antler fragments used in comb manufacture are none the less quite common in towns (ch. 6). There is no explanation for this other than that the antlers were collected and traded separately.[60] Game must have been a luxury.

Herbs helped to flavour food and to disguise unpleasant tastes in poor quality food. The same was true of salt, and honey—the only known sweetener. Salt was also used as a preservative, and honey was an important ingredient in the alcoholic drinks *mjǫðr* and *bjórr*. There is no information about the collection of salt in Viking Age Denmark. Salt produced at home may have been obtained by the evaporation of sea-water or by extraction from seaweed, while high quality salt may have been bought abroad.[61] Nor is anything known about bee-keeping in Viking Age Denmark, but it is likely it was a regular activity: the country was suitable for it, and several regulations concerning bee-keeping occur in thirteenth-century laws, and from this same period there is informa-tion about the quantities of honey paid in tax. Bees also provided wax, which was equally sought after, used as it was for candles and in moulding processes.[62]

Meat, apart from being salted, could also be preserved by three long-established, cheap methods: drying, smoking and pickling. Archaeo-logical evidence rarely indicates which method was used, but fish-bones found in Hedeby come from herring which must have been bought already smoked or salted. Other fish (flounder and large cod) was most likely dried, and groups of bones found in Viborg must derive from the dried or smoked chines of various domestic animals.[63] Many fruits and vegetables could also be dried.

Drink could be water, milk products, juice of fruit and berries, beer, *mjǫðr*, *bjórr* or wine. Drinking-water was usually fetched from wells, frequently found in the settlements of the period even when they were situated by streams (e.g. Lindholm Høje, Sædding, Trelleborg, Hedeby).[64] Milk products, including whey, were no doubt drunk in large quantities,[65] but beer is thought to have been the most important drink. In Denmark, beer must have been brewed from barley and was probably spiced, perhaps with hops and bog-myrtle.[66] *Mjǫðr* was another alcoholic drink, produced from honey and water with added flavouring.[67]

Although all these drinks are mentioned in Norse literature, *bjórr* is seldom referred to and appears to have been a sweet, strong drink, and rare—drunk in the halls of the great and in Valhall, and a component of magic potions. It was probably a strongly fermented cider, thus a drink which could easily attain an alcohol level of about 18 per cent, more than beer, *mjǫðr* and grape wine. The small silver vessels, many of which are known from Denmark (pls. 24 and 36) are very suitable for a drink such as this.[68] Finally there is wine (from grapes) which was probably imported in some quantity.[69] Archaeological evidence for the import of wine exists in the shape of barrels from Hedeby, which were put to

Pl. 24　*Silver vessels from Lejre, Ribe and Fejø. Top: three of the vessels from Lejre. Left: four of the vessels from Ribe. Right: four of the vessels from Fejø (the large cup is 9.7 cm high). The vessels from Terslev are shown in pl. 19.*

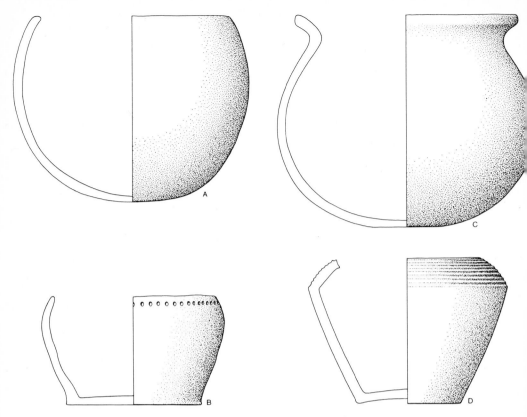

Fig. 33 *Four pottery types: A Jutland hemispherical vessel from Århus; B East Danish, flat-bottomed vessel from Trelleborg; C globular pot* (kugeltopf) *from Hedeby; D Baltic vessel from Lund. Scale about 2 : 7.*

subsequent use as well-linings; they are made of silver fir which did not grow in Denmark but was common in the wine-producing Rhineland. It is quite possible that these arrived in Hedeby filled with wine.[70] The rare drinking-glasses, most likely imported from the same regions (as well as from elsewhere), would make very suitable wineglasses, though they may of course have been used for other drinks too.[71]

Food could be prepared in many ways, and the archaeological finds give much evidence about cooking. As a rule, heating, boiling and roasting took place on the central hearth in the dwelling-houses. Fire was made by striking a strike-a-light against a flint and catching the spark in a piece of tinder of some kind.[72] Cooking-pots could be placed on stones above the fire or be hung over the hearth, perhaps on a chain with a hook like the fine example found at Trelleborg (fig. 32).[73] Cooking-pots were most frequently made of clay but could also be made of fireproof soapstone or of thin iron sheets riveted together. These latter are best known from Norway; only fragments survive in Denmark.[74]

Until about AD 1000, pottery was usually of poor quality. The vessels used for the storage and serving of food, as well as for cooking,

Fig. 32 *Iron cauldron chain and hook from Trelleborg. Length 115 cm.*

are often completely lop-sided; the rare decoration is usually haphazard and the clay often has a very coarse grit-tempering which protrudes on to the surface. Technically, the vessels were shaped by hand—the ones from Jutland usually coil-made—and fired at low temperatures on a fire or in a clamp. These can only have been home-made.[75]

The shapes, however, vary, and they reveal regional variations and contacts. Thus hemispherical vessels (fig. 33A) with rounded bases and inverted rims dominated in Jutland. This type, which occurs before the Viking Age too, can also have lugs (either the so-called 'swallows-nest lugs', or simply upright pierced flaps) and a tubular spout; they occur in sizes ranging from 'cooking-pot size' right down to small bowls; they are also common on Samsø and possibly on Fyn.[76] Flat-bottomed vessels (fig. 33B) were almost universal on Sjælland and east of Øresund. These must have been inspired by Slav pottery.[77] The type is also found on Langeland and other islands in southern Denmark.[78] The pottery vessels of Hedeby are unusual in Denmark in that many are globular (with rounded bases and everted rims, fig. 33C). Vessels of this shape, though common in north-western Germany, only appear in small numbers further north on the east coast of the Jutland peninsula. In West Jutland (in Ribe, for example)[79] they are more frequent—this vessel is a North Sea type. Many other pottery types have been found at Hedeby, and wheel-turned pottery also occurs here.

Slav-inspired pottery made great advances at the end of the tenth or beginning of the eleventh century. It became almost universal east of Øresund and on the Danish islands including Fyn until around AD 1200. It also occurs in Jutland. Genuine imported Slav pottery is also found, as earlier, but most pottery is doubtless of local production and is all referred to as Baltic pottery. These vessels, modelled on the so-called Late Slav types, are of a much better quality than earlier types. They are carefully formed and decorated with precision, often with concentric grooves and various stamps (fig. 33D). The rim has often been moulded and some pots have a raised mark on the base which is most likely the potter's stamp.[80] The hemispherical vessels with rounded bases continued to dominate in Jutland, but were eventually (perhaps in the eleventh century) overtaken by the globular vessels, and the pottery gradually became more carefully shaped and was fired at higher temperatures.[81]

Soapstone pots from Norway or south-western Sweden had many advantages over the locally made clay vessels.[82] They were comparatively solid, easy to clean, had good heat distribution and did not give the food an unpleasant taste. Like the Jutlandic pottery of the period, they usually have rounded bases and are undecorated (pl. 17), and they sometimes have iron fittings for iron handles. The largest soapstone vessel to survive in Denmark ended up as a font in Ørslev church in Fyn.[83] It has a diameter of 59 cm, though the diameter of such pots is usually less than 40 cm.

Fragments of soapstone pots are known from almost all Danish settlements of the period; in addition there are individual finds from graves and a fair number of stray finds, not least of pots dredged up from the sea.

The latter are presumably trade-goods lost *en route* to their destination (ch. 6). Usually, however, there are few soapstone fragments in comparison with the number of potsherds in the various settlements; only in Fyrkat are the numbers more balanced and this must be a sign of wealth.[84] In Denmark, soapstone vessels appear to be a purely Viking Age phenomenon. Their importation probably did not commence in Hedeby until the ninth century and it appears to have ceased before Hedeby was deserted around 1050.[85] In addition, though fragments of soapstone vessels occur in Lund in levels dated to between 1020 and 1050,[86] none such have been found in Schleswig, Hedeby's successor.[87] Perhaps there is a connection between the disappearance of the soapstone cooking-pots and the improved quality of the pottery.

Liquids could also be heated and brought to the boil by dropping hot stones into them. Frequently the stones burst from the sudden change in the temperature, and large quantities of these shattered pot-boilers occur in or near the Viking Age settlements. The advantage of cooking with stones is that use can be made of containers of non-heatproof materials such as clay, wood and hide. Pot-boilers seem to belong with the inferior pottery of the period and they disappear as it improves.[88]

Roasting over a fire was normally synonymous with spit-roasting—frying as we now know it is a later development. Splendid iron spits have been found in several parts of the country (fig. 34);[89] in all probability there were also small grilling spits intended for roasting meat over embers.[90] Gridirons (spiral grids of iron with long handles) are known from Norway, but so far not from Denmark. The same applies to circular iron plates with long handles,[91] which may have been used for baking flat-bread, but which could also be used for frying chunks of meat.

The dome-shaped baking ovens and the small ovens of the sunken-featured buildings mentioned above could be used both for baking bread and roasting meat. Meat was also roasted in earth-ovens (or cooking pits). This method is still employed in various parts of the world, and modern experiments have given very tasty results. A simple pit dug into the ground is half-filled with glowing stones, heated on a nearby fire. The roast, packed in clay or wrapped in large leaves, is placed on top and covered by more red-hot stones, after which the pit is filled with material such as earth or turf. The method takes only a normal cooking time—about one hour per kilo of meat. Viking Age earth-ovens such as this have been found at Lindholm Høje, at Sædding and elsewhere. They survive in the form of pits containing numbers of stones made brittle by heat (and there are also numerous Bronze Age examples in Denmark).[92]

Among other domestic equipment, wooden cheese- and butter-churns from Lund should be mentioned.[93] Assorted wooden troughs, ladles, bowls, beakers and large spoons, as well as turned bowls, cups and coopered buckets, sometimes with iron handles, occur on those sites where wood has survived, especially Hedeby, Lund, Trelleborg and Århus.[94] Buckets are also known from a number of graves, some with splendid ornamental fittings, and there was a bronze bucket in the Søllested grave on Fyn. These buckets were most likely for drinks other than water.[95]

Fig. 34 *Iron spit from Lund. Length 111 cm.*

Knives and whetstones of various sizes were naturally indispensable and have been found in large quantities. The handles of ordinary knives are very often of ash, but rarer sorts of wood, such as spindle-tree and bullace, were sometimes used for fine knives, bound with silver. A number of bone and antler handles probably belong to knives too.[96] The whetstones—usually slate—are often carefully shaped, and the small ones sometimes have a hole for suspension so that they could be carried together with the knife; knives and whetstones have indeed often been found close together in graves.[97] The whetstones, or the raw material at any rate, were for the most part imported, a large number apparently from Norway (ch. 6).

Many households possessed a hand-quern, either of native stone or of imported Rhenish lava, so-called Mayen basalt (pl. 17); others may have originated in Norway.[98] The axes in the Oseberg burial, in particular, seem to show that axes were used as household implements,[99] and it is likely that many of the much discussed small axes are quite simply kitchen-axes.[100] They are perfectly suited to kitchen use. Large iron forks were used for fishing the meat out of the soup and for serving.[101]

The layout of the houses shows that it was usual to cook and eat in the same room; the utensils used for preparation and storing of food cannot have been much different from those used for serving. Certain types of implements, however, and certain of the materials used in their production, are specifically luxury items, no doubt used on festive occasions and in wealthy circles.[102]

This applies to a number of the buckets mentioned above, as well as to pottery vessels imported from Western Europe. The latter include yellowy-white Pingsdorf ware with red painted decoration,[103] the black Tating ware[104] and glazed pottery.[105] The glass drinking-vessels mentioned above are also luxury items as are the drinking-horns: ox-horn with decorated silver or gilt-bronze fittings,[106] and cups and bowls of copper alloy, not least the splendid Hiberno-Saxon bowl from the Nørre Longelse grave on Langeland.[107]

The silver vessels from Ribe in Jutland, Fejø near Lolland, Terslev and Lejre in Sjælland (pls. 19 and 24) are the supreme examples of wealth and splendour. The first three of these finds consist of a large cup or bowl and, respectively, six, five and four smaller vessels of gradually decreasing size. They clearly belong together as sets, and the large vessels were presumably containers for a drink served in the smaller ones. The large cups from Ribe and Fejø are of Frankish and West or Central European origin respectively, while the large Terslev bowl may come from the East; the simple small bowls are considered native work. It is uncertain whether all four vessels from Lejre form a set. The largest bowl from this find is a Hiberno-Saxon hanging-bowl, while a smaller decorated cup is clearly of Scandinavian workmanship. None of these silver vessels were of large capacity, and they are too small for the serving of beer, mjǫðr and wine to thirsty people, although they are, however, quite suitable for the relatively strong bjórr.[108]

The small decorated silver cup from the royal grave at Jelling (pl. 36) fits satisfactorily in this context; attempts to identify it as a Christian chalice are not very convincing. Its capacity is about the same as that of the small silver bowls, and there is no doubt that the grave-furnishings of King Gorm and Queen Thyre were of great splendour. The Jelling cup must have been one of their drinking-vessels.[109] There is also a corner of a flat silver dish from the Jelling grave. Pieces of another silver dish come from the Ladby boat-grave.[110]

Large bowls of sheet bronze found in many of the rich tenth-century graves, both male and female, were used on fine occasions. A related bowl found in Kaupang in Norway was inscribed inside with runes I MUNTLAUKI ('in the hand-basin') and such bowls were no doubt used for washing the hands before (and after) the meal, particularly useful since knife and fingers were the chief eating implements. Spoons, though, were not unknown.[111]

Ideals of personal hygiene are also reflected in other ways in the archaeological finds. Pictures show people with well-groomed hair and beards (pl. 1),[112] and combs are common finds. They are usually antler and vary in quality, no doubt corresponding to different price-levels. Produced in many parts of the country, they must have been the work of specialists (ch. 6). The most splendid types, however, up to about 24 cm in length and of very beautiful workmanship, are of unknown origin.[113] Mention may also be made of a silver toilet-set in the Terslev hoard (pl. 19), consisting of a ring with short chains, from which hang two objects perhaps for nail care.[114] Small iron and bronze tweezers may also have been toilet articles.[115]

CLOTHES, FOOTWEAR AND JEWELLERY

Not much is known about Viking Age garments in Denmark. Only small fragments of textile have survived, but some characteristic brooches and their position in graves show that female dress was in principle the same as that reconstructed on the basis of more substantial textile fragments and brooches from the Birka graves in Sweden. The most characteristic element of female dress, the over-dress, was evidently current all over the North until some time in the tenth century. Women who emigrated took the fashion abroad with them.

Female dress in its typical form (though it can scarcely have been used by all women) consisted of a shift or under-dress, its neck-slit sometimes closed by a small disc brooch. The over-dress, worn on top of this, consisted of a rectangular piece of cloth wound round the body and reaching the armpits; this was held up by shoulder-straps, fixed in front on each shoulder by an oval brooch (fig. 35 and pl. 26). In some cases the dress seems to have been sewn up at the sides. A shawl or cloak could be worn on top of it, sometimes pinned in front by a heavy brooch such as a trefoil brooch (pl. 26). They may also have had jackets, and a tunic might be worn under the dress. Oval brooches disappear during the tenth century and the Scandinavian over-dress must consequently have gone out of fashion in Denmark before the end of the century, presumably to be replaced by a dress of West European inspiration. There were also

Fig. 35
*Reconstruction
Scandinavian
woman's dress
oval brooches,
pl. 26.*

Fig. 36 *Embroidered textiles
from the Mammen grave in
Jutland. Scale about 1:3.*

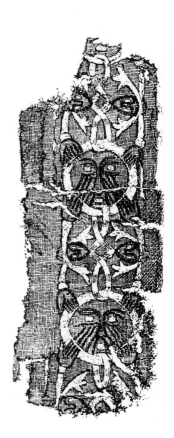

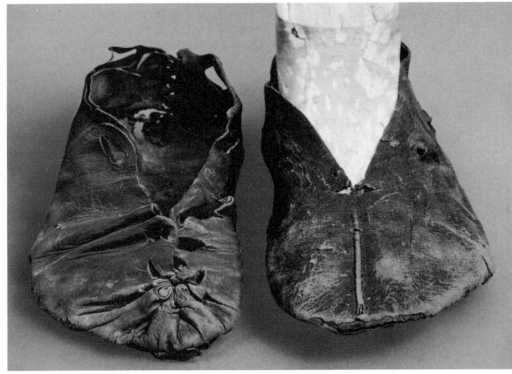

Pl. 25   *Shoes from Ribe. Left: a 'skin shoe'. Right: a 'sole shoe'.*

various kinds of head-dress, judging by Norwegian and Swedish pictures. Nothing is known about underwear and stockings, but women would hardly have been without them in the Danish climate.[116]

The appearance of male dress can for the most part only be reconstructed from pictures in Norway and Sweden; only a few exist in Denmark. As for centuries before and after the Viking Age, it consisted of trousers (wide or narrow), a shirt or a tunic, sometimes belted at the waist, and a cloak held together on the right shoulder by a large brooch, or ties. There were also various forms of head-dress.[117] Strap-fittings from three graves in Lejre—probably all male graves—are thought to have belonged to 'garters'. The most splendid set was found under the knees of the dead man,[118] and consists of buckles, strap-slides and strap-ends, all of gilt-bronze decorated in high relief.

Many textile fragments and impressions occur in graves, some from garments, some from rugs, pillows or similar articles, and some perhaps from shrouds. The materials—wool, linen and silk—are usually plain weave or twill. These textiles, of which the silk at least was imported, might be dyed and decorated with embroidered figures, as in the man's grave at Mammen (fig. 36), or with patterns, as in the woman's grave at Hvilehøj. Tablet-woven borders with gold and silver thread, fur-trimmings and many other refinements were also used to adorn garments.

The textiles in the graves at Mammen and Hvilehøj give the best impression of grand dress. The former grave also contained two so-called bracelets of silk with ornamental borders. A woman's grave on the Stengade II site at Langeland contains textiles from a more ordinary outfit.[119] Finds from Hedeby, Århus and Lund give further information about the textiles of this period.[120]

Some fragments of leather with stitch holes from the horseman's grave in Nørre Longelse may be the remains of shoes. There are also said to have been remains of shoes in the Hvilehøj grave.[121] All other known shoes and fragments of shoes from the Danish Viking Age are from settlements, especially Elisenhof, Ribe, Hedeby and Lund. These finds cover the entire Viking Age and represent ordinary shoes rather than rare and expensive ones corresponding to the fragments of grand dress from Mammen and Hvilehøj. The shoes can be divided into two main groups of which the second is by far the most common: first, 'skin shoes', with the sole and the uppers cut in one piece and laced or sewn together; and secondly 'sole shoes', with the sole and the uppers cut separately and sewn together (pl. 25). Where the leather has been analysed (from Hedeby and Ribe) it consists of goat, sheep and ox skins; soft goatskin was particularly desirable for the uppers. There are shoes, ankle-boots and higher boots. The uppers on sole shoes may be sewn together at the back, front or side, and the sole may be rounded at the back or run to a point, curving up behind the heel. Generally, shoes were fastened with a thong laced through holes around the opening or crossed over the instep. The thongs on boots were tied round the ankle through holes in the leg of the boot. Footwear could be reinforced around the opening, the uppers decorated with seams, and no doubt sometimes coloured.[122] Many shoes were manufactured in towns by shoemakers (ch. 6).

Though most jewellery is known from graves and hoards, there is now a fair amount from settlements. The dating of jewellery types is to a great extent based on the results of Jan Petersen's 1928 study of jewellery from Norwegian graves. Chronologically this survey covers pagan burial-customs until they ceased some time in the second half of the tenth century or around AD 1000. By this time, jewellery was no longer buried with the dead, but there is not a long gap before the earliest finds from Lund (founded around 1000). Hedeby too is a source of jewellery from the later Viking Age. Coin-dated hoards and the style of ornamentation also help in dating jewellery.[123]

The jewellery can be divided into two main groups: the functional and the decorative. Small disc brooches (tin, bronze, silver or gold), oval brooches (always bronze), and trefoil brooches (usually bronze), belong to the former group (pl. 26), and their function has been discussed above. Oval brooches were in such demand that they were mass-produced on a regular basis and widely copied; this accounts for their uniformity over extensive areas (ch. 6). Disc brooches and trefoil brooches were also standardised, though less widely distributed.[124] Rectangular brooches of bronze or iron with decorative plates continue to appear in the very earliest part of the Viking Age.[125] Bronze equal-armed brooches do not seem to occur after the ninth century. Large, circular, slightly domed

Pl. 26 *Two oval brooches and a trefoil brooch from a grave at Besser on Samsø. Oval brooches are shown in use in fig. 35. Scale about 2 : 3.*

brooches of silver and gold occur in tenth- and eleventh-century hoards (for example the silver brooches from Nonnebakken in Odense and the two gold brooches from Hornelund near Varde, pls. 20 and 41). They are among the best examples of goldsmith's work from the Viking Age.[126]

The small disc brooch, often of tin, with a domed centre is a particular eleventh-century type; many have been found in Lund. Rosette brooches of silver filigree also belong to that century. The so-called Urnes brooches (silver or bronze) with an openwork Urnes-style animal motif begin in the middle or second half of the eleventh century and continue into the twelfth. The Lindholm Høje brooch is one of the finest examples (pl. 43).[127] A few brooches fall outside all groups, such as a boat-shaped one, and another (pl. 39) probably representing an even more stylised ship.[128]

Finally, there are brooches of undoubted foreign manufacture as well as various foreign mounts which have been made into brooches in Denmark (Gotlandic drum-shaped brooches, Hiberno-Saxon brooches, Frankish strap-ends, fig. 52). Frankish items in particular inspired native jewellers. Women's trefoil brooches, which occur only in the ninth and early tenth centuries, were modelled on Frankish scabbard mounts—the Vikings got to know them well on their ninth-century expeditions into the Frankish Empire and took some home with them for their nearest and dearest.[129]

Buckles were used not only in male dress but also in horse-trappings, and it is not always possible to determine the function of a particular buckle. Iron, bronze and silver buckles have been found. The so-called 'garter' buckles from Lejre have already been mentioned; other particularly splendid buckles and strap-fittings are known from the Ladby grave, and from Jelling, both from the grave in the mound and from the grave in the church there (pl. 37). The Ladby buckle is Frankish, while the Jelling objects are Scandinavian. To complete the geographical picture, there is a strap-end from the North of England and a Hiberno-Scottish ornamental stud (for horse or man), both from Aggersborg.[130] Finally, annular brooches (often bronze) might be associated with male dress, and likewise ringed pins (a pin with a small ring through the head) of iron, bronze or silver, and some bone pins with pierced heads.[131]

Among the purely decorative objects the commonest are arm-rings. They can be bronze, silver or gold, but rarely was much work or imagination expended on them. They are usually standardised, and clearly served as treasure and bullion (pl. 44), sometimes even having 'small change' attached in the form of small rings (ch. 6).[132] Silver and gold finger-rings are fairly rare and usually very simple. The same applies to neck-rings. The largest, which is gold, is about 30 cm in diameter and weighs a little under 2 kg.[133] Besides being very wealthy, its owner— man or woman—must have had an exceptionally broad chest. Ear-rings were a Slav fashion, and most of the few Danish examples come from the south-east of the country. A couple of toe-rings from a Fyrkat grave are unique.

Among pendants, coloured glass beads predominate. There are also beads of gold, silver (both Scandinavian and Slav), copper alloy, amber, rock-crystal (some perhaps from Norway, others from the East), carnelian (from the East) and jet (from England).[134] Bronze, silver and gold chains are known, sometimes with animal-head terminals gaping across a ring from which the pendant itself is hung. Such pendants may be ornamental discs with various decorative features or complicated, cross-shaped motifs with a bird's-head-shaped loop, such as the magnificent gold jewellery from the island of Hiddensee near Rügen (pl. 45).[135] Several other forms occur. Some are obviously religious symbols, like the Thor's hammers (pl. 32)[136] and the crosses from the late Viking Age. Miniature chairs (fig. 30), sickles, scythes, staves and the like are possibly also pagan symbols. Coins were used both as pendants and as brooches.[137] Many pendants, incidentally, were suspended from a loop or a hole in the lower part of an oval or trefoil brooch rather than from a necklace.

PASTIMES

In daily life, women no doubt looked after house and children while men took care of most work in the fields and with the animals. Women did spinning, weaving and other work with textiles, and in their spare hours many people no doubt carved various things for themselves from wood, bone and other easily worked materials.

Games, sports and pastimes have not left a great many traces in the archaeology; people cannot have had much time for these activities anyway. Of children's toys only a couple of boat models from Hedeby and some skates have been found; there is a little more elsewhere in Scandinavia.[138]

By the Viking Age, hunting larger animals such as red deer, roe and boar was possibly a sport reserved for the great landowners. It is remarkable (as noted earlier in this chapter) that hardly any bones of large game occur in the settlements—even when vast numbers of bones have been examined, as at Hedeby. Is it possible that we may find bones from game on royal estates and estates of the ruling classes?[139] In this connection it may be mentioned that there are pictures of harts on some of the early Hedeby coins and on a couple of rune stones. The pictures on the former have no clear numismatic models and have been interpreted both as Christian and as pagan symbols, while the latter are seen as Christian.[140] These illustrations of harts should perhaps be seen instead as symbols of rank.[141]

The most important hunting weapons were spear, bow and arrow. Hunting-dogs and hunting-birds were known, and presumably the game was sometimes driven into pits.[142] A bone of a peregrine falcon perhaps used for hawking has turned up at Trelleborg,[143] and bones of dogs suitable for hunting have been found on many sites, some in richly furnished graves.[144] A couple of harness-mounts for dog-teams are also known, among them a beautiful example from the Ladby grave.[145]

Lap-dogs—or knee-dogs as they are called in medieval laws—also seem to have brightened the existence of some Viking Age folk. Thus bones of a dog with a shoulder-height of only about 38 cm were found in a grave at Lejre, and bones of dogs from Hedeby ranged in size down to about 25 cm.[146] The medieval laws of Skåne, for example, stipulated far higher fines for killing lap-dogs than other types of dog.[147]

The Arab at-Tartuschi, who visited Hedeby around 970, thought that the inhabitants there sang like dogs (see ch. 2). This interesting comment is from a person with a quite different musical background, but apart from this there is only sparse information about the music of the period. Some bone whistles have been found at Hedeby and elsewhere; there is also the bridge of a lyre from Birka, but so far no equivalent from Denmark.[148]

The equipment used for feasting is described above. Story-tellers and scalds entertained on suitable occasions.[149] Board-games were also among the amusements of the period, and many gaming-pieces are known. They are often turned, cube-shaped counters of antler with a hole drilled in the underside, perhaps for a peg which fitted into peg-holes on a gaming-board, as on the complete board from Ballinderry, Ireland. Counters of simpler shapes and materials also occur, such as stones and sea-urchin fossils, as well as the more precious specimens in amber and gold (pl. 2). Fragments of gaming-boards have been found in richly equipped graves.[150]

The most highly regarded game was *hnefatafl*. Only sparse information about its rules exists, but we know it was played by two people with a dice and about twenty-four counters of similar shape divided into two sets, often of different colours, as well as a specially shaped counter or *hnefi*. Other board-games were known too. A gaming-board was found in the Norwegian Gokstad ship, for example, with the same marking as used today for the game of Nine Men's Morris.[151] The game of chess, on the other hand, does not appear to have arrived in the North until some time in the twelfth century.[152]

This account covers many aspects of daily life in Viking Age Denmark which can be demonstrated archaeologically. New finds and new publications will in time certainly supplement the picture sketched here. There are also many aspects of daily life which archaeology will never be able to illumine, many of them the sort of things which made life exciting and occupied people's thoughts—story-telling and poetry, politics, gossip and scandal, news from foreign countries, precise recipes of good food and drink, the composition of a meal, the course of a good feast and much else. Some of this can be glimpsed through the written sources[153] but it is rather sad to think that sounds and smells, those basic components of daily life, are inevitably almost completely lost. It is all the more fascinating when these things can be revived. A very well-preserved bell (pl. 14) found in Hedeby harbour doubtless still sounds the same as it did in the Viking Age. The stench of mud from the town's old shore-line (whence 'smell-samples' have been dug) is no doubt the same too.

8 Arms and Fortification

Military aspects of the Viking Age have always attracted keen interest. Events such as the conflicts with Charlemagne, the siege of Paris, raids in the Mediterranean and the conquest of England excite imagination. Foreign writers recorded strife above all else. Many scaldic poems do the same, and numerous rune stones were raised to the memory of men of military or semi-military status, or by fathers to sons who died young and on service. In a few instances the stones mention actual battles, while many rich hoards reflect times of general unrest. Correspondingly, weapons constitute a fairly large part of the finds from men's graves. Weapons have also been found in fields and bogs, lakes and streams (a large number of the latter may be sacrifices).[1] In addition, the elegant warships and not least the great fortifications are among Scandinavia's most impressive monuments. Many of these are royal monuments, reflecting the consolidation of Denmark into an independent nation under one king. Some of the structures can be associated with particular persons or political events known from written sources, and the associations will doubtless increase as more are dated precisely by dendrochronology.

WEAPONS AND WARFARE

Life could be violent on many levels—from regular defensive wars and acts of aggression led by a king to common fights. But there are few archaeological traces of battles or strife in Denmark. A man in the Langeland Stengade II cemetery appears to have died from an arrow in the neck.[2] There is some evidence of unrest in the pre-fortress civilian settlement at Trelleborg in the form of human skeletal remains in wells; and in the fortress itself in the form of numerous arrows embedded in the exterior of the rampart; there is also one grave containing ten people, one of whom had an unhealed wound above the knee that might well have been fatal, and two graves each containing five bodies. The remains of a couple of skeletons from Hedeby also show signs of battle-wounds.[3]

But weapons are common finds, as already stated, and the numbers found in men's graves (often along with riding equipment) reflect their importance in Viking Age life. It is weapons from Danish burials of the period c. 900–50 that we know best, but much information on early

Pl. 27   *Swords. Top: found in the river Tude on Sjælland; bottom: from Sønder Sø in North Jutland. The third is of unknown provenance.*

Viking Age weapons can be obtained from Norwegian graves. Of course, the richest graves illustrate the equipment of the upper classes, not that of the common man.

No study of the whole corpus of Danish material has ever been carried out,[4] and typology and datings therefore continue to depend largely on the results of Jan Petersen's classification of the weapons found in Norwegian graves, which are much richer and cover a wider period than the Danish ones.[5] The following weapons were used: sword, axe, spear, javelin, bow and arrow. Defensive weapons consisted of helmet and mail-shirt, possibly also lamellar armour (made from small overlapping plates), and shield. Various other items are mentioned in written sources (for example siege machines); and there may have been other defensive and offensive equipment of a sort unlikely to leave any trace in archaeological, pictorial or literary sources—such as helmets and body armour of leather, for example, or stone slings.

Some single-edged swords are known from the early Viking Age but the common sword of the period is the two-edged slashing sword (pl. 27) with a blade about 75–80 cm long and a broad blood-groove or fuller. The hilt usually has a lower guard, a grip formed by the tang (or tongue) covered by material which has often disappeared, and an upper guard and pommel.[6] The scabbard might be fitted with a metal chape—examples are known in decorated bronze.

Some swords are thought to come from England[7] while others are presumably Frankish—despite the often repeated ban on selling swords to the Vikings—and a number of sword-blades, found both in Scandinavia and elsewhere, are furnished with inscriptions such as *Ulfberht*, *Ingelrii*, or debased forms of these. They were most likely manufactured in several places on the Continent, in the Frankish Empire for instance.[8] No systematic investigation of markings on sword-blades found in Denmark has been made and so far no Viking Age swords with such inscriptions have been reported. The swords found in graves are often in too poor a condition to determine whether or not they were originally inscribed. But investigations in Norway seem to indicate that some blades, including pattern-welded blades, may in fact have been manufactured in Scandinavia[9] and it is easy to believe that the smiths in Danish Viking fortresses produced high-quality weapons,[10] but we have no conclusive evidence that they did. Indeed, many questions about the provenance of sword-blades remain unanswered.

The sword-hilts, however, are frequently native products, often superbly decorated with animal ornament in silver and copper, as on two swords from Bustorf near Hedeby (fig. 49).[11] The sword was the period's most elaborate and most costly weapon. Swords occur in most undisturbed, richly furnished men's graves and the sword is the weapon praised above all other in scaldic verse.

It may be only a myth that the axe was the Viking weapon *par excellence*, a myth inspired perhaps by St Olaf's attribute, the axe, and by pictures such as that on the famous Lindisfarne stone with its axe-wielding men. Axes were cheaper than swords, and were thus probably used by those who could not afford swords, as an alternative to swords or spears.[12] Axes do not occur very often along with other weapons in graves, and they are not mentioned much in scaldic verse,[13] although a man carrying an axe is depicted on one of the Hunnestad stones (fig. 2).[14]

Axes found in graves must normally be weapons, since it was customary in Denmark to bury men with their war equipment but not with agricultural implements or craftsmen's tools. Battle-axes are also known from the Viking fortresses and elsewhere.[15] However, a number of the axes found in connection with settlements must have been tools rather than weapons (ch. 6), although firm identification is often difficult. In addition there are a number of ornamental axes from graves, such as those inlaid with silver from Mammen (pl. 28) and Trelleborg, and the badly preserved but perhaps once still more splendid one from Hadbjerg decorated with silver and copper.[16] These axes may have served a ceremonial purpose. The same may apply to the openwork cross-marked axes from a couple of graves which were obviously unsuitable for practical purposes.[17] Some grave-goods may of course have been made specifically to accompany the dead. Though this is difficult to prove in general, burial-customs certainly included symbolic features such as ship-settings instead of ships, and cart bodies instead of complete carts.

Pl. 28   *Iron axe with silver inlay from the Mammen grave in Jutland. The blade is about 10.5 cm across.*

The results of some metallurgical and wood analyses are of interest here.

A metallurgical examination of one axe blade from a grave showed that, though usable, it was not good quality. Its haft was maple and the hafts of two other axes from the same burial-ground were maple and birch; a maple axe-haft was also found on another cemetery. While maple is often used for smaller handles, one would expect ash to be used for such weapons. Furthermore, the birchwood haft was badly executed: it was quite unusable. Thus it is possible that these axes were produced specifically for the burial.[18] This may also apply to some of the small axes of disputed function found in graves.[19]

Axes must generally have been of native production. However, twelve axe-heads fixed to a spruce pole (pl. 18) were found near the beach at Gjerrild in Djursland, which, as neither the iron nor the spruce originated in Denmark, reflect the importation of axes, most probably from iron-rich Norway.[20]

Spear-heads can be as long as half a metre, but many are shorter.[21] Pattern-welding has been demonstrated on only one Danish example, a blade from Hedeby,[22] but on the other hand the material has not been systematically surveyed to see whether others occur. Some spear-heads are winged. The sockets can be decorated with silver (pl. 29).[23] Fragments of a shaft have been identified as ash.[24] Spears occur frequently in richly furnished male graves. They were important weapons for both battle and hunting.

Throwing spears or javelins are not part of the grave equipment in Denmark. But there are several stray finds of spear-heads, including

29   *Spear-head*
h silver-inlaid
ket. From a grave
Rønnebæksholm
Sjælland. Length
cm.

a fine example about 26 cm long from the guard-house of the Fyrkat fortress and another from Trelleborg.[25] Javelins are also mentioned repeatedly in written sources.[26]

Arrow-heads occur in a few graves, such as the Ladby and Hedeby boat-graves,[27] as well as in fortresses and other settlements.[28] The heads take various forms, but a slender leaf-shaped blade is common. Fragments of the butt ends of arrows have survived in the Hedeby grave, with bronze fittings notched to take the bow-string. Incisions in the shaft were presumably for the string holding the feather in place.[29] A complete yew bow is also known from Hedeby.[30] From the same site there are several blunt-headed wooden arrows for hunting birds and small animals.[31]

Helmets and lamellar armour are unknown in Denmark. Only one fragment of a mail-shirt survives, from Lund, 15 cm in length,[32] but the garment shown on the small wooden male figure found in the Jelling burial may be a mail-shirt, as suggested by the cut, the colour and the stylised finish.[33] These defensive garments were hardly very common, but their absence in rich male graves in Denmark is presumably because their deposition was not part of the burial conventions (see ch. 9). The likely appearance of a Viking Age helmet (without horns) is illustrated in finds from Gjermundbu in southern Norway which also include remains of a mail-shirt. Fragments of lamellar armour occur at Birka.[34]

No shields have survived in Denmark either, but hemispherical iron shield-bosses with flat flanges occur in a number of graves. A couple of examples are also known from Trelleborg and Lund,[35] and a horseman with a small round shield is depicted on a rune stone from Álum in North Jutland (fig. 37). There may have been two kinds of shield: small round shields such as at Álum, with parallels in other pictures on rune stones and of which a few medieval examples have survived in Scandinavia,[36] and large round shields such as those known from Gokstad and elsewhere, and shown in pictures of boats on coins (fig. 22) and rune stones (ch. 3). Abbo of Paris mentions the painted, round shields of the Vikings,[37] a rune stone from Rønninge on Fyn refers to a certain Ásgaut with a red shield, and early scaldic poems describe shields painted with narratives of gods and heroes.[38]

Fig. 37 *Rider shield and standa carved on a rune stone at Álum, North Jutland.*

Much information about the weapons, and the fighting customs and technique of the Viking Age may be obtained from a systematic and critical investigation of contemporary written sources and scaldic poems.[39] Only a selection from easily accessible sources will be given here. The Frankish annals record siege-machines such as battering rams, and military standards, and the Anglo-Saxon Chronicle mentions a raven banner.[40] The latter may perhaps have looked like the pennant on the Álum rune stone just mentioned. A similar pennant (or perhaps a weather-vane) can be seen on a Viking coin struck by a York moneyer around 950.[41] It is also said that Vikings rattled their quivers and shouted battle-cries and abuse at the enemy as battle was joined.[42]

The chief functions of ships in war were as means of transport and places of refuge; but they were sometimes directly involved in attacks on places situated on river-banks. Naval battles also took place, when it was a matter of boarding the enemy's vessel.[43]

But most fighting was on land and on foot, and written sources such as Abbo's description of the Paris battles in 885–6, and the Anglo-Saxon poem on the Battle of Maldon in 991 give detailed descriptions of the conduct of battles. Both the Frankish annals and the Anglo-Saxon Chronicle describe the Viking armies as very inventive and mobile, excelling in sudden attacks and in the quick erection of fortified camps and field-fortifications of wood and earth. In the Battle of Dyle in 891, the Frankish army had to descend from their horses and fight on foot because of these field-fortifications.[44]

It has been argued that the horsemen's graves with their riding-gear and weapons, and the introduction of the stirrup (chs. 3 and 9), show that a regular cavalry on the Frankish pattern also existed in Denmark. Written sources have also been used to support this theory,[45] but in them horses seem to be referred to only as a means of transport. Like the ships, they were of great significance for the mobility of the army. Obviously encounters on horseback might occur, but I know of no sources which record that the Vikings had any regular mounted forces.[46] The word *equitatus*, for example, in the entry for AD 804 in the Frankish annals ('Eodem tempore Godofridus rex Danorum venit cum classe sua necnon et omni equitatu regni sui ad locum, qui dicitur Sliesthorp ...') could mean horsemen or knights, possibly the nobility.[47] The weapons which occur in the horsemen's graves cannot be identified specifically as cavalry weapons either. The big spear-heads in particular have been noted in this connection, but similar weapons were used by late medieval foot-soldiers, for example, and could also be hunting spears, as already mentioned. The contents of these graves seem to possess a strong element of display, and it is highly likely that the chief purpose of horses and horsemen's equipment placed in them was to ensure that the dead man could travel to the next world in style (ch. 9). In short, there is no evidence that cavalry existed in Viking Age Denmark. Current opinion holds that cavalry did not become a regular instrument of war there until the twelfth century.[48]

FORTIFICATION

According to the written sources mentioned above, Viking armies abroad often entrenched themselves inside solid buildings such as stone churches and fortresses, built fortified camps, or camped on islands.[49] But it has been almost impossible to demonstrate the existence of such camps and entrenchments, presumably because of their temporary character and small dimensions. Similarly, it is very difficult to prove the brief use by Viking forces of a construction already in existence. Hague-Dike for example, an earth rampart in Normandy which cuts off the La Hague peninsula, has often been associated with the Vikings. But C-14 datings of charcoal from the interior of the rampart show instead that it belongs to the Hallstatt period, that is c. 900–800 BC. Nevertheless, this does not preclude the possibility that the rampart with its Scandinavian name was also used by Vikings.[50] So far the only archaeological

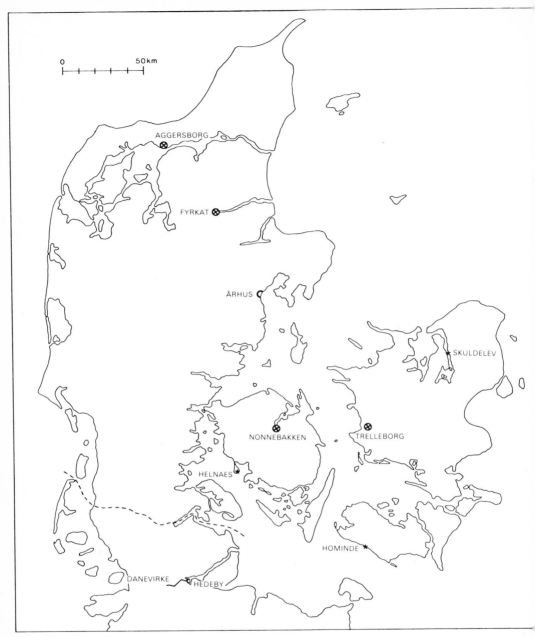

Fig. 38 *Important military constructions: ramparts, fortresses and sea-barriers.*

evidence of fortification abroad which can perhaps be ascribed to the Vikings is some trenches associated with Repton church in North-amptonshire, which together isolate an area between two rivers. The Anglo-Saxon Chronicle records that the Vikings wintered in Repton in 874/5, and from the stratigraphy it appears that this may indeed be their fortified camp. In addition there are ramparts round some of the towns which the Vikings took over.[51]

The Vikings' familiarity with fortifications is best demonstrated by the Danish ramparts, fortresses and ship-barriers which are of a permanent character and large dimensions: the Danevirke, which protected the kingdom's southern border; the semicircular ramparts which protected Hedeby and Århus; the circular fortresses of the Trelleborg type; and several barriers obstructing the access of ships.

All fortifications on land are built of earth and/or turf and many were reinforced or extended with timber. A number of tools employed in the construction of such earthworks have been found in the infill of the Danevirke, the Jelling mounds and Trelleborg. These include shovels and spades, some of which had iron shoes (fig. 16), hand-barrows (pl. 8), as well as bits of wagons and carts.[52] The consumption of building materials, the quantities of tools, the amount of human labour and the numbers of draught-animals involved must have been enormous, and it is natural to see royal power as responsible for them. But only in one case is royal involvement mentioned in contemporary written sources. The Frankish annals relate that King Godfred was behind the planning of a vast construction of ramparts by the southern border in AD 808 and continue: 'After he (Godfred) had now distributed the work among his leaders, he returned home ...'.[53] We know nothing more of how building work was organised, here or elsewhere in Denmark.

The Danevirke

The Danevirke (fig. 39, pl. 30) is one of the largest of northern Europe's ancient defensive works. The entire complex consists of several different ramparts with a total length of about thirty kilometres, running from the head of the Schlei fjord in the east to the rivers Rheide and Treene in the west. It thus effectively cuts off the land approach to Denmark, since the western approach was barred by rivers and broad, swampy river-valleys. The main north–south traffic route, the Army Road (Hærvej) or Ox Road, cut through the Danevirke close to Hedeby. South of the rampart was a belt of uninhabited forest some twenty kilometres wide running to the border river, the Eider. Beyond this lived the Saxons and various Slav tribes.

Until recently only two kings, Godfred in 808 and Valdemar the Great in the second half of the twelfth century, were known to have been responsible for building activities on the Danevirke, and these were also the only two dated building phases. Consequently numerous theories were advanced to explain the origin of the Danevirke and its many ramparts.[54] The 1969–75 excavations have now provided more dates by dendrochronology and the C-14 method, but absolute datings are still only available for a few stretches of the ramparts and a few building phases. Nevertheless, these datings and our increased knowledge of the individual structures and their orientation lend plausibility to the most recent theory, which divides the Danevirke into three successive complexes, each functioning for varying periods:[55]

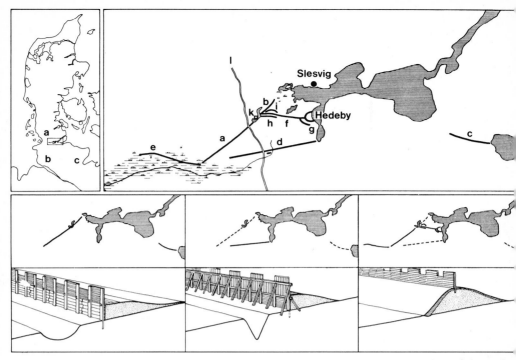

Fig. 39 *The Danevirke. Top left: a Danes; b Saxons; c Slavs. Top right: the positions of the walls. a Main Wall; b North Wall; c East Wall; d Kovirke; e Crooked Wall; f Connecting Wall; g Semicircular Wall at Hedeby; h Double Wall; i Curved Wall, k Thyreborg; l Army Road (Hærvej or Ox Road. The walls measure about 30 km overall. Bottom: course of walls 1–3 with schematic reconstruction of walls and ditches.*

1 The North Wall, the earliest phase of the Main Wall and perhaps the East Wall.
2 Kovirke? (of uncertain date).
3 Hedeby's Semicircular Wall and the Fore Wall etc., the Connecting Wall with the Double Wall and the Curved Wall, reinforcements on the Main Wall, the Crooked Wall.

The building of phase 1 (the North Wall, built in one phase, and the earliest phase of the Main Wall) is dated by dendrochronology to AD 737. The wall was about 7 km long, 10 m wide and 2 m high. It was constructed of earth faced with horizontal timbers, held in place by vertical posts at 2 m intervals. The lower ends of some posts have survived, but mostly only the post-holes remain. A U-shaped ditch, about 1.5 m deep and 5 m wide, ran along the south front of the wall at a distance of 1.5–2.5 m from it. Where the wall had to cross a narrow swampy stretch to the east, it had a solid foundation of logs, branches and stones, and along another stretch the front of the wall was further strengthened below ground by a wooden facing. No wall crossed the swampy area immediately to the west of Thyreborg (a fort of unknown

Pl. 30 *Aerial photograph of the Main Wall of the Danevirke. Seen from the west where it meets the Crooked Wall. In the background, Schleswig town, see fig. 39.*

date) but here the lines of communication with the Main Wall were secured by a causeway on a foundation of logs and branches. One section of the causeway was laid on a continuous series of large, sunken, block-built oak boxes. When excavated, one sunken box, 6 × 4 × 1 m and filled with sand and earth, was found to contain a very naturalistic wooden phallic figure.

The East Wall which protected the Svansen peninsula against enemies from the south was 3.3 km long. Certain features in common with the section of the wall just described may indicate that the East Wall is of the same age, though there are no scientific datings to confirm this.

There cannot be much doubt that this great wall-structure of around 737 was built by order of a Danish king, presumably in response to threats from Saxon neighbours or perhaps more likely from the acquisitive Slavs. The king may have been Ongendus. At any rate we know that Willibrord, the missionary to the Frisians, who died in 739, undertook a mission to Denmark and met this king of the Danes. There may well be a connection between the idea of this earliest Danevirke, a wall on a scale hitherto unparalleled in northern Europe, and the linear earthworks built in the same century in England, such as Offa's Dyke (later than Danevirke) which marks the border with Wales.[56]

In the entry for the year 808, the Frankish annals related that King Godfred:

> ... decided that he wished to fortify the border of his kingdom towards Saxony by means of a rampart so that a defensive wall should stretch from the eastern sea which the Danes call Ostersalt (the Baltic) to the North Sea and along the entire northern bank of the Eider, the wall to be broken by only one gate through which wagons and horsemen could go out and return home again ...[57]

According to this, the wall was constructed because of the hostility which had existed for several years between Godfred and Charlemagne.

This wall is not actually identified, and it must be emphasised that the description of the wall may not be reliable, because the Frankish annals were written a long way from Denmark. Godfred's wall may not have been completely new but a repair so far undetected by archaeologists, or an extension of the earlier wall of 737. Secondly, the annals describe an undertaking which would have taken some time to complete but give no indication that the wall was actually built according to the plan. On the other hand, we do know that Godfred was killed by one of his own men in 810, and his successor Hemming made peace with Charlemagne immediately afterwards.[58] This altered the entire political background, and the building of the wall may have stopped altogether. The only way to identify Godfred's wall would be to find a wall or phase which could be precisely dated to the years 808–10.

Kovirke (wall system 2) is a possible candidate. The wall runs to the south of Hedeby between Selk Nor and the marshes of the river Rheide. It is 6.5 km long, apparently of a single building phase, and it contains the only gate so far demonstrated in the Danevirke. Some C-14 datings of small charcoal fragments from post-holes are compatible with this idea. But it has been pointed out that the Kovirke, with its uncompromisingly straight route, its facing of dressed timbers, its deep V-shaped ditch and its brief period of use, has certain features in common with the tenth-century fortresses of the Trelleborg-type and also that two C-14 datings on wood from the embankment section of the Crooked Wall correspond equally well to the supposed dates of Godfred's structure.[59] The course of the Crooked Wall and its facing (see below) suggest, however, that it—or at any rate its rampart section—may be more recent.

The 'Great Wall' of the Danevirke (wall system 3), 14 km long, makes a vast zigzag across the country from Hedeby in the east almost as far as Hollingstedt in the west, where the rivers Rheide and Treene meet before merging with the Eider. The abrupt angles in its course clearly show that this rampart consists of sections from different periods.

The nucleus is the Old Main Wall of 737, apparently now in its second building phase (this is not scientifically dated). It was converted to an earth rampart 12–13 m wide and about 3 m high, its steep front covered with turf. It has not been possible to identify any associated ditch. A wooden palisade was presumably constructed on the crest of the rampart, as indicated by a few post-holes. The same features appear in the first phase of the Connecting Wall and the first phase of the rampart section of the Crooked Wall. It is also to be found in the so-called second phase of Hedeby's much-rebuilt Semicircular Wall. All these sections presumably form a whole. The stratigraphy seems to indicate that Hedeby's Semicircular Wall was established in the mid tenth century at the earliest. This Hedeby rampart is a logical prerequisite for the Connecting Wall, and two samples from the earliest phase of the latter (the northern Double Wall) have been dated by dendrochronology to 968, and to c. 951–61.

This is in brief the basic evidence for the datings of the mighty Danevirke, now including the fortress of Hedeby. Though several points remain unclear, there are still good reasons for assuming building activity on a grand scale around the mid tenth century or a little later, perhaps concentrated around 968 as indicated by the date of the Connecting Wall. In that case, it must have been King Harald Bluetooth (c. 940–86) who commissioned the building and who was also responsible for vast structures elsewhere in the kingdom. The political background can only have been the acute antagonism between Denmark and the German Empire, and the building of the Danevirke strongly contradicts the often-advanced theory that the Saxons dominated Denmark for the greater part of Harald Bluetooth's reign.[60]

In 974, the year after the death of Emperor Otto I, there was already fighting at the Danevirke, which was in fact taken by Otto II. The precise significance of this defeat has been, and still is, the subject of much debate, but it is certain that in 983, after the death of Otto II, the Danes captured the fortress (not identified by name) which the Emperor had built against them after the battle in 974. In the same year, the Danes, together with the Slav prince Mistivoj, harried Holstein and burnt Hamburg. According to the Sønder Vissing rune stone (pl. 46) he was the father of a wife of Harald the Good, probably Harald Bluetooth. Battles of this decade may actually be mentioned on two rune stones raised in memory of two Svein Forkbeard's followers, Skarði and Erik, who fell at Hedeby, though they may have died later.[61]

During the eleventh and twelfth centuries, the Danevirke was extended several times, partly as a defence against Slav attacks which began in the eleventh century after the death of Cnut the Great, partly against the Germans. The crowning glory was Valdemar's wall of brick, built in the second half of the twelfth century and mentioned on the lead tablet at Valdemar the Great's grave in Ringsted as one of his major achievements. After the thirteenth-century reorganisation of the border areas, the significance of the Danevirke dwindled. But the old ramparts were used once more and extended for the last time in 1864 when the Prussians attacked Denmark.

Urban defences

Fortified settlements appear to be unknown in Scandinavia until the tenth century, when Birka in Sweden and Hedeby and Århus were surrounded by earth banks. Birka and Hedeby were considerably older, but the earliest settlement so far found at Århus was contemporary with the bank. These towns, surrounded by ramparts, were to all intents and purposes fortresses.

Hedeby's Semicircular Wall, roughly 1300 m in length, encloses an area of 24 ha (pl. 13) and actually constitutes part of the Danevirke.[62] As stated above, the rampart is thought to be mid tenth century at the earliest, and its relationship with the Connecting Wall is such that it can hardly be much younger. Investigations in the past have shown that the Hedeby rampart was extended many times before it reached its present impressive size: about 8 m in height and 25 m wide. On the seaward side, the settlement and harbour-area were protected by curved rows of posts; these probably linked up with the Semicircular Wall. In the mid eleventh century the role of Hedeby as a town was taken over by Schleswig, but it seems unlikely that the Semicircular Wall was left to decay completely; after all, it still formed part of the Danevirke defences.

The area south of the Semicircular Wall was also fortified. Its ditch lies close to the outside of the rampart, and the Fore Wall is about 250 m away, running from the south right up to the Connecting Wall. Investigations in the 1960s uncovered another two ditches between the Fore Wall and the Semicircular Wall which also apparently joined the Connecting Wall. One with a U-shaped section is about 30 m from the Semicircular Wall; the other is a V-shaped ditch running about 130 m from the Semicircular Wall. It is uncertain whether any ramparts were associated with these ditches which on the basis of stratigraphy and their relationship with the Connecting Wall can hardly be older than the mid tenth century. The Fore Wall may be contemporary with the Connecting Wall, which seems to have been established around 968. However, both the Fore Wall and the ditches described above may also be younger. In Hedeby's earlier, unfortified phase, the inhabitants may have used the nearby 'Hochburg' (of unknown date) as a refuge.[63]

The ramparts around Århus are not visible today, but the line they followed can be traced in the streets of the town. The excavations of 1963 and 1964 produced evidence for dating them to the Viking Age.[64] The inner face of the rampart and a small area along the interior base were excavated. Smaller supplementary investigations have been undertaken since then. The wall was presumably semicircular and enclosed an area of 4–5 ha. It was of earth, with a sloping inner face bordered by a wood-paved road (pl. 16). Definite information about the front of the rampart, and its height and width, is not yet available. There was an outer ditch except on the south side, which was protected by the river. There is no evidence of harbour-fortification as at Hedeby and if any such existed we must assume it has long since been destroyed by later harbour works.

Traces of a bank and its ditch have also been found around the Viking Age settlement at Löddeköpinge in Skåne. But they are small and we do not know when they were constructed. Even if contemporary with the settlement—which is interpreted as a trading-station with seasonal habitation—it is doubtful whether they had a defensive purpose; it has been suggested that they simply delineated the boundary of the trading-station.[65]

The king must have had considerable influence in the towns as upholder of peace and possibly as property owner (ch. 5), and it is thus conceivable that he was behind the building of the Hedeby and Århus ramparts. After all, both these walls belong to the series of impressive tenth-century structures many of which can be dated to the reign of Harald Bluetooth, as we have seen.[66] It is thus reasonable to suppose that it was he who instigated the building of town walls. Threats from pirates and other raiders were no doubt an incentive, but there may have been a political wish to turn some towns into fortresses. This is particularly evident at Hedeby.

Fortresses

Fortresses as such existed for only a very brief period in the Viking Age. Three or four closely related structures (fig. 40)—Trelleborg near Slagelse on Sjælland, Fyrkat near Hobro in north-east Jutland, Aggersborg on the northern shore of Limfjord in North Jutland, and probably Nonnebakken in Odense on Fyn—were all built in the second half of the tenth century and were soon abandoned. Given the striking similarities in layout and dating, these fortresses were undoubtedly built at the command of central authority in the person of the king.

The first fortress to be recognised by modern scholars was Trelleborg, excavated from 1934 to 1943 and published in 1948.[67] The results led to a complete revaluation of the technical and organisational capacities of the Viking Age, and seriously undermined the current views of the extent of royal power in tenth-century Denmark.[68] The search for more circular fortresses was then already under way. The period and character of the Aggersborg ramparts were recognised in 1945, and excavations continued with interruptions from then until 1954. In 1970, a smaller supplementary excavation was carried out in the area of the fortress, and in 1976 the floor of the church immediately outside the circular ramparts was excavated.[69] Fyrkat (pl. 31) was excavated between 1950 and 1963, and published in 1977.[70] Nonnebakken was located in 1952 and minor excavations have been undertaken there at intervals, even though the earthworks are now completely levelled and covered by modern Odense. Very little is known about the appearance of the fortress there, but its apparently circular form (best seen on a 1593 engraving), its correspondence in diameter to Fyrkat, its turf bank, and not least the dating of the Viking Age artefacts from the area, make it likely that Nonnebakken belongs to this group of fortresses.[71]

The most important features these fortresses had in common are the

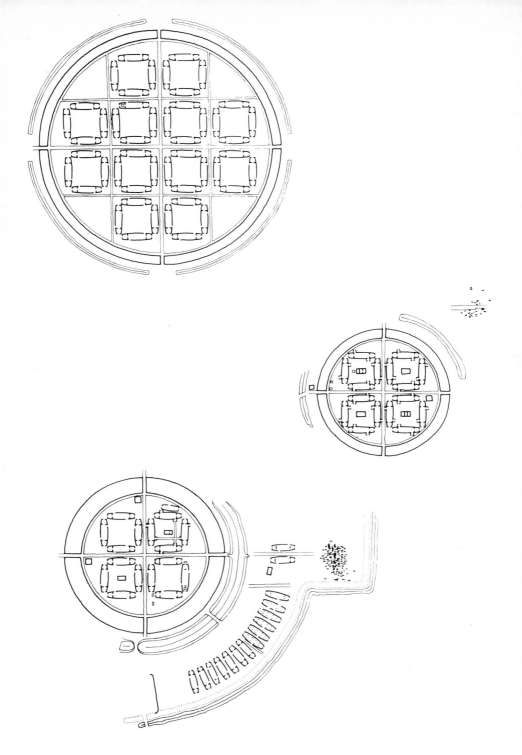

Fig. 40 *Reconstructed plans. Top: Aggersborg. Centre: Fyrkat.*
Bottom: Trelleborg. Scale 1:4000.

31 *Aerial photograph of Fyrkat seen from the north-west. The cemetery is in the foreground on the*

following (fig. 40): outer circular walls with gates at the four points of the compass; ramparts with interior timber supports, timber facings and sloping fronts (fig. 41); gates that were covered, and linked by two timber-paved axial roads and a ring-road around the inside of the rampart; ditches of V-shaped section concentric with the walls but separated from them by a berm; large, bow-sided buildings divided into three rooms, arranged in a quadrangle in each of the quarters of the fortress's ground area; a smaller rectangular building in the centre of every courtyard; building materials mostly earth, turf and wood.

It was chiefly in size that the fortresses differed. The most important measurements (in metres) are as follows:

	Internal diameter of fortress area	Width of ramparts	Width of berm	Width of ditch	Length of buildings
Aggersborg	240	11	8	4	32.0
Trelleborg	136	19	5	18	29.4
Fyrkat	120	12	11	7	28.4
Nonnebakken	120	17?	8?	7?	?

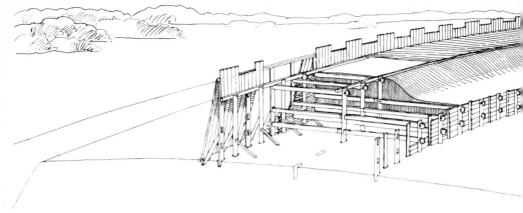

Fig. 41 *Fyrkat ramparts. Possible reconstruction.*

There was thus space for forty-eight large houses within the circular wall at Aggersborg compared with sixteen in the other fortresses. The outer fortress at Trelleborg contained a further fifteen large buildings bringing the total number there to thirty-one. The constructional details of Trelleborg's ramparts and large buildings differed from those at Fyrkat and Aggersborg; the latter pair differed from each other only in size.[72] Existing settlements had to be cleared at Trelleborg and Aggersborg (though perhaps only partially at Aggersborg) to make room for the fortress, but Fyrkat was apparently built on a site last inhabited in the Bronze Age. Enormous infilling was necessary, however, at Fyrkat and Trelleborg (and levelling too at Fyrkat) to make space on the chosen site for the planned fortress. Finally it must be mentioned that the cemeteries at Trelleborg and Fyrkat lie immediately outside the circular walls—at Trelleborg within the low bank of the outer fortress. Nothing is known at present of the Aggersborg and Nonnebakken cemeteries; the excavations beneath Aggersborg church have at least shown that the burial-ground is not there.

The appearance and construction of the large buildings (figs. 40 and 42) have been the subject of a good deal of discussion; only post-holes have survived.[73] All the buildings were about 30 m long, had curved long walls and straight gables, and two similar gable-rooms. They were made of oak, the walls consisted of vertical staves, and the roofs were probably covered with shingle. In the middle of the central room of some houses was an oblong hearth, and some contain traces of what were probably broad wall-benches. The outer rows of post-holes were interpreted as evidence of an outer gallery in the reconstructed Trelleborg house of 1942, with the weight of the roof carried on the large posts of the dividing walls. But it was subsequently observed that the outer post-holes sloped inwards towards the walls, and the posts must therefore have been angled in order to absorb the outward pressure of the roof on the walls. They may either have been extensions of the rafters that continued right into the ground or of sloping braces which supported

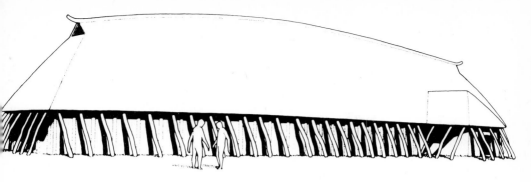

Fig. 42 *Bow-sided building at Fyrkat. Possible reconstruction.*

the wall-plate on which the rafters rested. In either case the large posts of the dividing walls functioned essentially only as wall-posts. It has also become clear that there were small porches in front of the outer doors set in the long walls. These were first demonstrated at Fyrkat, and subsequent excavations strongly suggest that they existed at Trelleborg too; they have not been looked for at Aggersborg. Apart from the large bow-sided buildings, smaller rectangular houses have been found in the courtyards of Trelleborg and Fyrkat. There are also a few sunken-featured buildings.

Trelleborg was described in 1948 as a fortress 'in which active young warriors were trained under strict discipline and fixed rules for the craft of war and the demanding expeditions across the sea . . .', in other words a kind of training-camp or barracks; and each building was thought to have had room for the crew of a longship, about seventy-five men. It was believed to be associated with the westward expeditions of Svein Forkbeard, which culminated in his conquest of England in 1013.[74]

This exciting and cogent theory was later developed and extended to apply to all the fortresses and was accepted almost without question. It was later modified[75] and has now been completely discredited. The reasons for dismissing it are manifold, but a decisive one is new dendrochronological dating of the foundation of Trelleborg to the year 980 or 981 (the end of Harald Bluetooth's reign).[76] The great raids on England belong to the reign of Svein Forkbeard (*c.* 986–1014) and to the early years of that of his son, Cnut the Great. There were a few in the 980s, but they did not start seriously, and Svein Forkbeard is not known to have taken part in them, until the 990s and later.[77] The fortresses belong to quite a different political situation.

The basis for dating will be discussed first.[78] The antiquities from Trelleborg are of an age that fits well with the date of the fortress's foundation in 980. Together with the fact that the buildings show no sign of repairs, they indicate that the fortress functioned for only a relatively short time. It could well have been abandoned before AD 1000. The same applies to Fyrkat, which judging by its artefacts and burial-customs must have been founded between 950 and 990, and abandoned around 1000 at the latest. The results of new dendrochronological analyses correspond well to the dating of Trelleborg but have so far failed to determine the actual year of Fyrkat's foundation. The silver found at Nonnebakken (thirty-three coins and several pieces of silver jewellery) also corresponds to the dating of Trelleborg. It shows that there was activity here some time between 975 and 990. If, as seems increasingly likely, Nonnebakken was a fortress of the same type as the others, the silver and other finds may be from an earlier settlement razed to make way for the fortress (compare the gold arm-ring which was found hidden in one of the houses of the earlier settlement at Aggersborg). Alternatively, they may have been hidden away when the fortress was vacated or destroyed (a couple of silver arm-rings were found concealed in the wall of a Fyrkat house and Trelleborg had certainly been under attack, see p. 134 above). The dating of Aggersborg had been much discussed, but for the present the best evidence is the very close relationship of this fortress to the others of the same type and the fact that they all appear to have been short-lived.

Secondly, the geographical locations of the fortresses will be considered.[79] It has long been recognised that their locations were well suited to the control of the country. All were situated on, or very close to, major roads. Only Aggersborg was on an important waterway, but also at an important crossing of Limfjord. Fyrkat was on the river Onsild about 3 km from the place where it now runs into Mariager fjord. We do not know whether the river was navigable as far as Fyrkat in the Viking Age, and in addition, the head of the very long and narrow Mariager fjord with its strong currents is an impractical site for a naval base: under most wind conditions, crews would have had to row nearly all the long way in and out of the fjord. Nonnebakken lies in practically the same situation by the Odense river at the head of the long Odense fjord. A narrow, winding channel, the last part of which is in fact man-made, links the sea and the town today, which is important as a junction of major roads. Finally, recent scientific investigations have shown that it was impossible to sail from the Great Belt to Trelleborg, since the river Næsby was dammed. The locations of the fortresses (other than Aggersborg) made them completely unsuitable for the mustering of fleets, for training-camps and barracks for crews, and for control of sea-ways. They must rather have been built chiefly to safeguard control of the interior of the realm and the important main roads.

Aggersborg's colossal dimensions have always been difficult to explain, but its location on Limfjord (fig. 38) must be the key to an understanding of them. Limfjord was the most important waterway between the Baltic and the North Sea, and it could be controlled from Aggersborg, where customs duties and other tolls could be collected. Aggersborg was presumably also intended to play some sort of role in connection with Norway, with which Denmark had extensive trade-links (ch. 11) and where Harald Bluetooth was in power for some time. It was apparently possible to sail directly from Limfjord, from a point just west of Aggersborg, north to Jammer Bay or Vigsø Bay, and from there it was only a twelve-hour sail to South Norway. That means it never took more than twenty-four hours to get from Aggersborg to the Norwegian coast, and the Danish king's men could easily meddle in

Norwegian affairs. If Aggersborg had been built as a base for raids on Western Europe, it would presumably have been sited at the western end of Limfjord rather than half-way along it, to be sure to benefit from a favourable wind for the trip across the North Sea.

A third point, significant for understanding the fortresses' function, is the kind of life led in them as far as we can reconstruct it on the basis of the buildings and their internal arrangements, the cemeteries and the artefacts. It is clear that not all the buildings were dwelling-houses/barrack-rooms as it used, to be thought,[80] and that women, children and craftsmen lived there alongside some sort of military group. The picture is clearest at Fyrkat where there is no earlier settlement to distort it (though it must be remembered that only three-quarters of the fortress has been excavated). Here we can see that the buildings alongside the wall functioned variously as smithies, storehouses and possibly stables or byres (cf. the contemporary farms, ch. 4), and that the dwelling-houses lay along the main east–west street. The west gate, flanked by a small guard-house, was the main entrance. Originally there may also have been dwelling-houses along the main north–south street, but one of these buildings was definitely used at some time by gold-smiths and another had apparently been very little used at all. One of the smaller buildings, too, was used by goldsmiths, and there is in general clear evidence of craftsmen working in the fortress. Many similar features occur at Trelleborg, but the material from Aggersborg does not permit conclusions of this nature to be drawn—in fact we cannot even be sure that this fortress was ever finished and actually used.

The old idea of the fortresses housing purely male communities can no longer be maintained, either. The military features of the Trelleborg cemetery have often been mentioned, but they are in fact restricted to a few multiple graves which, with other finds, show that there was fighting around the fortress. Women's and children's graves occur both at Trelleborg and Fyrkat, and there is much evidence of women inside the fortresses.

None of the fortresses has yielded finds which reflect direct contact with England, but there is clear evidence of contact with the rest of Scandinavia and with the Baltic. Both the architecture and the finds show that the fortresses were associated with the upper classes. It is easiest to explain the civilian character which emerges in what are obviously military structures if we see them functioning as normal royal estates where the king's agents collected and kept his revenues, and where his possessions in general could be protected. The fortresses may also have been intended to maintain law and order in the appropriate areas, to provide safe housing for mints and to act as centres for organising major offensive expeditions. They may also have been suitable residences for craftsmen in royal employ who produced weapons, riding equipment and jewellery for the king and his men. There must also have been a number of warriors stationed in each fortress.

No direct models for the architecture of the fortresses are known. A series of circular fortresses along the coasts of the Low Countries exhibit certain common features, and on excavation one of these, Souburg on the Walcheren, has proved to have both a circular rampart with gates at the four points of the compass and axial streets. But Souburg also has many features which distinguish it from the Danish fortresses, and so far we cannot tell whether it is earlier or later. There may have been influences in either direction, or they may share a common prototype as yet unknown. There is little doubt, however, that the Danish fortresses represent a combination of very different elements, some Scandinavian (such as the building materials and the bow-sided houses) and others presumably inspired by Carolingian and Ottonian monumental architecture (for example the geometric arrangement in general, the quadrangles and the suggested arcades along Fyrkat's ring-road). The purpose behind the building of the fortresses was to create monumental architecture to fulfil certain political needs.[81]

The idea of a series of royal fortresses each controlling a particular region seems to have been new in later tenth-century Denmark. Certainly no earlier examples of fortified royal estates or private fortifications are known. However, there are parallels in numerous contemporary and earlier Slav fortresses and in the fortresses constructed in Western Europe—both on the Continent and in England—during the ninth and tenth centuries, partly in response to the harrying of the Vikings and partly in attempts to secure newly conquered territory (in the Danish areas of England for example). The 'great Danevirke', the two town walls and the circular fortresses show that the tenth century was also a great period of fortification in Denmark.[82]

In order to define the political situation behind the building of the fortresses and their subsequent demise, we must return to the dating and consider the fragments of extant information we possess concerning the major events and historical developments of the period. The erection of the fortresses must have caused a good deal of agitation among the Danes a thousand years ago, and their rediscovery has caused perhaps little less among their descendants of the last generation or two. The process of interpretation is by no means complete.

As stated above, Trelleborg was founded at the end of the reign of Harald Bluetooth and there is general agreement that he was killed between about 985 and 987 at the latest. The other fortresses must be of approximately the same date, and they correspond well to the picture of Harald suggested by history and archaeology, as a great builder and king (fig. 53). He was responsible for the Jelling monuments and he probably founded the precursor of Roskilde Cathedral (ch. 9). He must also have instigated the great bridge across Ravning Enge which, like Trelleborg, was constructed around the year 980. King Harald may also have had the ramparts raised around Hedeby and Århus, and likewise the Danevirke's 'Great Wall', and it was he who resumed the regular issue of coins after a long gap. In the words of the large Jelling stone, he 'won for himself all Denmark and Norway and made the Danes Christian', and it was in his reign, in AD 983, that the Ottonians were repulsed from the southern border where they had gained some ground after their defeat by Harald in 974 (see p. 145). It is also known that the last years of Harald's reign were characterised by unrest. His son,

Svein Forkbeard, led a revolt which resulted in his father's flight and death.

It is precisely in connection with the problems of power 'in all Denmark and Norway' that the fortresses fall into place as the king's local centres of authority—fortresses of coercion as it were—from which an area could be kept under control and the rights and duties of the king maintained. It was probably these very rights and duties which Harald sought to extend. Trelleborg, certainly, must have existed when the Hedeby area was retaken in 983, North Germany plundered and Hamburg burnt; the troops from this fortress no doubt took part in those events. Aggersborg may have been intended to play an important part in the reconquest of Norway, which had been lost to Harald Bluetooth in the last part of his reign.

The fortresses may thus express the efforts of a still powerful old monarch to retain power, and strengthen it, in a kingdom which had lost important regions and which was suffering great internal conflicts. Part of the realm was regained in 983, as stated above, but the internal unrest continued, and the brief life of the fortresses and the evidence of fighting at Trelleborg may well be due to the civil war between Harald and Svein in the 980s. If the new wielders of power led by Svein identified the fortresses with Harald's political system and ambitions, these might make good reasons for giving them up. In any case, the outcome was that they were soon abandoned, and consigned to total oblivion.[83]

Sea-barriers

> ... therefore they trusted in neither weapons nor fortifications; so as to restrict access to pirates, arms of the water were barricaded with very long poles and stakes.[84]

This is how Saxo, writing around 1200, described the situation when the Slav attacks on Denmark reached a climax half a century before, in about 1150. A number of sea-barriers have in fact been discovered in the east and south of the country. But they are of widely different dates. Some, such as the two barriers in Haderslev fjord 'Æ Lei' and 'Queen Margrethe's bridge' have been dated by C-14 to the Roman Iron Age, but the former, 'Æ Lei', may have been improved during the late Viking Age.[85] Others were built towards the end of the Middle Ages. Barriers are also known from other countries; they are the logical means of preventing sudden attacks from sea-borne enemies and barring the passage of any unwelcome ships. People with local knowledge knew the openings in permanent barriers or used other, often very complicated, sailing channels.[86]

C-14 datings of sea-barriers seem to indicate, however, that many were constructed in the late Viking Age and early Middle Ages, when Denmark was plagued by Slavs, Norwegians and Swedes.[87] The best known barrier is that formed by the Skuldelev ships (ch. 3). These were filled with stones some time in the eleventh century and sunk in the Peberrende, an important channel leading to Roskilde. This was

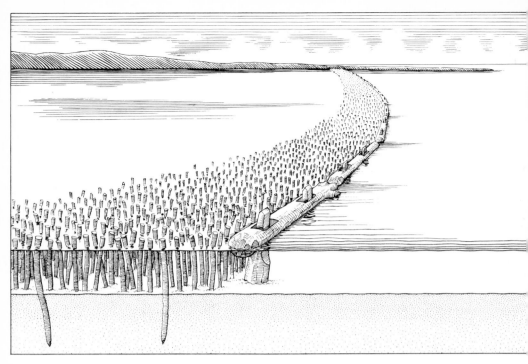

Fig. 43 *Sea-barrier at Hominde on Lolland. Reconstruction.*

apparently carried out in two separate operations so that the two last ships to be sunk (wrecks 2 and 6) acted as reinforcement of an earlier barrier consisting of three ships (wrecks 1, 3 and 5). In addition to the ships and stones, the barrier was composed of poles and fascines which may have been part of a larger barrier system. Certainly other barriers have been demonstrated in this part of Roskilde fjord.[88]

Another method of obstruction was employed (fig. 43) at Hominde, off Lolland. Here a broad belt of close-set piles was driven down, sometimes as many as ten per square metre, with horizontal timbers along the inside. A C-14 date suggests this barrier was built in the late Viking Age or early medieval period.[89] Here the strength lay in the sheer mass of material. By contrast, the strength of the Helnæs barrier barring access to Fyn lay in the careful fashioning of a considerably smaller number of timbers. The barrier consisted of two parallel rows of piles with horizontal sticks through their lower part to ensure they were not driven too far into the bottom, and with notches close to their sharp lower ends to ensure that they could not be pulled up. Horizontal 'floaters' connected each pair of piles in the two rows. The barrier was presumably several hundred metres long and has been dated by C-14 to the late Viking Age or early Middle Ages.[90] Finally, the Bussevik barrier in Blekinge in Sweden (close to Skåne) has been dated to the late Viking Age on the basis of a number of C-14 datings.[91] It is uncertain whether the king, local magnates or the local communities were responsible for these massive sea-barriers which protected considerable areas.

MILITARY ORGANISATION

We know only a little about military organisation in the Viking Age. But the structures mentioned above are clear evidence of some form of organisation, and other sources also provide information. It is highly probable that a system of land defence went into operation in response to a sudden attack. All able-bodied local men were then bound to report for duty on receipt of a prearranged signal. There is only sparse evidence of this system from much later written sources, however.[92] Warnings could be transmitted over quite large distances by beacons on prominent sites; so far there is no evidence that they were used in the Viking Age, but it is likely.[93] There is no doubt that the king was the supreme military leader and that he could claim some form of military service—King Godfred and his successors were already mentioned in the ninth century as the central figures in acts of war and peace-negotiations. In 808 Godfred also took the initiative in building part of a massive Danevirke, and in 974 the Norwegian Earl Hákon fought on Harald Bluetooth's side at the Danevirke. There are many more examples in the written sources.

The ramparts and fortresses of the period are almost inconceivable unless we assume that the king conscripted labour as did his colleagues in Western Europe.[94] The Viking Age was probably also familiar with a levy organisation, but we cannot be sure how far back the system goes, nor of its form in the Viking Age. Levy is only known in Denmark from post-Viking Age sources (the first mention is in St Cnut's deed of gift to the church in Lund in 1085) and then the system is constantly changing.[95] Historians studying the Danelaw have suggested that Danish Viking Age kings led armies whose members were soldier-farmers giving military service in return for rights of cultivation on royal land.[96] Even if this were true, it has also been argued that it is very doubtful whether the Vikings' situation abroad can be directly applied to their home countries.[97]

Nomenclature found on rune stones (though of disputed value) gives some further insight into military organisation or at least one aspect of it (cf. ch. 2). Fundamental seems to have been the *lið* (the company of warriors) whose members were *félagi* (companions). They had a *dróttinn* (leader) to whom the others, his *hempægar* (home-companions) owed loyalty. Both the king and other great men could be a *dróttinn* and have a band of retainers. The *þegn* and *dreng* probably had a relationship of dependence on or sworn loyalty to the king, and some were doubtless members of his *lið*. A *þegn* was probably often older and of greater importance than a *dreng*. Viking armies that operated independently abroad seem to have been organised on a *lið* system, an army consisting of a number of such bands, each of which was led by a *dróttinn* but under the overall command of a person often referred to as king.[98] Moreover, the motley international composition of the Viking armies is reflected in a number of inscriptions on Swedish rune stones. These commemorate Swedish Vikings who took part in expeditions to England and elsewhere (one died in Jutland before ever reaching England) and in some cases the leader of the expedition is mentioned, among others the well known historical figures Thorkell the Tall and Cnut the Great.[99]

Archaeological research on the horsemen's graves in Denmark will produce more information on the organisation of armies and the relations of the upper classes with the king in tenth-century Denmark. The chronology of the graves is at present rather vague within the confines of the century, but there is a remarkable uniformity in their grave-goods, which also have clear associations with the finds from the fortresses and with the Jelling material. Detailed analysis will doubtless reveal that certain artefacts were the products of the same workshop (whether in the Viking fortresses or on ordinary royal estates). Such correspondences between finds from royal structures and from graves imply a close association between the king and the important men around the country.[100] Many of those who lie buried in the richly furnished tenth-century men's graves are no doubt the same as those called *þegn, dreng* and *hempægi* on the rune stones, and some are no doubt the heroes familiar to us from the sagas and histories of later times.

It was in the Viking Age, around AD 960, that Denmark officially re-
nounced paganism and accepted Christianity. This was one of the most
important decisions made there in the last couple of millennia, with all
that it entailed in the way of a gradually changing world picture: different
religious practices and organisation, and closer links with other countries
through the international ecclesiastical establishment. Christianity was
introduced in Norway at the beginning of the eleventh century and in
Iceland in the year AD 1000. The huge country of Sweden, which was
further away from Western Europe, was not converted until *c*. 1100.

PAGAN RELIGION AND RELIGIOUS PRACTICES

Before the conversion, the Scandinavian countries probably for the most
part shared the same pantheon of gods and the same mythology.
Scattered information about the gods and their personalities exists in
Viking Age scaldic verse and on rune stones. We learn a little, too, from
a few pictures and religious symbols. Furthermore, place-names and
personal names compounded with names of gods yield information about
the popularity of the gods concerned and sometimes about the places
in which they were worshipped; and offences under Christian law sometimes reflect ancient pagan customs not yet entirely eradicated. Foreign
written sources also reveal something of Norse paganism, while archaeology throws light chiefly on beliefs concerning the after-life. But most
information about pagan faith and worship in the Viking Age comes
from poems and stories written down in the thirteenth century. The
Poetic Edda and Snorri Sturluson's handbook for poets, the *Prose* or
Snorra Edda, are the most important sources. Both of these are Icelandic
sources and represent Norwegian–Icelandic tradition. But as these texts
were written down a couple of hundred years after the transition to
Christianity, when people were no longer familiar with the pagan
religion, much has no doubt been distorted, misunderstood or forgotten.
Recent research suggests that some of the mythological poetry may even
have been composed in the Christian period itself. Similar problems exist
with regard to information about paganism in the *Gesta Danorum* written
by Saxo Grammaticus in very elaborate Latin about AD 1200.

Thus in general it is the case that nearly all literary sources about

Pl. 32 *Soapstone mould for Thor's hammer, crosses and ingots from Trendgården in North Jutland. Si[*
Thor's hammers from Rømersdal on Bornholm, Mandemark on Møn and Sejrø.

pagan faith and worship were written by foreigners, Christian or Muslim
(and often we do not know how much writers saw for themselves and
how much they actually understood), or were written down a long time
after the introduction of Christianity. Fortunately, several of the Viking
Age sources mentioned above (rune stones, pictures, scaldic verse,
religious symbols, burial-customs and so on) to some extent confirm
the information offered in these later written sources.[1]

The Scandinavian pagan religion was not dogmatic. It was composed
of many different concepts which were not organised according to a
logical system. Unlike Christianity, there were many gods each with a
more or less clearly defined major role. They were conceived and
depicted as human beings, with human behaviour and foibles. They were
divided into two main tribes, the Æsir and the Vanir, who lived in
communities much like the well-to-do farmers of the period.

Odin was the head of the Æsir. He was the god of strife, wisdom and
poetry, and had a number of strange talents. He had exchanged one of
his eyes for a drink from the well of wisdom, and he learnt of everything that took place in the world from his two ravens. He presided
over Valhall: a splendid hall where warriors killed in battle spent the
after-life in fighting and feasting. Odin rode an eight-legged horse—just
such horses can be seen on Gotlandic picture stones. Around 1070 Adam

of Bremen described a cult statue of Odin—whom 'they chisel armed'—in the large pagan temple in Uppsala in Sweden. In Denmark there is no pictorial evidence of Odin, but his name appears on a piece of human skull inscribed with runes from Ribe. It also occurs in place-names such as Odense (Odin's *vé*, 'Odin's sanctuary') indicating that this mighty god was worshipped in Denmark, presumably by those of the highest social status and in particular by the more or less professional warriors.[2] Their grave-goods are also appropriate to the concepts of Valhall, as we shall see later in the chapter.

Thor was one of Odin's sons. He ruled over the sky and the weather and must have had influence over the crops; in addition he was the mighty god who fought the evil giants and tried to fish the equally evil world-serpent out of the sea surrounding all lands. His weapon was the hammer Mjǫllnir; and when he drove across the sky in his chariot drawn by goats, it thundered (the name Thor means 'the thunderer'). Thor was extremely popular throughout the extensive Viking world and he was presumably worshipped in far wider social circles than Odin. Thus an Anglo-Saxon source relates that he was the god most prized by the Danes.[3] His name occurs in many personal and place-names (ch. 2),[4] and his hammer became a much-used religious symbol, made of gold, silver, bronze, amber or iron (fig. 8, pl. 32) and worn as jewellery like the Christian cross. Such Thor's hammers are known from many places.[5] The symbol was also carved on rune stones and Thor is the only pagan god to be invoked by name on Danish rune stones; the large Glavendrup stone (pl. 4) is one of the three examples.[6] The story of his struggle with the World Serpent is depicted both in Denmark (Hørdum in Thy, pl. 33)

Pl. 33   *Scene of Thor's fishing on the stone at Hørdum church in Thy. Thor has caught the World Serpent on the hook and hauls it in with such force that his foot goes through the bottom of the boat. But the giant Hymir stands with raised axe about to cut the line to free the serpent.*

and elsewhere[7] and other depictions of this scene are described in scaldic verse.[8] Finally, we should include a small seated figure from Iceland holding something like a hammer in his hands. This is presumably an amulet of Thor.[9] According to Adam of Bremen, there was a large cult statue of him in the Uppsala temple.

Among the most popular divine beings were the Vanir brother and sister Frey and Freyja. They were gods of fertility, and Frey is also said to have exerted influence over trade and shipping. His name occurs (though rarely) as a prefix in both personal and place-names in Denmark, but is found far more frequently in Sweden, presumably reflecting the greater extent of his worship there. A small seated bronze figure from Södermanland in Sweden, with an immense erect penis, is thought to be an image of Frey. It was with this characteristic feature that Adam of Bremen described his image in the temple at Uppsala, after saying 'he bestows peace and pleasure on mortals'.[10]

In addition to these two groups of major divinities there were the female beings called Dísir who had influence on fertility and daily prosperity. They were associated with Freyja, who was their leader. There were also the goddesses of Fate—the Norns—and the Valkyries, women who led warriors killed in battle to Valhall. Valkyries may possibly be represented by small bronze and silver figures from Sweden, some of whom offer drinking-horns.[11] In addition there were mysterious dwarfs, who often figure in literature as craftsmen, and the malevolent giants whom the gods spent such a large part of their time fighting and tricking, but whom, according to the stories, they might also marry. All the divine figures mentioned, and a number of others besides, are characters in the mythological stories and poems. Many natural features were also worshipped: springs, hills, groves and so on.[12]

Miniature harvesting implements such as scythes and sickles may have been religious symbols or amulets, representing gods or less individualised powers with influence on fertility and crops: Frey and Freyja, Thor or others. But we cannot be sure of this. Like the Thor's hammers, and the chairs, staffs and other miniature objects (perhaps also symbols of divinities), these were worn as jewellery and are known both in Denmark and elsewhere.[13] The shape of one type of brooch may well have been inspired by ideas about Thor: on top of it are two sculptured goats flanking a boss shaped rather like a fossilised sea-urchin—a thunder-stone according to folk belief.[14] Other pictures on Danish stones may have mythological significance, besides the Hørdum example mentioned.[15] A forceful phallic figure carved in wood and found in the foundations of the earliest Danevirke may not be associated with any particular god or even with the supernatural in general. On the other hand, we do know that phallic figures were worshipped.[16] A small bronze frog from a female grave in Jutland which is shown clasping a large cleft and two domed projections is perhaps an amulet to assist childbirth.[17] A strange assortment of things, including owl-pellets, henbane seeds and part of the lower jaw of a young pig found in another female grave (at Fyrkat) may also have been used to make contact with the supernatural.[18] Finally, it should be emphasised that it is hazardous to identify small objects, pictures and figures with particular pagan gods or with the supernatural in general unless they possess distinctive attributes—such as Thor's hammer—or elements from an easily recognisable scene, for example Thor's fishing for the world-serpent. Some small figures thought to be images of gods may well be gaming-pieces.[19]

The actual mode of worship of pagan gods is also problematic. As already mentioned, Adam of Bremen describes the magnificent temple at Uppsala with its statues of Odin, Thor and Frey. Adam goes on to speak of priests and sinister ceremonies involving the sacrifice of nine males of every species, accompanied by the singing of songs so indecent that he thinks it best to pass over them in silence.[20] Around 1015 the German Thietmar of Merseburg writes about Danish rites as follows:

> ... But I have heard strange stories about their ancient sacrificial feasts which I will not leave unmentioned. There is in those regions a place, the capital of the realm (*caput istius regni*) by the name of Lejre in the province called Sjælland where they all gathered every ninth year in the month of January after our celebration of the birth of the Lord, and there they offered to their gods ninety-nine people and equal numbers of horses, as well as dogs and cocks (instead of hawks), as bloody sacrifices; as I have said, they thought it certain that these rites would serve their purpose with the powers of the Underworld and placate them after crimes had been committed.[21]

Lejre, which lies about eight kilometres from Roskilde, is thus referred to as an ancient cult centre. Legends about kings and heroes in later written sources are also connected with Lejre, and tenth-century archaeological finds and memorials confirm the significance of the site at that time.[22] Soon, however, Roskilde took precedence. Judging by their names, Odense and Viborg are also to be identified as ancient cult places (both with *vé*, meaning a sanctuary, a sacred enclosure) as well as important assembly places (ch. 5).

The king or some other leader in a particular region presumably took charge of the major cult activities.[23] The designation *goði* ('priest') occurs on a couple of rune stones, so such people with special religious functions actually existed. The designation *þulr*, which also appears on a Danish rune stone, may have had a related meaning. The *goði* of the Glavendrup stone is also called a *þegn* and as such was presumably associated with the power-system centred on the king (ch. 2).[24]

Nothing is known of pagan cult buildings in Viking Age Denmark. No mention of such buildings is made in the description of Lejre or in any other written sources, and there is no archaeological evidence of any either. It used to be taken for granted that existing churches were located on ancient cult sites, thus obliterating cult buildings. But there are no traces of any such buildings—or of any paganism at all even beneath the earliest churches, for example Jelling. It is probable that, generally speaking, the earliest churches do *not* lie beneath existing church sites, and there is as yet no sign of any continuity between pagan and Christian cult places in Denmark.[25]

But we gather from place-names, poems and other literary sources that gods were worshipped at various places and chiefly in the open air:

at a *vé*, a *hǫrgr* (a rock outcrop, stony mound or cairn), in groves and on hills, and by other natural features such as crags and springs. The *hǫrgr* may have been a place mainly for a private or local cult; and it is possible that some kind of shelter was built at it. Otherwise the only indoor celebrations we know of were held in a *hof*, the designation given to a farmstead important and large enough to provide the facilities for cult rites and feasting but probably not distinguished in any particular way from other dwelling houses.

In the nature of things it will hardly ever be possible to provide archaeological proof of the existence of cult sites such as these, and certainly nothing of the kind has so far come to light in Denmark. Even the temple at Uppsala has left no convincing traces, despite—according to Adam of Bremen—its splendour and size.[26] The church at Mære in Norway, however, may lie on an old cult site with a cult building, though evidence of its use in the Viking Age is rather shaky,[27] and many people hold that there are remains of at least one *hof* in Iceland (Hofstaðir).[28] All in all, we have virtually no archaeological evidence of pagan cult places in Viking Age Scandinavia, and it is quite possible that large cult images and specialised religious buildings were extremely rare. Descriptions in thirteenth-century literary sources must of course be approached warily, because they may well have been influenced by Christian concepts of worship.[29]

PAGAN GRAVES AND MEMORIALS

We are on archaeologically firmer ground in considering graves, mounds and memorials to the dead in general. Precise dating of Danish Viking Age graves is still, it is true, dependent on Jan Petersen's 1919 and 1928 chronology of artefacts based on Norwegian grave-finds. But much Danish material indicates what kind of care was taken of the dead, and archaeological evidence can sometimes confirm, illuminate or supplement the evidence of the written sources concerning concepts of the after-life and other matters.

Pagan burial customs in Viking Age Denmark were variable in the extreme. Cremations and inhumation graves, with and without grave-goods, occur throughout the period over most of the country. Cremations and inhumation graves rarely occur in the same cemetery, however, and we do not know why some were cremated with their grave-goods and others were not. The inhumation burial appears to be by far the most common. But this impression may of course be due to the fact that cremations leave little trace and are therefore less easily discovered and examined.[30]

The dead were sometimes buried in coffins, sometimes not, or they might be placed in a burial-chamber[31] or in a ship[32] on a bier of some sort. Instead of a purpose-made coffin (those we know show various constructions),[33] a suitable object from daily life could serve as a container: a boat (rare in Denmark),[34] the body of a cart (figs. 8 and 44),[35] a chest (fig. 29)[36] or perhaps just a fragment of one of these.[37] Other items such as sledges may also have been used, but no evidence survives.

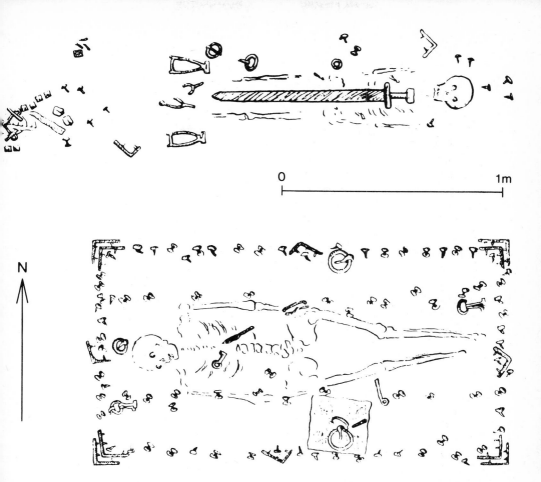

Fig. 44 *Top: man's burial with sword, riding equipment and horse. Bottom: woman's burial in wagon-body decorated with Thor's hammers, cf. fig. 8. Her grave-goods included knife and whetstone, and a box containing, among other things, a Danish coin struck c. AD 900–50. The graves were in a cemetery at Ketting on Als excavated from 1925 to 1931.*

Usually (but not always) graves are orientated east–west, and usually (but not always) the dead were placed in them flat on their backs, their arms down their sides, and their heads to the west (fig. 44). Though it is clear they were often dressed,[38] only small fragments of clothing have survived.

The grave-goods range from the simplest (for example a knife) to splendid equipment including weapons, horse- and riding-gear inlaid with silver in male graves, and jewellery, textile implements and boxes in female graves. Furniture is sometimes found (ch. 7). Dogs accompany the dead in a number of graves, large greyhound-like dogs in some male graves and a lap-dog in one female grave.[39] A few axes must have had a purely ceremonial function[40] and tools of an occupational nature other than weapons of war are extremely rare—unlike the finds in Norwegian graves.[41] In some places, remains of food and drink have also been found

Pl. 34   *Aerial photograph of Jelling seen from the south. The rune stones can be seen in front of the church porch.*

and many containers for them have survived.[42] There are also examples of slaves or other sacrificed persons buried alongside their masters. In general, grave-goods must be seen as a selection of the deceased's personal property, symbols of rank as well as necessities such as food. The presence of grave-goods clearly presupposes ideas of a life after death. But some quite unpractical items in a couple of graves[43] may indicate that people did not always take such concepts quite literally. And if cart-bodies and ship-settings are to be understood as symbolic carts and ships, these may indicate the same attitude.

The construction of graves ranges from quite simple flat graves to those with a stone-covering, a stone surround of some sort, or a small mound; and from these to impressive monuments with burial-chambers, large mounds, big ship-settings, rune stones and so on, which serve not only as a grave but also as a memorial, the largest and grandest of course being Jelling (pl. 34). But presumably many of those graves which today are flat were originally marked in some way, by a post, a couple of stones, or a piece of wooden sculpture. There is only sparse evidence of this, however.[44] Many ship-settings—which incidentally when they *did* contain burials seem to have enclosed cremations only—have also been removed in the course of time for use in roads and bridges and so on, without leaving any trace in the landscape. The impressive fleet of stone ships at Lindholm Høje has thus survived only because it was so soon covered by vast sand-drifts.[45] The very rich graves are often isolated, but groups of graves on differently sized cemeteries are usually associated with a farm (as possibly at Sønder Onsild in North Jutland), a village (as apparently at Hesselbjerg in Central Jutland and Stengade II on Langeland), a town (such as Hedeby, where there were thousands of graves), or a fortress (such as Trelleborg and Fyrkat—these fortress-cemeteries, however, belong to the transitional period between paganism and Christianity).[46]

Nothing is actually known about pagan burial-ceremonies in Denmark or about possible grave cults. Traces of fires and pits have been found between graves on some burial-grounds, though they cannot necessarily be associated with the graves themselves. In some places the settings are clearly older than the graves.[47] Ship-settings may in fact have defined areas where religious ceremonies were conducted, but we can only guess at this. A timber structure in the centre of Fyrkat's burial-ground is so far unique. It may have had a ritual purpose but its precise construction and appearance are uncertain,[48] and like the fortress itself it belongs to the period just after the introduction of Christianity.

While rich grave-goods and large burial monuments are naturally determined by the wealth of the deceased or his relatives, scanty grave-goods or the lack of them altogether are not necessarily evidence of poverty or low social status. For everything points to the fact that throughout the Viking Age people were frequently buried without possessions for religious or ideological reasons, not economic or social considerations. For example, the few Danish graves known so far where a slave accompanied his master in death are not particularly well furnished (pl. 3).[49] A tradition of simple graves probably survived from the Germanic Iron Age.[50] In addition, there was some Christian influence, certainly from the conversion period onwards, opposed as the faith was to grave-goods, ship-settings and mounds.

Not all people received a proper burial. Slaves who ended up as grave-goods have been mentioned, and graves of infants are conspicuous by their absence in pagan cemeteries—though plenty are found in Christian ones.[51] As the introduction of Christianity hardly led to increased infant mortality, we must suppose that in pagan times infants were buried in a different manner from adults.[52] The Arab at-Tartuschi in the second half of the tenth century recounted that unwanted children in Hedeby were thrown into the sea (ch. 2), and in the pagan period in Scandinavia it was probably normal to expose unwanted children and leave them to their fate. Perhaps this tough view of the life and death of infants (against which the Church reacted strongly)[53] explains why those infants who died a natural death were not normally buried in adult cemeteries either. What became of them is uncertain. Scattered human bones frequently turn up when the bones from a settlement are examined. These sometimes come from destroyed cemeteries, but not always. A number of them must be those of people hastily buried—the complete skeleton of an adult male who had suffered this fate was found in Århus and several children's skeletons were lying in wells at Trelleborg.[54] Similarly macabre is a child's skeleton found under the fireplace of a house in Hedeby. As with the child's skeleton from Elisenhof, on the west side of the Jutland peninsula, this is probably a case of a foundation sacrifice,[55] although another possible explanation is that people thought to keep in touch with the dead child in this way.

Monuments of the sort discussed above were not always associated with graves. Thus only doubtful traces of graves occur in association with the large ship-settings at Glavendrup (pl. 4), Bække and Lejre, which were possibly only memorials or perhaps both memorials and sanctuaries. These have all been restored. Originally they were about 60, 45 and 80 m long, respectively. The first two each project from a Bronze Age mound, and at each prow stands a rune stone. The inscriptions inform us that the Glavendrup monument was raised by wife and sons to husband and father, and that the Bække monument was raised by sons to their mother. Incidentally, the wife on the Glavendrup stone, Ragnhild, also raised a monument in Tryggevælde on Sjælland to her husband by another marriage. Only the huge rune stone has survived, but the inscription also mentions a mound and a ship (*skaiþ*), doubtless a ship-setting.[56]

Only a few rune stones are known to have stood on a grave or to have been directly associated with one. Their function was primarily commemorative (ch. 2) and so they were presumably erected on sites where many people gathered or passed by, just as modern memorials are.[57] Nor did all mounds contain graves. This is the case with Denmark's largest prehistoric mound, for example, the South Mound at Jelling discussed in more detail below. Some of the empty mounds are, one imagines, memorials, to people who died elsewhere perhaps (though bodies of fallen heroes may well have been brought back from expeditions preserved in salt, as happened in the twelfth century). And, as mentioned earlier in this chapter, some mounds may well have been cult sites, and maybe also arenas for formal meetings: there is lots of space on the large flat top of Jelling's South Mound.[58]

The information in scaldic verse and other literary sources about life after death in the imagination of the pagan Viking Age is far from unambiguous. But it corresponds well to the very varied burial-customs outlined above and to the fact that graves appear to have been associated in a number of ways with very different types of memorials.[59] A certain development in grave types, however, can be identified, and this may reflect changing attitudes towards the Other World. Ninth-century (and earlier) graves are generally simple, rarely containing much in the way of grave-goods. This probably explains why not a great many have been found. On the other hand, graves and cemeteries of the tenth century are well known. This is true both of the cemeteries associated with farms and villages, and of the really rich graves which sometimes had associated memorials. It also applies to the memorials themselves: large mounds, large ship-settings and rune stones (though a few of the latter occur earlier).[60] Within the pagan part of this century (to c. 960–80) the burial-customs appear quite standardised, if we distinguish between the ordinary farm, village and town graves on the one hand, and the richly furnished graves of the wealthy on the other. This is certainly true of the inhumation graves which have been most thoroughly examined. There are a number of examples of richly furnished graves in cemeteries of otherwise ordinary character. In the Hedeby area, however, there were apparently large burial-grounds for ordinary people and small ones for the upper classes with richly furnished graves arranged in timber chambers of different sizes.[61] On Langeland a similar distinction may exist between three small, rich cemeteries, Stengade I, Nørre Longelse and Skebjerg, and the large Stengade II site with about eighty-five graves which presumably belonged to a village.[62] The grave-furnishings in such burial-grounds often seem a pale reflection of the rich graves, but they are difficult to interpret more precisely. The richly furnished graves of the upper classes illuminate best contemporary beliefs—at any rate those of the class in question—and the splendour and glory of the age.

By far the greatest number of these rich graves have such common features in their layout and furnishings and in many of their individual objects that they must represent the two or three generations who died in, or perhaps a little before, the reign of Gorm the Old (probably died between 935 and 945) and in the reign of Harald Bluetooth (died c. 986). Much of the material was presumably manufactured by a small number of craftsmen and, as it has been pointed out, these craftsmen may well have had royal patronage. The men's equipment usually comprises a horse and magnificent riding-gear, a sword and/or other weapons, a bucket to contain drink, and sometimes drinking-vessels, a hand-basin, a dog and so on.[63] Many of the women of similar rank were buried in the body of a wagon like that from Oseberg (figs. 8 and 44) or even in a complete wagon with horses, and were furnished with splendid textiles, jewellery, needlework implements, boxes for personal property, a container for drink, a hand-basin and other goods.[64]

Against this background, we may convincingly identify many of the men in these standard warrior graves with king's men, the *þegn* and *dreng* of the rune stones (chs. 2 and 8). It is then tempting to interpret the riding-gear and weapons as royal gifts. In addition, these graves illustrate vividly concepts central to the traditional picture of Valhall. Valhall was Odin's residence, the place where warriors and great kings led a life of fighting and feasting after death. Several scaldic poets make these activities the ideal mode of existence in this world, too. And what could be better to take to Valhall than your horse and weapons? Horses resplendent in their trappings were suitable for high-ranking men—even though they were not likely to have been used in battle (ch. 8)—and presumably they also had to bear their masters to the Other World. Weapons were obviously necessary, and the other grave-goods were no doubt useful both for the journey and for feasting on arrival (for example food and hand-basin). But, as those who were killed in battle were restored to life in Odin's hall, armour may have been thought unnecessary, and that may explain why it is not found in Danish Viking Age graves.[65]

Apart from the Valkyries who fetched the dead warriors, there do not seem to have been any women in Valhall. We do not know what was thought to become of them after death, but people could hardly have believed that everyone ended up in Hel, the dismal kingdom of the dead, for everything indicates that dead women were the object of just as much ceremony as men of similar rank and status. Many were buried in the bodies of wagons—the suitable conveyance for women (ch. 3). Like those of the men, their grave-goods comprised items for suitable occupations in the next life, including needlework. The occupants of these graves must represent the class of women who raised rune stones and to whom rune stones were raised.[66]

Some means of transport was a fairly fixed component in rich graves and this must mean that a journey to the Other World was envisaged for which conveyances were necessary or at least convenient. So, unlike the other grave-goods, the means of transport was not just intended for use in the next life. Horses for men and wagons for women have already been mentioned, while some particularly rich graves—among them the large Søllested grave on Fyn—may well have contained a complete wagon with draught-horses and their magnificent equipment (ch. 3 and pl. 7). Ships and boats also occur in connection with graves: large warships, such as the Ladby ship and the ship from Hedeby's boat chamber-grave for great men, and small boats for others. Even the symbol of a ship—a ship-setting—may have been thought sufficient to carry the dead to their destination in reasonable comfort. Other people presumably walked—as they would have had to on earth.[67] Finally, it is possible that some coins found in graves may be travelling expenses, like the pennies demanded from the dead for crossing the river Styx by Charon, the ferryman of classical antiquity.[68]

A few graves are distinguished by quite outstanding magnificence, though the concepts revealed in their furnishings are generally the same.[69] But several of these particularly elaborate graves were broken into in antiquity and the original layout destroyed. Others, found by chance, were destroyed by eager treasure-seekers. Mention has just been made of the Søllested grave. This is Denmark's largest chamber-grave, about 10 × 3 m, inside a mound.[70] A similar grave containing carriage equipment is known to have existed at Møllemosegård, also on Fyn, but even less information about it has survived.[71] The Mammen grave near Viborg in Jutland is known especially for its silver-inlaid axe (pl. 28), the ornamentation of which gave the Mammen style its name, and for its splendid textiles (fig. 36) which were unfortunately torn to bits when the grave was found in the nineteenth century. This grave contained neither horse- nor riding-equipment and thus falls outside the normal pattern of rich male graves. But this may be the result of Christian influence, since the grave dates from *c.* 950–1000, judging by the axe's ornament.[72]

The boat-graves at Ladby on Fyn and at Hedeby, however, clearly belong to the pagan period and also to men of the highest rank. Unlike those just mentioned, both graves have been expertly examined (in 1935–1936 and 1908 respectively) and comprehensively published.[73] Both were covered by mounds and contained sumptuous furnishings (for the ships, see ch. 3), matching the traditional image of a Viking chief. Some of the Ladby grave-goods were missing and some destroyed when the mound was broken into in ancient times. But there were the remains of weapons (arrow-heads and one shield-boss), more than four sets of riding equipment, at least eleven horses, several dogs and a dog-harness, splendid tableware, a hand-basin, a gaming-board and fragments of fine clothes. The number of dead contained in the ship is unknown, since there were no human bones and no traces of bodies, but there may well have been more than one. The mound with the boat-grave was associated with a small cemetery of normal farm or village character. There were no remains of bodies in the Hedeby burial either, to indicate the number of dead. But the transverse division of the chamber, the distribution of grave-goods within it, the three swords, and the three horses in a pit outside the chamber indicate that there was more than one. In character the grave-furnishings correspond to Ladby's, though not quite so abundant. On the other hand, this Hedeby grave was in all probability undisturbed.

JELLING

The grandest Viking Age grave and monuments in Denmark—one can almost say in the whole of Scandinavia—are at Jelling. According to inscriptions on the two rune stones, they are associated with King Gorm and Queen Thyre, and their son Harald Bluetooth. In addition to the rune stones, the elements of the monument known today (pl. 34) are a burial-mound (the North Mound), a mound without a grave (the South Mound), remains of a large stone setting and a large wooden church built in association with a chamber-grave. The church was succeeded by two wooden churches and lastly by the present church built of calcareous tufa about the year 1100. A fragment of another rune stone was found in the churchyard wall a couple of years ago, but does not necessarily belong to the rest of the complex. The interpretation of all these features is still under discussion, and the newly found grave and the first wooden church are as yet unpublished. But the complex can be explained in brief as a grave for King Gorm and possibly also Queen Thyre, as a memorial to King Gorm, Queen Thyre and King Harald, and finally as a proclamation of Denmark's official conversion to Christianity.[74]

The smaller rune stone (pl. 35) is 140 cm high and carries the inscription: 'King Gorm made these memorials to Thyre his wife, Denmark's improvement'. Its original site is unknown but the large rune stone (pls. 35 and 42) most likely still stands on its original site, exactly half-way between the two mounds. It is a huge stone of unusual shape, with three large faces; most of one of these is covered with bands of

Pl. 35 *The royal rune stones at Jelling. The small stone is 140 cm in height (above ground-level), the large one 243 cm.*

inscription which continue below the pictures on the other two faces. The inscription runs: 'King Harald commanded these memorials made to Gorm his father and to Thyre his mother. That Harald who won for himself all Denmark and Norway and made the Danes Christian'—proud words dramatically confirmed by Denmark's greatest Viking Age structures. On one of the pictorial faces of the stone, a proud advancing beast is shown entwined with a snake. On the other, Christ is depicted with a crossed halo and bound in interlacing ribbons. Unlike many rune stones, the inscription is carved in horizontal bands and the pictures are executed in low relief; there is no doubt that they were further emphasised by paint. The stone is the most magnificent of all surviving rune stones and it is highly probable that it served as a model for subsequent pictorial stones.[75]

The North Mound, today 65 m in diameter and 8.5 m high, is the largest burial-mound in Denmark. It is built of turf over a timber grave-

Pl. 36 *The Jelling cup. It was found
in 1820 in the burial-chamber of the
North Mound. Silver with niello
inlay, gilt details and gilt inside.
Height 4.3 cm.*

chamber, 6.75 m long, 2.6 m wide and 1.45 m high, dug into a much smaller Bronze Age mound. One end of the chamber was divided into two by a plank set on edge, as if for two people. At an early stage, however, the grave was broken into and no human remains at all were found when the chamber was first examined in 1820. But, among the few remnants of what were clearly sumptuous furnishings, there are examples of characteristic male grave-goods such as riding-gear. There also appear to be the remains of a box, a characteristic of women's graves. Some of the most significant finds are the small silver cup (pl. 36) which gave the Jellinge style its name, and a number of carved, painted pieces of wood, among them the oldest painted representation of a figure known in Denmark. The form and decoration of the objects date the grave to the first half of the tenth century or around 950, and, all things considered, it is highly likely that it was King Gorm who was buried here in magnificent pagan fashion, and possibly also Queen Thyre. The burial itself and the completion of the mound must have been due to King Harald.[76]

The most debated feature of the Jelling complex is the remains of a large stone-setting, the V-shaped southern part of which survives beneath the South Mound (probably not including a number of stones found here and there in the churchyard). The extended lines of the V-shape enclose the North Mound, and a line bisecting the V-shape cuts through its burial-chamber and Harald's rune stone. This is presumably the remains of an enormous ship-setting erected in association with the North Mound; the excavator interpreted this as the point of a large V-shaped sanctuary (a *vé*), but none such is known elsewhere. If the stones represent a ship-setting, it was doubtless Denmark's largest, at least 150 m long.[77] Otherwise the longest one we know of was at Vejerslev near Viborg, 80–90 m long.[78]

The South Mound is even larger than the North Mound. Today it is 77 m in diameter and 11 m high, and so the largest prehistoric mound in the country. It is constructed of the same materials as the North Mound, and apparently had several building phases. The big 1941 excavations revealed the enormous amount of work involved in building it. They also uncovered a V-shaped timber structure, at first thought to

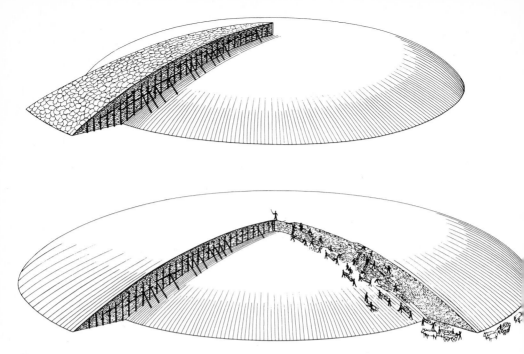

Fig. 45   *Schematic representation of the erection of a large mound. Top: a section of one phase built in a V-shaped timber construction such as that known from the South Mound at Jelling and elsewhere. Bottom: about three quarters of the mound completed with the timber structure acting as a template.*

have been for cult purposes but subsequently convincingly interpreted as a 'template' used to give the mound the same curve all over (fig. 45). Mounds on this scale were in fact works of architecture, as can also be seen from the proud inscriptions by three mound-builders on a rune stone in Bække. As already mentioned, the South Mound does not contain a burial and is presumably a memorial, a cult site, a meeting place or possibly all three.[79] But the remains of a building on top of the mound has nothing to do with its original function, because it is dated to *c.* AD 1100.[80] As the mound covers a section of the stone-setting described above, which in turn seems to be associated with the North Mound, and as the placing of the large rune stone also seems to presuppose the existence of the South Mound, then this mound must also have been built by Harald Bluetooth.

Jelling's earliest church was very large and built of wood, but only parts of it have been examined. The site alone, and the fact that there were three churches on this site before the present one of around 1100, make it reasonable to associate the first one with King Harald, who introduced Christianity in about AD 960.[81] This first church contained a chamber-grave made at the same time as the church was built. It measured some 4 × 2.6 m and contained many human bones. These were lying in great disorder and had clearly been moved from elsewhere. In addition, the grave contained a large number of gold threads from textiles as well as two

Pl. 37 *Strap-end from the chamber-grave in the oldest church at Jelling. Silver-gilt with niello inlay. Length about 7.5 cm.*

exceptionally well-preserved and beautifully executed silver strap-mounts with gold and niello (pl. 37) which are closely related to several finds both from the Jelling burial-mound and from others of the richest tenth-century graves, such as Ladby and Søllested. Anthropologists have now agreed that the human remains are those of a middle-aged man (just after excavation it was thought that there were two people because of some peculiarities of the teeth and because some bones were distinctly male, while others seemed to be female).[82]

The grave, its position in the church, and its grave-goods show clearly that this man belonged to the very highest echelons of tenth-century society. In addition, recent examination of old drawings strongly suggests that the earlier breaking in to the grave-chamber of the North Mound was actually carried out in an orderly fashion and was not simple grave-robbing. Under these circumstances there can be little doubt that the bones are those of King Gorm, and that King Harald wished to mark his conversion to Christianity and that of his people by giving his great monument a Christian character: his father was moved from the pagan burial-mound to receive a Christian burial in a prominent place in the large new church.[83]

This does not completely rule out the possibility that Thyre was also buried in the North Mound. For she died before Gorm, and if she was cremated—which is quite possible—there would hardly be any remains to move to the church, and almost certainly none to excavate. And just outside the church Harald had the massive rune stone raised, its magnificent pictures and long memorial inscription to his parents and himself no doubt carved especially for the occasion. The inauguration must have been a tremendous event.

King Harald must primarily have had a political aim in view when he built the lavish Jelling complex: to establish the ruling dynasty by greater and more splendid memorials than ever before seen in Denmark. Apart from the church, all the features clearly derive from a native tradition—they may also be a symbol of nationalist feeling aimed at the German Empire and its expansionist policies.[84] The magnificent complex undoubtedly set a fashion, at first for pagan monuments, later for Christian ones, and other people may have opened up old graves else-where in order to transfer their dead kinsmen to churches newly built. A good example may be the Ladby grave in which, despite good conditions of preservation, there were no skeletal remains.[85] From Harald onwards, all Danish kings were interred in churches. According to Adam of Bremen, Harald himself died in exile from wounds received in battle against his rebellious son, Svein Forkbeard, and was then returned to Denmark and buried in the church he had built in Roskilde, the precursor of the cathedral in which Danish kings are buried today.

THE CONVERSION

When Harald Bluetooth 'made the Danes Christian' around the year 960, the new religion was already well known in Denmark and it seems that no major political upheaval resulted.[86] Danes had met Christians and had got to know churches and monasteries (and their wealth) on their journeys and expeditions abroad. Foreign relatives—in England and Normandy for example—had long since become Christians, and in the course of time a number of Danes had received the *prima signatio*, the sign of the cross, as a fairly non-committal precursor to baptism and 'had full contact with Christians and heathens, but kept whatever faith they were inclined to'.[87] Others were given a proper baptism abroad. Thus Scandinavian chieftains and kings would let themselves and their people be baptised as part of peace-treaties in return for certain allowances, and political alliances were sometimes confirmed by baptism, whereby a king would receive a king or an emperor as his godfather and would be presented with gifts. In some cases, however, it was clearly a matter of camouflaged Danegeld and, even though some undoubtedly received baptism with integrity, far from everybody actually remained Christian.[88]

Many foreign Christians went to Denmark, both merchants and missionaries, and the German Empire gave vigorous support to missionary activities. In the mid ninth century, Ansgar received permission from the Danish king to build churches in Hedeby and Ribe, and to sound a bell in the former place. He baptised a number of people and gave others the *prima signatio*,[89] but the activities of Ansgar and his successors can hardly have had any lasting significance. Bishops of Schleswig/Hedeby, Ribe and Århus are none the less mentioned in 948 (and presumably there were also churches in these places then) and again in 965.[90] By the latter date, of course, Denmark was officially Christian.

There were undoubtedly several reasons for taking this step. In a violent age, the Christian message of charity was no doubt appealing, and the foreign god had proved 'powerful'. This religion was also less ambiguous than the pagan one, which could always manage to add a new member to its already numerous gods. This liberal attitude to religion is amply illustrated by various finds: a woman in a grave at Thumby-Bienebek near Hedeby was accompanied both by crosses and Thor's hammers, and moulds for hammers and crosses together (pl. 32) show that craftsmen were responsive to public demand.[91]

We may also presume that the king saw political advantages in introducing Christianity. In particular it would eliminate the excuse for crusades, an important element in German expansionist policy, and both written sources and the improvements to the Danevirke around 968 (ch. 8) show that the south posed an acute threat at this time. Internally, the king could see to it that the new religion was not enforced too rigorously to start with, but at the same time consolidate his power by filling the important church positions with sympathetic, loyal people—as happened in Christian countries abroad. Harald Bluetooth's need for consolidation is shown, among other things, by the large fortresses (ch. 8) and by the unrest leading to Svein Forkbeard's successful revolt. There is little reason to see the introduction of Christianity as a sign of weakness in face of the German Empire. The missionary Poppo, who according to an almost contemporary German source converted Harald by undergoing the ordeal of carrying hot coals, has a German or Frisian name but we do not know his ecclesiastical allegiance. Formally, however, the Danish church belonged to the archbishopric of Hamburg/Bremen until Scandinavia obtained its own archbishopric in Lund in 1103/4.[92]

The actual transition to Christianity seems to have occurred gradually from south to north and west to east. In 988 a bishop of Odense is mentioned, together with the bishops of Schleswig/Hedeby, Ribe and Århus. Skåne got a bishop in the reign of Svein Forkbeard, and the reign of Cnut the Great (around 1020) saw the establishment of the Sjælland bishopric at Roskilde. Skåne and Fyn still had a bishop each. But the whole of Jutland, with the exception of the Schleswig bishopric, was now subject to Odinkar the Younger, who was bishop of Ribe from about 1000 to 1043. He was succeeded by one Vale, who in 1049 was called Vale of Viborg, Bishop of the Danes. It was not until about 1060, in the reign of Svein Estridsson, that Denmark was divided into regular dioceses, with bishoprics in Schleswig, Ribe, Århus and Viborg, with Vendsyssel (north of the Limfjord) in Jutland, Odense on Fyn, Roskilde on Sjælland, and Lund and nearby Dalby in Skåne, though this last-named see was quickly abolished. In the reigns of Cnut the Great and his successors there was strong English ecclesiastical influence, with several bishops of English origin in Danish sees.[93]

The archaeological material only confirms the impression of a peaceful conversion. People gradually went over to invoking God and St Michael instead of Thor on rune stones, and these were now sometimes decorated with crosses.[94] Thor's hammers, whether as carved or incised ornaments or as jewellery, disappeared in the second half of the tenth century. The same applies to grave-goods[95] and it is symptomatic of this that the youngest coin from the total of twenty-two pagan graves containing coins known from Viking Age Denmark was minted between 959 and 975.[96] As late as c. 980 the dead might be buried with some of their possessions, even in Harald Bluetooth's own fortresses, as shown by the Trelleborg and Fyrkat finds. Here several examples of women's graves occur with the traditional pagan feature of a wagon body, but it may be due to Christian influence that there are no horsemen's graves and that there are a number of children's graves at Fyrkat.[97] Clear Christian features are to be found in a couple of graves in other parts of the country which contained openwork axes marked with crosses, dated to the end of the tenth century.[98]

At some point, however, people must have made a complete break with their past and chosen new burial-grounds, for no pagan burials occur in regular Christian cemeteries or beneath churches.[99] There are

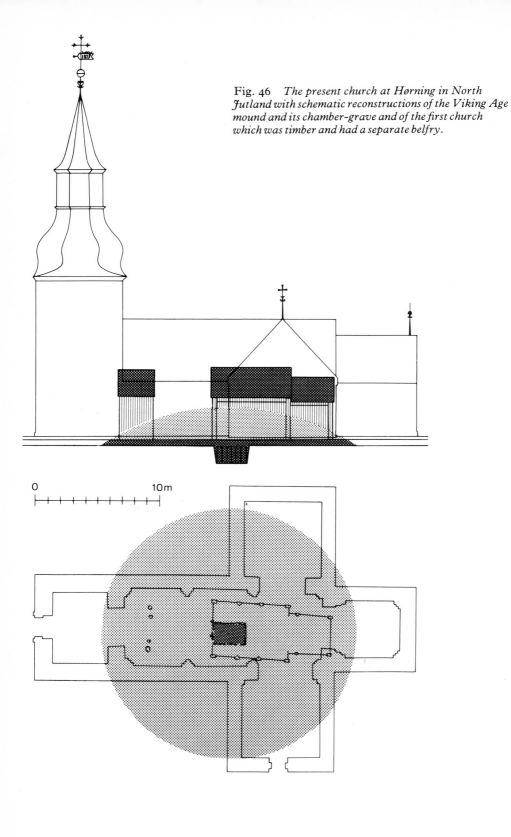

Fig. 46 *The present church at Hørning in North Jutland with schematic reconstructions of the Viking Age mound and its chamber-grave and of the first church which was timber and had a separate belfry.*

0   10m

not even the slightest traces of paganism below the church at Aggersborg, which lies immediately outside the fortress and quite close to the civilian settlement, though there must have been a large pagan cemetery for the Viking Age civilian settlement and perhaps a semi-pagan one for the fortress.[100] There is, it is true, the church at Hørning, built over a levelled Viking Age mound containing a woman in a well-furnished chamber-grave (fig. 46). But the oldest church, the ground-plan of which is known from excavation and which is dated by the carved, painted Hørning plank (pl. 38), need not be older than the beginning of the twelfth century and is certainly not older than the second half of the eleventh.[101] As there is thus probably a century or more between the grave and the church, it may only be coincidence that the church lies on top of the mound. There are several examples of Bronze Age mounds and many examples of prehistoric mounds on or near churchyards. This proximity may be explained by the fact that high points in the landscape were chosen both for burial-mounds and for churches.[102] In the case of Hørning, normal respect for the deceased—perhaps a grandmother or great-grand-mother—might explain why the grave was not destroyed and why she was finally 'churched' and christianised in a proper manner.

CHRISTIAN CEMETERIES

A number of eleventh-century cemeteries reflect the earliest Christian burial-customs known to us.[103] In several cases, these sites have turned out to be enclosed by shallow ditches,[104] a feature unknown in pagan and transitional burial-grounds. Grave-goods now no longer occur, and the dead are shrouded rather than clothed. As before, they nearly always lie flat on their backs with their arms at their sides and their heads to the west—later it became the custom to put both hands over the loins. Graves are with or without coffins, and in the first half of the eleventh century, at least, the coffins are even more varied in construction than earlier. Any kind of container from daily life seems to have been serviceable; and proper coffins, both rectangular and trapezoid, were made in many different ways. We get to know this material from the well-preserved graves of the earliest cemetery on the Thule site and on the PK Bank site in Lund (c. 1000–50), but similar coffins can be seen in Löddeköpinge, also in Skåne. The coffins of the burial-ground belonging to the stave church built c. 1050 on the sites in Lund just mentioned, however, are fairly standardised.[105]

Long sticks, 'grave-sticks', have been found in many of the early Christian graves, especially in Lund. They are generally hazel, but other sorts of wood occur. They have been interpreted as symbols of rebirth or resurrection: giving the dead a couple of sticks from a healthy tree to accompany him in his grave was a good way to look after his future. The custom was widespread, both in time and place, and presumably also occurred in the transitional period between paganism and Christianity, for similar sticks have been found in the chamber-grave below Hørning church, among other places.[106] Examples of the so-called 'charcoal' graves occur in Lund. These are graves in which the coffin rests on a thick layer of charcoal and sometimes also contains it in large quantities. The custom was probably due to English influence: similar 'charcoal' graves of the tenth century and earlier have been demonstrated in Winchester.[107] Burials inside churches are rare in this period. They were, one suspects, reserved for the select few, such as the founders of churches and their families, high-ranking clerics and persons of similar standing.[108]

CHURCHES

No church has been found in association with the earliest cemetery (*c.* 1000–50) at Lund, with the early Christian graves below Aggersborg church and below St Ib's in Roskilde, or with the burial-ground begun in early Christian times some 300 m from the present Stenløse church on Sjælland.[109] Churches may of course have been located outside the excavated area, or their traces may be unrecognisable. But we may assume that churches were not always located on the earliest Christian cemeteries; after all, a certain time must have elapsed before the whole country was served by churches. Around 1070, a century after the official conversion to Christianity, Adam of Bremen relates with pride that there were three hundred churches in Skåne, half that number on Sjælland and a third as many on Fyn. We do not know how reliable this is, however.[110]

Several early Christian cemeteries also occur outside the churchyards of later parish churches, as is the case at Stenløse and Lund. In addition there is the Löddeköpinge cemetery mentioned above, thought to have been begun *c.* AD 1000 and abandoned about 1150. Here traces have also been found of a wooden church about 20 m long, thought to have been built in the first half of the eleventh century. The present Löddeköpinge church, a Romanesque stone church presumably of the twelfth century, lies 300 m away.[111]

We do not know whether there were precursors of the Stenløse and Löddeköpinge churches on their present sites and of the same age as the cemeteries mentioned. The Stenløse burial-ground continued in use long after the building of the present church, but it seems possible that the early church and churchyard at Löddeköpinge may have moved simulta-

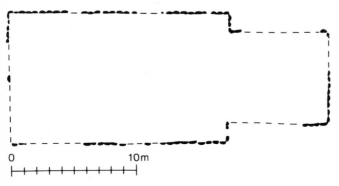

0   10m

Fig. 47 *Outline of the stave church of around 1050 on the Thule and PK Bank site at Lund. The roof was carried on two interior rows of posts.*

38 *The Hørning plank. The carved and painted plank was originally the wall-plate (connecting the wall and roof) in the wooden church at Nørre Hørning, see fig. 46. The decoration is Urnes style.*

neously to the present church site. In any case, the location of neither churches nor cemeteries can have been so stable as once assumed. In spite of many excavations in existing churches, it is extremely rare to find coins or anything else which can date previous churches on the sites to the eleventh century,[112] apart from churches in those towns known to be of that age or older. As we saw earlier, it is hardly likely that the country became rapidly and uniformly served by churches, and it now seems that many of the earliest were not built on the same sites as the existing ones. It was apparently not until the end of the Viking Age or early Middle Ages that village sites were fixed (ch. 4), and it is highly probable that the churches accompanied them. They were, after all, timber buildings which were easy to move and usually had short lives.[113]

The sizes of churches varied greatly. The Jelling church was large. The stave church on the Thule site and the PK Bank site in Lund, dated by dendrochronology to around 1050, had a total internal length of 25.7 m (fig. 47) and had two internal rows of posts to support the roof.[114] Another wooden church in Lund, St Maria Minor, thought to be about the same age, and also having internal posts for roof support, was probably a little smaller,[115] while Löddeköpinge's wooden church was about 20 m long. Hørning church, on the other hand, was only about 9.3 m long (fig. 46).[116] The churches in Lund, Löddeköpinge and Hørning had rectangular naves with rectangular or square chancels, no doubt the normal layout; traces of a belfry were found immediately west of the churches at Lund and Hørning. The carved and painted Hørning plank (pl. 38) with other carved planks from early medieval churches[117] show that the churches (and no doubt the houses of the wealthy too) could be splendidly decorated. But generally only traces of earth-fast posts remain (as at Jelling and Hørning) or the lowest parts of the posts themselves (as in the Lund churches). The stone packing which indicates the wall-course of Löddeköpinge church has not been satisfactorily interpreted. However, it is clear that walls of Viking Age or early medieval wooden churches were often stave-built—as in the partly preserved stave church at Greensted, Essex, for example. It is equally clear that the roof was sometimes, but not always, supported internally by two rows of posts, corresponding to contemporary vernacular buildings. But no Danish churches have been found corresponding to the famous Norwegian stave churches with their raised central sections. These, however, are all from the Middle Ages and represent a later stage of development in Scandinavian wooden architecture.[118]

In the eleventh century a completely new building-material for churches was introduced: calcareous tufa. This was quarried in a few areas of Denmark, and when newly quarried is so soft it can easily be sawn or split. It hardens under the influence of carbon dioxide in the air. The earliest stone church recorded in Scandinavia is said to have been built about 1030 by Estrid, sister of Cnut the Great, as a successor to the church of Harald Bluetooth in Roskilde (which had possibly already been rebuilt by Svein Forkbeard). Here Cnut the Great had had Estrid's husband, Earl Ulf, killed; and here the Earl was buried. There is no archaeological evidence of either Harald's wooden church or Estrid's stone church. The earliest building traces identified below Roskilde Cathedral are from Bishop Svein Nordmand's calcareous tufa church of the 1080s.[119]

However, traces of the only other Danish stone church known to have been built before c. 1050 have actually been found in Roskilde. Excavations in St Jørgensbjerg church (originally St Clement's) located the foundation trenches of a totally demolished calcareous tufa church which can be dated to around 1040 by means of a hoard of 110 coins placed in the trenches as a foundation sacrifice. The church had a chancel, a nave and a western section—presumably a tower—and its total length was about 19 m. Several calcareous tufa blocks turned out to have been reused in the present church, as also were a number of architectural features, for example the north doorway, which had Anglo-Saxon elements. It would not be surprising if a foreigner were responsible for building a church in a completely new material. Nor would it be surprising if he were an Anglo-Saxon, since at this time Harthacnut was king of both Denmark and England. Between about 1020 and 1029 Roskilde also had an English bishop, and during the reigns of Cnut and Harthacnut English moneyers operated there. It has been very plausibly suggested that the craftsmen who built Estrid's church then went to work on St Jørgensbjerg.[120]

But these two churches are so far unique. Not until the second half of the eleventh century, after Svein Estridsson's new division of the country into dioceses, is there evidence of other stone churches. These, with the exception of the partly surviving church at Dalby,[121] were all situated in towns. The bishop of Roskilde, Svein Nordmand, built all of four calcareous tufa churches: two in Roskilde, one in Slagelse and one in Ringsted.[122] The oldest surviving church interior in Denmark, the restored crypt below the Church of Our Lady in Århus, dates to this period too.[123] Around 1100, a number of calcareous tufa churches could be seen in the countryside, and most of the granite churches, thought of today as typical Danish village churches, were built in the twelfth and early thirteenth centuries.[124] The inscription on a rune stone found at Lund runs: 'Toke had a church built and ...'. The stone is dated to 1000–50, so Toke's otherwise unknown church was presumably of timber. But the inscription shows that it was not only the foremost members of the royal family and the bishops who were responsible for building churches, and it emphasises the fact that church-building was regarded as an estimable deed, worthy of commemoration.[125]

10 Art and Ornament

The originality and vigour of the period is perfectly illustrated by its decorative art. This was rooted in a style of animal ornament ultimately derived from the end of the Roman Iron Age and the beginning of the early Germanic Iron Age (fourth to fifth centuries AD) but which reached new peaks of accomplishment in the Viking Age. Internal developments and new impulses—some from abroad—were absorbed and adapted, imbuing with new strength the art of the late Germanic Iron Age whose motifs had become disjointed almost beyond all recognition.

The art of the Viking Age was self-assured and imaginative. Nevertheless it was subject to rules, and these make it possible to classify it in styles which developed one from another and which overlapped chronologically and succeeded one another. The poetry of the period—best known from the scaldic poems—was also subject to rules. Some of these are explained in the *Edda*, the handbook on the art of poetry written by the Icelander Snorri Sturluson about 1220, and the style, contents and intricacy of the poems have long fascinated literary historians, philologists and others, in many countries.[1]

Danish art-historians, on the other hand, have displayed an almost total lack of interest in the decorative art of the Viking Age, and there is little interest elsewhere except in archaeological circles.[2] This is rather odd, because Scandinavian art of this period makes a notably original contribution to European art. Perhaps one reason for this lack of interest is that no key on the lines of Snorri's *Edda* exists to the interpretation of the art. A contributory factor may also have been the attitude of earlier times, expressed for example in Sophus Müller's classic work of 1880, that Scandinavian art was essentially adapted from foreign models. Ireland was thought to have been especially influential.[3] It has long since been demonstrated, however, that Irish and Scandinavian art developed independently in the pre-Viking and most of the Viking period. Furthermore, the Dublin finds have demonstrated that in fact Scandinavian art styles in the late Viking Age influenced Irish art.[4]

Notwithstanding this neglect, a good many archaeologists and others have been fascinated by the splendour-loving and imaginative quality of Viking art, with its strong sense of style. In addition, the art styles are invaluable in helping to date decorated objects and also the contexts in which they are found. Sometimes the decoration of an object can also illuminate connections over considerable distances—such as between England and Denmark—and decorated artefacts can provide social and economic information.

The history of Viking Age art in Scandinavia has been discussed and described several times in recent years. This chapter is for the most part a short summary of this literature,[5] but here the characteristics and development of the art will be illustrated as far as possible by means of Danish examples. We may first remark that a basically similar mode of artistic expression seems to have existed over most of Scandinavia, and several of its phases are also well represented in many of the Scandinavian colonies, especially on the Baltic coast, in Russia and the British Isles. This widespread distribution must in part be due to itinerant craftsmen. In addition, there was probably extensive interchange of sketches, models and so on between various craftsmen, possibly through potential purchasers. Some of these sketches and models may have resembled the motif-pieces which are especially well known from the Dublin excavations (pl. 48). Finally there was extensive copying of jewellery and other objects with a varying degree of adaptation of form and style, sometimes resulting in products that reveal an interesting mixture of the tastes of different cultures.[6]

The art that has survived was chiefly employed for the decoration of functional objects—buildings, furniture, textiles, caskets, brooches, rune stones, shields (as known from some poems), and so on. Three-dimensional images are rare. But we know that sculpture in the round was produced on both a small and a large scale. We have a few small figures, often gaming-pieces, and there are animal or human heads forming terminals on objects such as strap-ends, harness-bows, chains (pls. 7, 19 and 37), and on the wagon and sledges and other pieces of the Oseberg burial. Written sources also tell us about dragon-heads on ships, and idols in Uppsala's pagan temple.

The motifs were almost exlusively stylised animals and various forms of ribbon interlace. Birds and snakes occur too, but rarely human figures.

Pl. 39   *Gold brooch from Gåbense on Falster: a highly stylised ship. Length 7.3 cm.*

Fig. 48   *Centre: graffiti on a piece of slate from Löddeköpinge in Skåne;*
bottom right: on bone handle from Viborg; the other two: on a piece of
amber from Elsehoved on Fyn. Scale 1:1.

Nor was any particular interest displayed in plant ornament until the mid
tenth century, though it is true that some plant ornament of Frankish or
English inspiration appears on a number of trefoil brooches (ch. 7). But
after about 950 plant motifs become increasingly dominant, in the end
almost taking over from animal ornament. Naturalistic pictures are rare,
and the deeper meaning behind the individual designs is almost always
hidden, even in the case of such important pictures as the great beast on
King Harald's large rune stone at Jelling (pl. 42). We may none the less
delight in the vitality, the imagination, the strength and the perfect craftsmanship in the high quality art.

A few examples of identifiable narrative art have survived—in
Denmark, a scene from mythology, Thor's fishing for the World Serpent
(pl. 33). As we saw in ch. 9, scaldic poems indicate that both shields
and the wooden panels of houses could be decorated with narrative
depictions.[7] There is no evidence in Scandinavia of illustrations of
history (as on the late eleventh-century Bayeux Tapestry) but heroic
legends (especially those concerning Sigurd the Dragon-Slayer) seem to
have been consistently popular.[8] No such Viking Age pictures have been
identified in Denmark, however, and it must be emphasised that the
secure identification of religious, heroic and historical figures depends on
the presence of well-defined and intelligible attributes.[9] Thus there is no
doubt as to the identification of Christ on one face of the large Jelling
stone (pl. 35); he is equipped with a crossed halo. But a triquetra on the
carved wooden figure of a man from the Jelling burial-chamber is not
sufficient basis for identifying it as Christ or any other sacred person.[10]

Casually scratched sketches of ornaments, artefacts and rather im-
pressionistic scenes also exist (fig. 48) and give charming glimpses of
what engaged the carver's mind—often it was ships. They also show that
a more naturalistic mode of expression existed alongside formalised art.[11]
Such graffiti may sometimes represent the working out of a new motif
to be employed in the formalised art.[12]

Most of the surviving decorated objects are in metal: jewellery,
weapons and mounts. But wood must have been preferred for decoration,
though very little of it has survived in Denmark. Chief among the extant
examples are the wooden carvings from the burial-chamber in the Jelling
mound, a walking-stick from Lund (fig. 50) and the wall-plate from the

first church at Hørning (pl. 38). The finds from the Oseberg grave and the carvings in Urnes church (both Norwegian) give some idea of what magnificent works have been lost.[13] Nor have many carvings in bone, antler or ivory survived. The chief pieces are the Cammin casket, destroyed in the Second World War, and the Bamberg casket (pl. 23), which may be of Danish origin.[14] Even fewer textile remains are known, but fragments of figure embroidery from the Mammen grave (fig. 36), and the Oseberg tapestry and others give an impression of what once existed. Other textile fragments found in Denmark reveal the great technical skill that went into their production.[15] Picture stones were virtually unknown in Scandinavia (except on Gotland) before the mid tenth century. The massive Jelling stone, perhaps inspired by English stone-carving, may have started a fashion, for immediately after its erection a number of decorated stones were carved in Denmark. Most are to be found in Skåne (fig. 2), and stones decorated with pictures and ornament were raised in Sweden (and on the Danish island of Bornholm) long after the practice had become unfashionable in Denmark.[16]

Today the colours which originally brightened the now subdued memorial stones have all but vanished. The large Jelling stone must have been painted (though not like the copies in the courtyard of the National Museum in Copenhagen and at the Danish Church in London). Here and on other stones irregularities in the carving could be camouflaged by paint; and text, ornament and pictures could be picked out. It is conceivable that some memorial stones were only painted and not carved at all; obviously these can rarely be identified as memorials today. It is also conceivable that part of the decoration of a stone (such as the text) was painted, while the rest was carved. The Sjellebro stone with the large mask, which has no inscription, and several of the Hunnestad stones may originally have been of this kind. On some Swedish rune stones the carved runes expressly state that the stones were also painted, and traces of paint on stones in Sweden and England show which colours were used and in what combination. One of the best known examples is the stone from St Paul's churchyard in London (pl. 51) from the time of Cnut the Great. In addition, several wooden objects in the Oseberg burial have faint traces of colour, and, in Denmark, colours can be seen on a fragment from the Ladby ship-burial, on the Hørning plank and on wooden carvings in the Jelling burial-chamber—the colours on the small male figure, originally gaudy but now decayed, have recently been reconstructed. Red and black were most common, but there are also examples of blue, brown, yellow and white. Green was also used on the inner side of the Hørning plank.[17] Thus neither stone nor wood was originally left in its natural state, so appealing to many modern eyes. Incidentally, the slightly later granite sculptures in churches were equally brightly coloured.[18]

Sources for understanding Viking Age art in Denmark have an unequal chronological spread. Examples from the rest of Scandinavia have to be included in order to obtain anything like a coherent picture. Stray finds of decorated objects occur in Denmark throughout the Viking Age, but they are concentrated in hoards deposited between *c.* 950 and

1000, and to a lesser extent in the eleventh century. The art of the tenth century is far better represented than that of the preceding hundred and fifty years, partly because of the different burial customs (ch. 9). Pagan burials with grave-goods became less common in the second half of the tenth century, and our knowledge of Viking Age art thereafter depends mainly on pictures on rune stones, on an ever-increasing number of decorated objects from fortresses, towns and other settlements, and on the hoards mentioned above. Just recently, however, well-dated decorated objects have turned up in mid eighth-century contexts, for instance in Ribe (ch. 5). These finds include oval brooches of the so-called Berdal type, previously thought to be of ninth-century date. Thorough studies of the Ribe finds (in progress) will contribute significantly to the classification and dating of early Viking Age art styles, an area with so far only few fixed chronological points.

By the beginning of the Viking Age—perhaps from the mid eighth century or a little earlier—art styles known as E and F were current. Style E is a further development of the earlier Scandinavian animal styles (A–D), and is part of the so-called Salin's Style III. The style is not particularly well represented in Denmark (only eleven finds were known in 1966), and a description of Style E often takes the gilt-bronze mounts from Broa in Gotland as examples. In addition to the gripping beast described below, the following animals appear:

1 An animal with a double-contoured rounded body and a small head often having a lappet, its legs pierced at the hip and intertwining with tendrils around the body; heart-shaped areas often occur where the body's double contours end. The flowing lines of the animals are often broken by a framework which divides the surface of the mounts into fields.

2 An animal or a bird without double contours but otherwise generally similar to the animal described in 1.[19]

Style F is clearly inspired by so-called Anglo-Carolingian art which was cultivated in and disseminated from the Anglo-Saxon missionary areas on the Continent. It belongs especially to the region around the mouth of the Rhine, as well as to present-day South Germany and Switzerland. The most important manifestation of Style F is the Tassilo chalice, produced for the Austrian monastery of Kremsmünster between the years 777 and 788. Genuine Anglo-Carolingian art is beautifully represented on the imported silver cup from Fejø (pl. 24). The inspiration for Style F, which in general has small, compact, articulated animals in compositions covering the surface within delineated fields, may have been imported along the trade-route from the Rhineland to western Denmark so well illustrated by the finds from Ribe's earliest phase (ch. 5). It has been suggested that it was brought by Christian missionaries in the form of mounts on their books, but there is no need to define the source so narrowly. Style F does not seem to have lasted long. It was soon absorbed into the established Scandinavian art.[20]

Styles E and F may have gone out of fashion in Denmark shortly after the year 800, but it is hard to say with any certainty until all the

Pl. 40 *Gripping beast. Enlarged detail of an oval brooch from Lisbjerg near Århus.*

decorated objects attributed to the early Viking Age have been systematically examined. Style E is certainly represented both in the Oseberg grave-goods—the dead woman is thought to have been buried in the first half of the ninth century—and on the Broa mounts from Gotland. Another motif appears on material from both these finds: the lively gripping beasts which at this early stage usually occur *en masse*. These were previously thought to have appeared first around AD 800, but are now known on oval brooches from Ribe that are half a century older. Sometimes the gripping-beast motif in conjunction with Style E motifs are designated 'early Viking Age styles'. Gripping beasts (gripping people also exist) are so called because their feet grip anything in the vicinity: a framing band, a neighbour, or their own body. They are usually plump, with cat-like heads (pl. 40). Their precursors occur in earlier Scandinavian art, and they continue well into the tenth century, in the later phase, however, usually as individual animals. Gripping beasts became immensely popular both in Denmark and in the rest of Scandinavia.[21]

The next Scandinavian art-style is the Borre style, named after a richly furnished grave in Borre in southern Norway, containing decorated gilt-bronze bridle mounts. The style has three main elements:

1 The so-called ring-chain, which consists of a symmetrical pattern of two-strand interlace, bound by rings, enclosing hollow-sided lozenges.
2 A single gripping beast in the form of a comparatively easily distinguished quadruped with a cat- or mask-like face and a ribbon body curving between shoulders and hips (pl. 41); the feet often grip the frame or some other part of the animal itself.
3 Backward-looking animals of fairly normal proportions and with spiral hips and a tail.

This style was developed at the latest by about the mid ninth century and continued until the end of the tenth century.[22] Its motifs are well known in the rich tenth-century Danish finds, executed in gold, silver and bronze. Among the most splendid examples are the silver-inlaid stirrups (pl. 6) from the horseman's grave in Nørre Longelse on Langeland and the silver brooch (pl. 41) from Nonnebakken in Odense.[23]

The Jellinge style is named after a silver cup from the Jelling burial-chamber decorated with a characteristic animal (pl. 36) with a ribbon-

Pl. 41   *Silver brooch with late Borre-style gripping beasts from Nonnebakken in Odense. Scale 1:1.*

shaped, scaly and double-contoured body. In this style the head appears in profile with a small lip lappet, and the animal usually has a small tail. The hip is often marked by a spiral, and the animals are often surrounded by, or intertwined with, ribbon interlace, while leaf-like shoots may branch from their bodies. The style may have evolved in the second half of the ninth century and was certainly in full flower before the middle of the tenth; it had come to an end before AD 1000. Thus for a long time it was contemporary with the Borre style.[24] Among the many outstanding examples of the Jellinge style in Denmark are the two strap-mounts from the grave in Jelling church (one in pl. 37), the harness-bows from Søllested (pl. 7) with gaping animal-head terminals and the sword from Bustorf (fig. 49). The style is also represented on more humble objects such as bronze brooches.[25]

The Mammen style is named after the site where a silver inlaid axe was found, near Viborg in North Jutland (pl. 28). The style obviously develops from the Jellinge style and is sometimes difficult to distinguish from it. But in their characteristic form, the Mammen animals (as on the axe) are far more fleshy than the Jellinge animals and their extremities often develop into solid tendrils—plant elements are important in this style. It is thought by many to have been inspired by the art of southern England, but Ottonian art has also been suggested as the source of inspiration.[26] Several other central examples of this style also come from Denmark: first and foremost the great beast on King Harald's rune stone at Jelling (pl. 42), which was raised between about 960 and 986; the carved wood from the Jelling burial-chamber (earlier than the stone); and the large masks decorating a number of rune stones. In addition, the splendid casket from Bamberg (pl. 23), which is decorated with

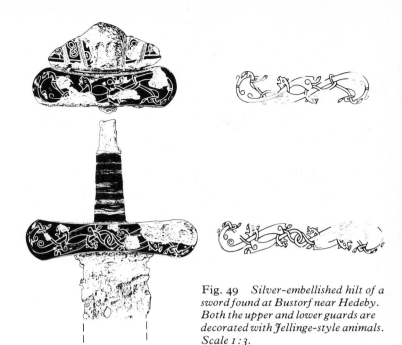

Fig. 49 *Silver-embellished hilt of a sword found at Bustorf near Hedeby. Both the upper and lower guards are decorated with Jellinge-style animals. Scale 1:3.*

50 *Upper part wooden ing-stick from d, with erike-style ment. Scale 1:2.*

animals, birds, plants and masks, may be Danish. A precise dating of the style is difficult, but we are hardly far off if we place it between 950 and 1010.[27]

As already mentioned, the great beast of the Jelling stone apparently set a fashion, and the main motif of the succeeding Ringerike style is a large, substantial animal in vigorous movement. Other motifs are the serpent (also to be seen on the Jelling stone) and finally a mass of elongated tendrils.[28] These motifs are seen together in their classic form on the St Paul's stone (pl. 51), probably raised in memory of one of Cnut the Great's men. Traces of colour survive on the stone, and its inscription in Scandinavian runes refers to people with Scandinavian names. An almost identical though more primitive beast can be seen on a silver brooch from Skåne, and slightly clumsier animals appear on some rune stones in Skåne too (fig. 2).[29] But the style also appears in different form in Denmark, as shown by the animal-head with an immense mane of tendrils on a walking-stick from Lund (fig. 50), a tendril on one of the Skuldelev ships, and the handsome birds on some gilt-bronze drinking-horn mounts from Århus.[30] The style, named after a group of decorated stones in southern Norway made of Ringerike sandstone (from the Oslo area), flourished in the first half of the eleventh century; it probably originated at the end of the tenth. The Ringerike style became so popular in England that it was even used in the illumination of ecclesiastical manuscripts, for it belonged to the age when Danish kings ruled the country and was not very far removed from the contemporary Winchester style.[31]

Pl. 42   *The great beast and the serpent on Harald Bluetooth's rune stone at Jelling, one of the best examples of the Mammen style. The motifs stand out particularly clearly (cf. pl. 35) because the background has been blackened with soot.*

Pl. 43 *Silver brooch in Urnes style from Lindholm Høje. Width 3.2 cm.*

The Urnes style concludes the many centuries of Scandinavian animal ornament. It is named after the magnificent wood-carvings of an older church at Urnes in West Norway, which were reused in the surviving twelfth-century church. These carvings include the characteristic motifs of the style: slim, elegant, rather lethargic quadrupeds, snake-like animals and thin, thread-like interlacing ribbons, sometimes with animal-heads—all writhing around one another and biting one another in elegant confusion. A simpler form of the Urnes style is represented on a number of characteristic brooches which were widely used in Denmark and elsewhere. A workshop for such brooches has even been found, in Lund. One of the most beautiful of all examples of the style is the silver brooch from Lindholm Høje (pl. 43). The animal-head terminals on the gold chain from the island of Orø in North Sjælland, the bone head of a walking-stick from North Jutland, with incised sketches, and not least the Hørning plank (pl. 38) must also be mentioned. The style was developed just before 1050 and remained popular for a century.[32] Reminiscences of it can be seen on the portals and carved ashlar of some of the twelfth-century stone churches,[33] but by then European Romanesque art had the upper hand—no doubt due to strong ecclesiastical influence—and was employed for all important monuments.[34] The Hørning plank itself is in fact transitional, for, while the outer side is decorated with Urnes-style ornament, the inner has painted Romanesque leaf scrolls. Politically and artistically the Viking Age was over.

But the end of the nineteenth and beginning of the twentieth century saw an Indian Summer of Viking art. It inspired the rich animal world which gambolled happily about on Copenhagen's telephone kiosks, allotment cottages and summer-houses, picture-frames, cruets and much else. It was against this revival that Sophus Müller reacted with notable lack of success in his work of 1880.

11 Foreign Contacts

The Vikings' extensive, varied and often dramatic relations with other countries are ever fascinating and a distinctive feature of this period. They are also the main reason why the Viking Age is so popular. The previous chapters refer to numerous contacts between Denmark and other countries as indicated by archaeological finds and written sources. The foreign impact was felt both in the countryside and in the towns, even in everyday household utensils. This chapter gives a more systematic survey of Denmark's relations with other countries, including military and commercial developments, and the settlements in Eastern and Western Europe.

Denmark's foreign relations in the Viking Age must be seen partly against a background of the country's external contacts in the preceding centuries[1]—presumably mostly trade—and partly against a background of that explosive Scandinavian expansion which characterises the period as a whole. In Western Europe, Scandinavian incursions probably began in the last decades of the eighth century. The famous or infamous attack on the monastery of Lindisfarne on 8 June 793 is the first raid about which we are told, but it can hardly have been the first ever made. For in the previous year King Offa of Mercia was already aware of Kent's danger from 'seagoing pagans with roaming ships', and in the year 789 a representative of the king of Wessex had been killed by Vikings.[2] Alcuin of York, who was in charge of Charlemagne's court school in Aachen, commented on the attack on Lindisfarne in a number of letters and wrote among other things:

> Lo, it is nearly 350 years that we and our fathers have inhabited this most lovely land, and never before has such terror appeared in Britain as we have now suffered from a pagan race, nor was it thought that such an inroad from the sea could be made. Behold the church of St Cuthbert spattered with the blood of the priests of God, despoiled of all its ornaments; a place more venerable than all in Britain is given as a prey to pagan peoples.[3]

This raid and various other acts of plunder during the following years in the north and west of the British Isles were most likely the work of roving Norwegians. In the course of the Viking Age, Norwegians colonised Shetland, the Faeroes, the Orkneys, the Hebrides and part of Scotland. They settled Iceland, and from there Greenland was colonised. Norsemen even reached North America. Norwegians were also the protagonists in the Irish adventure, which started with raids and ended with flourishing towns, Ireland's first. In addition, they settled the Isle of Man, and some put down roots in England, chiefly in the north-west. They even provided some tenth-century kings of York. The most important Swedish expansion took place in the coastal regions of the Baltic, where their colonisation was already in full swing before the Viking Age, and in Russia. They acted extensively as traders, but they also mounted raids and some Swedes made permanent homes east of the Baltic. In Russia the Swedes also became political leaders, and their role in the formation of the Russian state has for long been a subject of vigorous debate, often with nationalistic overtones. They reached Byzantium (Constantinople) and many spent some time in the imperial guard, as did other Scandinavians, for example Harald Harðráði ('the Ruthless'), later king of Norway. One Halfdan left his name in runes in Hagia Sophia, the city's grandest church, now a mosque. At home in the North, such military service gave enormous prestige and was commemorated on rune stones. The Swedes no doubt shared the southern shores of the Baltic with the Danes, but otherwise the latter had their chief sphere of interest in the Frankish Empire, including Frisia and Normandy, and in England. Some were active in Ireland, too. Naturally there were also internal connections among the Scandinavian countries.[4]

The specific areas of contact between the individual countries are explained by their geographical locations (fig. 51). From Denmark one could easily and quickly sail both to Eastern and Western Europe and to the Scandinavian mainland. At the same time, east–west passage through Denmark was easy, by ship through Limfjord or overland by way of Hedeby, and the country had common borders with both the western Slavs and the Saxons immediately south of Hedeby (fig. 39).

The sources which deal with the character of Danish foreign affairs and of Danish settlements abroad are very uneven. Nearly all the written sources are West European works and primarily treat the situation in the places where they were written. Military and political affairs loom largest, and since they are naturally seen through the eyes of Western Europe, not Denmark, the accounts are often very biased. Denmark's relations with the rest of Scandinavia and with Eastern Europe, and commercial and other peaceful activities, only very occasionally leave traces in these sources. An exception is missionary activity in Denmark, which of course interested the ecclesiastical writers and which incidentally often had political overtones. Knowledge of Scandinavian settlements abroad, for example, and the nationality of the colonisers is in fact best gained from place-names and in some degree from loan words, as well as from archaeological finds, which become increasingly important sources as they grow in number and are examined in detail. It is this last group of sources which also illustrates the nature of Viking Age trade most clearly.

Nor do written sources always relate from which country a Viking

Fig. 51 *Europe*

army or raiding party came, though no doubt many of them were of mixed nationality. Swedish rune stones, for example, show that Swedes took part in the exploits in England from *c.* 1000 to 1050, usually led by Danes,[5] and there were undoubtedly Swedish traders in England and Frisia, and Danish traders in Russia. It must further be noted that numbers are often exaggerated in the written sources. A reference to 10,371 Danes killed in a battle in Saxony in 884 and to 700 ships at the siege of Paris in AD 885-6 must be taken to mean only that many Danes were killed in the first instance and that they had many ships in the second.[6] The Vikings' paganism and their unfamiliar culture also made them particularly abhorrent to Christian writers, and it is they who have provided us with the conventional modern image of the Vikings. But they were neither better nor worse than their opponents and other robbers and conquerors of their times, apart from their total lack of respect for religious foundations. The age was rough and cruel, and even Christians sometimes plundered churches and monasteries. Taken together, however, the many different sources draw a multi-faceted picture of Viking activity abroad. The aim was profit (through acquisition of easily convertible assets, land, political dominance yielding taxes, and trade) and excitement and fame. Behind this lay their formidable adaptability and their capacity for taking advantage of new situations. Their excellent ships were an important prerequisite.

Foreign relations naturally made an impact on Denmark, for many people went abroad, many returned home, and foreigners also came to Denmark. But information is scanty, and written sources do not tell much about the consequences. We hear a fair amount about fights on the southern border, and some rune stones from around AD 1000 were raised to the memory of men who had been to Norway, Sweden, England, 'northwards', 'eastwards' or 'westwards'.[7] These rune stones mostly refer to contacts of a military nature—as do most of the passages relevant to Danish foreign affairs in West Norse scaldic poems and later Norse literary sources. We do sometimes hear—but only exceptionally—of meetings between kings and leaders (when magnificent gifts were often exchanged), of political refugees in Denmark, of church matters, of the trade links of towns, and—even more exotically—of the impressions the country made on visiting Spanish Arabs. Finally, many archaeological finds in Denmark are evidence of contact with other countries, and these also include objects from the Baltic and Eastern Europe, about which the written sources tell very little. It must be noted here—as often before —that finds from ninth-century hoards and graves are scarce, and much evidence of imports in that period is not to be expected. We have to be cautious in basing conclusions on the absence or scarcity of finds in particular categories, bearing in mind, among other factors, the frequent dearth of systematic investigation of the material that is available.[8] This also applies to coins, which are good indicators of contact because usually their provenance and date can be determined. Furthermore, much of the merchandise traded was perishable or consumable and has seldom left any archaeological trace. This is true of slaves, furs, textiles, wine, agricultural produce—not to mention music, poetry, fashions and so forth.

It can rarely be determined how finds classed as imports (i.e. foreign-made) arrived in Denmark. Mass-produced objects such as soapstone pots and whetstones from Norway, as well as quernstones from the Rhineland, must largely have come by trade, though some may possibly have been paid as taxes, and many of the English coins are no doubt Danegeld and soldiers' wages. But with most other material it must remain open to question whether an object arrived as plunder, Danegeld, tax, gift, souvenir, trade goods, bride-price or dowry, or whatever, and whether it was brought to Denmark by a Dane or a foreigner. The Viking Age was long, and life was varied and turbulent: in explaining objects of foreign origin, allowance must be made for the many complexities of the period. But, irrespective of their character, imported goods reflect some contact with the place of manufacture, whether directly or in-directly, and whether conveyed by Danes or by foreigners, or by both together. It is also indisputable that the many different activities drew enormous riches to the North—all its gold and silver for example—and that they contributed to the internal expansion and consolidation which took place in Scandinavia in the Viking Age.

NORWAY AND SWEDEN

The Scandinavian countries were closely connected. The distances between them were short, in languages and culture they were intimately related, and the variations in natural resources could promote fruitful trading relations between them. But the ambition to dominate one over the other was a frequent factor to reckon with, and neighbourly attacks by land and sea, small-scale and large, were not uncommon. It is often impossible to decide whether an object is a local product or import from another Scandinavian country, because they shared so many common forms and followed the same lines of artistic and technical development. The provenance of certain materials can, however, be determined, and the same applies to a few distinctive jewellery types.

Danish political interest in Norway can be traced back to the beginning of the ninth century. Under the year AD 813, the Frankish annals relate that two Danish kings, co-regents, subdued a revolt in Vestfold, on the western side of Oslo fjord, where, we may note, the trading centre of Kaupang was situated.[9] From time to time, written sources allow us a glimpse of political relations between the two countries in the succeeding period, too. Most famous is Harald Bluetooth's proclamation on the large rune stone at Jelling that he won Norway. But the country slipped from his grasp in the last years of his reign. From about AD 1000 until his death in 1014, his son Svein Forkbeard was master of Norway; and from 1028 to his death in 1035, Svein's son Cnut the Great also held sway over that country. From 1042 to 1047 it was the other way round, for the Norwegian king Magnus the Good was also king of Denmark.[10]

The obvious Danish interest in Norway was undoubtedly prompted by the riches of that country, which included furs, down for eiderdowns and cushions, walrus ivory for carving and walrus hides for ropes, iron, soapstone for pots, and slate for whetstones. Around AD 890, the trader

Ohthere sailed all the way from northern Norway to Hedeby and on the way put in to *Sciringes heal*, probably Kaupang in Vestfold (fig. 51). The virtually imperishable Norwegian products—soapstone vessels and whetstones—appear in vast numbers in Denmark (see ch. 6). Norwegian iron has probably been identified too, and around 1070 Adam of Bremen mentions several different sailing routes between Norway and Denmark.[11] A rune stone at Egå in Jutland was raised in memory of Manni, who was *landhirþir* (estate manager or similar) of Ketill the Norseman,[12] evidence of yet another form of peaceful contact: a Norwegian who owned land in Denmark.

Swedes were geographically closer than Danes to the wonders of the Orient[13] and doubtless often acted as middlemen in the importation of Eastern riches. Like Norway, Sweden itself had a wealth of desirable resources, for example furs and iron, and connections between Sweden and Denmark are mentioned in numerous written sources. For instance, it is related that around 850 the missionary Ansgar carried a letter of recommendation from the Danish king Horik to the Swedish king Olaf in Birka. There is no certain evidence of formal Danish rule over Sweden or Swedish rule over Denmark. It is true that at the beginning of the tenth century a ruling family best known from rune stones near Hedeby (pl. 15) is thought by some to have been of Swedish origin; but it is not certain how much of Denmark they ruled, and their Swedish beginnings have been questioned. Fighting and raiding among Swedes and Danes were not rare, however, and are mentioned, on rune stones for example, both in Denmark and in Sweden.[14] So far, archaeology has been unable to reveal much about contacts between the two countries, other than that they were close. The forms of objects largely correspond. But some distinctive forms existed on Gotland and jewellery from there found its way to Denmark, reflecting contact with that wealthy island. Among the pieces of Gotlandic origin is a magnificent brooch, a so-called box- or drum-shaped brooch, from the richest of the women's graves at Fyrkat. One or two runic inscriptions prove that Danes certainly visited Gotland, and Danish coins and silver jewellery have been found in Gotlandic hoards.[15]

THE EASTERN BALTIC, RUSSIA, THE EAST, BYZANTIUM

The Danes travelled even further east.[16] In the *Life* of Ansgar, mention is made of an unsuccessful Danish foray to Kurland (on the south-east Baltic coast) around 850. It is further related that the area had earlier been under Swedish rule, and evidence confirming this is found in cemeteries excavated at Grobin a little further north (fig. 51). The merchant Wulfstan, who around 890 related how one sailed from Hedeby to Truso, also described conditions among the Estonians. He may thus have sometimes travelled further east. Contacts between the eastern Baltic and Denmark have also left traces in jewellery found in Denmark, for example dress-pins from the decades around 1000.[17]

Contacts further to the east and south-east, with Russia and the Orient, are revealed especially by silver finds. Cufic coins—particularly coins minted in the eastern part of the Caliphate—found their way to the North in vast numbers and are known from many tenth-century Danish silver hoards deposited before c. 970–80. A few hoards containing Cufic coins may well have been hidden away before about 900, but, as we have seen, silver hoards from the ninth century and the beginning of the tenth are for unknown reasons not very numerous in Denmark and rarely contain coins. When the influx of Cufic coins into Scandinavia stopped, c. 970, their place was taken by coins mainly from Western European mints. This change was the result of several factors: the eastern trade-route through Russia gave way to a more westerly one; large silver mines were opened up in the Harz mountains in Germany; Danish campaigns in England gained momentum from about 980.[18]

Altogether nearly 5000 Cufic coins have been found in Denmark (including Skåne, Halland and Blekinge with a total up to 1976 of 1140 pieces).[19] But it was not only minted silver that was imported. It also came in the form of so-called Permian rings: spiral rings with faceted terminals which were produced according to a system of weight. These came from the central Russian districts of Perm and Kirov (Viatka) and occur in Danish hoards deposited between c. 850 and 950. A contemporary variant of this type, with everted terminals, possibly comes from the same area (pl. 44), but is thought by some to be a Scandinavian imitation of the Permian type.[20] Some Eastern silver is no doubt also contained in those pieces of jewellery of Scandinavian manufacture made before c. 970. In an age when one either bartered or paid in silver by weight, it was in many ways practical to keep one's silver in the form of jewellery rather than as coins. It is most likely that the system of payment in silver by weight was ultimately derived from the Islamic world (see ch. 6).

Apart from silver, Eastern Europe and the Orient also furnished luxury goods such as beads of amethyst, rock crystal and carnelian. A quantity of high quality rye from the Fyrkat fortress is probably of East European origin, and pollen grains found elsewhere seem to indicate that Eastern contacts in the Viking Age resulted in the introduction of several plants. Exotic curiosities like glazed pottery eggs from Kiev and pink spindle-whorls of Volhynian slate from the same district also found their way to Denmark.[21] Special mention may be made of a ninth-century lead seal from the Byzantine Empire and of a brooch of similar age made from a Byzantine coin. Both objects were found in Hedeby. To this can doubtless be added most of the silk which reached the North during the Viking Age. Danish coins from the reigns of Harthacnut and Magnus the Good, and especially of their successor Svein Estridsson (1047–74) sometimes show strong Byzantine influence—this also applies to the coins of many other West European countries at this time—and a pair of small bronze brooches from eleventh-century Lund are imitations of Byzantine coins.[22] Slaves and furs were presumably also obtained from the countries to the east of Denmark, but these belong among perishable goods and thus their existence can rarely be demonstrated.

44 *Hoard from Duesminde on Lolland from c. 850–900. It consists of a two-stand gold arm-ring and* *silver spiral rings (ring-money). Among them (centre left) is one with faceted terminals of the so-called* *'ermian' type from central Russia. The other silver rings may also be from Eastern Europe.*

How the riches and curiosities of Eastern Europe and the Orient reached Denmark is open to debate. Was there direct or indirect contact? Eastern traffic has generally been thought to have been the prerogative of the Swedes, but information in written sources suggests otherwise. There is evidence that Danes sailed to Birka, Gotland and Kurland, and around 1070 Adam of Bremen wrote that from Hedeby/Schleswig 'ships usually proceed to Slavia or to Sweden or to Samland, even to Greece'.[23] Given this information, and Denmark's access to the Baltic, it is reasonable to assume that Danes were involved to some extent in Russian commerce and in trade even further south and east, as well as in other sorts of expeditions to these regions. This conclusion may find further support in the eastern imports, which are after all comparable in number with those from England, with which we know from written sources there was close contact. We may also recall the woman buried at Fyrkat with grave-goods that appear to have been gathered from various places on the eastward trade routes and could well be souvenirs. Her small silver toe-rings may also have been an Eastern inspiration.[24] And if some of the beads of semi-precious stone and rock crystal were worked in Scandinavian towns and trading-centres, as has been suggested, then the technique must have been learnt in south-east Europe, or in the East, or from craftsmen who originated there.[25] There must have been some direct contact between Denmark and Eastern and Central Europe and the Orient in the Viking Age—contact which meant not only the import of material goods and luxuries but also knowledge of quite a different world.

THE WEST SLAV AREAS

South of the Baltic—in what is now Poland, East Germany and the north-eastern part of West Germany—lived the West Slav tribes. They were Denmark's neighbours. There was a common border at the base of Jutland, and the Baltic Sea was no barrier (figs. 39 and 51). Right from the beginning of the Viking Age, and no doubt earlier, there were contacts between Scandinavia and these regions. Along the southern shores of the Baltic, a series of trading-posts were founded in the eighth and succeeding centuries, with industry and commerce as major occupations; some of these later developed into towns. They acted as entrepôts for the movement of goods between Scandinavia and the Slav countries, but no doubt they were primarily stations on the network of east–west trade-routes. Several had a Scandinavian element in their populations, buried their dead according to Scandinavian customs, with Scandinavian objects. But the Scandinavians presumably formed only part of a population which was extensively Slav but often of motley origin.[26]

A large silver hoard deposited c. 850 at Ralswiek on Rügen is among the finds which bear witness to distant connections. It consisted of about 2200 whole and fragmentary Arabic coins with a total weight of 2750 g, and one fragment of an arm-ring, a variant of the Permian type described above. Remains of three boats were also found here, and archaeologists have investigated part of the settlement and many graves, some of which were Scandinavian.[27] Another trading-centre which began to operate in the early ninth century, or perhaps already before 800, was at Menzlin, near the mouth of the river Peene. Here are Scandinavian graves placed in ship-settings and Scandinavian objects in the associated settlement.[28] Immediately to the east of this lay Wollin, near the mouth of the river Oder. Wollin was already of great importance in the ninth century, and c. 1070 Adam of Bremen says (no doubt in somewhat exaggerated terms) that the town was the largest in Europe, inhabited by Slav and other tribes, Greeks, barbarians, even Christian Saxons. Perhaps the renowned fortress of Danish Vikings, the Jomsborg of the sagas, was located here—if this fabulous stronghold populated by great

Pl. 45   *Scandinavian gold jewellery from the small island of Hiddensee near Rügen. It belongs to a major find comprising a neck-ring, the large disc brooch, ten cross-shaped pendants and four small pendants, all of gold. The pendants were no doubt part of a large necklace.*

Pl. 46   *The rune stone from Sønder Vissing in central Jutland. Height 245 cm. The inscription reads: 'Tova, Mistive's daughter, and the wife of Harald the Good, son of Gorm, had these memorials (kuml) made after her mother'. Mistive is probably the Slav prince Mistivoj and Harald Gormsson is no doubt Harald Bluetooth. Tova and her mother are not otherwise known.*

warriors ever existed. It is not mentioned in written sources until the late twelfth century, and no archaeological evidence of it is known.[29] Still further east lay Kołbrzeg (Kolberg), which presumably owed its existence to the salt-trade. Truso lay in the Gulf of Danzig, where the Vistula reaches the Baltic. The merchant Wulfstan visited it around AD 890, having sailed for seven days and nights from Hedeby (see ch. 3). The line of coastal trading-posts can be extended eastwards along the Baltic including Wiskiauten and Grobin, already mentioned.

It is difficult to determine whether the Scandinavians who were active in these coastal trading-posts and were buried here were from Denmark or Sweden—as previously stated, the provenance of Scandinavian objects can rarely be identified within Scandinavia, and most likely the people in question were not very conscious of their nationality. But we may certainly guess that some of the Scandinavians who lived in Ralswiek, Menzlin and Wollin, which lie due south of Viking Age Denmark, were people of Danish origin.

Further evidence from Slav regions of contact with Scandinavia comes from various hoards containing Scandinavian jewellery and coins. The most famous is the gold hoard from the small island of Hiddensee near Rügen (pl. 45).[30] But the fortresses of the upper classes, for example Alt Lübeck (near the present Lübeck) have also yielded Scandinavian material,[31] and the contacts were by no means limited to trade.

The earliest Danevirke, from AD 737, was possibly constructed to counter Slav expansion; and when at the end of the eighth century Charlemagne subjugated the Saxons, he acquired dangerous neighbours in both the West Slavs and the Danes. This meant that the Frankish annalists began to take an interest in their new borders and they record many conflicts on the northern marches.[32] The different national groups made shifting alliances and, as the Slavs were divided into several tribes, there were more than three main parties to consider. Such alliances often led to raids on the enemy of the moment, but usually it was the Saxons or Slavs who suffered. Among the most famous expeditions was that of King Godfred in 808, when, in conjunction with a Slav tribe, the Wilze, he harried the land of the Abodrites, also Slav (and allies of Charlemagne), and destroyed the trading-post at Reric (see ch. 5). It must also have been common practice to levy tribute: payments exacted from subjugated peoples are often mentioned.

But not many archaeological finds in Denmark bear evidence of contact with the Slavs until the middle or second half of the tenth century.[33] Then they become numerous and correspond quite well to the written sources. There were political alliances between Slavs and Danes directed against the German Empire, for example in 983, when the border area was reconquered and the allied forces sacked and burned Hamburg. Judging by the inscription on the Sønder Vissing rune stone (pl. 46), Harald Bluetooth was most likely married to the daughter of the Slav prince Mistivoj. Harald's son Svein Forkbeard was later married to a Polish princess who had previously been married to the Swedish king, Erik the Victorious. But there was also strife: Svein Forkbeard is said to have been captured by Slavs more than once and to have been ransomed for huge sums. And after the death of Cnut the Great in 1035 the Slav tribes grew restless and started harrying Denmark. They were repulsed by Magnus the Good (king of Norway from 1035 and of Denmark from 1042 until his death in 1047) in a great battle on Lyrskov Hede in South Jutland.[34]

It is archaeologically demonstrable that from about 970, when the trade-route to the East through Russia was abandoned in favour of a more westerly one, Slav silver jewellery becomes fairly common in Danish hoards. This is particularly true of small items such as beads and ear-rings.[35] The influence of Slav pottery on common East Danish domestic pottery is quite considerable. In addition, there is a certain amount of imported Slav pottery. Contacts with Slav regions may also lie behind such important constructions as bridges, the oldest of which so far found in Denmark are from this very period. Knowledge of Slav fortresses and their function may also have influenced the large Trelleborg-type circular fortresses, and some of the Danevirke's many building phases are no doubt due to threats from the Slav tribes. The location and date of many sea-barriers can also be explained as defences against Slav raids. Finally it may be mentioned that some place-names in the southern Danish islands probably indicate Slav immigration.[36]

THE CONTINENT

Denmark's relations with Western Europe can be far better illustrated than those with the regions discussed above. They are mentioned in numerous written sources, mostly annals (pl. 47), but there are also some relevant narrative sources, including such an important one as the *Life* of Ansgar. Place-names and archaeological finds also provide much information.[37]

At the beginning of the Viking Age there were well-established trade connections between Denmark and the Rhineland. This is especially reflected in the many imports to eighth-century Ribe, and in the art style which has been called Style F (see chs. 5, 6 and 10). Frisia and the Rhineland were not far away, but they were under the dominion of the Franks, and at the end of the eighth century King Charlemagne (crowned emperor in AD 800) also conquered Saxony and so became Denmark's immediate neighbour. This led to border conflicts and persistent Frankish attempts to interfere in Danish affairs—among other reasons, in order to prevent Danish raids on wealthy Frisia.

Frankish attempts to keep Denmark quiet took several forms. There were some military campaigns and threats of more; some political negotiations; an active interest in exiled pretenders to the Danish crown, who were sometimes granted fiefs in Frisia; and finally missionary activity. The most famous missionary was Ansgar, who arrived in the North for the first time in 826 and who visited Denmark and Sweden several times before his death in 865. In Denmark he was granted permission to build a church in each of the two important trading centres, Hedeby and Ribe. Otherwise neither his mission nor the other attempts to infiltrate Denmark met with any great success. The Eider remained

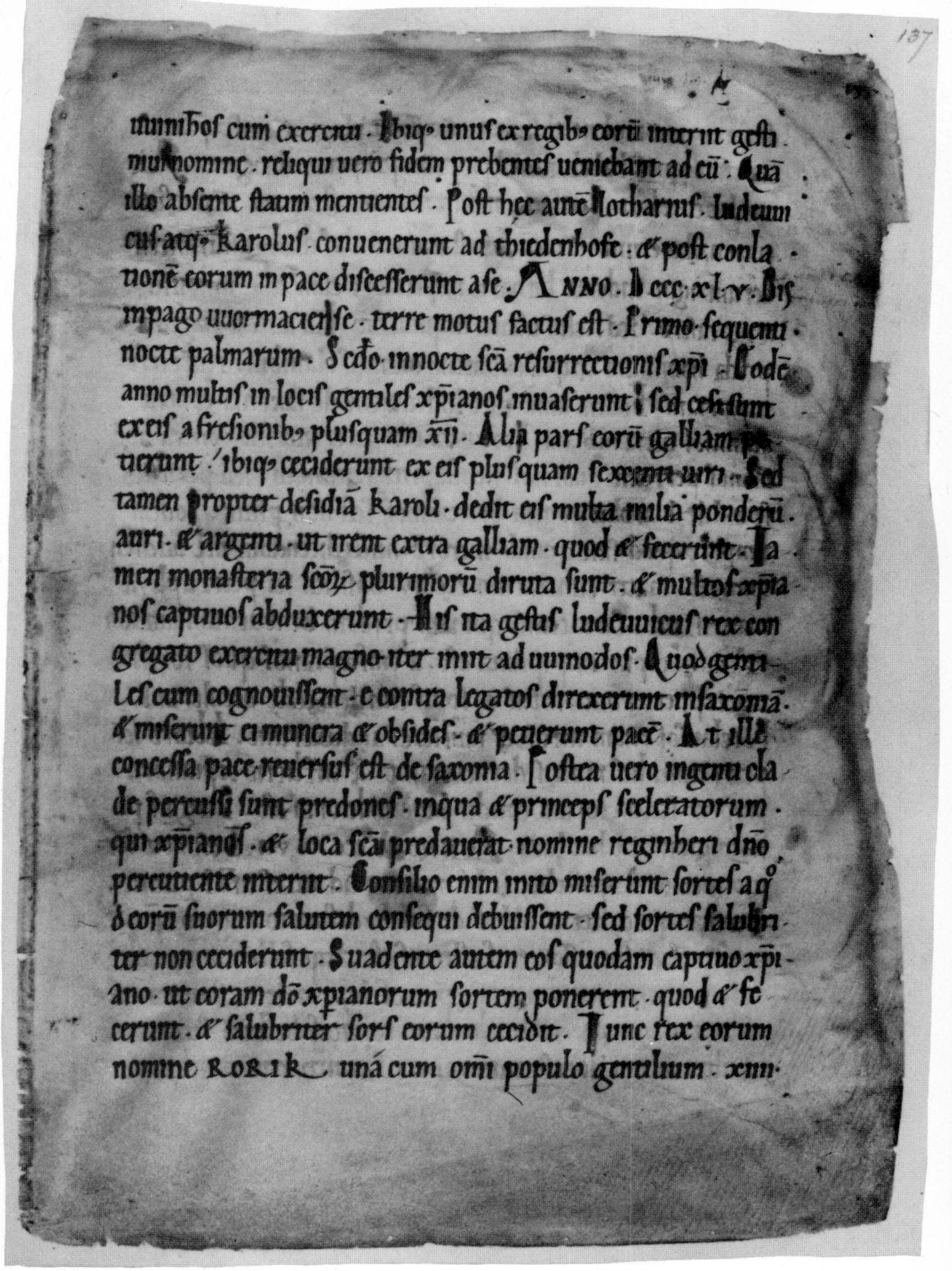

ununihos cum exercitu. Ibiq; unus ex regibz corũ interiit gesti
multnomine. reliqui uero fidem prebentes ueniebant ad eũ: Qua
illo absente statim mentientes. Post hec aũt Hotharius. Ludeuui
cus atq; karolus conuenerunt ad thiedenhofe: & post conla
tione eorum in pace discesserunt a se. ANNO. Dccc xl v. Dis
in pago uuormacien se. terre motus factus est. Primo sequenti
nocte palmarum. Scdo innocte sca resurrectionis xpi. Eodẽ
anno multis in locis gentiles xpianos inuaserunt: sed cesi sunt
ex eis a frehionibz plusquam xii. Alia pars corũ galliam pe
tierunt. Ibiq; ceciderunt ex eis plusquam sexcenti uiri. Sed
tamen propter desidiã karoli. dedit eis multa milia ponderũ.
auri. & argenti. ut irent extra galliam. quod & fecerunt. Ta
men monasteria scõɤ plurimorũ diruta sunt. & multos xpia
nos captiuos abduxerunt. His ita gestis Ludeuuicus rex con
gregato exercitu magno iter init ad uuinodos. Quod gentil
les cum cognouissent. e contra legatos direxerunt in saxonia.
& miserunt ei munera & obsides. & petierunt pacem. Et ille
concessa pace reuersus est de saxonia. Postea uero ingenti cla
de percussi sunt predones. inqua & princeps sceleratorum.
qui xpianos. & loca sca predauerat nomine reginheri dño
percutiente interiit. Consilio enim inito miserunt sortes a q̃
ð corũ suorum salutem consequi debuissent. sed sortes salubri
ter non ceciderunt. Suadente autem eos quodam captiuo xpi
ano. ut coram dõ xpianorum sortem ponerent. quod & fe
cerunt. & salubriter sors eorum cecidit. Tunc rex eorum
nomine RORIK una cum omi populo gentilium. xiiii.

Pl. 47   *One page of* Annales Xantenses *recording events in Western Europe in the year 845,*
among them the Viking attacks on Frisia and France, payment of the Danegeld, plundering
of monasteries and capture of Christians. In addition it is mentioned that a great catastrophe
befell the Vikings which brought about the death of their leader Reginher (Ragnar Loðbrók?).
At the bottom of the page there is a reference to their king, Rorik.

an effective border between Denmark and the Frankish Empire. As we saw in ch. 8, this border was fortified in AD 737 by an immense rampart, the earliest phase of the Danevirke, which may have been directed against the Slavs. But the extension of the Danevirke, initiated by King Godfred in AD 808, was clearly motivated by the conflicts with Charlemagne. He for his part extended the coastal defences of Western Europe, and these functioned more or less as intended in his lifetime (died 814). It is, however, related that a vast Danish fleet harried Frisia in AD 810 and that tribute was paid to it. But in the same year Godfred was killed by one of his own men and his successors made peace with the Emperor.

Subsequently the Franks sought to benefit from struggles for the Danish crown, and in 826 one of the pretenders, Harald Klak, was granted the fief of Rüstringen by the mouth of the Weser. This was conveniently close to Denmark. First Harald had been baptised with the Emperor as godfather, from whom he received munificent christening presents. It was after this that Ansgar travelled to the North. But, a few years later, internal dissension in the Frankish Empire opened the gates to the flood of Viking attacks on Western Europe, and it is clear from the written sources that these raids were very often made by Danes and often led by members of Danish royal families. Sometimes a reigning king instigated them.

Some Viking ships attacked Flanders and the mouth of the Seine in 820 but were repulsed by the coastal defences. In 834, however, Dorestad on the Rhine—one of the most important trading-centres in northern Europe—was sacked and burnt, and in each of the succeeding three years the Vikings enriched themselves in Dorestad and elsewhere in Frisia where the coastal defences were disintegrating. In 838 the Danish king Horik demanded formal recognition of his supremacy in Frisia—refused by the Emperor—and there are accounts of more depredation in Frisia in 839.

The death of Louis the Pious in 840 signalled a further escalation of the raids. His realm was divided between three frequently warring sons, and the Vikings now very successfully extended their activity to present-day France, with incursions into Spain and other Mediterranean countries. From now until the end of the ninth century nearly every year brings its tale of plunder and battle in one or more places, and the whole of the area from Saxony to the Mediterranean was exposed to attack. Large towns by the coast—Dorestad, Quentovic and Rouen for example—were sacked, but the Vikings also sailed far up the rivers. Paris thus suffered several times, and it is related that around 860 a band of Vikings thought they had captured Rome itself. But they were mistaken: it was the small town of Luna in northern Italy. Churches, monasteries, fortresses and country districts also suffered. The first time we hear of Vikings wintering abroad was in 843, on the island of Noirmoutier at the mouth of the Loire. This now became common, and especially in the second half of the ninth century there was frequently co-operation between the Vikings on the Continent and those across the Channel in England and Ireland.

During these years the Vikings exploited Western Europe with skill.

They plundered or let themselves be bought off for huge sums (Dane-geld), and they held prominent captives to ransom. They also acted as mercenaries in the internal struggles of West European countries, or they were hired to fight other Vikings. They held markets too, where no doubt many captives were sold as slaves. In the ninth century, Frisia was granted in fief to several Viking chieftains or kings. Others got land in France, and in 911 Rollo was given Normandy by the French king. This seems to be the only place in Western Europe where Scandinavians settled in any number. Place-names in particular provide evidence of this, and they also reveal that most of Rollo's men were of Danish origin, though some were Norwegian. Rollo himself may have been a Nor-wegian, but that is hard to decide. The most important pointer is that he had a daughter with a Norwegian name.[38] Rollo's family became established in Normandy and quickly lost its Scandinavian character. When his descendant William the Conqueror won the throne of England in 1066, he came as a Norman, not a Northman. The last Danish ruler of Frisia, Godfred, was killed in 885. So, during much of the ninth century, the area had had Danish rulers or had paid tribute to Danes. But it was apparently rather a case of political dominance and economic exploitation than of settlement. As a condition of co-operation with the Frankish rulers and a stipulation in several peace treaties, the Vikings received baptism (and large gifts), but they were far from always loyal to the new faith. Marriages were also arranged between Viking leaders and Frankish princesses.

So far, only a few archaeological traces of the Vikings' movements in Western Europe are known, despite frequent mention in written sources. But, as has been said before, they came to get rather than to give. The undisputed Scandinavian grave-finds are limited to a woman's grave with oval brooches in Pîtres between Rouen and Paris, and a man's grave in a ship on the small Île de Groix, off Brittany's south coast, with furnishings which correspond in character to what is known of Scandinavian boat-graves. Among other finds a gold arm-ring and finger-ring from Dorestad may be mentioned and a number of stray finds of weapons from various places.[39]

The expeditions brought enormous gain to the Vikings. In 866, for example, they received 4,000 pounds of silver in Danegeld; in 884, 12,000 pounds. It has been calculated that, on the Continent, in the course of the ninth century, they were paid 44,250 pounds in bullion, and this figure does not cover those payments whose value was not specifically recorded in the sources.[40] To this must be added income from plunder, the sale of slaves and so on, where we cannot even guess the sums involved. Some of this wealth must have reached Denmark in company with souvenirs of various kinds. It is said that Ragnar, the conqueror of Paris in 845 (perhaps the famous Ragnar Loðbrók, 'Hairy Breeches') returned home with an immense amount of gold and silver—as well as a beam from the famous monastery at St Germain and a bar from the town-gate of Paris![41] But no treasures have been found in Denmark—neither beam nor bar—which directly reflect these activities in Western Europe. The best illustration is perhaps the hoard from Hon in southern

Norway, which contains 2.5 kg of gold and, among other things, objects of Frankish manufacture.[42]

The many plundering onslaughts and other daring incursions no doubt left their mark on Western Europe. They were catastrophic for many of those who were the victims, and they helped to weaken already weak rulers. But Western Europe is a large area, and the forays took place over a long period and (apart from Frisia) were aimed at a variety of targets. Moreover, there is little doubt that the horrors have been exaggerated in the always biased written sources. For example, it sounds incredible that Dorestad could be sacked four years in succession (834–7) and still carry on, to be plundered in 846 and yet again in 857 and 863— even after being formally ceded to the Viking chieftain Rorik, who had conquered it in 850. One wonders whether it was always a case of actual sackings of the town.[43]

The last Danegeld we hear about on the Continent was paid in AD 926 by the West Frankish king Rudolf, and the picture changes with the establishment of a strong German royal and imperial power in the tenth century. The military confrontations with Continental countries were, in the last three quarters of that century, largely limited to battles on the South Danish border, where the Germans were victorious on several occasions. At the same time, the Christian church again sought to obtain a foothold in Denmark, but when around 960 Harald Bluetooth 'made the Danes Christian' it was presumably as part of his own policies (ch. 9). We know of three important border wars.[44] In 934 the German king, Henry the Fowler, undertook an expedition against the Danes who had raided Frisia. According to the German sources, he was victorious, made the Danes pay tribute and forced their king to be baptised, but we do not know if the defeat had further consequences for the Danes. In 968 it is recorded that a war against the Danes was imminent, and dendrochronological analysis of timber from the Danevirke seems to indicate that the rampart was extended enormously by the Danes at this very time. But it was not until 974 that fighting took place here. The Germans defeated Harald Bluetooth and his allies, but again nothing is known about further consequences of the German victory, apart from the fact that the Germans built a fortress 'in those border areas and secured it with a garrison'. Immediately after the death of Emperor Otto II in 983, the fortress was captured by the Danes and the soldiers were killed.[45] Thenceforth, for the rest of the Viking Age, there was peace on the Danish–German border and Cnut the Great made a formal agreement with Emperor Conrad recognising the Eider as the border between the two countries. The peace was sealed by the arrangement of a marriage between Conrad's son Henry and Cnut's daughter Gunhild/Kunigunde.[46]

So far we have chiefly been concerned with political and military confrontations and missions, and trade has only been mentioned in passing. But it is evident from many sources that there was no stagnation in commerce in these apparently very unsettled years. Towns were founded and flourished in Denmark as elsewhere, and the most important Danish towns, Ribe and Hedeby for example, had Saxon and Frisian

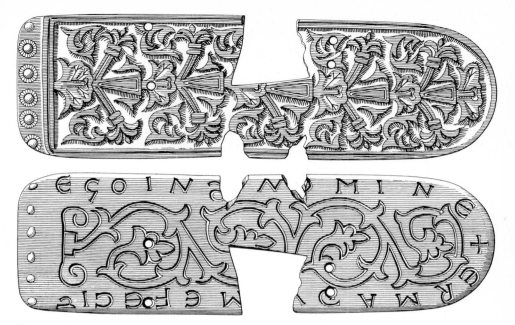

Fig. 52   *Frankish strap-end, silver-gilt and niello, found on Als. The four drilled holes show that it was altered to form a brooch. The Latin inscription on the reverse tells that the maker of the strap-end was Ermadus. It is probably from c. AD 800. Length 12.7 cm.*

connections. Dorestad is expressly mentioned as a trading partner of Hedeby, and an annal entry for 873 reports that King Sigfred of Denmark and King Louis the German agreed to secure the peace in their border districts so that merchants might travel to and fro, and trade in peace.[47] The evident Danish interest in Frisia was undoubtedly also due to its importance for trade. Domination of Frisian trade meant access to sought-after merchandise and duties levied on trade goods. Furthermore, the Scandinavians themselves traded in Western Europe with ordinary commodities, and with slaves and goods obtained in raids, spending the gold and silver they exacted as terrorists, won as robbers or earned as mercenaries.

Contacts with Western Europe have left many kinds of traces in Denmark.[48] Danes learnt to use sails on ships just before the start of the Viking Age and to use the mould-board plough probably in the Viking Age itself. The earliest towns, Ribe and Hedeby, must have been mainly founded on trade with Western Europe, and their organisation and administration may well have been inspired from there too. The earliest Scandinavian coins from around AD 800 or a little later (fig. 22) were struck on Carolingian patterns, probably in Hedeby, and a multitude of objects from Western Europe found their way to Denmark and have survived: quernstones (pl. 17), pottery, glass beakers, large silver cups (pl. 24), wine-barrels which can scarcely have been empty on arrival, weapons, silver mounts for scabbards and straps, many of which were fashioned into women's jewellery (fig. 52), buckles, and glass for the manufacture of beads. Undoubtedly we may also add much of the silver and gold used for Scandinavian-style jewellery—it may be noted at this point that, in spite of the large payments of precious metals from the West, there are only a few Western coins in Denmark and the rest of Scandinavia before the end of the tenth century. Western styles and the forms of Western objects were also influential on everyday Danish manu-factures. Women's trefoil brooches (pl. 26) were inspired by Frankish scabbard mounts, and West European globular pots (fig. 33) became popular in West Denmark in the late Viking Age. Style F was inspired by the so-called Anglo-Carolingian art of Central and Western Europe, and the plant ornament seen on a number of trefoil brooches probably derived from the same geographical area as the prototypes of the brooches. Christianity was introduced in part from the south and naturally made its mark in several spheres. The ideas of the Danish kings regarding their rights and duties and the way they exercised their power were in all probability also influenced by a knowledge of West European conditions.

In general the various relations with continental Western Europe made a considerable impression on Viking Age Denmark. What has been mentioned here is naturally only the tip of the iceberg, but even so it is not inconsiderable. The Danevirke was a defence against political and military domination from the South, but its mighty ramparts did not impede other forms of contact.

THE BRITISH ISLES

The great Viking ventures in the British Isles were just as varied as those on the Continent. The Danes were particularly active in England, but some of them went to Ireland too. On the other hand, as far as we know, they were not particularly interested in the Isle of Man, Scotland and the Atlantic islands. Those were in the orbit of Norwegian interest and it was Norwegians, too, who were chiefly responsible for the raids and settlements in Ireland. But we cannot always distinguish between Norwegian and Danish enterprises, and, as already mentioned, divisions on national lines were not always very clear-cut. It is also often uncertain whether a group of Vikings in the British Isles came from some other British area or from the Continent, or straight from home.[49]

Apart from the fleeting references to attacks on south-east England just around the year 800, mentioned in the introduction to this chapter, it is not until 835, the year after the first recorded sack of Dorestad in Frisia, that the Vikings appear in the written sources which tell of raids in England. But after this date they can be followed round the country almost year by year right up to 896. The chief source is the Anglo-Saxon Chronicle.[50] England was at the time divided into several kingdoms, of which the most important were Wessex, East Anglia, Mercia, and Northumbria with York as its capital. Only Wessex was able to keep out the Vikings.

At first the Danish expeditions took the form of occasional assaults, but in 850/51 the Vikings wintered in England and this became a regular occurrence. The first payment of Danegeld we hear of was in 864,[51] and events began to gather momentum in 865 when 'a great heathen host' arrived. The leaders were said to be sons of the legendary Ragnar Loðbrók: Ivar the Boneless, Halfdan and Ubbe, and the next year York was conquered and an Anglo-Saxon puppet king installed there. In the following years the army took control of the whole of eastern England apart from Wessex. According to the Anglo-Saxon Chronicle, 876 was the year when settlement began: 'In this year Halfdan divided the land of the Northumbrians and they were engaged in ploughing and making a living for themselves'. The next year the army shared out part of the kingdom of Mercia, and in 879 it was East Anglia's turn. The leader of this third group of Vikings, King Guthrum, had concluded peace with King Alfred the Great of Wessex (871–99) and was baptised along with thirty of his men in 878. But Guthrum soon broke the peace, after which another treaty was concluded, whose text survives. This fixed the border between independent Wessex and the independent part of Mercia on the one hand, and the Vikings' land on the other: in other words, it established the extent of the Danelaw.[52] In 892 a new Viking army came from the Continent. But King Alfred's defences were well organised on land with fortresses and a standing army, and at sea with ships built especially for combat with Viking ships, so this second army did not achieve anything spectacular. In 896 the army split up, some going to East Anglia, some to Northumbria, and a third group, those 'that were moneyless' (or without possessions), returned to the Continent to the Seine.[53]

All these events would have been forgotten but for records of them in written sources. They have left only sparse archaeological evidence. Some of the most important are a series of English coin-hoards, which are particularly numerous in the years of unrest after 865. In addition there are some possible traces of fire and other destruction,[54] and perhaps of defensive works built by the Vikings wintering in Repton 874–5 (ch. 8).

The successors of Alfred the Great worked with deliberation to unite England. Step by step the various kingdoms accepted the sovereignty of the kings of Wessex, who consolidated their power with fortresses and understood the need for local autonomy. In York, the last Scandinavian king, Eric Bloodaxe, was expelled and killed in 954. The English assumption of power here was facilitated by the fact that the kingdom had been in the hands of a series of frequently changing kings, who often had ambitious dreams of ruling both York and the Irish Viking colonies, especially Dublin. Several kings of York also came from Ireland and legitimised their claims by tracing descent from Ivar, one of the leaders of the 'great heathen host' of 865.

The Vikings in Ireland had begun by following the usual pattern: scattered raids were succeeded in the 840s by campaigns from fortified winter camps, and at this point the Danes started to assert themselves alongside the Norwegians. One of these camps was Dublin, which quickly developed into a permanent settlement. In the nineteenth century a large Viking burial-ground was found there, containing both

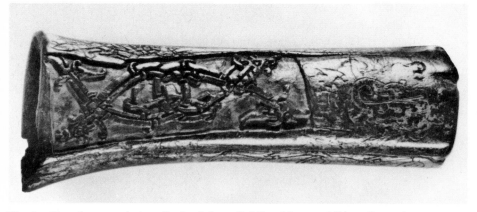

Pl. 48 *Bone fragment (a 'motif-piece') from Dublin with carved Ringerike-style ornament. Length 11.6 cm.*

men's and women's graves of this period.[55] But in 902 the Irish expelled the Scandinavians from Dublin. It may have been one of those who left then to settle in Scotland, the Isle of Man and north-west England, who hid away the enormous hoard of about 40 kg of silver which was found in its lead chest on a river-bank at Cuerdale, Lancashire, in 1840.[56]

Raids on Ireland were soon resumed, however, and many of the high round stone towers in Ireland were probably built as a defence against Vikings. Dublin was quickly reconquered, and eventually developed into a flourishing town with extensive trade connections. Around AD 997, King Sigtrygg Silkbeard had coins struck in the town. So Vikings struck Ireland's first coins, in the same way as they created the camps that became Ireland's first towns.[57] Dublin was at times under Danish/ Norwegian, at times under Irish, rulers but the Scandinavian influence was paramount. The recent excavations in Dublin have done much to reveal its Scandinavian character. Scandinavian house-types, jewellery and runic inscriptions have all been found, and the Ringerike and Urnes art styles were evidently extremely popular and employed by local craftsmen (pl. 48).[58] They even came to be used to decorate objects for churches and monasteries elsewhere in Ireland, and flourished there longer than in their countries of origin.[59] In Dublin, Norse was still spoken when Ireland was conquered by Normans from England in 1170.

Besides Dublin, the Vikings founded the towns of Wicklow, Arklow, Wexford, Waterford, Cork, Limerick and perhaps others. They became immensely rich—a little of their wealth is preserved in the many Irish gold and silver hoards of this period.[60] They appeared on the Irish scene as townspeople, traders and pirates, and they kept largely to the coastal regions. Only a few concerned themselves with farming, and they do not appear to have been interested in supremacy over the whole island— that was the business of the Irish. The two peoples complemented each other and in many ways got on well together.

To return to England: the consequences of the major conquests—the settlements—are hardly ever mentioned in written sources. But they have left many traces in place-names (especially names of settlements with the suffix -by, e.g. Grimsby, and with the suffix -thorp, e.g. Gunthorpe) and also in personal names, loan words into English and archaeological finds. During recent years there has been much discussion about the interpretation of these varied sources, but new research has thrown light on many obscure points[61] such as naming practices and land distribution, and excavations in York and Lincoln in particular now also reveal much of the conditions in the largest Danelaw towns.

The many Scandinavian and partly Scandinavian place-names are probably mainly due to an extensive redistribution of land carried out by the conquering Vikings. Huge estates—among them much of the land which had once belonged to the monastery at Lindisfarne—were divided into smaller units, which were henceforth owned and mostly named and cultivated by a large number of Scandinavians, for the army was probably supplemented by farmers from home. The great number of Scandinavian loan words in English, particularly relating to agricultural matters, and the many field-names with Scandinavian elements, seem to indicate this too. Place-names also allow us to distinguish between Danish and Norwegian settlement areas. The former are chiefly in the eastern part of the Danelaw, the others chiefly in north-west England, including the Isle of Man.[62] But we know virtually nothing so far of how Viking farms and estates were run in England, or of how they looked (cf. ch. 4). Only one or two farms thought to be Scandinavian have been excavated; the farm at Ribblehead in Yorkshire certainly dates from the time when Halfdan shared out the lands of the Northumbrians.[63]

All in all, there are only few archaeological finds which can illuminate the circumstances of rural Vikings. Stray finds of single objects cannot tell us much, but there are some graves with grave-goods in the traditional pagan pattern. These are few in number, partly because most ninth-century Danish Viking graves are rather simple and not easily discovered in any case (cf. ch. 9), and partly because the Vikings in England quite quickly became Christian or partly Christian and were buried in churchyards. A number of Viking graves have indeed been found in churchyards, even though we cannot expect to find many in such places because the ground has been dug over repeatedly in the last thousand years. But when the Vikings arrived they were pagan, and several of the kings who assumed power in York were also pagan. Pictures of Thor's hammer on coins struck in this town, stone sculptures, place-names and written sources all help to illuminate aspects of the religion of the Vikings.[64]

Almost all stone sculpture showing Scandinavian influence[65] is found in churchyards and in churches (often in villages with old Anglo-Saxon names), and it is obviously Christian, even though we occasionally glimpse pagan elements. For example, one of the best depictions of the god Thor's famous fishing expedition is found on a stone in Gosforth church in Cumberland (Cumbria). Most of the sculptures are house-shaped tombstones (hogbacks) and crosses, which may often have flanked the former. The hogbacks probably also reveal something of the appearance of Viking houses in England (pl. 49). They are named after their curved roof-ridges, which was a characteristic of many Scandina-

Pl. 49　*Three house-shaped tombstones (hogbacks) from Brompton church in Yorkshire. It is not clear what the muzzled bears signify. The stone in the foreground is 128 cm long.*

vian houses of the period. Similarly, their outward-curving sides reflect the bowed walls of contemporary houses (cf. figs. 14 and 42). These features are also known in Anglo-Saxon building tradition, however.[66] The house-shaped tombstones and the crosses occur almost exclusively in the North of England, and are often decorated in the Scandinavian or Anglo-Scandinavian Borre, Jellinge or Mammen styles. Most are presumably tenth century, and, as corresponding memorials of this period are unknown in Scandinavia, the types were probably created in the Viking colonies of the North of England. With a few exceptions, the most beautifully executed sculptures come from towns, particularly York, which must have had highly skilled stone-carvers. The rural sculptures are often crude (and very charming), such as a cross from Middleton, Yorkshire. On one face a pixie-like warrior is depicted surrounded by his weapons; on the other face is a sleepy-looking Jellinge-style animal. Many of these sculptures were apparently produced by village craftsmen, whom we can frequently follow from place to place, as they used templates for pictures and ornaments.[67]

The Vikings based their power on fortified towns or fortresses. The most famous ones are York and the 'Five Boroughs': Lincoln, Nottingham, Derby, Leicester and Stamford—in York and Lincoln they could make use of, and possibly extend, walls which went back to Roman times. During the Viking Age towns emerged and flourished in the Danelaw just as in the rest of England: parts of the present town plans in York and Lincoln probably originate in this period. By the end of the ninth century, Viking rulers in the Danelaw were already minting coins, often with interesting representations of Thor's hammers, weapons, standards, birds and so on. As implied by its name, the Danelaw also had its own characteristics in the field of law.[68]

The excavations in Viking Age York[69] and Lincoln[70] have yielded much information about craft techniques and trade, and also (in York) about dwellings and workshops. So far not many Scandinavian-type objects have been found in Lincoln, but York became strongly Scandinavian. Many street-names still remind us of the town's Viking Age, for example Coppergate, the street (Old Norse *gata*) of bowl-makers (Old Norse *koppari*, workers of vessels called *koppr*). Nordic personal names are known in plenty, and the archaeological finds include many objects in pure Scandinavian fashion—many were in all probability manufactured in the town (pl. 50). But eventually a mixed Anglo-Scandinavian culture developed in the Danelaw, expressed in stone sculpture, for example, and in decorative objects such as strap-ends and jewellery. One of the most interesting finds in the last category is also from York: a mould for a trefoil brooch with unique ornament.[71]

England was large and wealthy, and the Vikings were ready to take advantage when fighting broke out after the murder of King Edward in 978 and the assumption of power by his brother Æthelred.[72] In the years 980–2 and again in 988 the Anglo-Saxon Chronicle tells of raids in several parts of the country, and in 991 the Norwegian Olaf Tryggvason arrived with ninety-three ships and raided until he was bought off with a Danegeld of 10,000 pounds of silver. After this, England was harried almost every year until 1013, when the Danish king Svein Forkbeard took over the whole country in a lightning attack. In many ways the course of events followed the well-known pattern. In 994 Olaf

Pl. 50 *Left: lead object found in York. Centre: silver pendant from the Tolstrup hoard in North Jutland, deposited* c. AD 1000. *Right: bronze die from Hedeby. The last was used for production of jewellery in the same style as that from Tolstrup and Hiddensee (pl. 45). The object from York is most likely also associated with the manufacture of such jewellery. Scale 1 : 1.*

[217]

and Svein appeared jointly and were paid 16,000 pounds of silver in Danegeld, after which Olaf, who was apparently already baptised, was confirmed and received gifts (Svein had been brought up as some sort of Christian), and promised never again to visit England as an enemy. He even showed his good intention by sailing away—evidently somewhat to the chronicler's surprise—back to Norway where he was accepted as king, undoubtedly much assisted by his English silver. After some time the Vikings, who were chiefly Danes, started wintering in England, and some of them temporarily served as mercenaries under King Æthelred. Others won loot and Danegeld, immense sums of which went out of the country.

Shortly after the conquest of England, Svein Forkbeard died and the army sailed home to Denmark. But in 1015 his son Cnut returned and in 1016 became king of England. He married Æthelred's widow, Emma of Normandy, and in 1018, after his brother Harald's death, he also became king of Denmark. He succeeded so well in the monarchy that in both countries he was called 'the Great'. Cnut spent most of his time in England, however. He died in 1035 and was succeeded by one of his sons by Ælfgifu of Northampton, and later by his son by Emma, Harthacnut, who was also king of Denmark until his death in 1042. Both he and his parents were buried in Winchester Cathedral, and the bones of Cnut and Emma now lie mixed with those of other English kings and bishops in two caskets in the chancel of the present cathedral. Cnut the Great and Harthacnut were also the two first Danish kings, and Emma the first Danish queen, to be depicted in contemporary manuscripts. These two manuscripts were produced respectively in Winchester and St Omer on the Flanders border. But we do not know how far the pictures present a likeness.[73] Harthacnut was succeeded in England by Edward the Confessor, Emma's last son by Æthelred, and in 1051 he finally abolished the tax which had financed Scandinavian mercenaries ever since the time of Cnut the Great.

The Danish kings and the Scandinavian aristocracy who accompanied them to England were instrumental in promoting Danish art and culture whose influence now made itself felt in the South of England too. The Ringerike style was used to decorate objects produced here—most splendidly on the rune-inscribed and painted grave-stone from St Paul's churchyard in London (pl. 51). The style was even used for the illumination of sacred books. Although Danish supremacy ended in 1042, several examples of the succeeding Scandinavian style, the Urnes style, are known in both the North and the South of England—it is even to be seen on a crozier which may have belonged to the Norman bishop Flambard (died 1128).[74]

Svein and Cnut's conquest of England did not, however, entail any large-scale immigration, and it is characteristic that most of the objects which display Scandinavian associations (including a few from Winchester) belonged to the aristocracy. Among the Winchester finds are a silver-gilt strap-end, a beautifully worked mount for a (?)casket, a fragment of rune stone, a beautifully executed grave-stone in the Anglo-Saxon fashion but mentioning people with Scandinavian names,

Pl. 51 *Grave-slab in Ringerike style from St Paul's churchyard in London. It probably commemorates one of the many who accompanied Cnut the Great to England. The stone has faint traces of colour and along the edge an inscription in Scandinavian runes which reads: 'Ginna had this stone laid and Toki'. Width 56 cm.*

and a picture stone from the Old Minster, now demolished, which was in use during the reigns of Cnut the Great and Harthacnut. The stone was part of a frieze and probably depicts a scene from *Vǫlsunga saga* (the episode dealing with Sigmund and the wolf). A fascinating suggestion has been made that the frieze was put up at the command of Cnut, who wished to demonstrate his legitimate claim to the throne of England through its pictures: they showed that the common root of the Danish and English royal families was to be found, naturally, in the great heroes of the past.[75]

Some Vikings settled in England and Ireland, but others returned home with their loot. Many more evidently came from Denmark to join the conquerors when they heard of land to be had in England in the 870s and 880s. Women went too. Otherwise we would not have found Scandinavian women's jewellery in graves in the British Isles, and the parallel development of art in Scandinavia and in northern England,

Ireland and southern England—in that order—presupposes lasting contact. It is also likely that some Scandinavian craftsmen were active in the British Isles. In addition, family ties must have caused traffic back and forth across the North Sea. After all, the distance was not great. We can also assume general trading between Denmark and England, though there is not much actual evidence of it. But around 890 the merchants Ohthere and Wulfstan both visited Hedeby and afterwards went on to visit King Alfred (see ch. 3), and around AD 1000 it was recorded that York was brimming with wealth belonging to merchants, most of whom were Danish. Written sources also seem to indicate that there was considerable Danish trade with London, and around 1070 Adam of Bremen wrote that ships were going from Ribe to England.[76]

In Denmark there are only few archaeological traces of connections with England and Ireland until we reach the time of the great campaigns around AD 1000 and the period of joint rule. The older finds consist mainly of some coins and some Hiberno-Scottish and English ornamental mounts. A large bronze bowl from the horseman's grave at Nørre Longelse on Langeland and a silver bowl from Lejre are among the most splendid items. Mention should also be made of some silver arm-rings of a type occurring mainly in Denmark and Ireland, an Anglo-Scandinavian strap-end produced in England and a comb with the Englishman's name HIKUIN incised in Scandinavian runes.[77]

The comparatively few objects from the period of the early attacks and settlements—particularly the scarcity of coins—have led some people to believe that there was no communication back to Denmark from England and Ireland.[78] Far more objects from the British Isles (though not coins) have been found in Norway.[79] But quite a lot of gold and silver was undoubtedly melted down. Again, we also have to consider ninth-century burial-customs in Denmark and the paucity of hoards, and we may even have to take into account the mundane possibility that people in Denmark did not much care for English and Irish objects. The future excavation of settlements will doubtless produce more material, and an improved knowledge and analysis of Anglo-Scandinavian types will permit more certain conclusions.

From the 990s onwards, we have substantial evidence of contacts both ways across the North Sea, both from archaeological finds—though mostly coins—and from written sources. Large numbers of English coins reached Denmark in the 990s and the first half of the eleventh century, and some have survived—though not nearly as many as in Sweden. Many of these coins must either be Danegeld or wages for the Scandinavian guard, which, as mentioned above, was not dissolved until 1051. Svein Forkbeard was the first to strike coins along English lines, and Cnut the Great and Harthacnut followed his lead and issued an extensive coinage; in this period the country became accustomed to paying with coins instead of with silver by weight. Incidentally, the moneyers were often English, and it is likely that the association with England also played a part in the development of eleventh-century Danish towns.

Among objects from this period either coming from or associated with England are remains of two English swords with ornamented silver hilts, found in Skåne, a pair of stirrups from Velds in Jutland, and four Danish rune stones raised to commemorate men who had been in England or died there. There are also various items from Lund, among them the lid of a pen-case and probably a quantity of glazed pottery sherds.[80]

The first Danish stone churches were most likely built by Anglo-Saxon craftsmen or master-builders in Roskilde, and English bishops were installed in several Danish dioceses. Generally, English church practices were very influential. The Ringerike style was presumably subject to English influence, and written sources tell of journeys made between Denmark and England. There is no doubt that Viking Age connections with England, not least those of the period of joint rule, were very significant in Denmark—in many more ways than those mentioned here.[81]

Nor did the death of Harthacnut entail the severance of connections between the two countries or the relinquishing of Danish hopes of the English throne. In Denmark, English ecclesiastical influence continued,[82] and in England many people were conscious of their Scandinavian origins. In 1069–70, Svein Estridsson (ruled 1047–74) and members of his family supported a large northern English revolt against William the Conqueror. The rebellion was crushed, however, and large parts of the North of England were systematically ravaged and plundered.[83] In 1085, Svein's son Cnut (ruled 1080–86) made a last attempt to conquer England as his namesake had done seventy years earlier. But the result was different. When the Danish fleet gathered in Limfjord, the king was engaged on the southern border, and consequently the ships returned home in the late summer. The fines which King Cnut levied for this offence were the chief cause of a revolt against him in the following year. He was killed in St Alban's church, Odense, and was canonised soon after. He became, not a great Viking king, but Denmark's first royal saint, and lies in his shrine in the crypt of Odense Cathedral. The Viking Age was over.

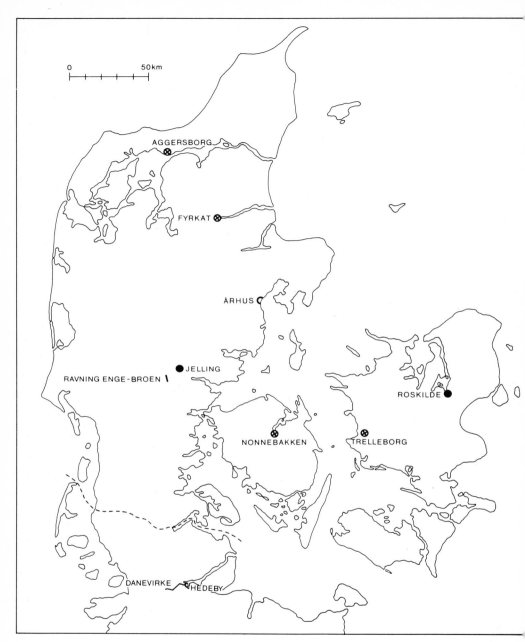

Fig. 53   *Royal building-works of the tenth century: the bridge at Ravning Enge (fig. 11, pls. 10–11), town defences at Hedeby and Århus (pls. 13 and 16), extension of the Danevirke (fig. 39, pl. 30), four circular fortresses (fig. 40–2, pl. 31), the Jelling monuments (pls. 34–5) and Roskilde Cathedral's earliest predecessor. Possibly all the work of Harald Bluetooth.*

12 Conclusion

The Viking Age saw both an immense expansion from Denmark and a rapid development within the country. At the end of the period, Denmark functioned in essential respects very differently from at the beginning. The same applies to the rest of Scandinavia, but Denmark with its central position between east and west and as Scandinavia's most southerly country was often first to receive innovations.

Towns and their fortifications are among the most important innovations in Denmark, as are royal fortresses, native coinage, Christianity, the Latin script, stone buildings and probably also ploughs and bridges. Much land was reclaimed for agriculture, and at the end of the Viking Age, or shortly after, the sites of villages became fixed: many present-day villages were founded at this time. Trade expanded greatly, and in addition to luxury goods it now included everyday commodities, and imports travelled far to reach farms and villages. The late Viking Age certainly had specialised ships with holds for cargoes. Payment with silver by weight—and gradually also with coins—was increasingly used instead of bartering. Some craftsmen were highly specialised, and the art of writing in runes became quite widespread.

At the end of the period, the king had considerable formal rights and duties which were extended in succeeding centuries. They had no doubt also developed during the Viking Age, but this cannot be traced, since the sources only afford glimpses. Two kings, however, emerge distinctly both in archaeology and in written sources. These are Godfred around AD 800 and Harald Bluetooth about a hundred and fifty years later. There is only very sporadic information about the activities of other kings, and then only in written sources. This is so until the beginning of the eleventh century, and for the remainder of the Viking Age in Denmark the only archaeological evidence of kings is provided by coins.

The many constructions which can be attributed, more or less certainly, to King Harald (fig. 53) imply a far stronger monarchy than has hitherto been thought to have existed in the tenth century. But Godfred's activities, too, imply great power, and Denmark was by then in all likelihood already one realm under one king. So Harald's constructions and his other exploits hardly reflect the initial formation of the kingdom —unless perhaps they were part of a reunification of the realm after a period of disunity. It is still not known precisely what Harald meant by his proclamation on the great Jelling stone 'won all Denmark for himself'. Incidentally, both Godfred and Harald were murdered—perhaps as a reaction to their exercise of power, which may have been linked to them as individuals rather than to the office of king. The monuments they raised and their other activities cannot as yet be connected with any continuous political development, but they show that some kings possessed considerable power. They also form part of the background to the ninth-century raids and settlements abroad, as well as to the expeditions of Svein Forkbeard and to his, and Cnut's slightly later, conquest of England. They give us an impression of Denmark's potential and demonstrate that, ever since the beginning of the Viking Age, the Danes had mastered the organisation of large-scale projects.

Scandinavian culture had its own modes of expression in many fields. But all through the Viking Age close connections with other countries resulted in strong influence, especially from Western Europe. These influences clearly played a large part in the development of society; and in religion and decorative art they gradually took over. By the end of the Viking Age, Denmark had in many respects become part of Europe.

Nor was it difficult for a Viking to be accepted in Western Europe, once he had become a Christian. Viking chieftains could be granted fiefs and marry the highest-ranking daughters of princes—Christian Vikings do not seem to have been considered barbarians by their contemporaries. The most notable example of this is Cnut the Great, who was accepted as king of all England and even married the former queen; later his daughter was married to the son of the German emperor. It is indeed remarkable that he was successful as king of Denmark as well as England. It emphasises the fact that the son of the Viking king Svein Forkbeard was well informed and well educated, and that Danish society of about AD 1000 was not fundamentally different from English. Cnut became one of the great monarchs of the past and is very far removed from the traditional image of the Viking as a barbaric and dirty pirate, unkempt and wild.

Danish society in the Viking Age was a civilised society with its own roots. But it was in the process of vigorous development and had close contacts with other societies as widely different as Western Europe, the Slav areas south of the Baltic, and the rest of Scandinavia. Its expansion is only one aspect of these contacts. It is, however, one of the most dramatic and has left permanent traces both at home and abroad. It would indeed be interesting to know why it began and why it succeeded. But, as is the case with most historical phenomena, the actual background is complex, and moreover the sources are few and scattered. Thus no clear and simple answer can be given, but behind the waves of expansion there was obviously a search for something which could be more easily obtained abroad than at home. Nor is it certain that the ninth-century raids and settlements had quite the same background as the expeditions around the year 1000 and the political domination of England. The early raids can be explained in part as an offshoot of that movement which led to the expansion of Denmark's agricultural land, with its simultaneous increase in population. But we can only hazard a guess as to whether the impulses were in fact new agricultural possibilities, because of new crops, new methods of cultivation and new agricultural systems, or improved outlets abroad, or climatic improvement. Westward raids may have been resumed at the end of the tenth century because of the need to replace the Arab silver which until then had flowed into Scandinavia. Specific political circumstances following the successful revolt against Harald Bluetooth may also have played a part.

Underlying the expansion in all its aspects (expeditions, settlements and political domination) may be a general social instability created by a dynamic society lying between east and west, north and south. In conjunction with a prosperity and a familiarity with different social systems, this situation had accustomed the Danes and other Scandinavians to exploiting possibilities as they arose in rather untraditional ways, and it also enabled them to adapt readily to completely new conditions in new countries.

The Vikings possessed the practical tools: good weapons and excellent ships, and the organisational ability. Their thorough knowledge of many other countries told them when and where opportunities existed. Their energy and enterprise made them quick to exploit every advantage.

List of
Dates

c. 737 The first Danevirke constructed.

700s Ribe founded; Hedeby founded (*Südsiedlung*).

789 Vikings kill royal representative on Wessex coast.

793 Lindisfarne monastery plundered.

804 Confrontation between Denmark under Godfred and the Frankish Empire under Charlemagne. Hedeby (Sliesthorp) mentioned for the first time.

808 King Godfred ravages the land of the Slav Abodrites, destroys the trading-centre of Reric, which paid tax to him, and takes its merchants with him. Arrives at Hedeby (Sliesthorp) and orders the raising of a mighty border rampart (Kovirke?).

c. 800–25 First Scandinavian coins struck, probably at Hedeby. Re-founding of Hedeby with organised town-plan.

810 Expedition to Frisia which pays a large tribute. Godfred killed by one of his followers. His successor, Hemming, concludes peace with Charlemagne.

812 Hemming dies. Strife follows.

813 The Danish joint kings Harald and Reginfred put down uprisings in Vestfold (west side of Oslo fjord).

813–54 Reign of Horik the Older.

815 Frankish armed expedition against South Jutland to support Harald, pretender to the throne.

817 Danish-Slav armed expedition on Holstein and the fortress Esesfelth.

820 Vikings attack Flanders and other coastal areas of Western Europe.

821 Harald obtains part rule in Denmark.

826 Harald and his family and followers are baptised at court of Emperor Louis the Pious near Mainz. Rüstringen is conferred on him in fief. The missionary Ansgar accompanies Harald to Denmark.

827 Harald expelled from Denmark.

828 Harald raids Denmark. The Danish kings (including Horik) raid Holstein.

834–*c.* 900 Frisia, Utrecht and Dorestad are attacked 834. From then on, Danes plunder in Western Europe nearly every year until *c.* 900.

835–96 First recorded Danish raids on England (Sheppey) 835. From then on, plundering almost every year until 896.

838 King Horik demands from Emperor Louis overlordship of Frisia and the land of the Abodrites.

843 First recorded wintering of Viking troops on the Continent (Noirmoutier at mouth of Loire).

840s Vikings construct fortified bases for wintering in Ireland.

845 Hamburg plundered. Paris conquered. Settlement in France?

850 Rorik gets Dorestad and other regions in fief. Godfred plunders the Seine area and is given land for settlement. King Horik shares the kingdom with two nephews.

c. 850 King Horik the Older gives Ansgar permission to build a church and have a priest at Hedeby. Danish expedition to Kurland.

850/51 First wintering in England.

854 Horik the Older killed. Horik the Younger becomes king.

855 Rorik takes control of part of Denmark but is later driven out.

c. 860 King Horik the Younger gives Ansgar permission to have a priest and a church at Hedeby again and to build a church and have a priest at Ribe (first mention).

864 Payment of first Danegeld in England.

865 A 'great heathen army' arrives in England.

866 York conquered; in next few years, large parts of eastern England raided and conquered.

873 Agreement between King Sigfred of Denmark and Louis the German about peace in border regions for trading purposes.

876 Halfdan shares out the land of the Northumbrians amongst his followers.

877 Part of Mercia shared out.

879 Guthrum shares out East Anglia amongst his followers.

885 Godfred, who held Frisia in fief, killed.

885–6 Great siege of Paris.

c. 890 Ohthere and Wulfstan tell King Alfred of Wessex about their travels.

892–6 A great Viking army from the Continent operates in England. In 896 many return to area round Seine.

902 Scandinavians driven out of Dublin but soon return.

911 Normandy conferred on Rollo by French king.

926 Payment of last recorded Danegeld on Continent.

934 After a Danish expedition to Frisia, the Danish king is conquered by the German king Henry the Fowler and is baptised.

c. 935/45 Gorm the Old, king of Denmark, dies.

c. 935/45–*c.* 986 Reign of Harald Bluetooth.

948 Hedeby (Schleswig), Ribe and Århus mentioned as bishoprics (Århus mentioned for first time).

954 Last Scandinavian king, the Norwegian Eric Bloodaxe, expelled from York by the English king.

940s–c. 1000 Jelling monuments raised. Temporary Danish supremacy over Norway. Hedeby fortified. Århus fortified some time in tenth century. Danish coins produced in greater quantities than before. Harald Bluetooth probably has the first precursor of Roskilde Cathedral erected.

c. 960 Harald Bluetooth introduces Christianity to Denmark.

965 Hedeby (Schleswig), Ribe and Århus mentioned again as bishoprics.

c. 968 Building on Danevirke: the Great Wall probably erected. German Empire expects imminent battle.

974 Harald Bluetooth is defeated at Danevirke.

c. 970–80 Stream of Cufic coins to North ceases. Among foreign coins, Western European coins dominate from now on.

c. 979 Bridge over Ravning Enge erected.

980–90 Sporadic Viking raids on England.

980–1 Trelleborg constructed. Fyrkat, Nonnebakken and Aggersborg also probably built around this time.

983 Capture of German fortress established in 974 against Danes in border area. Together with Mistivoj, the Slav prince, the Danes carry out raids on Holstein and burn Hamburg.

c. 986 Svein Forkbeard's revolt against Harald Bluetooth. Death of Harald.

c. 986–1014 Reign of Svein Forkbeard.

988 Hedeby (Schleswig), Ribe, Århus and Odense mentioned as bishoprics (Odense mentioned for first time).

991 Olaf Tryggvason's expedition to England. Large payment of Danegeld.

992–1013 Danish raids on England nearly every year and many large Danegeld payments. Svein Forkbeard involved on occasions, first with Olaf Tryggvason in 994. Frequent winterings in England.

990s English influence on Danish coinage begins.

c. AD 1000 Temporary Danish supremacy over Norway once more.

1013 Svein Forkbeard conquers England.

1014 Svein Forkbeard dies. The army sails home again.

1014–18 Harald, son of Svein, is king of Denmark.

1015 Cnut the Great sails to England.

1016–35 Cnut the Great is king of England.

1018–35 Cnut the Great is king of Denmark.

c. 1000–35 Odinkar the Younger is bishop of Ribe; see consists of Jutland with exception of the Schleswig bishopric. Successor is Vale of Viborg.

c. 1020 Roskilde becomes a bishopric.

c. 1030–40 Cnut's sister Estrid has first stone church in Scandinavia built around 1030. Around AD 1040 St Clement's Church (now St Jørgensbjerg) erected, built of stone in Anglo-Saxon style. Both in Roskilde.

1000–50 Alborg, Viborg, Ringsted, Slagelse and Lund mentioned for first time, on coins. Lund probably founded around AD 1000. Many Danish coins struck; payment with coins now more common than with silver by weight. Both coinage and ecclesiastical life strongly influenced by England; influence of English Church continues.

c. 1030 Norway conquered. Border treaty with German Empire. Marriage treaty between Henry, heir to German throne, and Cnut's daughter Kunigunde/Gunhild.

1035–42 Harthacnut is king of Denmark.

1040–2 Harthacnut is king of England. On his death, Danish overlordship of England ceases.

1042–7 Magnus the Good of Norway is also king of Denmark. Slavs conquered at Lyrskov Hede in South Jutland.

1047–74 Svein Estridsson is king of Denmark.

c. 1050 Schleswig flourishes as Hedeby declines. Lund (or part) levelled and a large stave church erected.

1051 Edward the Confessor abolishes the tax which had financed Scandinavian mercenaries since time of Cnut the Great.

c. 1060 Denmark's Church reorganised with major division into dioceses.

1066 William the Conqueror takes England.

1069–70 Great revolt against William in the north of England, supported by Denmark, but fails.

c. 1070 Adam of Bremen's description of the North.

1074–80 Harald Hen is king of Denmark.

1080–6 St Cnut is king of Denmark.

1085 St Cnut's deed of gift to St Lawrence's Church, Lund: Denmark's oldest known document. Cnut's planned raid on England abandoned.

1086 Revolt against St Cnut, who is killed in St Alban's Church, Odense.

Notes

Chapter 2: The Country and the People

1 Summaries in Christensen 1969, pp. 25ff.; *idem* 1977, p. 225; Lund 1980. The sources: see especially *Quellen zur Karolingischen Reichsgeschichte* I (the Frankish annals; excerpts in Danish in Albrectsen 1976; English translation until AD 829 in *Carolingian Chronicles*); *Quellen des 9. und 11. Jahrhunderts . . .* (the *Life* of Ansgar); Sweet ed. 1883, pp. 19f. (the *Orosius* of King Alfred); Rydberg ed. 1877, no. 23 (the border-treaty between Denmark and Sweden).
2 Christensen 1969, pp. 30ff.
3 See e.g. *Danmarks Natur* I.
4 The figures are from *Gyldendals Tibinds Leksikon*: 'Danmark'.
5 Mertz 1924. Voss, Müller-Wille and Raabe 1973, pp. 61ff. (Langballigau); Strand Petersen 1975; cf. Roesdahl 1980 (the Limfjord area); Crumlin-Pedersen 1978 (Roskilde fjord).
6 See Strömberg 1961, I, pp. 190ff; Wulff Andersen 1979.
7 cf. *Danmarks Natur* I, pp. 432ff; Berglund 1969.
8 Criticism of Adam's description, see for example Levin Nielsen 1978, pp. 14ff. (on the description of Jutland); Lund 1980.
9 Adam of Bremen IV: 1–8, *et passim*.
10 Eckstein 1977 (Hedeby); Bartholin in Mårtensson ed. 1976, pp. 145ff; Bartholin 1978; *idem* 1979 (especially on Lund). The conclusions follow Bartholin's.
11 On the quantity of timber used in the Viking fortresses, see Jessen in Nørlund 1948, pp. 163ff; Wagner in Roesdahl 1977a, pp. 209ff.
12 Bartholin 1979.
13 Bartholin, *op. cit.* in n. 10.
14 Aaby 1974. The difficulties of establishing what Denmark's climate was like in defined historical periods such as the Viking Age have been strongly emphasized by Bent Aaby of *Danmarks Geologiske Undersøgelser*, in a lecture given on 28 November 1979 at Moesgård and in conversations. Cf. ch. 4, n. 23.
15 Jensen 1979, p. 189 (presumably on the basis of Christensen 1938, pp. 46ff).
16 Schaefer 1963, pp. 180f; Helmuth 1977 (Hedeby); Brøndsted 1936, pp. 224ff; Nørlund 1948, p. 112; Gilberg in Skaarup 1976, pp. 220ff (present-day Denmark); Persson in Mårtensson ed. 1976, pp. 171ff (Lund).
17 Schaefer 1963, p. 181.
18 *Statistisk Årbog* 1978, p. 43; cf. Helmuth 1977, p. 48.
19 Skaarup 1976, pp. 56ff, 224ff; skull shapes are discussed in Steffensen, 1953.
20 Nørlund 1948, pp. 112ff; Schaefer 1963, pp. 205ff; Jacobsen in Skaarup 1976, p. 228; Helmuth 1977. On other diseases see Schaefer, *loc. cit.*; Helmuth 1977.
21 *loc. cit.* in ch. 8, nn. 2–3.
22 Nørlund 1948, pp. 112ff; Schaefer 1963, pp. 211ff; Gilberg in Skaarup 1976, pp. 220ff; Jacobsen in Skaarup 1976, pp. 228ff; Persson in Mårtensson ed. 1976, p. 171; Roesdahl 1976, p. 40 and fig. 15; Helmuth 1977, pp. 46f and *passim*.
23 Foote and Wilson 1970, pp. 92ff; *KLNM* XI, 'Lægekunst', 'Lægemidler'. Cf. Helmuth 1977 (including an example of amputation and of possible trepanning).
24 Helbæk on Olsen and Schmidt 1977, p. 36; Roesdahl 1977a, p. 143.
25 Leuner 1968; Foote and Wilson 1970, pp. 403f; *KLNM* XV, 'Sejd'.
26 Hald 1971 with references; *idem* 1974 with references; Knudsen *et al.* ed. 1940–64; Jacobsen and Moltke 1941–2, Text col. 526ff; Moltke 1976, pp. 281ff; *KLNM* XIII, 'Personnavn'.
27 Compare for example Moltke 1976, pp. 23f; Moltke and Lund 1977, p. 201f; Liestøl 1971; *idem* 1973; *KLNM* XIV, 'Runer', with references.
28 The figure comes from Jacobsen and Moltke 1941–2, Text col. 1041f, supplemented with information from Moltke 1976, pp. 408ff, and from Stocklund and Moltke 1978.
29 Liestøl 1971; *idem* 1973. On the Bergen inscriptions, see Liestøl 1968.
30 Here following Liestøl 1973, p. 108. cf. *Quellen des 9. und 11. Jahrhunderts . . .*, pp. 42f. Thanks to Peter Foote for comments on the translation of *deformatis*.
31 Liestøl 1971, p. 77.
32 All the runic inscriptions of Viking Age Denmark known before 1976 were published in Jacobsen and Moltke 1941–2, and in Moltke 1976. These two works are the main source for the inscriptions and interpretations given here. But cf. *op. cit.* in n. 29, and *KLNM* XIV, 'Runer', 'Runinskrifter', 'Runemagi', 'Runemønter', with references. For St Cnut's deed of gift see *Diplomatarium Danicum*, ser. 1, vol. 2, no. 21; Christensen 1977, pp. 248f.
33 For general surveys see especially Christensen 1969, *passim*; Moltke 1976, pp. 147ff, 233ff; Skovgaard-Petersen 1977, *passim*; Lund 1980.

All contain bibliographical references.

34 H. Andersen 1960, pp. 26ff; Skaarup 1976, pp. 56ff; cf. Ramskou 1963–5.

35 Moltke 1976, pp. 258f.

36 A number of sources concerning slaves are collected in Sørensen 1978, pp. 90ff. See also Lund 1980; *KLNM* XIX, 'Træl'.

37 *loc. cit.* in n. 33; Christensen 1977, p. 225. A rather less military interpretation of the terms *þegn* and *dreng* can be found in Foote and Wilson 1970, pp. 100ff.

38 Moltke 1976, pp. 182f, 233ff.

39 Jacobsen and Moltke 1941–2, Text col. 767ff, *passim*; Moltke 1976, pp. 233ff.; Lund 1980; cf. Moltke and Lund 1977.

40 Jacob 1927, p. 29; Birkeland 1954, pp. 103f (at-Tartuschi, cf. n. 41); Jacob 1927, pp. 37ff; Birkeland 1954, pp. 83ff (Al-Gazal in Ibn Dihya; there is some doubt about the historicity of this account, see Birkeland 1954, p. 153, n. 1a).

41 Translation after Birkeland 1954, pp. 103f. at-Tartuschi's account is included in Al-Qazwini's *The Countries' Monuments and Information about the People* compiled in the mid thirteenth century (Birkeland 1954, p. 101). The account is translated into German and printed with a commentary in Jacob 1927, p. 29. Birkeland translated the text into Norwegian after Arabic editions (and probably with an eye on Jacob's translation). Hægstad 1964 has raised doubts as to whether the town described is Hedeby. He prefers to think it was a Slav town but his arguments are not convincing.

42 Adam of Bremen, IV: 6.

43 Foote and Wilson 1970, p. 326.

Chapter 3: Transport and Communications

1 Brøgger and Shetelig 1950; Grieg 1928, pp. 3ff.

2 Olsen and Crumlin-Pedersen 1967; *idem* 1969.

3 *Encomium Emmae Reginae*, pp. 18ff.; cf. also *ibid.*, Appendix Va, pp. 94ff (translated into English by Campbell).

4 Foote 1978.

5 *KLNM* XV, 'Skibstyper'.

6 *ibid.*; Malmer 1966, pp. 60ff, p. 340, pls. 1, 33, 34; Moltke 1976, p. 216; Ohlsson 1975–6, fig. 81.

7 For Viking ships in general, see the following works with references: *op. cit.* in n. 5; Christensen 1972; Crumlin-Pedersen 1968, 1972, 1977a.

8 See for example Moltke 1976, p. 216.

9 *KLNM* XIV, 'Rigg'.

10 Thorvildsen 1961; Crumlin-Pedersen 1972a; Müller-Wille 1976b, fig. 50 with references; Mårtensson ed. 1976, pp. 135ff.

11 Thorvildsen 1957; cf. Crumlin-Pedersen 1969, p. 29; Müller-Wille 1976b, p. 27.

12 Müller-Wille 1976b.

13 Crumlin-Pedersen 1969.

14 *op. cit.* in n. 2; Crumlin-Pedersen 1968, 1972, 1977a, 1978 *passim*. The C-14 dates given are uncalibrated.

15 Crumlin-Pedersen 1977b, pp. 174f.

16 Crumlin-Pedersen 1960.

17 Thorvildsen 1957, pp. 42f. (Ladby); Bencard and Stief Aistrup 1979 (Ribe); for the dating of Ribe cf. Bendixen 1978.

18 Nørlund 1935, pl. 9.

19 Crumlin-Pedersen, for example 1972 and 1978; *op. cit.* in n. 5.

20 Olsen and Crumlin-Pedersen 1967, pp. 153ff; 1969, pp. 129ff.

21 *KLNM* XV, 'Skibstyper', col. 486.

22 Müller-Wille 1978a, pl. 7:12. A ship's prow, corresponding to the reconstructed prow of the Oseberg ship (Munksgaard 1968), is incised on a piece of amber from Fyn, see fig. 48.

23 cf. also Müller-Wille 1978a, pp. 64f.

24 Malmer 1966, pl. 1; Moltke 1976, p. 216; Brøndsted 1936, fig. 116.

25 *op. cit.* in n. 9; Crumlin-Pedersen 1968, p. 34; *idem* 1975a; *idem* 1977a, p. 7. Håsum 1974 argues that the ships did not sail particularly well.

26 Foote and Wilson 1970, pp. 232ff with references.

27 Crumlin-Pedersen 1975a; *idem* 1978, p. 49; *Vikingeskibshallens Bådelaug* 1980.

28 Sweet ed. 1883, p. 19.

29 *ibid.* See Neugebauer 1968 for the identification of Truso.

30 Marcus 1953; Binns 1968; Foote and Wilson 1970, pp. 255f. Cf. Ramskou 1969.

31 Hingst and Kersten 1955; Crumlin-Pedersen 1969, p. 7; cf. e.g. Schietzel 1975, pl. 2. The 1979 excavation was kindly shown me by Kurt Schietzel.

32 Ambrosiani *et al.* 1973; Blindheim 1969.

33 Ramskou 1960a; *Museumsmagasinet* 1978: 6–3; cf. *KLNM* XII, 'Naust'.

34 cf. Steenstrup 1876, pp. 355ff; Schledermann 1974.

35 Stiesdal 1960; *idem* 1964; new research, 1977, by Tage E. Christiansen (unpublished).

36 Tauber 1966, p. 113. According to information kindly sent by Henrik Tauber, the calibrated date is 815 ± 100 years.

37 Adam of Bremen, for example IV: 1, 3, 4, 6.

38 'Ice-legs' are very common in Viking period finds, see for example Nørlund 1948, p. 135; Blomqvist and Mårtensson 1963, pp. 207f; Andersen, Crabb and Madsen 1971, pp. 141f; Mårtensson ed. 1976, pp. 383ff; Bender-Jørgensen and Skov 1978, p. 35. Ferrules for spiked sticks have been identified at Lund, see Blomqvist and Mårtensson 1963, p. 208; Mårtensson ed. 1976, p. 385.

39 Reproduced in Mårtensson ed. 1976, fig. 336; MacGregor 1976, fig. 2.

40 MacGregor 1976. Here he dismisses the theory put forward in several places that some 'ice-legs' were in fact implements for smoothing textiles.

41 Blomqvist and Mårtensson 1963, pp. 166f; Mårtensson ed. 1976, p. 386; cf. la Cour 1961, pp. 217f.

42 *KLNM* XV, 'Skidor'.

43 Grieg 1928, pp. 33ff; 212ff.

44 Nørlund 1948, pp. 134f; Mårtensson ed. 1976, p. 385.

45 Berg 1935.

46 Brøndsted 1936, p. 219 and *passim*; Thorvildsen 1957, pp. 56ff; Müller-Wille 1976a, pp. 27ff with references; *idem* 1977a. A saddle is said to have been found at Elisenhof near Tønning. For saddles in Norway, see Petersen 1951, p. 39.

47 Petersen 1951, pp. 32ff; Callmer 1973–4, pp. 282ff. He dismisses the traditional identification of an object from Vendel grave XIV as a stirrup and in this agrees with White jr. 1964 (p. 24 and n. 5).

48 *op. cit.* in n. 47; cf. Stein 1967, p. 85.
49 Nørlund 1948, pp. 133f.
50 *op. cit.* in n. 46 and 47; Almgren 1963, pp. 234ff.
51 See for example Andersen, Crabb and Madsen 1971, p. 217; Müller-Wille 1973, pp. 30ff.
52 Horseshoes from Hedeby: Müller-Wille 1973, p. 32; shoes from Lund: Blomqvist and Mårtensson 1963, pp. 166, 276; a fragment has also turned up in association with the Risby road which was built about AD 1000 (Schou Jørgensen 1977a, p. 50). It must be mentioned that a horseshoe is thought to have come from a horseman's grave in South Schleswig, which has not been professionally examined. (Müller-Wille 1977a, catalogue no. 16, and pl. 6:13).
53 Nørlund 1948, p. 134.
54 *op. cit.* in n. 50.
55 *op. cit.* in n. 46; Laursen 1970.
56 Brøndsted 1936, no. 33; Wilson 1964, pp. 44, 47, 50, pl. 9.
57 For example Blomqvist and Mårtensson 1963, pp. 164ff; Nørlund 1948, pp. 133f.
58 Grieg 1928, pp. 3ff.
59 Schou Jørgensen 1977a, p. 46, and figs. 8, 11; Nielsen 1977, p. 62 and fig. 2; Ramskou 1960b, p. 25.
60 Schou Jørgensen 1977a, p. 46 and fig. 10; Nielsen 1977, p. 62.
61 Dyggve 1942a, p. 71. There are probably more fragments of wagons from the Jelling mounds, cf. Kornerup 1875, p. 13.
62 Müller-Wille 1976a, pp. 13ff, 44ff; Wagner 1976; Roesdahl 1977a, pp. 131ff.
63 Brøndsted 1936, nos. 79 and 80 with references; Wulff, Andersen and Hatting 1978 with references; Müller-Wille 1974a.
64 Brøndsted 1936, nos. 34, 79, and 80 with references; Müller-Wille 1974b. A similar mount, but smaller and probably used on a saddle or on a light vehicle or sledge, has been found in Skåne. It belongs to a group with distribution in Norway and Sweden, see Strömberg 1964–5.
65 cf. Müller-Wille 1974b, p. 145.
66 Müller-Wille 1976a, p. 45; *KLNM* XIX, 'Vagn'.
67 Schou Jørgensen 1977a, Ramskou 1977; Olsen and Schmidt 1977, p. 64; Marseen 1959, fig. 16.
68 Albrectsen 1976, p. 16; *Carolingian Chronicles*, p. 89; *Quellen zur Karolingischen Reichsgeschichte* I, pp. 88f.
69 Roesdahl 1978.
70 Dyggve 1964, fig. 20 and p. 35; Andersen 1977, p. 32; the complete list of the many wooden finds from Hedeby has been kindly shown me by K. Schietzel. Cf. *KLNM* XVIII, 'Trillebør'. I saw similar hand-barrows in use in 1977 in the middle of Leningrad.
71 Illustrated in Madsen 1977, p. 15. The block in question has elsewhere been interpreted as part of a loom (Grenander Nyberg 1977).
72 Blomqvist and Mårtensson 1963, p. 200 and figs. 227–9; Mårtensson 1968; Liebgott 1978c.
73 General remarks, see Wittendorff 1973, pp. 56ff; Bredsdorff 1973; Hansen and Nielsen 1977. For the situation in the late Roman Iron Age, see also Schou Jørgensen *et al.* 1978, pp. 74ff.
74 Schou Jørgensen 1977a; *idem* 1977b with references; Hansen and Nielsen 1977; Mogens

Schou Jørgensen has kindly given me information about a Viking-period roadway excavated in the summer of 1979 and also about a possible bridge over Halleby river in western Sjælland. It is also possible that the embankment at Pine Mølle near Trelleborg represents a roadway (Christiansen *et al.* forthcoming).
75 Hansen and Nielsen 1977, pp. 106f (*Varpelev*: C-14 datings from three samples, conventional AD 980 ± 100, AD 1030 ± 100, AD 1040 ± 100); Schou Jørgensen 1977a; *idem* 1977b (*Risby*: C-14 dating from one sample, conventional AD 910 ± 75, calibrated AD 960 ± 75; in addition a number of C-14 datings of stratigraphically both older and more recent levels); Ramskou 1977 (*Ravning Enge*: dendrochronology gives 979 ± *c.* 2 years; there are corresponding C-14 dates); Schou Jørgensen 1979 (*Falgård*: C-14 datings from two samples, conventional 950 ± 55 years, 960 ± 70 years; calibrated AD 990 and 1000). My thanks to Mogens Schou Jørgensen for much helpful information about the construction of these bridges; see also n. 74.
76 Nørlund 1948, pp. 33f, p. 65.
77 Schuldt 1975; *RGA* 3, 'Brücke', pp. 578ff.
78 Schou Jørgensen 1977a; *idem* 1977b; Mogens Schou Jørgensen has kindly given me a list of all the C-14 dates for the constructions mentioned here.
79 Similar sledges for the transport of heavy objects are known from more recent times (Berg 1935, pp. 74ff, pl. xx:1 and fig. 31).
80 Ramskou 1977.
81 Wilson 1978a; Brooks 1971.
82 Christensen 1978, pp. 275ff, gives a short survey of the situation in medieval Denmark from the thirteenth century onwards; cf. Abitz 1950, pp. 84ff, 125ff.
83 Matthiessen 1930, pp. 68ff; Wittendorff 1973, pp. 32ff, 298ff; Lidegård 1977, pp. 43ff.
84 Skovgaard-Petersen 1977, pp. 133ff; cf. ch. 5.
85 Moltke 1976, pp. 332f, with references.
86 *ibid.*, p. 206 and *passim*.
87 Matthiessen 1930, pp. 75ff.
88 Jansson 1962, pp. 85ff; Olsen 1941, p. 192ff.
89 Adam of Bremen, IV:1 and 5; Kaalund 1913, pp. 54, 64ff, 94ff.

Chapter 4: Settlement and Survival

1 Hald 1965.
2 e.g. Skovgaard-Petersen 1977, pp. 73ff.
3 e.g. Christensen 1969, pp. 36ff.
4 The problem is discussed in Becker 1975; Grøngård Jeppesen 1977; *idem* 1978a; *idem* 1979a; *idem* 1979b.
5 Steensberg 1952; Steensberg *et al.* 1968; Steensberg and Østergaard-Christensen 1974. A survey in Steensberg 1973. As far as I know, no objects have been found in any of these settlements to justify a Viking Age date. cf. Finds List 1 (see n. 8).
6 Grøngård Jeppesen 1978a; *idem* 1979a; *idem* 1979b, with references. The investigations have been carried out as part of the project 'The origin and development of the village (on Fyn)' led by Torben Grøngård Jeppesen and Erland Porsmose Christensen.
7 Stoumann 1977; *idem* 1978, *idem* 1979 (Sædding); Skov 1972–3; Bender Jørgensen and Skov 1978 (Trabjerg); Hvass 1976; *idem* 1977a; *idem* 1977b; *idem* 1979a; *idem* 1979b (Vorbasse);

L. C. Nielsen 1976; *idem* 1977 (Omgård). The work has been carried out with large grants from *Det arkæologiske bopladsudvalg* of the Danish Research Council for the Humanities, chairman C. J. Becker. A survey by C. J. Becker will be published in *Proceedings of the Eighth Viking Congress, Århus 1977* (ed. H. Bekker-Nielsen, P. Foote and O. Olsen), Odense 1981.

8 See Finds List 1, p. 249f.

9 Grøngård Jeppesen 1979b; Grøngård Jeppesen and Thrane 1978; Stoumann 1979. Niels H. Andersen of Moesgård has kindly informed me that traces of settlement have been discovered near Århus by the same method. However, as such evidence is rarely published and can only be given a date somewhere between about AD 700 and AD 1100, this has not been marked on the map, fig. 12, cf. Finds List 1. See ch. 7 for the use of pot-boilers.

10 *op. cit.* in nn. 5–8. Lejre: Finds List 1, no. 21 (cf. n. 8); cf. however, Grøngård Jeppesen 1979a, p. 72, pp. 110ff.

11 Olsen 1926; cf. ch. 9.

12 Grøngård Jeppesen and Thrane 1978, pp. 37f; Grøngård Jeppesen 1979b; Stoumann 1979; cf. Finds List 1 (see n. 8).

13 Brøndsted 1936; Ramskou 1950; cf. ch. 9.

14 Karby on Mors, Trabjerg, Aggersborg and Löddeköpinge, among others, seem to have originated in the eighth century (Finds List 1, nos. 5, 8 and 4; see n. 8); Ohlsson 1975–6; the settlement at Lindholm Høje is thought to be even older (Finds List 1, no. 1).

15 In particular Grøngård Jeppesen 1978a; *idem* 1979a, with references; *idem* 1979b; other reports in Thrane ed. 1979.

16 cf. n. 15; Becker 1973–4, with references.

17 See ch. 5.

18 Jørgensen 1977; Lisse 1974.

19 Hvass 1979.

20 *Trap Danmark, Ribe Amt*, pp. 918ff.

21 Fyn: Grøngård Jeppesen 1978b; cf. Brøndsted 1960, pp. 298ff.

22 Hedeby and Ribe: ch. 5; Danevirke: ch. 8.

23 Information kindly provided by Bent Aaby, of the Danish Geological Survey. Based on pollen analysis in Store Vildmose, Jutland. Cf. Berglund 1969, and ch. 2 (nn. 10–14).

24 cf. Brøndsted 1960, p. 362. Many deserted settlements of various periods have also been noted in other countries; cf. Janssen 1977.

25 e.g. Thrane ed. 1979, *passim*.

26 Finds List 1, no. 1 (see n. 8).

27 *ibid.* nos. 20 and 4.

28 Porsmose Christensen 1977; *idem* 1979.

29 Noe 1976; Græbe and Roesdahl 1977, p. 14. Ramskou (1957a and b) thinks that the fields at Lindholm Høje were ploughed with 'a light mould-board plough', while Veibæk (1974, pp. 77f) argues that an ard may have been used. Plough marks at Hedeby are mentioned by Schietzel (1969, p. 51) but Veibæk (1974, pp. 71f) questions whether a mould-board plough rather than an ard was employed. Ohlsson 1973 refers to furrows at Löddeköpinge in Skåne; these are also dismissed by Veibæk (1974, pp. 55f). On the other hand he emphasises the presence of furrows at Alt Archsum on Sylt (1974, pp. 66ff). See also Kossack, Harck, Reichstein 1974, p. 363.

30 Bencard 1973, pp. 36ff; Bencard *et al.* 1978;

Ohlsson 1973; cf. Veibæk 1974, pp. 55ff.

31 Vensild 1970. C–14 datings of Danish ploughing implements are currently being published by Lerche in *Tools and Tillage* (first given in Lerche 1968).

32 Haarnagel 1977, pp. 279ff.

33 *op. cit.* in n. 28; cf. Glob 1951; Vensild 1970; Veibæk 1974.

34 Ramskou 1957a and b; *idem* 1960b, pp. 37f; Marseen 1959, pp. 64f. Cf. Steensberg 1973, p. 76.

35 Andersen 1958; Wulff Andersen 1977a, pp. 21f.

36 cf. Veibæk 1974, pp. 74ff.

37 Steensberg *et al.* 1968, especially text volume pp. 40f; Steensberg 1973, pp. 66ff.

38 V. Nielsen 1970, p. 31; Veibæk 1974, pp. 73ff; *RGA* 2; 'Bejsebakken'. The traces of fields at Bejsebakken near Ålborg are of the same type as the fields at Lindholm Høje.

39 These theories have been advanced by Porsmose Christensen 1977; *idem* 1979.

40 *ibid.*; cf. the idea of soldier-colonists (Kristensen 1975).

41 Arup 1926, pp. 64ff; Christensen 1969, pp. 52ff; V. Nielsen 1970; cf. Vensild 1970; Veibæk 1974.

42 Stoumann, *op. cit.* in n. 7.

43 Andersen, Crabb and Madsen 1971, pp. 40ff.

44 Sunken-featured buildings in Denmark were first identified as houses by C. G. Schultz (1949). Sunken-featured buildings: in particular Bencard 1969; Madsen 1969; Strömberg 1969–70; *op. cit.* in n. 43; Ohlsson 1975–6; Strömberg 1978. On the relations with the Icelandic *dyngja* cf. Strömberg 1978, p. 37.

45 At Aggersborg and Trelleborg, pits have been examined in the end rooms of three houses. If it were not for their position these would have been classified as sunken-featured buildings (Olsen and Schmidt 1977, pp. 113f). In England, too, a number of constructions similar to sunken-featured buildings seem to have been cellars (Rahtz 1976, pp. 70ff).

46 cf. Rausing 1979.

47 Skov *op. cit.* in n. 7; Bender Jørgensen and Skov *op. cit.* in n. 7.

48 Hvass *op. cit.* in n. 7.

49 Nielsen *op. cit.* in n. 7. Leif Chr. Nielsen has kindly shown me the finds and the site plans.

50 Bantelmann 1975.

51 fig. 12 and Finds List 1.

52 Olsen and Schmidt 1977, pp. 146f. Heid Gjöstein Resi has examined the distribution of the many soapstone fragments in the large house. As virtually all of these were in the eastern end, she reached the same conclusion as Schmidt, that animals were kept at the other end.

53 Andersen 1960; Wulff Andersen 1977a.

54 Nørlund 1948, pp. 44f.

55 Nancke-Krogh 1978; Grøngård Jeppesen and Thrane 1978; Grøngård Jeppesen 1979b; Nørlund 1948, pp. 36ff; Olsen and Schmidt 1977, p. 154.

56 Stoumann 1978, pp. 44f; L. C. Nielsen 1977, p. 76 and fig. 18.

57 Ramskou 1957b; *idem* 1960b, pp. 20f and 36f.

58 Schmidt 1973; Olsen and Schmidt 1977, pp. 107ff, with references; cf. Rahtz 1976.

59 Stoumann 1978; Olsen and Schmidt 1977, p. 119.

60 e.g. Strömberg 1961, vol. 1, pp. 19ff, 171ff;

Ohlsson 1975–6; Strömberg 1978 with references.

61 Blomqvist and Mårtensson 1963, pp. 109ff; Mårtensson ed. 1976, pp. 41ff.

62 Ohlsson 1975–6.

63 *KLNM* XVII, 'Stolpe'; cf. Herrmann ed. 1970, pp. 138ff.

64 Liebgott 1979.

65 See ch. 5; cf. Bantelmann 1975, pp. 186ff.

66 Moltke 1976, pp. 180ff and *passim*.

67 Olsen and Schmidt 1977, pp. 139ff; Rahtz 1976.

68 For domestic animals in general see Degerbøl in Nørlund 1948, pp. 241–64; Møhl 1968; Strömberg 1969–70, pp. 262f; Møhl in Andersen, Crabb and Madsen 1971, pp. 321–9; Ekman 1973; Reichstein and Thiessen 1974; Ohlsson 1975–6, pp. 140f; Stoumann 1978, pp. 54f; Strömberg 1978, pp. 78ff; Levin Nielsen 1978, pp. 43ff. According to a MS (1979) by Tove Hatting and Knud Rosenlund of the Zoological Museum, Copenhagen, the same animals occur at Aggersborg.

69 See also Degerbøl in Thorvildsen 1957 (from the horseman's grave at Errindlev and from the Ladby ship-burial); Wulff Andersen and Hatting 1978, pp. 30f (the Gryderup horse). Tove Hatting kindly informs me that the horse from the horseman's grave at Stengade in Langeland was about 15 hands (i.e. with a shoulder-height of about 150 cm), the same as the Gryderup horse and the Errindlev stallion.

70 *KLNM* VII, 'Hästkött'; Møhl 1968; Hatting and Rosenlund (MS) 1979. According to Reichstein and Thiessen (1974, p. 41) horses were not eaten at Hedeby.

71 Degerbøl in Nørlund 1948, p. 242; Andersen, Crabb and Madsen 1971, pp. 141f; Hatting and Rosenlund (MS) 1979, report on the bone from Aggersborg.

72 Andersen, Crabb and Madsen 1971, p. 109.

73 Ullemeyer 1970; Mårtensson ed. 1976, pp. 219ff; Bencard *et al.* 1978.

74 See for example Sawyer 1978b, p. 24.

75 Andersen, Crabb and Madsen 1971, p. 141; Hatting and Rosenlund (MS) 1979, report on the bone from Aggersborg.

76 Andersen, Crabb and Madsen 1971, pp. 208f; Brade 1978; Bencard *et al.* 1978; Hatting 1979.

77 Ullemeyer 1970; Mårtensson ed. 1976, p. 222; Bencard *et al.* 1978; Hatting and Rosenlund (MS) 1979, report on the bone from Aggersborg.

78 For eiderdowns and pillows, see ch. 7. Bullocks and castrated sheep have been detected at Aggersborg (Hatting and Rosenlund (MS) 1979).

79 Brøndsted 1936, p. 220; Degerbøl in Nørlund 1948, pp. 255ff; Degerbøl in Thorvildsen 1957, pp. 114ff; Wulff Andersen and Hatting 1978; Wendt 1978. Cf. *KLNM* VII, 'Hund'.

80 Glob 1951, p. 77 and fig. 96; according to Veibæk (1974, pp. 45f) there is an arrow-shaped wooden blade from the South Mound at Jelling.

81 Ramskou 1957a; *idem* 1957b; *idem* 1960, p. 35.

82 See ch. 8.

83 Jankuhn 1943, pl. 50; Stoumann 1978, pp. 54f; Roesdahl 1980, fig. 10; cf. Petersen 1951, pp. 157ff.

84 Steensberg 1943, pp. 111ff; Andersen, Crabb and Madsen 1971, p. 167; Mårtensson ed. 1976, p. 225; Stoumann 1978, p. 54; Roesdahl

1980, fig. 10.

85 Jessen 1953–4; Hjelmqvist in Blomqvist and Mårtensson 1963, pp. 233–70; Behre 1969; Helbæk 1970; Jørgensen in Andersen, Crabb and Madsen 1971, pp. 289–304; Fredskild in Andersen, Crabb and Madsen 1971, pp. 307–318; Helbæk in Olsen and Schmidt 1977, *Excursus*; *KLNM* VII, 'Hvede'.

86 For peas, beans and other vegetables, see ch. 7. In recent years fragments of linen textiles have proved to be fairly common in the graves of the period (ch. 7). Various implements, possibly used in the preparation of flax, have also been found (ch. 6). Cf. Tidow in Müller-Wille 1976a, p. 62.

87 *op. cit.* in nn. 7 and 8.

88 Bones of wild animals are rare in the settlements of the period, see ch. 7.

89 Stoumann 1978, pp. 55f; Levin Nielsen 1978, pp. 45f.

90 Nørlund 1948, p. 139; Blomqvist and Mårtensson 1963, pp. 163f; Mårtensson and Wahlöö 1970, no. 131; Andersen, Crabb and Madsen 1971, p. 118, 169; Ohlsson 1975–6, p. 114; Mårtensson ed. 1976, p. 223 and figs. 172–4; Roesdahl 1980, fig. 10.

91 Brandt 1970; Andersen, Crabb and Madsen 1971, pp. 232f.

92 Møhl in Andersen, Crabb and Madsen 1971, pp. 321ff; Ekman 1973, pp. 56ff; Rosenlund 1976, pp. 44ff and *passim*; Lepiksaar and Heinrich 1977; Strömberg 1978, pp. 78ff.

93 Lepiksaar and Heinrich 1977, pp. 113f.

94 Finds List I (see n. 8), nos. 1 and 4.

Chapter 5: The First Towns

1 For definitions of towns, see Jankuhn *et al.* ed. 1973–4; Jankuhn 1974; Biddle 1976; Lund 1980.

2 e.g. Jankuhn *et al.* ed. 1974 (including articles on Kaupang and Birka); Biddle 1976; for Birka, see also Arbman 1939. For the processes of urbanisation in Sweden and Norway, see, respectively, Andersson 1979; Herteig, Lidén, Blindheim 1975.

3 cf. Jankuhn *et al.* ed. 1973–4 and chs. 4 and 6.

4 The project 'The medieval town' under the auspices of the Danish Research Council for the Humanities, chairman Olaf Olsen, coordinator Ole Schiørring.

5 For mints in the various towns, see Hauberg 1900; Olsen 1972a.

6 An immense amount of literature about Hedeby is available. Some is listed below: Jankuhn 1976 and earlier editions of this work, especially 1943; Schietzel 1968; *idem* 1969; *idem* 1974; *idem* 1975; Schietzel and Ulbricht 1977; Eckstein and Schietzel 1977; Schledermann 1966; *idem* 1967; Steuer 1974. The finds are currently presented in *Berichte über die Ausgrabungen in Haithabu*, ed. K. Schietzel, Neumünster 1969ff. Also available are seven volumes of monographs, *Die Ausgrabungen in Haithabu*. A review of Hedeby research by Kurt Schietzel is at press (1979). For the Schleswig excavations see Vogel 1974; *idem* 1977.

7 Albrectsen 1976, pp. 12ff; *Carolingian Chronicles*, p. 83, 88; *Quellen zur Karolingischen Reichsgeschichte* I, pp. 78f, 88f.

8 e.g. Mecklenburg (Herrmann 1976) and Alt Lübeck (H. H. Andersen 1979).

9 Most recent Skovgaard-Petersen 1977, pp. 115f.

10 *Quellen des 9. und 11. Jahrhunderts ...*, pp. 78ff, 100ff.

11 Jacobsen and Moltke 1941–2, nos. 1–4 and 6; Moltke 1976, pp. 156ff. On the so-called Swedish dynasty, cf. ch. 11, n. 14.

12 For summaries of Viking Age Ribe and interim reports on the excavations, see Bencard 1973; *idem* 1974a; *idem* 1974b; Bencard and Wiell 1975; Olsen 1975a; Brinch Madsen 1976; Bencard 1976; *idem* 1978; Bencard *et al.* 1978. The excavations will be published in a series: *RIBE: Excavations 1970–1976* (South Jutland University Press, edited by M. Bencard). One part, dealing with the coins and the written sources, by K. Bendixen and I. Skovgaard-Petersen, is expected to be published in 1981. For the quotation, see Adam of Bremen IV: 1.

13 Bencard *et al.* 1978.

14 Søgaard 1961; Andersen and Madsen 1966; Andersen, Crabb and Madsen 1971; H. H. Andersen 1974; Madsen 1975a. Churches: *Danmarks Kirker, Århus Amt.* Rune stones: Moltke 1976, *passim.*

15 Levin Nielsen 1966; *idem* 1968; *idem* 1974; *idem* 1975; *idem* 1978. Oldest antiquities from the town: Roesdahl 1977d; a disc brooch with Jellinge-style ornament is unpublished. The rune stone: Moltke 1976, *passim.* The assembly: *KLNM* XVI, 'Snapsting'; Christensen 1969, pp. 75f. For Vale of Viborg, see *Diplomatarium Danicum*, ser. 1, vol. 1, no. 494. I am indebted to Erik Levin Nielsen for much help with the section on Viborg.

16 Blomqvist 1951; *idem* 1974; Blomqvist and Mårtensson 1963; Mårtensson ed. 1976 (the new datings presented in the latter). The water-mill: Thun 1962–3; it is interpreted as a possible bath-house in Blomqvist and Mårtensson 1963, p. 119. The document of 1085: Christensen 1977, pp. 248ff. The rune stones: Jacobsen and Moltke 1941–2, nos. 314–15; Moltke 1976, p. 197.

17 Skovmand 1942, nos. 28–30 (pp. 84–6); cf. Roesdahl 1977a, pp. 167f; Albrectsen 1970; Grandt-Nielsen 1971; Bartholin and Grandt-Nielsen 1974; Bartholin 1976; *Trap Danmark, Odense Amt*, pp. 106ff with references. For Nonnebakken, see ch. 8. For the assembly, cf. Christensen 1969, pp. 75f. A single fragment of soapstone has been found in the town, see fig. 21, no. 37.

18 Roskilde in general: *Trap Danmark, Københavns Amt*, pp. 1017ff with references; *Danmarks Kirker, Københavns Amt* 3; Olsen 1960; *idem* 1963; Krins 1968, pp. 5f *et passim*; Nielsen and Schiørring 1979 (here the 'Viking Age' stretches to 1074 and thus also includes the reign of Svein Estridsson). The two brooches mentioned are in the National Museum in Copenhagen, 1. Dept., no. 7323 and no. dnf. $\frac{9}{52}$. My thanks to Stine Wiell and Elisabeth Munksgaard for information about these. Soapstone: fig. 21, no. 43.

19 Kock 1975; *Trap Danmark, Ålborg Amt*, pp. 894ff with references.

20 Adam of Bremen IV: 1.

21 *Trap Danmark, Sorø Amt*, pp. 663ff (Ringsted), pp. 687ff (Slagelse) with notes. Slagelse: Olsen 1972b. The assembly in Ringsted: cf. Christensen 1969, pp. 75f.

22 Hauberg 1900, pp. 73ff. The location of Toftum: Kousgård Sørensen 1958, p. 160, n. 2.

23 e.g. Sawyer 1978b; cf. ch. 8.

24 Jankuhn 1963, pp. 175ff; cf. ch. 11, n. 47.

25 e.g. Biddle 1976; Herrmann 1976, pp. 130ff; Sawyer 1978b.

26 Jankuhn 1963, pp. 175ff; Christensen 1969, pp. 127ff; Skovgaard-Petersen 1977, pp. 139ff; Sawyer 1978b.

27 *Quellen des 9. und 11. Jahrhunderts ...*, pp. 80f.

28 Biddle 1976.

29 cf. Levin Nielsen 1966, pp. 30ff; *idem* 1978, pp. 59f; Blomqvist 1951; *idem* 1974. My thanks to Ole Schiørring for his comments on this chapter.

Chapter 6: Trade, Industries and Crafts

1 The Frisian theory was advanced by e.g. Arup 1926, pp. 89ff. It is discussed and dismissed by e.g. Christensen 1966; *idem* 1969, pp. 108ff, pp. 185ff. On the role of the Scandinavians in trade generally: Foote and Wilson 1970, pp. 191ff; Skovgaard-Petersen 1977, pp. 123ff, pp. 136ff; Sawyer 1978b; Wilson 1980a.

2 e.g. Sawyer 1978b; Wilson 1978b; *idem* 1980a.

3 See e.g. Roesdahl 1977a, p. 150; Blindheim 1978.

4 Skjølsvold 1961; Resi 1978; *idem* 1979. Cf. fig. 21 and Finds List 2.

5 Roesdahl 1977a, p. 59; Resi 1978. Cf. ch. 7, n. 97. My thanks to Heid Gjöstein Resi for helpful discussions on whetstones.

6 Quernstones: ch. 7, n. 98. For reindeer antler, see Resi 1978; Ulbricht 1978, p. 106 *et passim*; cf. Ekman 1973, p. 49.

7 Müller-Wille 1973, pp. 23ff; Resi 1978. Cf. Müller-Wille 1977b, pp. 137ff.

8 Bencard 1978, pp. 18f; Bencard *et al.* 1978.

9 cf. Sawyer 1978b.

10 Liestøl 1973.

11 Skovmand 1942; Munksgaard 1969; *idem* 1971; Hårdh 1976; *idem* 1977–8.

12 Steuer 1973; *idem* 1978; Hatz 1974, pp. 108ff; Roesdahl 1976, p. 44 with references; *idem* 1977a, pp. 40f, p. 137.

13 Munksgaard 1969; Roesdahl 1977a, p. 33, with references.

14 Skovmand 1942, pp. 174ff *et passim*; Hårdh 1976; *idem* 1977–8.

15 cf. ch. 5, n. 12.

16 Viking Age coins in Denmark: Hauberg 1900; Skovmand 1942; Galster 1951; *idem* 1964, pp. 21ff; Malmer 1966; Håstrup 1969; Malmer 1974; Hatz 1974; Hårdh 1976, p. 32; Kromann in Skaarup 1976, pp. 192–9 (here the number of Anglo-Saxon coins in Denmark is incorrect, see Galster 1964); Bendixen 1976; *idem* 1977; Blackburn, Dolley and Jonsson 1979. There is a survey in Bendixen 1978.

17 Roesdahl 1980.

18 Sweet ed. 1883, pp. 17ff; cf. ch. 5.

19 *KLNM* X, 'Köpman'; Lund 1980.

20 See ch. 5, with references.

21 *op. cit.* in Finds List 1 (p. 249).

22 Nørlund 1948; Roesdahl 1977a, pp. 41ff, 153ff, 161ff.

23 Hvass 1977a, p. 26; *idem* 1977b, p. 379; *idem* 1979 (Vorbasse); Leif Chr. Nielsen has kindly provided information on industries at Omgård.
24 cf. Lund 1980.
25 Roesdahl 1975; *idem* 1977a, p. 156; cf. Janssen 1977, pp. 306ff.
26 Foote and Wilson 1970, p. 318.
27 Berg 1955; Arbman 1961, pls. II–V.
28 Moltke 1976, pp. 258ff; p. 418, no. 108.
29 *KLNM* xvi, 'Smed'. Foote and Wilson 1970, p. 327.
30 H. Andersen 1963; Wulff Andersen 1977a, pp. 15f (so far only one smith's grave has been found in Denmark).
31 Stoumann 1978, pp. 44f.
32 Petersen 1951, pp. 71ff; Blindheim 1963.
33 Foote and Wilson 1970, pp. 181ff, pp. 316ff; *KLNM* xvi, 'Smed'.
34 Moltke 1976, pp. 258ff; Lund 1980; cf. Janssen 1977, pp. 306ff.
35 Bencard *et al.* 1978.
36 Linen: Hald 1950, pp. 126ff; *op. cit.* in ch. 7, nn. 119–20, *passim*. Wooden mallets: Hald 1950, pp. 126ff; Nørlund 1948, pl. 47: 7–10; Blomqvist and Mårtensson 1963, p. 173; Schietzel 1970, fig. 7: 1; Mårtensson ed. 1976, fig. 210; cf. Grieg 1928, pp. 183f. Hackles: Nørlund 1948, p. 142; Andersen, Crabb and Madsen 1971, p. 139; cf. Petersen 1951, pp. 319ff.
37 Roesdahl 1977a, pp. 28f; Hoffmann 1974, pp. 284ff.
38 See *op. cit.* in Finds List 1 (p. 249).
39 Major groups of spindle-whorls have been published: Nørlund 1948, p. 141; Blomqvist and Mårtensson 1963, p. 173f; Andersen, Crabb and Madsen 1971, pp. 225ff; Ohlsson 1975–6, pp. 115f; Roesdahl 1977a, pp. 29ff; Bencard *et al.* 1978. Amber spindle-whorls are mentioned in *KLNM* xiii, 'Rav'. There are 128 spindle-whorls from Aggersborg, 111 of fired clay, 6 of soapstone, 9 of heads of femurs (caput femeri) of domestic ox, 1 antler and 1 lead. Wooden spindles: Bencard *et al.* 1978; Schietzel 1970, fig. 8:3 – (?)4; Grieg 1928, p. 181.
40 Grieg 1928, p. 182, pp. 187ff.
41 Blomqvist and Mårtensson 1963, p. 174.
42 See n. 38; major groups of loom-weights are published in the works referred to in n. 39.
43 Hoffmann 1974.
44 *ibid.*; *KLNM* xix, 'Vevstol'; Andersen, Crabb and Madsen 1971, pp. 250ff.
45 Liebgott 1977, pp. 155ff; Andersen, Crabb and Madsen 1971, pp. 225ff.
46 Petersen 1951, pp. 285ff; Aggersborg no. A3–1514.
47 Andersen, Crabb and Madsen 1971, p. 111: CEC; the Aggersborg examples are nos. A3–132, A3–207–B, A3–346; A3–402–B. Cf. Wilson 1976b, pp. 271f. They are also thought sometimes to have been of wood (*ibid.*, p. 280, n. 235). Cf. Geijer 1938, p. 57.
48 Nancke-Krogh 1978, p. 91; cf. Grieg 1928, p. 193 and fig. 126c; Geijer 1938, p. 57 and pl. 39.
49 Hald 1950, pp. 227ff; Mårtensson ed. 1976, p. 363 and fig. 314; cf. Grieg 1928, p. 180. There are also weaving tablets from Hedeby (thanks to Kurt Schietzel for this information).
50 Hald 1950, pp. 100ff. Gold and silver thread

in textiles: Roesdahl 1977a, p. 137 with references.
51 Hald 1950, pp. 243ff.
52 Grieg 1928, pp. 175ff.
53 Hald 1950, pp. 291ff. The rune-inscribed bone needles: Blomqvist and Mårtensson 1963, p. 176; Moltke 1976, pp. 375ff.
54 Grieg 1928, pp. 178ff; for the technique, see Hald 1950, p. 249ff.
55 Roesdahl 1977a, p. 136 with references. The scissors from Birka and Hedeby: Arbman 1940, pls. 175:2, 176:2; Jankuhn 1943, p. 127.
56 Schultz 1949, fig. 9; Andersen, Crabb and Madsen 1971, p. 221; cf. Arbman 1940, pls. 167ff; Petersen 1951, pp. 324ff.
57 e.g. Blomqvist and Mårtensson 1963, pp. 176ff; Andersen, Crabb and Madsen 1971, pp. 109ff; Schwarz-Mackensen 1976.
58 Jankuhn 1943, pp. 110f; Ramskou 1976, fig. 140; Skaarup 1976, pp. 91ff; cf. Petersen 1951, p. 328f.
59 Petersen 1951, pp. 328ff.
60 cf. Geijer 1972, pp. 95ff.
61 cf. Bencard *et al.* 1978.
62 Brøndsted 1936, p. 222; *KLNM* ix, 'Kvinnearbeid'; cf. Petersen 1951, pp. 285ff.
63 For this see chs. 3 and 7 in particular.
64 Wagner 1976; Wagner in Skaarup 1976; Wagner in Roesdahl 1977a; Eckstein 1977.
65 Ch. 3.
66 Krogh and Voss 1961.
67 On the subject in general: Olsen and Crumlin-Pedersen 1967, pp. 154ff; Blomqvist and Mårtensson 1963, pp. 169ff; Olsen and Schmidt 1977, pp. 116ff; cf. Møller 1953; Wilson 1968, *idem* 1976b.
68 See n. 27.
69 Petersen 1951, pp. 188ff.
70 Andersen, Crabb and Madsen 1971, pp. 264f.
71 Such axes may perhaps be seen in Nørlund 1948, pl. 38:2–3; Blomqvist and Mårtensson 1963, figs. 170–71.
72 Nørlund 1948, p. 140 and pl. 47:2–3. Andersen, Crabb and Madsen 1971, p. 155 (wedges). Olsen and Crumlin-Pedersen 1967, fig. 63 (splitting of logs with axe and mallet). For mallets, see also *op. cit.* in n. 36.
73 Olsen and Crumlin-Pedersen 1967, p. 158.
74 e.g. *op. cit.* in n. 66; Nørlund 1948, pp. 71ff; Blomqvist and Mårtensson 1963, pp. 116ff; p. 131ff.
75 Møller 1953, pp. 146ff.
76 Müller-Wille 1973, p. 28 and fig. 4:10; cf. *op. cit.* in n. 27; Foote and Wilson 1970, p. 180; cf. Petersen 1951, figs. 134–35.
77 Müller-Wille 1973, p. 26 and fig. 3; Thomsen 1971a, pp. 30ff.
78 Brøndsted 1936, fig. 9. The description of the shape is my own.
79 Nørlund 1948, pp. 136f, pls. 36f.
80 *op. cit.* in n. 27; Petersen 1951, figs. 119–20. The sockets of a couple of tools published in Andersen, Crabb and Madsen 1971, p. 253 and fig. EAA, and in Blomqvist and Mårtensson 1963, fig. 172, are hardly strong enough for adzes.
81 Nørlund 1948, p. 140, pl. 45:2–3; Müller-Wille 1973, fig. 4:9; Roesdahl 1977a, p. 56; an example from Aggersborg, no. A3-3342-A (draw-knives). Nørlund 1948, p. 140, pl. 45:4; Andersen, Crabb and Madsen 1971, p. 133; two examples from Aggersborg, nos. A3-10

and A3-797-E (gouges). Petersen 1951, fig. 118 and pp. 222ff (augers).
82 Wilson 1976a, p. 257.
83 Olsen and Crumlin-Pedersen 1967, p. 161 *et passim*; Krogh and Voss 1961, pp. 22ff; Kornerup 1875, pl. 17:2–3; cf. Petersen 1951, pp. 226f. and fig. 121.
84 Andersen, Crabb and Madsen 1971, pp. 139f.
85 Nørlund 1948, p. 140 and pl. 47:4–6; Andersen, Crabb and Madsen 1971, p. 217. Stoumann 1978, p. 57 (chisels). Andersen, Crabb and Madsen 1971, p. 117; Stoumann 1978, p. 57; some examples from Aggersborg, nos. A3-424a-E, A3-449-E (mandrels).
86 Nørlund 1948, p. 140, pl. 46:14–16; Blomqvist and Mårtensson 1963, p. 170 and fig. 174; Andersen, Crabb and Madsen 1971, pp. 210f; Roesdahl 1977a, p. 56; an example from Aggersborg, no. A3-299-H; an example, about 33 cm long, from the Halleby River find (National Museum Copenhagen, 1st Dept.); Olsen and Crumlin-Pedersen 1967, p. 161.
87 Petersen 1951, fig. 124.
88 Andersen, Crabb and Madsen 1971, p. 157, fig. BT; there is also a fly-wheel from the Halleby River find (National Museum Copenhagen, 1st Dept.); cf. Petersen 1951, fig. 128 and pp. 235ff.
89 Stoumann 1978, p. 57; cf. ch. 7, nn. 99–100; ch. 8, n. 19.
90 e.g. Schietzel 1970, pp. 77ff.
91 Andersen, Crabb and Madsen 1971, p. 220; cf. Petersen 1951, pp. 232ff.
92 See ch. 7, n. 96.
93 Brandt 1970; Andersen, Crabb and Madsen 1971, pp. 232f; Körber-Grohne 1977. On minor finds: Thorvildsen 1957, p. 42; Olsen and Crumlin-Pedersen 1967, p. 129; Mårtensson ed. 1976, fig. 174. Ohthere's account: Sweet ed. 1883, pp. 17f.
94 Andersen, Crabb and Madsen 1971, p. 162, fig. CVA, p. 233; Mårtensson ed. 1976, fig. 173; Nancke-Krogh 1978, pp. 81f.
95 Ullemeyer 1970; Mårtensson ed. 1976, pp. 219ff; Bencard *et al.* 1978.
96 Ullemeyer, 1970; Bencard *et al.* 1978; Mårtensson ed. 1976, pp. 215ff; cf. *op. cit.* in ch. 7, n. 122. For shoe lasts, I refer to the list of wooden objects from Hedeby, which K. Schietzel has kindly provided. Cf. Wilson 1976b, pp. 274f.
97 Mårtensson and Wahlöö 1970, no. 104. Simple knife sheaths: Blomqvist and Mårtensson 1963, p. 197 and figs. 218–20; Ullemeyer 1970, fig. 13; Roesdahl 1977a, p. 133.
98 Mårtensson ed. 1976, p. 215 and fig. 160.
99 See ch. 4.
100 Aggersborg, unpublished; cf. Schwarz-Mackensen 1976; Bencard *et al.* 1978.
101 Bencard *et al.* 1978.
102 Ch. 7; n. 106.
103 Especially Ulbricht 1978; cf. *op. cit.* in n. 6.
104 Ulbricht 1978 (Hedeby); Bergquist and Lepiksaar 1957, pp. 20ff (this material belongs to the period *c.* 1020–1400); Mårtensson and Wahlöö 1970, no. 146; Ekman 1973, pp. 48ff (Lund); Andersen, Crabb and Madsen 1971, pp. 120ff; Møhl, *ibid.*, p. 327 (Århus); Bencard *et al.* 1978 (Ribe); Nørlund 1948, pp. 130f; Degerbøl, *ibid.*, p. 263; Roesdahl 1977a, p. 166 (Trelleborg). Cf.

Wilson 1976b, pp. 259f.
105 Unpublished.
106 *op. cit.* in nn. 103–4, particularly Ulbricht 1978.
107 Ulbricht 1978; cf. ch. 7.
108 e.g. Ó Ríordáin 1971, p. 75 (Dublin).
109 cf. Bencard *et al.* 1978.
110 Ch. 7, n. 113.
111 Ulbricht 1978.
112 *ibid.*, pp. 33ff.
113 Bencard *et al.* 1978.
114 Unpublished; National Museum Copenhagen, 1st Dept. nos. A3-56; A3-915-B; A3-532B-P.
115 Bencard *et al.* 1978 with references.
116 Jankuhn 1963, pp. 247f.
117 Bencard *et al.* 1978; Bencard 1978, pp. 18f.
118 Brinch Madsen 1976; Bencard *et al.* 1978. Final publication (by Helge Brinch Madsen) is in progress.
119 Capelle 1968, *passim*; *idem* 1970; Ulbricht 1978, pp. 75f.
120 Ramskou 1957b, p. 199.
121 Mårtensson ed. 1976, pp. 199ff.
122 Andersen, Crabb and Madsen 1971, p. 218.
123 Roesdahl 1977a, pp. 50f, p. 65.
124 For example at Trelleborg (Nørlund 1948, p. 140; Roesdahl 1977a, pp. 164ff); Aggersborg (unpublished); Fyrkat and other sites (Roesdahl 1977a, p. 48); Hedeby (Resi 1979); cf. Oldeberg 1966, pp. 79ff.
125 Hvass 1977a, pp. 24ff; *idem* 1977b, pp. 379ff; Roesdahl 1977a, pp. 65 and 68f. Cf. Müller-Wille 1977b, p. 137ff.
126 Boye 1858, p. 199.
127 *op. cit.* in n. 118. My thanks to Helge Brinch Madsen for information on the distribution of the Ribe bronze-worker's products.
128 cf. n. 118; cf. Zachrisson 1960.
129 Such moulds are published in *op. cit.* in n. 119, as well as elsewhere.
130 Oldeberg 1966; Lund Hansen 1975; *loc. cit.* in n. 124; Roesdahl 1977a, pp. 45ff.
131 e.g. Skovmand 1942.
132 Roesdahl 1974, pp. 212f.
133 e.g. one of the Hornelund brooches and the Hiddensee brooch (pls. 20 and 45).
134 For the brooch from Nonnebakken and the jewellery with a bird's-head-shaped loop (such as the Hiddensee jewellery) see Roesdahl 1977a, pp. 35ff, pp. 163f, pp. 167f with references. For the Hornelund brooches, see ch. 7, n. 126. A number of dies are illustrated in Capelle 1968, pl. 28.
135 Roesdahl 1977a, p. 157 *et passim*.
136 Workshops: Roesdahl 1977a, pp. 41ff (Fyrkat); Hvass 1977a, pp. 24ff; *idem* 1977b, pp. 379ff; *idem* 1979b (Vorbasse); Stoumann 1978, pp. 56f (Sædding); Ramskou 1960b, p. 35 (Lindholm Høje). Slag: Andersen, Crabb and Madsen 1971, p. 211 (Århus); Schietzel 1975, pp. 67ff (Hedeby); Bencard *et al.* 1978 (Ribe); Bender-Jørgensen and Skov 1978 (Trabjerg); Skov 1979 (Herrup); there is unpublished slag from both Trelleborg and Aggersborg. Smiths in general: Müller-Wille 1977b.
137 For the Tjele find, see Boye 1858; for the Halleby find, see Ohlhaver 1939, p. 128 and pl. 15; Mogens Schou Jørgensen has kindly shown me the unfinished bronze mount. For the smith's grave in Lejre, see H. Andersen 1963; Wulff Andersen 1977a, pp. 15f. For

various tools, see Nørlund 1948, p. 140;
Müller-Wille 1973, pp. 24ff. Norwegian
finds: especially Petersen 1951, pp. 71ff;
Blindheim 1963. The Mästermyr find: *op. cit.*
in n. 27. Forging tools in general: Ohlhaver
1939; Müller-Wille 1977b. As far as I know,
a couple of tool sets from Ålebæk, Borre
Sømose on Møn (Ohlhaver 1939, pp.
129f) and Skovlunde Mark in Ballerup parish near
Copenhagen do not contain anything which
dates them to the Viking Age, though they
sometimes have been associated with this
period.
138 Roesdahl 1977a, pp. 41ff.
139 *ibid.*, pp. 61ff; Thomsen 1971d; Bencard *et al.* 1978; Stoumann 1978, pp. 56f.
140 Glob 1959; Thomsen 1971d; Roesdahl 1977a, p. 45.
141 Müller-Wille 1973, pp. 23ff with references; Stoumann 1978, p. 57.
142 R. Thomsen 1967; *idem* 1971 a–d; Naumann 1971; Pleiner *et al.* 1971; R. Thomsen 1975; Fabritius Buchwald 1976; cf. Liestøl 1951.
143 cf. n. 142.
144 Oldeberg 1966, pp. 195ff; Lund Hansen 1975, pp. 150ff.
145 *loc. cit.* in n. 144; Brøndsted 1936, pp. 167ff and pls. 4ff; Hundt in Müller-Wille 1972, pp. 108ff; Hundt 1973; Thomsen 1975, pp. 89ff.
146 Thomsen 1975, p. 91.
147 Roesdahl 1977a, pp. 95ff, 135f with references; *idem* 1977d.
148 Roesdahl 1977a, pp. 156ff.
149 The identification by Steensberg (1952, pp. 52ff) of a structure at Bolle in Vendsyssel as a water-mill from the pre-Roman Iron Age is vigorously rejected by V. Nielsen (1971). But cf. Steensberg 1978.
150 L. C. Nielsen 1977, p. 77 (Omgård); ch. 5, n. 16 (Lund); Steensberg 1959; *idem* 1978. My thanks to Henrik Tauber for further information on the C-14 datings, nos. K-2716 and K-2817 (Ljørring).
151 Wilson 1976b, pp. 275f.

Chapter 7: Daily Life

1 Schietzel 1975, fig. 3; Eckstein and Schietzel 1977.
2 Levin Nielsen 1975; *idem* 1978, pp. 55ff.
3 Blomqvist and Mårtensson 1963, pp. 111ff; Mårtensson ed. 1976, pp. 41ff.
4 Jankuhn 1963, pp. 117ff; Schietzel 1969, pp. 28ff; Olsen and Schmidt 1977, pp. 119ff. Some buildings with turf walls examined at Nødskov Hede in West Jutland are difficult to date (Steensberg 1952, pp. 259ff); ? from the early Middle Ages.
5 Olsen and Schmidt 1977, pp. 128ff.
6 cf. Jessen 1953–4, p. 132.
7 Zippelius 1969; Olsen and Schmidt 1977, pp. 124ff.
8 Blomqvist and Mårtensson 1963, p. 115; Olsen and Schmidt 1977, p. 132; Stoumann 1978, pp. 44f.
9 Schietzel 1969, pp. 28ff; cf. Olsen and Schmidt 1977, pp. 120f.
10 cf. n. 9.
11 Blomqvist and Mårtensson 1963, p. 115, p. 124; Roesdahl 1977a, p. 14.
12 Nørlund 1948, p. 125 and pl. 21; Blomqvist

and Mårtensson 1963, pp. 124ff; Andersen, Crabb and Madsen 1971, pp. 183f; Olsen and Schmidt 1977, figs. 83–4.
13 Olsen and Schmidt 1977, p. 131. Krogh and Voss 1961 (Hørning); Schetelig 1920 (Oseberg); Wilson and Klindt-Jensen 1966, pp. 147f (Urnes).
14 Olsen and Schmidt 1977, p. 132; Levin Nielsen 1975, p. 55; Stoumann 1978, pp. 44f.
15 Stenberger ed. 1943, pp. 83f and *passim*; *KLNM* I, 'Benk'.
16 Andersen, Crabb and Madsen 1971, pp. 40ff.
17 In the reconstructed Hedeby house, one quickly discovers the practical nature of the broad wall-benches.
18 Olsen and Schmidt 1977, pp. 130ff.
19 Nørlund 1948, pp. 83f; Ramskou 1960, p. 38; Schietzel 1969, pp. 36ff; Andersen, Crabb and Madsen 1971, pp. 40ff; Mårtensson ed. 1976, pp. 45ff; Olsen and Schmidt 1977, p. 132; Strömberg 1978, pp. 46ff.
20 Andersen, Crabb and Madsen 1971, p. 87 with references; Mårtensson ed. 1976, pp. 260f.
21 Petersen 1951, pp. 430ff.
22 Worsaae 1869, p. 212; Vellev 1973, p. 51; Kornerup 1875, p. 26.
23 cf. *KLNM* II, 'Bonad'; III, 'Duk'; IV, 'Fjär och dun'; VI, 'Handkläde'; XV, 'Sengeutstyr'.
24 Hald 1950, pp. 110ff, p. 116; Kornerup 1875, p. 26.
25 *KLNM* II, 'Bonad'.
26 Eldjárn 1953.
27 My thanks to Kurt Schietzel for this information.
28 e.g. Nørlund 1948, pp. 125f; Blomqvist and Mårtensson 1963, pp. 138ff; Andersen, Crabb and Madsen 1971, pp. 184ff; Mårtensson ed. 1976, pp. 399ff; Roesdahl 1977a, p. 14; Stoumann 1978, p. 58.
29 Andersen 1969a; *idem* 1969b; Wulff Andersen 1977a, pp. 19ff.
30 Roesdahl 1977a, pp. 119ff, 131.
31 Brøndsted 1936, pp. 191f and figs. 102–3.
32 Grieg 1928, pp. 118ff; Berg 1955; Stenberger 1964, fig. 302; Karlson 1928, pp. 94ff.
33 Karlson 1928, pp. 94ff; pls. 23f.
34 The description of the chest and the preserved parts: Kornerup 1875, pp. 9, 22 and 26; Roesdahl 1974, p. 219. The plaited hair and the board are not mentioned here. They are in the National Museum Copenhagen, 1st Dept. (no number) along with other unnumbered finds from the Jelling grave.
35 Müller-Wille 1976a, pp. 21ff.
36 e.g. Karlson 1928, pls. 23f.
37 My thanks to Mogens Schou Jørgensen for information about the Halleby river chest.
38 *KLNM* XII, 'Nyckelbärare'; XIX, 'Tyveri'.
39 *loc. cit.* in n. 28; Roesdahl 1977a, pp. 27f; *idem* 1977d.
40 Goldschmidt 1918, pp. 58f and pls. 62–9; Wilson and Klindt-Jensen 1966, pp. 124ff.
41 Roesdahl 1974, pp. 215ff; *idem* 1975.
42 Andersen and Wulff Andersen 1976; Müller-Wille 1976a, p. 41 and pls. 36f; Roesdahl 1977a, pp. 95ff, 134f.
43 Roesdahl 1976; Nordqvist 1976; Roesdahl 1977a, pp. 95ff, 115f, 122ff, 134f.
44 Brøndsted 1936, p. 221 with references; *op. cit.* in nn. 41–3.

45 Blomqvist and Mårtensson 1963, pp. 218ff, 224.
46 Grieg 1928, pp. 105ff.
47 *op. cit.* in n. 45.
48 cf. Eames 1977, p. 181.
49 Roesdahl 1977a, pp. 14of with references.
50 Blomqvist and Mårtensson 1963, p. 138 and fig. 115; Mårtensson and Wahlöö 1970, p. 28 (Lund); the stool from Hedeby is exhibited at Schloss Gottorf, Schleswig.
51 Anker 1968, pp. 14f; *KLNM* II, 'Bord'; I, 'Benk'. From the Oseberg grave there is a four-legged stool or bench, with a seat or top of about 33 × 92 cm (Grieg 1928, pp. 166f).
52 Krogh and Voss 1960; Krogh and Voss 1961, pp. 22ff; *KLNM* II, 'Bord'.
53 Grieg 1928, pp. 81ff.
54 My thanks to Kurt Schietzel for this information.
55 Kornerup 1875, pp. 22ff and pls. 15–17; Roesdahl 1974, pp. 219f. The small figure of a man: Moltke 1974, pp. 202ff; Marxen and Moltke 1978.
56 Schetelig 1920, pp. 233ff.
57 Brøndsted 1936, p. 224.
58 Jessen 1953–4; Helbæk 1959; Hjelmqvist in Blomqvist and Mårtensson 1963, pp. 233–70; Behre 1969; Jørgensen in Andersen, Crabb and Madsen 1971, pp. 289–304; Fredskild *ibid.*, pp. 307–18; Eckstein 1977. Bullace: Skaarup 1976, p. 94, n. 47. Nuts: Worsaae 1869, p. 210; Vellev 1973, p. 50; Levin Nielsen 1978, p. 43. Pollen from walnut trees and several other plants: Christiansen *et al.* (at press), Appendix A. Cress from Oseberg: Holmboe 1927, pp. 19ff.
59 *op cit.* in ch. 4, n. 68; Ulbricht 1978, p. 123.
60 Ulbricht 1978, pp. 123ff. Cf. ch. 6.
61 *KLNM* XIV, 'Salt', 'Salthandel'; Hellerup Madsen 1977.
62 *KLNM* I, 'Biskötsel'; VI, 'Honung'; XIX, 'Vax'.
63 Lepiksaar and Heinrich 1977, p. 114 (Hedeby); Møhl 1968, p. 88; Levin Nielsen 1978, pp. 43f (Viborg).
64 Marseen 1956; Stoumann 1978, p. 49; Nørlund 1948, pp. 39ff; Schietzel 1969, pp. 39ff.
65 *KLNM* XI, 'Mjölkhushållning'.
66 *KLNM* XX, 'Øl'. For hops, see Behre 1969, p. 33.
67 *KLNM* XI, 'Mjöd'.
68 Fell 1975a; *idem* 1975b.
69 *KLNM* XX, 'Vinhandel'.
70 Behre 1969, p. 10ff.
71 Dékowna in Müller-Wille 1976b, pp. 63–6; Lund Hansen 1973, pp. 28f; Ellmers 1964/5.
72 For strike-a-lights, see e.g. Nørlund 1948, pl. 29:11–15; Andersen, Crabb and Madsen 1971, p. 141; Mårtensson ed. 1976, p. 240; Roesdahl 1977a, pp. 25f. For tinder, see Seehann 1977.
73 Nørlund 1948, p. 124 and pl. 19:10.
74 Petersen 1951, pp. 369ff; Nørlund 1948, p. 125; Roesdahl 1977a, pp. 66f.
75 The pottery of the Viking Age in general: Brøndsted 1936, *passim*; Ramskou 1950, *passim*; Selling 1955; Hübener 1959; Andersen, Crabb and Madsen 1971, pp. 64ff; Madsen 1972; Steuer 1974; Wahlöö 1976; Liebgott 1978a; *idem* 1978b.
76 *op. cit.* in n. 75; Ramskou 1976, *passim*; Roesdahl 1977a, pp. 16ff; Grøngård Jeppesen

and Thrane 1978, pp. 33ff; Bender Jørgensen and Skov 1978, pp. 25f; Nancke-Krogh 1978, pp. 87ff; Stoumann 1978, pp. 51f.
77 *op. cit.* in n. 75; Nørlund 1948, pp. 115ff; Strömberg 1961, I, pp. 166f; Ohlsson 1975–1976, pp. 122ff.
78 See also Skaarup 1976, pp. 170f.
79 Bencard 1973, pp. 39f.
80 *op. cit.* in n. 75; Blomqvist and Mårtensson 1963, pp. 147ff; Mårtensson ed. 1976, pp. 251ff; Liebgott 1977.
81 *op. cit.* in n. 75; Andersen and Madsen 1966.
82 Soapstone in general: Skjølsvold 1961; Resi 1978; *idem* 1979. Soapstone finds in Denmark: fig. 21.
83 Olsen 1956.
84 Roesdahl 1977a, pp. 20ff.
85 Resi 1978; *idem* 1979. Cf. ch. 6.
86 Blomqvist and Mårtensson 1963, pp. 145f; Mårtensson ed. 1976, pp. 263ff.
87 Resi, *op cit.* in n. 85.
88 Madsen 1965; Andersen, Crabb and Madsen 1971, pp. 161f.
89 Brøndsted 1936, pp. 196f (identified here as a whip-handle); Mårtensson ed. 1976, pp. 235ff; Roesdahl 1977a, pp. 91f, p. 133.
90 A spit has been found at Aggersborg (National Museum Copenhagen, 1st Dept., no. A3-240-B) which is about 37 cm long including the tang. This is a stray find.
91 Petersen 1951, pp. 419ff, 429f.
92 Ramskou 1960b, p. 36; Lerche 1969; Stoumann 1978, p. 49; Eskildsen 1979.
93 Blomqvist and Mårtensson 1963, p. 161.
94 Schietzel 1970; Blomqvist and Mårtensson 1963, pp. 153ff; Mårtensson ed. 1976, pp. 233ff; Nørlund 1948, p. 123 and pl. 18; Andersen, Crabb and Madsen 1971, pp. 241ff.
95 *Antiquarisk Tidsskrift* 1861–3, pp. 18f; Brøndsted 1936, p. 223; Müller-Wille 1976a, p. 41; *idem* 1976b, pp. 132ff; Roesdahl 1976, pp. 32ff, 44; cf. Ellmers 1964/5.
96 Blomqvist and Mårtensson 1963, pp. 197ff; Andersen, Crabb and Madsen 1971, pp. 158f, 208; Madsen 1975b; Mårtensson ed. 1976, pp. 241ff; Wagner in Skaarup 1976, pp. 217ff; Wagner 1976, p. 85; Roesdahl 1976, pp. 28, 32; Roesdahl 1977a, pp. 27, 132f.
97 Andersen, Crabb and Madsen 1971, pp. 133ff; Roesdahl 1977a, pp. 57ff, 133; Resi 1978. Cf. ch. 6.
98 There are quernstones of Rhenish lava from all the places mentioned below. The list comprises only finds from present-day Denmark, and Hedeby. Nørlund 1948, p. 125 and pl. 20 (Trelleborg); Jankuhn 1963; pp. 198ff (Hedeby); Bencard 1969, p. 34 (Okholm); Andersen, Crabb and Madsen 1971, pp. 162ff (Århus); Stoumann 1978, pp. 53f (Sædding); Bender Jørgensen and Skov 1978, p. 36 (Trabjerg); Hvass 1979 (Vorbasse); unpublished examples from Aggersborg. Cf. Madsen 1969. Quernstones of other materials are published in many of the same works and in Roesdahl 1977a, p. 14. On the possible exportation of quernstones from Norway: Rønneseth 1968.
99 Grieg 1928, pp. 162f.
100 cf. Roesdahl 1977a, pp. 141f; Petersen 1951, pp. 337ff.
101 Nørlund 1948, p. 125 and pl. 19:8–9; Roesdahl 1977a, p. 25.

102 cf. Ellmers 1964/5; Müller-Wille 1976b, pp. 132f.

103 Hübener 1959, pp. 36ff, pp. 122ff (Hedeby); Stoumann 1978, p. 52 (Sædding); Bender Jørgensen and Skov 1978, p. 30 (Trabjerg); Hvass 1979 (Vorbasse).

104 Hübener 1959, pp. 40, 133ff (Hedeby); Bencard 1973, p. 40 (Ribe); Hans Jørgen Madsen tells me there is also Tating ware at Aggersborg.

105 Mårtensson ed. 1976, pp. 267f.

106 Müller 1900b; Müller-Wille 1976a, pp. 41f and pls. 30ff; Roesdahl 1977a, pp. 91f, 133. At the National Museum Copenhagen, 1st Dept. there is also a collection of silver drinking-horn mounts (C24116), but of unknown provenance.

107 Brøndsted 1936, pp. 173ff and pl. 10; Skaarup 1976, pp. 94, 175f; Roesdahl 1977a, pp. 93f, 134.

108 Skovmand 1942 no. 16 (p. 75), no. 35 (p. 93), no. 45 (pp. 111ff), no. 52 (pp. 115ff); Friis Johansen 1912; Wilson 1960a; idem 1960b; Ørsnes 1966, pp. 239ff; Fell 1975a; idem 1975b. In each of the hoards from Kulhusgärde and Kongens Udmark there is a fragment of a silver vessel (Skovmand 1942, no. 48 (p. 114) and no. 61 (p. 128), and the hoard from Lackalänga, Skåne has a complete vessel (Hårdh 1976, pl. 39). There are also fragments in several southern Swedish hoards (Hårdh 1976, p. 76).

109 Kornerup 1875, pp. 9, 20f; Roesdahl 1974, pp. 212ff; Fell, op. cit. in n. 108. The theory that the cup was a Christian chalice was first put forward by Schultz 1952.

110 Kornerup 1875, pp. 18, 22; Roesdahl 1974, p. 214; Thorvildsen 1957, p. 86.

111 Liestøl 1953; Müller-Wille 1976b, pp. 132ff; Roesdahl 1976, pp. 32, 42 and 44; cf. KLNM VI, 'Handkläde'. Spoons from Hedeby have kindly been shown me by Kurt Schietzel; cf. Jankuhn 1943, p. 164. There are also spoons from Birka: Arbman 1940, pl. 151.

112 KLNM VII, 'Hår- og skægmoder'.

113 Nørlund 1948, pp. 130ff; Schultz 1949, fig. 9; Blomqvist and Mårtensson 1963, pp. 200ff; Andersen, Crabb and Madsen 1971, pp. 143ff; Ohlsson 1975-6, pp. 113f; Mårtensson ed. 1976, pp. 317ff; Ulbricht 1978. For combs in graves, see Brøndsted 1936, p. 222; Müller-Wille 1976b, pp. 132f. Cf. ch. 6.

114 Friis Johansen 1912, pl. 2; Skovmand 1942, no. 45 (p. 112).

115 Nørlund 1948, p. 130; Ohlsson 1975-6, p. 104; Ramskou 1976, figs. 79, 138A and 221.

116 Geijer 1938, pp. 134ff; KLNM III, 'Drakt'; Hägg 1974; Munksgaard 1974, 'passim; Müller-Wille 1976a, pp. 33ff; Bender Jørgensen in Skaarup 1976, pp. 215f. On the disappearance of oval brooches, cf. Roesdahl 1977a, p. 33 with n. 98, p. 148.

117 Geijer 1938, pp. 134ff; KLNM III, 'Drakt'; Moltke 1976, p. 213; Marxen and Moltke 1978. If the figure mentioned in the last work had a head-dress, it might have looked like that on one of the Hunnestad rune stones (fig. 2). This is not necessarily a halo, as has been suggested. On Danish fashions, cf. Whitelock ed. 1979, no. 232.

118 Andersen 1969a.

119 Hald 1950, pp. 98ff (includes the most important material from present-day Denmark found before 1950 but not the many fragments and traces of textiles which are preserved in connection with brooches and other metal objects); Thorvildsen 1957, pp. 78ff; Krogh and Voss 1961; Bender Jørgensen in Skaarup 1976, pp. 208ff; Tidow in Müller-Wille 1976a, pp. 60ff; Østergård 1976; Østergård in Roesdahl 1977a, pp. 102ff; ibid., p. 137. On dyeing: Hald 1950, pp. 138ff.

120 Schlabow 1940; Ullemeyer 1970; Ellen Andersen, in Andersen, Crabb and Madsen 1971, pp. 229ff; Blomqvist and Mårtensson 1963, pp. 220ff; Mårtensson ed. 1976, p. 284.

121 Brøndsted 1936, pp. 176, 220, 222; Engelhardt 1881, p. 179.

122 Blomqvist and Mårtensson 1963, pp. 180ff; Ullemeyer 1970; Hald 1974; Bencard et al. 1978. My thanks to Ingrid Nielsen for help with this section.

123 Brøndsted 1936; Ramskou 1950; Ramskou 1976 (grave-finds); Friis Johansen 1912; Skovmand 1942; Hårdh 1976; Liebgott 1978a (hoards); Strömberg 1961 (Skåne); Capelle 1968; idem 1970 (Hedeby); Bencard 1973; Bencard et al. 1978 (Ribe); Andersen, Crabb and Madsen 1971, pp. 108ff, 199ff, 206, 215ff (Århus); Blomqvist and Mårtensson 1963, pp. 190ff; Mårtensson ed. 1976, pp. 293ff (Lund); Nørlund 1948, pp. 126ff, 143 (Trelleborg); Roesdahl 1977a, pp. 32ff, 137ff, 161ff (Fyrkat, Nonnebakken); Schultz 1949; Roesdahl 1977a; idem 1980 (Aggersborg). Cf. Wilson and Klindt-Jensen 1966.

124 cf. n. 123; cf. Petersen 1928; Arbman 1940. Trefoil brooches and Frankish strap-mounts from the old Danish area have been collected by Stine Wiell (unpublished MA thesis 1973, Copenhagen University); for such brooches, see also Bencard and Wiell 1975.

125 See also Ørsnes 1966, pp. 136ff.

126 The Nonnebakken brooches: Roesdahl 1977a, pp. 167f. On the type: Stenberger 1958, pp. 32ff. The Hornelund brooches: Brøndsted 1934; Stenberger 1958, pp. 39f; Wilson and Klindt-Jensen 1966, p. 140 (Brøndsted considers them Frankish, especially as they are so perfectly executed; Stenberger thinks they were produced by one or two continental master craftsmen working in Denmark; Wilson and Klindt-Jensen apparently believe that they are Scandinavian workmanship. Their splendour is no argument for the opposite view, and they fit very properly into the Danish brooch tradition.)

127 Ramskou 1955, p. 184 and fig. 12; idem 1957b, pp. 199ff; Marseen 1959, pp. 62ff; Mårtensson ed. 1976, pp. 206ff.

128 Brøndsted 1934; Glob 1977.

129 Arbman 1937; Wiell op. cit. 1973 in n. 124; Bencard and Wiell 1975.

130 Thorvildsen 1957, pp. 77f (Ladby); Roesdahl 1974, p. 218; Krogh 1980a (Jelling); Roesdahl 1980, figs. 4 and 6 (Aggersborg).

131 Bone pins: Schwarz-Mackensen 1976.

132 Arm-rings: Munksgaard 1969.

133 Wulff Andersen 1977b; Munksgaard 1977.

134 See also Callmer 1977; von Müller 1970; Arrhenius 1978. One jet bead from Aggersborg has been identified.

135 Paulsen 1936.

136 Müller-Wille 1976a, pp. 38ff and Finds List 4, pp. 57f; Schwarz-Mackensen 1978.

137 H. H. Andersen 1971; Roesdahl 1977a, pp.

140f; cf. Arrhenius 1961. The theory is disputed by Schwarz-Mackensen 1978 (on miniature tools). Hatz 1970 (on coin jewellery).

138 Graham-Campbell and Kidd 1980, cat. nos. 10–11; Gräslund 1972–3. Skates: ch. 3.

139 But cf. Janssen 1977, p. 305. Some bones of wild animals have been found at Trelleborg (Degerbøl in Nørlund 1948, pp. 262f), but the stratigraphical conditions are uncertain.

140 Coin pictures: Malmer 1966, pl. 2 and pp. 63ff. Rune-stone pictures: Moltke 1976, pp. 212, 223, 235.

141 cf. also the stag on the sceptre from the royal grave at Sutton Hoo (Bruce-Mitford 1979, pp. 27f).

142 KLNM VII, 'Jakt', 'Jaktfåglar'.

143 Degerbøl in Nørlund 1948, p. 263; cf. n. 139.

144 Ch. IV, n. 79.

145 Thorvildsen 1957, pp. 50ff.

146 Wulff Andersen and Hatting 1978, p. 31; Wendt 1978, p. 65.

147 KLNM VII, 'Hund'.

148 Brade 1978; KLNM XI, 'Lyra'; Addyman 1979, p. 8.

149 Foote and Wilson 1970, pp. 319ff.

150 Gaming-pieces: Nørlund 1948, p. 132; Ramskou 1950, p. 166; idem 1976, graves 1086 (fig. 77) and 2196; Blomqvist and Mårtensson 1963, pp. 205f; Mårtensson ed. 1976, pp. 379f; Andersen, Crabb and Madsen 1971, p. 212; Schou Jørgensen 1975, p. 73 and fig. 69; Ulbricht 1978, p. 78; cf. Grieg 1947, pp. 53ff; KLNM II, 'Brettspill'. The gaming-board from Ballinderry: Hencken 1933. Gaming-boards from Danish graves: Thorvildsen 1957, p. 86; Laursen 1970, p. 99.

151 KLNM II, 'Brettspill'.

152 ibid. The small gold figure (pl. 2), often identified as a chessman, has no characteristics which might connect it with this game in particular. For example, it clearly does not represent a bishop (early medieval bishop-pieces sometimes actually look like bishops). Judging from the long hair and dress it is more likely to represent a woman (cf. Schou Jørgensen 1975, fig. 69, text p. 73, information on the find etc. pp. 97f).

153 See e.g. Foote and Wilson 1970 passim.

Chapter 8: Arms and Fortification

1 Wilson 1965, pp. 50ff; Behrend 1970.

2 Skaarup 1976, pp. 105f.

3 Nørlund 1948, p. 41f, 105f, 137f (Trelleborg); Schaefer 1963, p. 204 (Hedeby).

4 Brøndsted 1936; idem 1960, pp. 438f; Ramskou 1950; Strömberg 1961, pp. 134ff; Müller-Wille 1977a; cf. KLNM XIII, 'Pil'; XVI, 'Spjut'; XVII, 'Sverd'; XX, 'Øks'; Foote and Wilson 1970, pp. 272ff.

5 Petersen 1919.

6 Swords: Müller-Wille 1972 and 1976b.

7 e.g. Strömberg 1961, pp. 138ff; Müller-Wille 1977a, p. 43. Cf. Wilson 1964, pp. 45f. David Wilson has kindly informed me that he is now of the opinion that the swords from Vrångabäck and Dybäck were made in England.

8 Ban on exports: Jankuhn 1951, p. 228; Thomsen 1971b, n. 4. Also KLNM XVII, 'Sverd', with references.

9 ibid.

10 Roesdahl 1977a, pp. 156f.

11 Müller-Wille 1972; other swords with ornamental hilts, see op. cit. in n. 4, passim; Laursen 1970; Mårtensson ed. 1976, pp. 388f.

12 cf. la Cour 1959, pp. 29ff.

13 Brøndsted 1936, p. 218; Müller-Wille 1976b, p. 129; KLNM XX, 'Øks'.

14 cf. Moltke 1976, p. 213:5, p. 225.

15 Nørlund 1948, pp. 135ff; Roesdahl 1977a, pp. 38f, 136.

16 Nørlund 1948, p. 136; Worsaae 1869; Brøndsted 1936, pp. 98f.

17 Schiørring 1978.

18 For the metallurgical analysis, see Fabritius Buchwald 1976. For the hafts, see Wagner 1976, p. 85; Wagner in Skaarup 1976, p. 219. For the graves in question see Roesdahl 1976, graves IV–VI; Skaarup 1976, pp. 66ff.

19 Roesdahl 1977a, pp. 141f with references. Corresponding small axes are, however, also known from civilian settlements (Stoumann 1978, p. 57), some of which may very well have had practical use. On the function of these small axes, see also ch. 7.

20 Thorvildsen 1950.

21 Laursen 1960, p. 93; cf. Ramskou 1950, pp. 174f; Skaarup 1976, pp. 56ff, 177.

22 Thomsen 1971b.

23 Ramskou 1950, pp. 174f; Skaarup 1976, pp. 56ff, 177.

24 Wagner in Skaarup 1976, p. 219.

25 Roesdahl 1977a, pp. 38ff; Nørlund 1948, p. 137 and pl. 40:1.

26 KLNM XVI, 'Spjut'; Skyum-Nielsen 1967, p. 110 (Abbo II, 17).

27 Thorvildsen 1957, pp. 82f; Müller-Wille 1976b, pp. 8off.

28 e.g. Nørlund 1948, pp. 137ff; Andersen, Crabb and Madsen 1971, pp. 204f; Ohlsson 1975–6, pp. 110f. There are also several examples from Aggersborg.

29 Müller-Wille 1976b, pp. 8off.

30 Information kindly provided by Kurt Schietzel.

31 From the list of wooden objects from Hedeby, kindly provided by Kurt Schietzel.

32 Mårtensson ed. 1976, fig. 303.

33 Marxen and Moltke 1978. Here, however, the figure is interpreted as a saint or Christ.

34 Grieg 1947 (Gjermundbu); Thordeman et al. 1939, p. 226 and fig. 232:1–6 (Birka).

35 Brøndsted 1936, p. 218; Thorvildsen 1957, pp. 82f; Müller-Wille 1976b, pp. 78ff; Nørlund 1948, p. 139; Mårtensson ed. 1976, p. 395.

36 Moltke 1976, p. 213, cf. p. 135; Grieg 1943.

37 Skyum-Nielsen 1967, p. 85 (Abbo I, 119).

38 Moltke 1976, p. 258; Foote and Wilson 1970, pp. 36of.

39 Steenstrup 1876, pp. 262ff; Foote and Wilson 1970, pp. 272ff; Zettel 1977, pp. 250ff; KLNM, loc. cit. in 4.

40 e.g. Albrectsen 1976, pp. 77, 113, 131; Whitelock ed. 1979, p. 195; cf. Zettel 1977, pp. 257ff.

41 Dolley 1965, fig. 35.

42 e.g. Albrectsen 1976, p. 132; Quellen zur Karolingischen Reichsgeschichte III, p. 295.

43 Naval battles are mentioned in the Anglo-Saxon Chronicle (Whitelock ed. 1979, p. 186ff, e.g. annal for 882); Zettel 1977, pp. 258f; cf. Foote and Wilson 1970, pp. 282f.

44 Zettel 1977, pp. 250ff; cf. Skyum-Nielsen 1967; Whitelock ed. 1979, pp. 186ff, pp.

319ff; Albrectsen 1976, *passim*. Field fortifications in the Frankish Empire: Skyum-Nielsen 1979. Battle of Dyle 891: *loc. cit.* in n. 42.

45 Almgren 1963; Callmer 1973–4.

46 cf. Foote and Wilson 1970, pp. 283ff; Zettel 1977, p. 260.

47 Albrectsen 1976, pp. 12f; *Carolingian Chronicles*, p. 83; *Quellen zur Karolingischen Reichsgeschichte* I, pp. 78f.

48 *KLNM* IX, 'Krigskunst'; XIV, 'Rytteri'.

49 *loc. cit.* in n. 44.

50 Arbman 1961, pp. 84f; Dillmann 1974, nos. 76–84.

51 Wilson 1976a, pp. 439f; *RGA* 4, 'Burg', pp. 215f; cf. ch. 11. My thanks to Martin Biddle for information on the recent excavations in Repton.

52 Lerche 1975; *idem* 1976; Nørlund 1948, pl. 19:11–12; *KLNM* XV, 'Skovl'; XVI, 'Spade'. Wagons/carts and hand-barrows: ch. 3.

53 Albrectsen 1976, p. 16; *Carolingian Chronicles*, pp. 88f; *Quellen zur Karolingischen Reichsgeschichte* I, pp. 88f.

54 The main works are Müller and Neergaard 1903; Jankuhn 1937; la Cour 1951; Andersen, Madsen and Voss 1976.

55 Andersen, Madsen and Voss 1976; Andersen 1977.

56 Wilson 1978a; Sawyer 1978a, pp. 108f.

57 *loc. cit.* in n. 53.

58 Albrectsen 1976, p. 18; *Carolingian Chronicles*, pp. 92f; *Quellen zur Karolingischen Reichsgeschichte* I, pp. 94ff.

59 la Cour 1968.

60 This theory has most recently been disputed by the historians Christensen 1969, pp. 230ff; Skovgaard-Petersen 1977, pp. 170ff.

61 On the wars of 974 and 983, see Thietmar von Merseburg III:6 and 24 (p. 90f, 112f); cf. *op. cit.* in n. 60; H. H. Andersen 1977, pp. 51ff. Rune stones: Moltke 1976, p. 162f (Sdr. Vissing), pp. 157ff (Hedeby).

62 On the Semicircular Wall and the fortifications outside it: *op. cit.* in n. 55 with references.

63 Jankuhn 1963, pp. 84ff.

64 Andersen, Crabb and Madsen 1971.

65 Ohlsson 1975–6, pp. 141ff.

66 Roesdahl 1977a, pp. 172ff; *idem* 1980; Wilson 1978a; cf. below.

67 Nørlund 1948.

68 e.g. Christensen 1969, pp. 246ff.

69 Preliminary reports in Schultz 1949; Olsen and Schmidt 1977, *passim*; Roesdahl 1977a, p. 167; *idem* 1977b; 1977c; 1980. On the church excavation: Græbe and Roesdahl 1977.

70 Olsen and Schmidt 1977; Roesdahl 1977a.

71 Olsen and Schmidt 1977, pp. 86f; Roesdahl 1977a, pp. 167f.

72 Survey in Olsen and Schmidt 1977, pp. 86ff.

73 Schmidt 1973; Olsen and Schmidt 1977, pp. 108ff.

74 Nørlund 1948, pp. 161f.

75 The theory in full: Olsen 1962; *idem* 1975b; *idem* 1979; in modified form: Olsen in Olsen and Schmidt 1977, pp. 96ff.

76 e.g. Christensen 1969, pp. 246ff; Christiansen 1970; Wilson 1976a; *idem* 1978a; Schmidt in Olsen and Schmidt 1977, pp. 149f; Roesdahl 1977a, pp. 161ff; *idem* 1980; Christiansen *et al.* at press. For further attempts at interpre-

tation see Olsen and Schmidt 1977, pp. 96ff with references. The dendrochronological dating of Trelleborg was given by Tage E. Christiansen at the symposium of historians 'Danish Medieval History—New Currents' in Copenhagen, September 1979, and published in Bonde 1979. On the date of Harald's death, see e.g. Christensen 1969, pp. 240f; *idem* 1975, pp. 9f.

77 e.g. Stenton 1967, pp. 369ff.

78 Nørlund 1948; Roesdahl 1977a, pp. 161ff (Trelleborg); Roesdahl 1977a, pp. 168ff (Fyrkat); *ibid.*, pp. 167f (Nonnebakken); Roesdahl 1977a, p. 167; *idem* 1980; but cf. Olsen in Olsen and Schmidt 1977, p. 97 (Aggersborg). The dendrochronological analysis of timber from Fyrkat was undertaken 1979–80 at the instigation of Olaf Olsen who has kindly given me the results.

79 Location of Aggersborg: Roesdahl 1980. Location of Fyrkat: Olsen and Schmidt 1977, pp. 32ff. I should like to refer to a trip I made in a sailing boat down the entire length of Mariager fjord in the summer of 1979. Location of Trelleborg: Nørlund 1948; Christiansen 1970; Christiansen *et al.*, at press.

80 Roesdahl 1977a.

81 Olsen and Schmidt 1977, pp. 89ff, 149f; Roesdahl 1977a, p. 173. Souburg: Trimpe Burger 1973; *idem* 1975.

82 Wilson 1978a; *RGA* 4, 'Burg'.

83 Most of these ideas are presented and discussed in more detail in Roesdahl 1980.

84 *Saxonis Gesta Danorum* I, p. 395.

85 Crumlin-Pedersen 1975b.

86 Wåhlin Andersen 1964.

87 Crumlin-Pedersen 1973. The article summarises the information available in 1973 about sea-barriers in Danish territory.

88 Olsen and Crumlin-Pedersen 1967, pp. 91ff; Crumlin-Pedersen 1978, p. 33ff.

89 Schultz 1936; Crumlin-Pedersen 1973, p. 31. The C-14 dating is from parts of a pile, the tree being about seventy years old before the trunk in question was felled. The result: AD 930 ± 100 years (K 1156). Henrik Tauber has kindly informed me that the calibrated date is AD 975.

90 Crumlin-Pedersen 1973. C-14 dating of a wood sample from one of the floaters gave the result AD 1060 ± 100 years (K 1095). According to information from Henrik Tauber, the calibrated age is AD 1090.

91 Atterman 1969.

92 *KLNM* X, 'Landvärn'; Kjersgaard 1966.

93 Crumlin-Pedersen 1978, pp. 51f with references. *KLNM* I, '-bavn'; XIX, 'Vete I'.

94 Brooks 1971; Wilson 1978a; Lund 1980.

95 Skovgaard-Petersen 1977, pp. 194ff; Christensen 1977, pp. 248ff; *KLNM* X, 'Leidang'.

96 Kristensen 1975.

97 Lund 1980.

98 Moltke 1976, pp. 233ff; Lund 1980; cf. Skovgaard-Petersen 1977, pp. 194ff.

99 Jansson 1962, pp. 48ff; *idem* 1966.

100. Roesdahl 1977a, pp. 134ff, 156f; *idem* 1977d; Müller-Wille 1978b.

Chapter 9: Pagans and Christians

1 There is an enormous amount of literature on pagan faith and religious practices. The

works mentioned here are to be seen as an introduction to the subject. *KLNM* III, 'Döden och de döda'; 'Edda, den yngre'; 'Eddadiktning'; V, 'Gudediktning'; 'Guder og gudeætter'; XVIII, 'Trosskiftet'; Olsen 1966; *idem* 1969; *idem* 1970; Foote and Wilson 1970, pp. 387ff. The temple in Uppsala and the sacrifices there: Adam of Bremen IV:26–27.

2 *KLNM* XII, 'Oðinn'; XIX, 'Valhall'; Hald 1965; *idem* 1969, pp. 50ff; *idem* 1971, pp. 36ff; cf. Kousgård Sørensen 1974; Moltke 1976, pp. 120f.

3 *KLNM* XX, 'Þórr'.

4 See also Hald *loc. cit.* in n. 2.

5 *loc. cit.* in ch. 7 n. 136; Resi 1979, pp. 64ff.

6 Jacobsen and Moltke 1941–2, text, cols. 1007, 1012; Moltke 1976, pp. 180ff, 222.

7 Brøndsted 1955.

8 Foote and Wilson 1970, pp. 360f; *KLNM* I, 'Billedbeskrivende dikt'; V, 'Gudediktning', col. 535.

9 Eldjárn 1956, fig. 175 and pp. 362f.

10 *KLNM* IV, 'Freyja'; 'Freyr'; Hald *loc. cit.* in n. 2; Lindquist 1962. Cf. Adam of Bremen IV:26–7 (on the temple and sacrifices at Uppsala).

11 *KLNM* III, 'Diser'; XII, 'Norner'; XIX, 'Valkyrje'. Some of the female figures mentioned are illustrated in Wilson and Klindt-Jensen 1966, pl. 24: c–e.

12 *loc. cit.* in n. 1; Hald 1965; *idem* 1969, pp. 59ff.

13 *loc. cit.* in ch. 7, n. 137.

14 Ramskou 1962, p. 249.

15 Moltke 1976, pp. 199ff.

16 Andersen, Madsen and Voss 1976, p. 58 and fig. 104; H. H. Andersen 1977, p. 33; *KLNM* IV, 'Falloskult'.

17 Brøndsted 1942, pp. 315–18; Madsen 1970.

18 Roesdahl 1977a, pp. 143, 150.

19 e.g. a small figure of walrus ivory from Lund (Lindquist 1962; Mårtensson and Wahlöö 1970, no. 108). Incidentally, similar figures are known from Denmark (illustrated in Lauring 1973, p. 183 and elsewhere) and Iceland (Eldjárn 1956, fig. 174 and p. 361; this is interpreted as a gaming-piece).

20 Adam of Bremen, IV:26–7.

21 Thietmar von Merseburg, pp. 20f.

22 See especially H. Andersen 1960; Wulff Andersen 1977a with references; Skovgaard-Petersen 1977, pp. 36ff with references.

23 e.g. Foote and Wilson 1970, pp. 136ff; Skovgaard-Petersen 1977, pp. 98ff.

24 Jacobsen and Moltke 1941–2, text, cols. 655f, 729f; Moltke 1976, pp. 145, 180ff.

25 The thesis is advanced and defended in Olsen 1966.

26 Olsen 1966; *idem* 1969; *idem* 1970; Hald 1965; *idem* 1969, pp. 54ff; Foote and Wilson 1970, pp. 393ff; *KLNM* VII, 'Hov og horg'.

27 Lidén 1969 (the gold plates are important in identifying it as a cult place, but are difficult to date more precisely).

28 *loc. cit.* in n. 26 (Olsen; Foote and Wilson; *KLNM*).

29 *loc. cit.* in n. 26.

30 Cremation burials are surveyed in Ramskou 1950; Strömberg 1961, pp. 49ff; Voss, Müller-Wille and Raabe 1973, fig. 113 and List 1; Ramskou 1976. Inhumation graves in Denmark: Brøndsted 1936; in Skåne: Ström-

berg 1961, pp. 38ff. Nearly all known inhumation graves from Viking Age Denmark are listed in Müller-Wille 1976b, fig. 50 and Finds List 3. But see also Müller-Wille 1976a; Ramskou 1976; Skaarup 1976; Roesdahl 1976; *idem* 1977a; Wulff Andersen 1979. A survey of Viking Age burial-customs: Brøndsted 1960, pp. 330ff; cf. Skaarup 1976; Roesdahl 1977a, pp. 145ff.

31 Brøndsted 1936, pp. 214ff; Müller-Wille 1976b, pp. 116ff with references.

32 Thorvildsen 1957; Müller-Wille 1976b, p. 120, with references (the lists also include small boats used as coffins). Boat-graves: *RGA* 3, 'Bootgrab'.

33 e.g. Skaarup 1976, p. 164f; Roesdahl 1977a, p. 130.

34 *loc. cit.* in n. 32.

35 Müller-Wille 1976a; Roesdahl 1976; *idem* 1977a; *idem* 1978; *idem* at press.

36 Ch. 7, nn. 29–31.

37 Roesdahl 1977a, p. 132.

38 But cf. Roesdahl 1977a, p. 148.

39 Brøndsted 1936, p. 222; Degerbøl in Thorvildsen 1957, pp. 114ff; Voss, Müller-Wille and Raabe 1973, p. 111; Ramskou 1976, pp. 107ff; Müller-Wille 1976b, Table 1, p. 129; Wulff Andersen and Hatting 1978.

40 Ch. 8, nn. 16–17.

41 Brøndsted 1936, p. 219; H. Andersen 1963; cf. Petersen 1951 (on Norwegian graves).

42 e.g. Brøndsted 1936, pp. 223f; Skaarup 1976, pp. 170f; Müller-Wille 1976b, pp. 132ff; Ramskou 1976, pp. 107ff.

43 Ch. 8, nn. 18–19.

44 Brøndsted 1936, p. 216; Ramskou 1950, *passim*; Roesdahl 1977a, p. 145, with references.

45 Ship-settings: Brøndsted 1936, no. 3; Ramskou 1950, nos. 7 and 11; Strömberg 1961, pp. 51ff; Ramskou 1976; Wulff Andersen 1979, nos. 49, 51, 53; *op. cit.* in nn. 56 and 57. Survey in Brøndsted 1960, pp. 331f.

46 Roesdahl 1976 (Sønder Onsild); Andersen and Klindt-Jensen 1970; Skaarup 1976 (Hesselbjerg and Stengade II); Jankuhn 1963, pp. 124ff; Steuer 1974, pp. 19ff, 33ff (Hedeby); Nørlund 1948, pp. 105ff; Roesdahl 1977a, pp. 73ff (Trelleborg and Fyrkat).

47 Andersen and Klindt-Jensen 1970; Skaarup 1976, pp. 132ff; Roesdahl 1977a, pp. 74ff, 130; cf. Strömberg 1961, pp. 51ff.

48 Roesdahl 1977a, p. 129, 145.

49 Ch. 2, n. 34.

50 Brøndsted 1936, pp. 226f; cf. Ramskou 1950, pp. 178ff.

51 Compare e.g. *op. cit.* in n. 30 with Blomqvist and Mårtensson 1963, pp. 47f; Mårtensson ed. 1976, p. 171ff; cf. *op. cit.* in ch. 2, n. 22.

52 cf. Skaarup 1976, pp. 182f.

53 *KLNM* I, 'Barneutbering'. (The Church however allowed the exposure of seriously deformed children.)

54 Nørlund 1948, pp. 36ff; Andersen, Crabb and Madsen 1971, p. 46; Schietzel and Ulbricht 1977.

55 Schietzel and Ulbricht 1977, p. 61; Bantelmann 1975, p. 79.

56 Albrectsen 1958; *idem* 1959 (Glavendrup); Voss 1959 (Bække); H. Andersen 1960; Wulff Andersen 1977a (Lejre); Moltke 1976, pp. 180ff. *et passim*.

57 Jacobsen and Moltke 1941–2, text, col. 909ff;

Moltke 1976, pp. 248, 252 et passim.

58 H. Andersen 1951. Salted bodies brought home: Roesdahl 1979.

59 *KLNM* III, 'Döden och de döda'; XIX, 'Valhall'; Foote and Wilson 1970, pp. 406ff; cf. Almgren 1904, who attempts in an inspiring way to combine literary sources and archaeology.

60 Brøndsted 1936, pp. 213ff; *idem* 1960, pp. 330ff; Moltke 1976.

61 Jankuhn 1963, pp. 124ff with references; Müller-Wille 1976a; *idem* 1976b.

62 Skaarup 1976, p. 183; cf. Brøndsted 1936, nos. 87–9.

63 Müller-Wille 1976b, pp. 125ff. See also Brøndsted 1936, *passim*; Müller-Wille 1976a, pp. 27ff; *idem* 1977a.

64 *op. cit.* in n. 35; Brøndsted 1936, nos. 32 and 70:18; cf. Müller-Wille 1974a; Wulff Andersen and Hatting 1978.

65 Several of the ideas put forward here are proposed in Müller-Wille 1978b. Concepts of Valhall and other ideas about life after death: *loc. cit.* in n. 59; cf. Foote and Wilson 1970, pp. 331, 359ff.

66 See nn. 65 and 67.

67 Müller-Wille 1976a, pp. 44ff; *idem* 1978b; Roesdahl 1978; *idem* at press.

68 e.g. Kromann in Skaarup 1976, pp. 192ff; cf. Gräslund 1965–6. Coins in Danish Viking Age graves: *op. cit.* in n. 96.

69 Müller-Wille 1978b.

70 *Antiquarisk Tidsskrift* 1864, pp. 16ff; Brøndsted 1936, no. 79.

71 *Antiquarisk Tidsskrift* 1864, pp. 19ff; Brøndsted 1936, no. 80.

72 Worsaae 1869; Vellev 1973; on its possible Christian character, see e.g. Müller-Wille 1978b, p. 638, with references.

73 Thorvildsen 1957; Müller-Wille 1976b.

74 The literature on Jelling is vast. The standard work is Kornerup 1875. Dyggve 1948 and *idem* 1964 contain a survey of his ideas on the whole complex, several parts of which he excavated in the 1940s. In *Mediaeval Scandinavia* 7, 1974, important parts of the monument and their interpretation are discussed by various authors (*Jelling Problems. A discussion*); this contains references to older literature. The latest overall view is in Moltke 1976, pp. 162ff, where the small rune stone from the churchyard boundary wall is also mentioned. The most recent excavations: Krogh 1980b.

75 See especially Jacobsen and Moltke 1941–2, nos. 41–2. Also Klindt-Jensen and Wilson 1965, pp. 86ff (the large stone as a work of art); Glob 1969a (who thinks that the inscription on the large stone was carved in two stages); Christensen 1975 (who thinks that the stone was executed in several phases); Moltke 1974, *idem* 1976, pp. 162ff (who rejects this); Johansen and Liestøl 1977 (who consider the stone with particular reference to technique and materials).

76 Kornerup 1875; Dyggve 1948; Roesdahl 1974 (who in particular discusses the grave's association with Gorm and Thyre, and rejects the claim that many Christian elements can be detected in the grave-goods); *idem* 1975; Moltke 1976, pp. 174ff (who still sees Christian elements in the ornament on the small wooden figure from the mound);

77 Dyggve 1964; Glob 1969a and b; Olsen 1974, with references.

78 Brøndsted 1960, p. 332.

79 Dyggve 1942; *idem* 1948; *idem* 1964; H. Andersen 1951 (on empty mounds); *idem* 1972; *idem* 1974 (on the interpretation of the wooden construction as a template; cf. Thrane 1978); Moltke 1976, pp. 185, 200f; cf. Nielsen 1974, pp. 172ff (on the rune stone at Bække).

80 According to new dating by dendrochronology and C-14 (for which my thanks to Henrik Tauber; this dating modifies that published in Christiansen 1975).

81 There were several excavations in Jelling church before those current in 1979, see Dyggve 1948, pp. 195ff; *idem* 1964; Krogh 1966; cf. Olsen 1974.

82 cf. Krogh 1980a; *idem* 1980b.

83 The idea of the translation of the bodies was first proposed by Ejnar Dyggve, see Dyggve 1948, pp. 196f. It is discussed and considered unlikely in Roesdahl 1974, pp. 221f.

84 cf. Skovgaard-Petersen 1977, pp. 164ff.

85 cf. Müller-Wille 1978b, p. 633.

86 In general: Olsen 1969; Christensen 1969, pp. 226ff; Skovgaard-Petersen 1977, pp. 148ff.

87 The conversion of the Vikings in England: Wilson 1967 with references. *KLNM* XIII, 'Primsigning'. The quotation is from *Egils saga*, trans. C. Fell, p. 74.

88 e.g. *Quellen zur Karolingischen Reichsgeschichte* I, pp. 144ff; Albrectsen 1976, pp. 24, 55f, 111 *et passim; Carolingian Chronicles*, p. 119.

89 *Quellen des 9 und 11 Jahrhunderts . . . , passim.*

90 *Diplomatarium Danicum*, ser. 1, vol. 1, nos. 319 and 330.

91 Müller-Wille 1976a, p. 47 and pl. 19; Resi 1979, p. 66 and fig. 61:1; Brøndsted 1960, p. 380.

92 *op. cit.* in note 86. Harald's conversion is described by the Saxon Widukind: Widukind III:65.

93 *op. cit.* in n. 86; Krins 1968, pp. 2ff; Christensen 1969, pp. 266ff; *idem* 1977, pp. 226ff; Jørgensen 1908.

94 Moltke 1976, pp. 195ff, 217ff, 222, 228f.

95 Thor's hammers: n. 5 above. Graves: Brøndsted 1936, pp. 226f; Ramskou 1950, p. 182; Roesdahl 1977a, pp. 150f.

96 As far as I know there are forty-two coins from a total of twenty-one graves, with an unknown number of coins from yet another grave. References: Roesdahl 1977a, p. 151, n. 28 (present Denmark); Müller-Wille 1976a, p 42 nn.174, 176 and 177 (including the district south of the present Danish border). On the coin mentioned: Kromann in Skaarup 1976, pp. 192ff. Among the other coins, one was minted between 936 and 962, and another is attributed to *c.* 950–65. The others (as far as they are identified) belong to the first half of the tenth century or possibly to the very last years of the ninth c.

97 Nørlund 1948, pp. 105ff; Roesdahl 1977a, pp. 73ff.

98 Brøndsted 1936, pp. 181f; Schiørring 1978.

99 Olsen 1966, pp. 267 ff; cf. below on the locations of the earliest churches.

100 Græbe and Roesdahl 1977.
101 Krogh and Voss 1961. Dating of the plank, which is in the Urnes style: Wilson and Klindt-Jensen 1966, p. 147ff.
102 Olsen 1966, pp. 267ff. Slangerup church in Gammel Frederiksborg amt also lies on a levelled Bronze Age mound (information from Henrik Græbe).
103 Olsen 1963; Blomqvist and Mårtensson 1963, pp. 43ff, 89ff; Mårtensson ed. 1976, pp. 87ff; Græbe and Roesdahl 1977; Stiesdal 1977; Ohlsson 1977; Ohlsson and Cinthio 1979, pp. 49ff; Cinthio 1979–80.
104 Mårtensson ed. 1976, p. 87; Græbe and Roesdahl 1977; Ohlsson 1977; Ohlsson and Cinthio 1979, pp. 53f; Cinthio 1979–80.
105 Blomqvist and Mårtensson 1963, pp. 43ff, 89ff; Mårtensson ed. 1976, pp. 92ff; Ohlsson 1977; Ohlsson and Cinthio 1979, pp. 50ff; Cinthio 1979–80.
106 Blomqvist and Mårtensson 1963, pp. 48ff, 92ff; Krogh 1965; Mårtensson ed. 1976, pp. 105ff.
107 Mårtensson ed. 1976, pp. 112ff. According to information kindly provided by Olaf Olsen, there is also a charcoal grave at Snoldelev, Gammel Københavns amt.
108 cf. below under the individual churches.
109 loc. cit. in n. 103, respectively Mårtensson ed., Græbe and Roesdahl, Olsen, Stiesdal. For the present Stenløse church, see Danmarks Kirker, Frederiksborg Amt, 1976, pp. 2353ff.
110 Adam of Bremen, IV:7.
111 Ohlsson 1977; Ohlsson and Cinthio 1979, pp. 49ff; Cinthio 1979–80.
112 cf. Møller and Olsen 1961; Krogh and Voss 1961; Krins 1968, pp. 126ff; Olsen 1960, fig. 32; Steen Jensen 1977.
113 Møller and Olsen 1961; Møller 1963; Krins 1968, pp. 2ff, 126ff.
114 Mårtensson ed. 1976, pp. 116ff.
115 Blomqvist and Mårtensson 1963, p. 39 and fig. 18.
116 Krogh and Voss 1961.
117 The wooden church fragments, see Møller 1963; Krins 1968, p. 127 with references.
118 Møller and Olsen 1961. Danish secular buildings: Olsen and Schmidt 1977, pp. 119ff; Stoumann 1978; cf. ch. 4. Greensted church: Taylor and Taylor 1965, pp. 262ff; Christie, Olsen and Taylor 1979. Norwegian stave churches: Dietriechson 1892; Hauglid 1969; Anker 1970, pp. 200ff; idem 1977 (the most recent critical account of Norwegian churches and their dating).
119 Danmarks Kirker, Københavns Amt, 3; Olsen 1960, passim; Krins 1968, pp. 5f, 46ff.
120 Olsen 1960; Krins 1968, pp. 59ff.
121 Krins 1968, pp. 27ff.
122 Krins 1968; Olsen 1972b.
123 Danmarks Kirker, Århus Amt, 3, pp. 1003ff.
124 Mackeprang 1944.
125 Jacobsen and Moltke 1941–2, no. 315; Moltke 1976, pp. 197, 343; Krins 1968, p. 7.

Chapter 10: Art and Ornament

1 Foote and Wilson 1970, pp. 319ff.
2 The Norwegian art-historians Peter Anker (Anker 1970) and Signe Horn (Nordhagen) Fuglesang (e.g. in Horn Fuglesang 1980) are among the few who have worked on the art of the Viking Age. The Danish art-historian Erik Lassen (Lassen 1972, pp. 10–31) has touched on the subject.
3 Müller 1880; see also Brøndsted 1920 or 1924; idem 1960, pp. 377ff.
4 Wilson and Klindt-Jensen 1966, pp. 143f, 155ff; Ørsnes 1968; Graham-Campbell and Kidd 1980, pp. 153ff.
5 op. cit. in n. 4; Foote and Wilson 1970, pp. 286ff. In the following I make general reference to these works. Cf. Arbman 1961, pp. 118ff; Anker 1970.
6 See also Horn Fuglesang 1980; Lang ed. 1978; Bailey 1980; cf. ch. 11. On the Irish motif-pieces: O'Meadhra 1979.
7 Ch. 9, nn. 7–8.
8 ibid.; M. Blindheim ed. 1972; idem 1973; Margeson 1980.
9 cf. Foote and Wilson 1970, p. 336.
10 Moltke 1974; idem 1976, pp. 174ff; Marxen and Moltke 1978 (the latter work takes a putative halo—it is not actually there—as a distinctive attribute. But the figure may have been shown in a hat like the one depicted on a Hunnestad stone (fig. 2). There is a recent drawing and a photograph of it in Moltke 1976, pp. 213 and 225). Cf. Roesdahl 1974, p. 220.
11 Munksgaard 1968; Ohlsson 1975–6, fig. 81; Ulbricht 1978, pls. 34:17 and 43:19 and 21; Levin Nielsen 1978, p. 60; Liebgott 1978c.
12 Wilson and Klindt-Jensen 1966, pp. 27f, 78ff.
13 Kornerup 1875, pp. 22f, and pls. 15f; Marxen and Moltke 1978 (Jelling); Mårtensson 1968 (Lund); Krogh and Voss 1961 (Hørning); Schetelig 1920 (Oseberg); Wilson and Klindt-Jensen 1966, p. 147 and pl. LXIX (Urnes).
14 See ch. 7, n. 40.
15 Worsaae 1869 (Mammen); Krafft 1956 (Oseberg); cf. ch. 7); n. 119.
16 Moltke 1976, pp. 199ff; Jansson 1962, pp. 136ff.
17 Jansson 1962, pp. 147ff; Moltke 1976, passim; Johansen and Liestøl 1977, pp. 77ff (the Jelling stone); Wilson 1974; idem 1980b, p. 165, fig. 12; Moltke 1976, pp. 264ff (the St Paul's stone); Schetelig 1920, pp. 233ff (Oseberg); Thorvildsen 1957, pp. 87f and pl. 2 (Ladby); Krogh and Voss 1961, pl. 1 (Hørning); Kornerup, loc. cit. in n. 13; Marxen and Moltke 1978 (the Jelling carvings).
18 Kryger 1976; idem 1977.
19 Wilson and Klindt-Jensen 1966, pp. 37, 71ff; Ørsnes 1968, pp. 54f, 224ff et passim.
20 Ramskou 1963; Wilson and Klindt-Jensen 1966, pp. 38 ff; Ørsnes 1966, pp. 50ff, 224ff.
21 Wilson and Klindt-Jensen 1966, pp. 50ff, 75; Ørsnes 1968. For more Danish examples of gripping beasts see e.g. Brøndsted 1936, passim; cf. Ramskou 1962, col. pl. opposite p. 416. My thanks to Helge Brinch Madsen for information on the Ribe brooches.
22 Wilson and Klindt-Jensen 1966, pp. 87ff; Wilson 1978c.
23 ibid.; see also Skovmand 1942, passim; Brøndsted 1936, pp. 167ff and pls. 5ff (Nr. Longelse) et passim; Roesdahl 1977a, p. 167f with references (Nonnebakken).
24 Wilson and Klindt-Jensen 1966, pp. 95ff; Wilson 1978c.
25 ibid.; see also Krogh 1980 a and b (Jelling); Antiquarisk Tidsskrift 1861–3, pp. 16ff (Søllested); Müller-Wille 1972 (Bustorf); on bronze jewellery: e.g. Capelle 1968, pl. 12.
26 Compare Wilson and Klindt-Jensen 1966, pp.

95ff and Horn Fuglesang 1980, pp. 77ff., 118 ff. *et passim*. See also Horn Fuglesang 1978.

27 Wilson and Klindt-Jensen 1966, pp. 95ff; Wilson 1978c; Horn Fuglesang 1978; Horn Fuglesang 1980, pp. 14ff. On the Jelling stone and other rune stones see also Moltke 1976, pp. 162ff, 205f, 210f *et passim*. On the Jelling wood, see also *loc. cit.* in n. 13. For the caskets see *loc. cit.* in n. 14. For masks on stones other than rune stones and the origin of the motif, see also Wilson and Klindt-Jensen 1966, p. 119 with references, pl. xxxvii: d (harness-bow from Søllested; this is illustrated more clearly in *Antiquarisk Tidsskrift* 1861–3, p. 20).

28 Wilson and Klindt-Jensen 1966, pp. 136f; Horn Fuglesang 1978; Horn Fuglesang 1980.

29 *ibid.*; see also Wilson 1974; Moltke 1976, pp. 211, 215, 221, 264ff.

30 Mårtensson 1968 (Lund); Olsen and Crumlin-Pedersen 1967, fig. 50 (Skuldelev); Müller 1900b (Århus). See also Schultz 1949, fig. 13; Horn Fuglesang 1980, cat. nos. 36, 103, *et passim*.

31 *op. cit.* in n. 28; Wilson 1974.

32 Wilson and Klindt-Jensen 1966, pp. 147ff; Horn Fuglesang 1978. Horn Fuglesang 1980, pp. 19ff; Urnes brooches in Lund: Mårtensson ed. 1976, pp. 206ff. Chain from Orø: Lindahl 1975. The North Jutland bone fragment: Liebgott 1978c. For the Hørning plank, see Krogh and Voss 1961.

33 Mackeprang 1948, *passim*.

34 e.g. Lassen 1972, pp. 32ff.

Chapter 11: Foreign Contacts

1 Shetelig ed. 1940, I, pp. 1–9; cf. Ørsnes 1966, pp. 180ff; Thorvildsen 1972.

2 Sawyer 1978a, pp. 114f with references; *Cartularium Saxonicum*, II, no. 848.

3 Whitelock ed. 1979, p. 842.

4 Surveys: Arbman and Stenberger 1935; Shetelig ed. 1940–54; Arbman 1955; *idem* 1961; Almgren *et al.* 1967; Christensen 1969; *Varangian Problems* (1970); Musset 1971; Graham-Campbell 1980; Wilson 1980b.

5 Zettel 1977, pp. 33ff; ch. 8, n. 99.

6 Sawyer 1971, pp. 123ff; Zettel 1977, pp. 229ff.

7 Jacobsen and Moltke 1941–2, nos. 3, 6, 37, 108, 216, 220, 259, 266, 279, 295–7, 334, 335, 337, 344, cf. nos. 42, 55, 107, 411.

8 Hoards: Skovmand 1942, Hårdh 1976. Graves: *op. cit.* in ch. 9, n. 30. Imports: Brøndsted 1960, pp. 329ff, 347f.

9 *Quellen zur Karolingischen Reichsgeschichte* I, p. 102f; Albrectsen 1976, p. 20; *Carolingian Chronicles*, p. 96. Kaupang: Blindheim 1969; *idem* 1976a, 1976b, 1978.

10 Stenton 1967, pp. 388ff; Christensen 1969; *idem* 1977; Skovgaard-Petersen 1977.

11 Kaupang/*Sciringes heal*: Blindheim *op. cit.* in n. 9. Ohthere's journey: ch. 3. Sailing routes: ch. 5. Norwegian iron: Thorvildsen 1950 (the axes from Gjerrild, ch. 8).

12 Jacobsen and Moltke 1941–2, no. 107.

13 Arbman 1955.

14 Ansgar's journey: *Quellen des 9. und 11. Jahrhunderts* ..., pp. 86f. Theories on the so-called Swedish rule: Skovgaard-Petersen 1977, pp. 161ff; Lund in Moltke and Lund 1977, pp. 197ff. Fighting between Danes and Swedes: Ellehøj 1953; Christensen 1969; Skovgaard-Petersen 1977; cf. Jacobsen and

Moltke 1941–2, nos. 279 and 295–7. See also n. 7.

15 Gotlandic jewellery and silver in Denmark: Skovmand 1942, pp. 216f; Hårdh 1976, pp. 92ff; Roesdahl 1977a, pp. 137f, with references; a tongue-shaped pendant found near Svendborg is in the National Museum Copenhagen, 1st Dept., inv. no. C 14584. Runic inscriptions: Jacobsen and Moltke 1941–2, nos. 220 and 259. Danish silver in Gotland: Stenberger 1947 and 1958.

16 Vikings in these areas generally: *op. cit.* in n. 4.

17 Expedition to Kurland: *Quellen des 9. und 11. Jahrhunderts* ..., pp. 94ff. Grobin: e.g. Arbman 1955. Wulfstan's account: Sweet ed. 1883, pp. 19–21. Baltic jewellery in Denmark: Nørlund 1948, p. 128 and pl. 25:2 and 11; Hårdh 1976, pp. 71, 94f; Roesdahl 1977a, p. 38.

18 Ch. 6, with references. See also Arbman 1955; Sawyer 1971, pp. 86ff, 219ff; *KLNM* I, 'Arabiska mynt'; II, 'Bysantinska mynt'.

19 Hårdh 1976, p. 32.

20 Skovmand 1942, pp. 30ff; Stenberger 1958, pp. 123ff; Munksgaard 1969, with references; Hårdh 1976, pp. 91f, 95f.

21 Beads: ch. 7, n. 134. Rye and pollen: Helbæk in Olsen and Schmidt 1977, excursus; Jørgensen in Christiansen *et al.* (at press), Appendix A. On the other items: Blomqvist and Mårtensson 1963, pp. 173f, 209f.

22 The seal and coin-brooch from Hedeby: Laurent 1978; Capelle 1968, pp. 19, 106f (no. 93), pl. 11:3. Silk: ch. 7, n. 119; Blomqvist and Mårtensson 1963, pp. 220ff. Later coins and coin imitations: Hauberg 1900, pp. 117ff; Mårtensson 1968, pp. 224ff; Hatz 1978, with references in n. 30.

23 Adam of Bremen IV:1. Locations of the various places: Arbman 1955, pp. 155ff; *KLNM* XX, 'Semgallerna'. Bornholm, which because of its location might seem a suitable stage on the way east, does not appear to have played any particular role in this capacity (*RGA* 3, 'Bornholm').

24 Roesdahl 1977a, pp. 137ff, 150, 159f.

25 Arrhenius 1978 and references.

26 See in general: Arbman 1955; Herrmann 1975; *idem* 1976; Żak 1975.

27 Herfert 1973; Herrmann 1978 and references; Warncke 1978 and references.

28 Schoknecht 1977.

29 Wollin: Filipowiak 1974; Jomsborg: Ellehøj 1953; Christensen 1969, pp. 255ff; Foote and Wilson 1970, especially p. 267.

30 Paulsen 1936; Malmer 1966, especially pl. 54ff; Żak 1963–7; *idem* 1975.

31 A trefoil brooch has been found here in recent excavations, as Hellmuth Andersen kindly tells me; cf. Andersen 1979.

32 *Quellen zur Karolingischen Reichsgeschichte* I; Albrectsen 1976; *Carolingian Chronicles*; cf. e.g. Skovgaard-Petersen 1977, pp. 152ff.

33 Żak 1970; *idem* 1975.

34 Ellehøj 1953; Christensen 1969, especially pp. 252ff; *idem* 1977, pp. 218f; Skovgaard-Petersen 1977, pp. 179ff. Danevirke: ch. 8.

35 Skovmand 1942, p. 217 (nos. 2, 4, 10, 11, 24, 26, 31, 32, 37, 41, 45, 55, 57, 61: altogether fourteen of the sixty-five finds which he dates to the period c. 900–1016; finds from later hoards should be added); Hårdh 1976, pp. 94f.

36 Hald 1965, pp. 225f; *idem* 1974, pp. 38ff.

Bridges, pottery and fortifications: ch. 3, 7 and 8.

37 See in general de Vries 1923; Joranson 1924; Arbman 1937; Shetelig ed. 1940, I and IV, pp. 101ff; Arbman 1961, pp. 74–88; d'Haenens 1967; Christensen 1969; Musset 1971; Wallace-Hadrill 1975; Regteren Altena and Heidinga 1977; Zettel 1977; Skovgaard-Petersen 1977. There is an annotated bibliography in Dillmann 1974. See also the following editions of sources: *Quellen zur Karolingischen Reichsgeschichte* I–III (certain passages are translated into Danish in Albrectsen 1976; and into English in *Carolingian Chronicles*); *Quellen des 9. und 11. Jahrhunderts* . . . ; Adam of Bremen; Widukind; Thietmar von Merseburg. See further Skyum-Nielsen 1967.

38 Adigard des Gautries 1954; Christensen 1969, pp. 158ff, 181f; Musset 1971.

39 Shetelig ed. 1940, IV, pp. 101ff; Regteren Altena and Heidinga 1977, pp. 53ff; Müller-Wille 1978a.

40 Joranson 1924; Albrectsen 1976, pp. 142f.

41 Skyum-Nielsen 1967, pp. 38f.

42 Grieg 1929.

43 Recent excavations in Dorestad: van Es 1973.

44 Christensen 1969, pp. 223ff; Skovgaard-Petersen 1977, pp. 159ff; Andersen 1977, pp. 46ff.

45 *op. cit.* in n. 44; cf. ch. 8, n. 61.

46 Stenton 1967, p. 402; Christensen 1969, p. 266; cf. ch. 7, n. 40.

47 *Quellen zur Karolingischen Reichsgeschichte* III, pp. 88f; Albrectsen 1976, p. 98.

48 A certain amount of Danish material is included in Arbman's standard work of 1937 on Swedish trade with the Carolingian Empire in the ninth century. No corresponding Danish work exists. Apart from Arbman 1937, the reader may refer to references in the previous chapters and in particular to the following works: Wiell, *op. cit.* in ch. 7, n. 124; Skovmand 1942, pp. 214ff *et passim*; Galster 1951; Capelle 1968, pp. 31ff; Bencard and Wiell 1975; Hårdh 1976, pp. 92ff; Müller-Wille 1976a, pp. 36f, and references, and pls. 35:18, 38:4.

49 Vikings in England and Ireland in general: Shetelig ed. 1940–54; Stenton 1967; Lund 1967; Christensen 1969; Sawyer 1971; Jensen 1975; Wilson 1976c; articles in *Proceedings of the Seventh Viking Congress* (1976); Loyn 1977; Sawyer 1978a; articles in *The Vikings* 1978; Morris 1979; Wilson 1980a; Graham-Campbell 1980; Roesdahl *et al.* ed. 1981. Many written sources have been collected in Whitelock ed. 1979 (1955).

50 Whitelock ed. 1979, pp. 145–286 or other editions of the Chronicle.

51 Joranson 1924, pp. 14–25.

52 Whitelock 1979, pp. 416f.

53 Whitelock 1979, p. 205; cf. n. 78.

54 Wilson 1976c; Sawyer 1978a, p. 120.

55 Shetelig ed. 1940, III, VI.

56 Shetelig ed. 1940–54 (Cuerdale hoard: IV, pp. 32ff, VI, pp. 243ff); Wilson 1976d.

57 Dolley 1965; de Paor 1976.

58 Ó Ríordáin 1971; *idem* 1976; *Viking Settlement to Medieval Dublin* 1978; O'Meadhra 1979.

59 Wilson and Klindt-Jensen 1966, pp. 155ff; Horn Fuglesang 1980.

60 Shetelig ed. 1940–54, III, p. 101ff; Graham-Campbell 1976.

61 See survey in Jensen 1975; cf. also below. The discussions were sparked off by the first ed. (1962) of Sawyer 1971.

62 Jensen 1968; *idem* 1972; *idem* 1975; Morris 1977; Gelling 1978, pp. 215ff; articles in *The Vikings* 1978; Jensen 1978.

63 Wilson 1980a; cf. Wilson 1976c. Ribblehead: King 1978.

64 Stenton 1967, pp. 427f, with references; Wilson 1967; *idem* 1976c; Dolley 1965; *idem* 1978. Stray finds: Shetelig ed. 1940–54, IV, pp. 57ff.

65 Surveys: Collingwood 1927; Lang ed. 1978; Bailey 1980; cf. Wilson and Klindt-Jensen 1966; Wilson 1967; Lang 1978.

66 Relationship between hogbacks and houses: Schmidt 1970; *idem* 1973; Rahtz 1976.

67 Bailey 1980.

68 Biddle 1976; Sawyer 1978a, pp. 204ff; Wilson 1980a. Coins: Dolley 1965; *idem* 1978. York and Lincoln in particular: *op. cit.* in nn. 69–70. Social structure in the Danelaw: Kristensen 1975; Loyn 1977, pp. 125ff. Law in the Danelaw: Fenger 1972.

69 Shetelig ed. 1940–54, IV; Waterman 1959; Hall 1976; Hall ed. 1978; Hall, Daniells and York 1978; Hall 1979; Addyman 1979. The provisional results of the excavations are published in the quarterly *Interim* (ed. York Archaeological Trust) and in *Excavations in York. Interim Reports* (published for York Archaeological Trust by the Council for British Archaeology, ed. P. V. Addyman). The final results are to be published in the series *The Archaeology of York* (Council for British Archaeology). My thanks to Peter Addyman and Richard Hall who have kindly shown me excavations and finds.

70 Shetelig ed. 1940–54, IV; Colyer 1975; Colyer and Jones ed. 1979. The provisional results of the excavations are published in annual reports: *Lincoln Archaeological Trust. Annual Report* and in *The Antiquaries Journal*. The final results come in the series *The Archaeology of Lincoln* (Council for British Archaeology). My thanks to M. J. Jones, Jenny Mann and Kate Foley who have kindly shown me the town and the finds from excavations.

71 Stone sculpture: especially Bailey and Lang, *op. cit.* in n. 65. Metalwork: Wilson 1976e. See also MacGregor 1978; Shetelig 1940–54, VI, pp. 113ff. The object from York in pl. 50 is published in Waterman 1959, pp. 79f and fig. 10:10; cf. Roesdahl 1977a, pp. 35ff. The mould mentioned, with a reconstruction, can be seen in e.g. Hall 1979, p. 20.

72 England in this period: Hill ed. 1978; cf. *op. cit.* in nn. 49–51.

73 Galster 1960.

74 Shetelig ed. 1940–54, IV and V, pp. 113ff; Wilson and Klindt-Jensen 1966, pp. 147ff, 154; Wilson 1974; *idem* 1976c, pp. 401f; Horn Fuglesang 1978; Horn Fuglesang 1980.

75 Biddle 1966; Kjølbye-Biddle and Page 1975, and references.

76 Stenton 1967, pp. 532ff; Adam of Bremen IV:1.

77 The list below (see also n. 80) includes many of the objects of British origin older than *c.* AD 1000 that have been found in present-day Denmark. The list also includes objects which show influence from the British Isles but which were produced in Denmark, or possibly in the Viking colonies in the North of England

or Ireland. During the next few years it will doubtless prove possible to identify more objects in the latter category and probably to define more precisely where in the British Isles imported items were produced. Some items ought perhaps to be in the list in n. 80. In the same way, some items in that list may in fact belong here. Some imported items from the British Isles found in Hedeby are published in Capelle 1968, pl. 25, and references. Skåne: Strömberg 1961; Hårdh 1976, pp. 92ff. Coins: especially Galster 1964, cf. ch. 6, n. 16.
List: Two mounts of unknown provenance (Wilson 1955; *idem* 1964, p. 15, cf. pl. 1b); brooch or mount from Vejleby, Lolland (Christiansen 1948, fig. 1a and p. 6); two mounts and a silver bowl from Lejre (Wilson 1960a; cf. Andersen and Wulff Andersen 1976); strap-end, enamelled decorative stud and jet bead from Aggersborg (Roesdahl 1980); silver arm-rings from several places (Graham-Campbell 1976, pp. 51–53; cf. Munksgaard 1969, pp. 59–63); bowl from Nørre Longelse (Brøndsted 1936, pp. 173ff and pl. 10); a comb with an Englishman's name in runes from Århus (Andersen, Crabb and Madsen 1971, p. 150; Moltke 1976, pp. 296, 298).

78 Sawyer 1971, pp. 99–101; cf. Jensen 1978, pp. 371f on interpretation of the word *fēohlēase*.

79 Shetelig ed. 1940–54, v; Blindheim 1976b; but cf. Graham-Campbell 1977, p. 429 (who thinks that a number of the objects Blindheim

considers to be insular were produced in Scandinavia); Morris 1979.

80 The introductory comments to the list in n. 77 also apply here. This list comprises items from about AD 1000 and the first half of the eleventh century. Relevant material from Lund, published in Blomqvist and Mårtensson 1963, and in Mårtensson ed. 1976, is included here, as are two swords from Skåne.
List: Ornamented swords from Vrångabäck and Dybäck, Skåne (ch. 8, n. 7); stirrups from Velds (ch. 3, n. 56); rune stones (Jacobsen and Moltke 1941–2, nos. 3, 6, 266, 337). Also: lid for pen-case from Lund (Blomqvist and Mårtensson 1963, pp. 213ff and figs. 241–2); strap-end from Lund (*ibid.*, p. 190 and fig. 205); glazed pottery from Lund (Mårtensson ed. 1976, pp. 266ff and col. pl. 5); comb with an English name in runes from Lund (Moltke 1976, pp. 373f); coin-brooch from Trelleborg (Nørlund 1948, p. 128 and pl. 25:8); sword fragment of unknown provenance (Prehistoric Museum, Moesgård, no. 224; Wilson 1964, p. 49; Evison 1967, p. 175 and pl. 16b).

81 See e.g. Christensen 1979, pp. 260ff; Skovgaard-Petersen 1977, pp. 189ff; cf. Kristensen 1975. Cf. chs. 5, 9 and 10.

82 Jørgensen 1908; Lassen 1972, pp. 32–40.

83 Stenton 1967, pp. 593ff.

84 *ibid.*, pp. 603, 608f; Christensen 1977, pp. 243ff. The shrine is published in Burman Becker 1886.

Appendix

Finds List 1 Viking Age settlements in present-day Denmark traced archaeologically (fig. 12)

The list comprises settlements dated to the Viking Age (*c.* 750–1050) on the basis of the type of objects found and/or scientific datings. Jewellery and coins along with scientific datings of relevant material are the most satisfactory basis for dating. Soapstone, preferably found in association with low-fired hemispherical or flat-bottomed pots of Viking Age types, and with loom-weights, conical clay spindle-whorls or sunken-featured buildings, is also a good indication of the Viking Age date of a settlement. However, it must be emphasised that soapstone vessels (at any rate in Hedeby) do not seem to become common until some time in the ninth century and that soapstone was commonly used in Norway right through the Middle Ages, which means that an occasional soapstone sherd may also turn up in medieval contexts in Denmark. The following artefacts and structures (found singly or in association) cannot be regarded as a sufficient basis for dating a settlement to the Viking Age: uncharacteristic pottery sherds of poor quality (these occur in various prehistoric periods and sporadically also in the Middle Ages), hemispherical vessels (low-fired types are known from the later Germanic Iron Age as well as from the Viking Age), Slav-inspired pottery of uncertain date (occurring in both the Viking Age and the early Middle Ages), loom-weights, and conical clay spindle-whorls (pre-Viking Age, Viking Age and presumably also very early medieval), sunken-featured buildings (Germanic Iron Age, Viking Age and, rarely, even medieval), houses with curved long walls (Germanic Iron Age, Viking Age and early medieval).

The catalogue does not include settlements whose existence in the Viking Age is known only from coins found elsewhere bearing the name of the settlement. It should be mentioned that a number of settlements have been traced on Fyn which will probably turn out to be Viking Age (information kindly given by Torben Grøngård Jeppesen).

1 Lindholm Høje: Ramskou 1953; *idem* 1954; *idem* 1955; Marseen 1956; Ramskou 1957a; *idem* 1957b; Marseen 1959; Ramskou 1960b; *idem* 1962, pp. 292–9; *idem* 1976.
2 Bejsebakken: Ørsnes 1959; *idem* 1966, pp. 256f; *RGA* 2, 'Bejsebakken'.
3 Svenstrup: according to information kindly provided by Erik Johansen, Ålborg Historiske Museum, about thirty sunken-featured buildings and pits were excavated here in 1969 and 1971. The finds include hemispherical vessels, loom-weights, soapstone, glass beads. A thermoluminescence dating gave the result 834 ± 50 years (ÅHM j. no. 143). A Borre-style pendant

was found earlier in Svenstrup (National Museum, 1st Dept., hereafter NM I, no. C28589).

4 Aggersborg: civilian settlement and fortress. Schultz 1949; Olsen and Schmidt 1977, pp. 146f and *passim*; Roesdahl 1977a, p. 167; *idem* 1977b; *idem* 1977c; *idem* 1980.

5 Karby: Nielsen and Noe 1977; cf. Finds List 2, no. 12.

6 Faarup: S. Nielsen 1976.

7 Herrup: Skov 1979.

8 Trabjerg: Skov 1972–3; Bender Jørgensen and Skov 1978. A full report will be published in *Acta Archaeologica* 50, 1979 (1980).

9 Omgård: L. C. Nielsen 1976; *idem* 1977. A full report will be published in *Acta Archaeologica* 50, 1979.

10 Viborg: lit., see ch. 5.

11 Fyrkat: fortress. Olsen and Schmidt 1977; Roesdahl 1977a.

12 Arhus: lit., see ch. 5.

13 Vorbasse: Hvass 1976; *idem* 1977a; *idem* 1977b; *idem* 1979a: *idem* 1979b. A full report will be published in *Acta Archaeologica* 50, 1979.

14 Sædding: Stoumann 1977; *idem* 1978; *idem* 1979. A full report will be published in *Acta Archaeologica* 50, 1979.

15 Gammelby: Thomsen 1969; Vorting 1970; *idem* 1972a; *idem* 1972b.

16 Ribe: lit., see ch. 5.

17 Okholm: Bencard 1969.

18 Søby: Nancke-Krogh 1978.

19 Nonnebakken: presumably a fortress. Olsen and Schmidt 1977, pp. 86ff; Roesdahl 1977a, pp. 167f.

20 Trelleborg: civilian settlement and fortress. Nørlund 1948.

21 Gammel Lejre: Andersen 1960; Wulff Andersen 1977a, p. 23. According to information kindly supplied by Steen Wulff Andersen, the finds from the excavation in the village included a soapstone fragment, a couple of pottery vessels of East Danish Viking Age type and a conical clay spindle-whorl.

22 Roskilde: lit., see ch. 5.

23 Lynæs (Skuldevig): Liebgott 1979.

Finds List 2 Soapstone in present-day Denmark (fig. 21)

The list has been compiled on the basis of Resi 1979, fig. 132, and supplemented with more recent finds as well as information on soapstone received from various people. It could without doubt be extended by means of systematic research on soapstone in all the museums in the country. For the dating of soapstone, cf. the introduction to Finds List 1.

1 Strandby: three fragments of vessels. Resi 1979, fig. 132, no. 8.

2 Præstegårdens Mark, Bjergby; two fragments of vessels. Resi 1979, fig. 132, no. 7.

3 Furreby: two fragments of vessels. Krogh 1969; Resi 1979, fig. 132, no. 6.

4 Lindholm Høje: many fragments of vessels, from settlement. Lit., see Finds List 1, no. 1; Resi 1979, fig. 132, no. 13.

5 Svenstrup: at least five fragments of vessels, from settlement. Information kindly supplied by Erik Johansen, Alborg Historiske Museum; Resi 1979, fig. 132, no. 14.

6 Egense: about half a vessel, found by digging on the beach. NM I no. C17832; Resi 1979, fig. 132, no. 10.

7 Hals Barre: two vessels found in the sea, pl. 17. NM I nos. C12529 and C12530; Resi 1979, fig. 132, no. 12.

8 Aggersborg: many fragments of vessels (c. 25 kg) and six spindle-whorls, from civilian settlement and fortress. Lit., see Finds List 1, no. 4; Resi 1979, fig. 132, no. 5.

9 Trendgården: mould. NM I no. C24451; Roesdahl 1977a, pp. 48f.

10 Fovlum: vessel, presumably from grave. NM I no. 8367; Brøndsted 1936, fig. 7; Resi 1979, fig. 132, no. 11.

11 Kammerhøj: vessel from a grave. Brøndsted 1936, p. 88; Resi 1979, fig. 132, no. 9.

12 Karby: five fragments of vessels and three spindle-whorls, from settlement. Information kindly supplied by Per Noe, Morslands Historiske Museum (hereafter MHM); for the settlement, see Nielsen and Noe 1977.

13 Bjørndrup: spindle-whorl. MHM no. 2197. Information kindly supplied by Per Noe.

14 Fjallerslev: fragment of vessel. In private collection. Information kindly supplied by Per Noe.

15 Faarup: spindle-whorl, from settlement. S. Nielsen 1976.

16 Øster Assels: spindle-whorl. MHM no. 5184. Information kindly supplied by Per Noe.

17 Torp: net weight. MHM no. 51x. Information kindly supplied by Per Noe.

18 Herrup: two fragments of vessels, from settlement. Skov 1979.

19 Trabjerg: twenty-five fragments of vessels and two spindle-whorls, from settlement. Bender Jørgensen and Skov 1979; Resi 1979, fig. 132, no. 23.

20 Omgård: fragments of vessels, from settlement. L. C. Nielsen 1976; idem 1977; Resi 1979, fig. 132, no. 22.

21 Viborg: fragments of vessels, from settlement. Information kindly supplied by Erik Levin Nielsen, Viborg Stiftsmuseum; lit. on the settlement, see ch. 5.

22 Fyrkat: fragments (172) of vessels, two spindle-whorls, three moulds, a bellows-shield and eight indeterminate pieces, from fortress. Roesdahl 1977a; Resi 1979, fig. 132, no. 16.

23 Sødringholm: two vessels. Found on the beach having drifted ashore, overgrown with seaweed. Olsen 1956; Resi 1979, fig. 132, no. 19.

24 Randers: fragment of handle and body sherd from vessel. Old find from the grounds of Kinopalæet. Information kindly supplied by Bjørn Stürup, Kulturhistorisk Museum Randers.

25 In the sea outside Katholm and Havknude: two complete vessels and half a vessel at Djurslands Museum; fragment of a vessel in the National Museum, Copenhagen. Found in the sea close to shore. The vessels at Djurslands Museum were found along with another two to four vessels. Djurslands Museum nos. 1476, 1481, 1482; NM I no. C23442. Hovesen 1968; H. H. Andersen 1968; Resi 1979, fig. 132, nos. 15, 17 and 18. My thanks to Djurslands Museum and the National Museum for further information on these finds; the earlier find information seems to have been confused, see Hovesen 1968; thus there do not actually seem to have been vessels from Grenå harbour or from the sea outside Fornæs.

26 Århus: two almost complete vessels, many fragments of vessels, a spindle-whorl, a fly-wheel, from settlement. Søgaard 1961; Andersen, Crabb and Madsen 1971; Resi 1979, fig. 132, no. 20.

27 Snaptun: bellows-shield. Found on the water's edge. Glob 1959; Resi 1979, fig. 132, no. 21.

28 Vorbasse: fragments of vessels, from settlement. Hvass 1979.
29 Sædding: fragments of vessels, from settlement. Stoumann 1978; Resi 1979, fig. 132, no. 25.
30 Gammelby: fragments of vessels, from settlement. Vorting 1972a; Resi 1979, fig. 132, no. 24.
31 Ribe: fragment of vessel, from settlement. Bencard 1973 p. 44; *idem* 1974a, p. 13; Resi 1979, fig. 132, no. 27.
32 Okholm: fragment of vessel, from settlement. Resi 1979, fig. 132, no. 26; for lit. on the settlement, see Bencard 1969.
33 Søby: six fragments of vessels, from settlement. Nancke-Krogh 1978.
34 Ørslev: vessel, used as a font in the church. Olsen 1956; Resi 1979, fig. 132, no. 3.
35 Nabbe: spindle-whorl, probably from a settlement. Information kindly supplied by Torben Grøngård Jeppesen, Fyns Stiftsmuseum, Odense.
36 Svendborg: fragment of vessel, from medieval settlement. Jansen 1974, p. 180; my thanks to Helle Reinholdt for further information on the fragment.
37 Odense: fragment of vessel. Found in excavations 1970, in deep layers in Skomagerstræde. Information kindly supplied by Jørgen Nielsen, Odense Bys Museer.
38 Stengade: spindle-whorl, from grave. Skaarup 1976, p. 176; Resi 1979, fig. 132, no. 4.
39 Egholm: mould. Müller 1900a; Resi 1979, fig. 132, no. 1.
40 Store Fuglede: two fragments of vessels, found in connection with graves. NM I nos. C27285, C27286.
41 Trelleborg: many fragments of vessels, twelve spindle-whorls and a mould, from civilian settlement and fortress. Nørlund 1948; Roesdahl 1977a, p. 166 and fig. 227; Resi 1979, fig. 132, no. 2.
42 Gammel Lejre: fragment of vessel, from settlement. Information kindly supplied by Steen Wulff Andersen, Haderslev Museum, cf. Wulff Andersen 1977a, p. 23.
43 Roskilde: fragment of vessel, old find from Blågårdsstræde-Bondetinget, as well as a mould, old find at Stændertorvet. Roskilde Museum no. 1000–59; NM I no. 13814; information kindly supplied by Ingrid Nielsen, South Jutland University Centre.
44 Lynæs (Skuldevig): fragment of vessel, from settlement. Liebgott 1979.

Sources of Illustrations

Note: Works in italics are in the Bibliography

Bibliography

Many of the books and articles with titles in Danish or another Scandinavian language have English or German summaries.

Abitz, E. A. 1950: *Vejenes Retsforhold.* Copenhagen.

Adam of Bremen: *History of the Archbishops of Hamburg-Bremen.* (Trans. F. J. Tschan). New York 1959. Cf. *Quellen des 9. und 11. Jahrhunderts ...; Adam Bremensis. Monumenta Germaniae Historica. Scriptores Rerum Germanicarum.* (B. Schmeidler ed.). 3rd edn Hanover 1917.

Addyman, P. V. 1979: 'Jorvik', *Skalk* 1979, no. 6, pp. 3–8.

Adigard des Gautries, J. 1954: *Les Noms de Personnes scandinaves en Normandie de 911 à 1066.* Lund.

Albrectsen, E. 1958: 'Runemonumentet ved Glavendrup', *Fynske Minder* 1958, pp. 83–96.

1959: 'Til en ræde vorde den –', *Skalk* 1959, no. 3, pp. 19–27.

1970: 'Vikingetidens Odense', *Fynske Minder* 1970, pp. 123–32.

1976: *Vikingerne i Franken. Skriftlige Kilder fra det 9. Århundrede.* Trans. E. Albrectsen. Odense. (Cf. *Quellen zur Karolingischen Reichsgeschichte* I–III).

Almgren, B. 1963: 'Vikingatidens höjdpunkt och slut', *Tor* 9, 1963, pp. 215–48.

et al. 1967: *The Viking.* Tre Tryckare, Gothenburg.

Almgren, O. 1904: 'Vikingatidens grafskick i verkligheten och i den fornnordiska litteraturen', *Nordiska Studier. Tillegnade Adolf Noreen.* Uppsala. Pp. 309–46.

Ambrosiani, B. et al. 1973: *Birka. Svarta jordens hamnområde. Arkeologisk undersökning 1970–1971.* Riksantikvarieämbetet. Rapport Cl. Stockholm.

Andersen, H. 1951: 'Tomme høje', *Kuml* 1951, pp. 99–135.

1958: 'Grydehøj', *Skalk* 1958, no. 4, pp. 15–18.

1960: 'Hovedstaden i riget', *Nationalmuseets Arbejdsmark 1960*, pp. 13–35.

1963: 'Smeden fra Lejre', *Skalk* 1963, no. 1, pp. 8–10.

1969a: 'Vikinger fra uvant synsvinkel', *Skalk* 1969, no. 1, pp. 3–8.

1969b: 'Lejrelåsen', *Skalk* 1969, no. 3, pp. 16–17.

1972: 'Om at gøre høj', *Skalk* 1972, no. 6, pp. 12–15.

1974: 'On building mounds', *Mediaeval Scandinavia* 7, 1974, pp. 223–6.

Andersen, H. and Wulff Andersen, S. 1976: 'Genskabt skrin', *Skalk* 1976, no. 6, pp. 16–17.

Andersen, H. H. 1968: 'Grydestenens veje', *Skalk* 1968, no. 5, pp. 4–9.

1971: 'Tordenguden', *Skalk* 1971, no. 3, pp. 4–8.

1974: 'Århus in der Zeit von 900 bis 1200 n. Chr.', *Vor- und Frühformen der europäischen Stadt im Mittelalter* (H. Jankuhn et al.). Göttingen. Pp. 94–100.

1977: *Jyllands vold.* Århus.

1979: 'Det bjerg, der kaldes Gamle Lybæk', *Skalk* 1979, no. 2, pp. 9–13.

Andersen, H. H., Crabb, P. J. and Madsen, H. J. 1971: *Århus Søndervold. En byarkæologisk undersøgelse.* Copenhagen.

Andersen, H. H. and Klindt-Jensen, O. 1970: 'Hesselbjerg. En gravplads fra vikingetid', *Kuml* 1970, pp. 31–41.

Andersen, H. H. and Madsen, H. J. 1966: 'Nygade i Århus', *Kuml* 1966, pp. 7–29.

Andersen, H. H., Madsen, H. J. and Voss, O. 1976. With contributions by H. Steuer and H. Tauber: *Danevirke.* Copenhagen.

Andersson, H. 1979: *Urbaniseringsprocessen i det medeltida Sverige.* Riksantikvarieämbetet och Statens Historiska Museer Rapport. Medeltidsstaden 7. Gothenburg.

Anker, P. 1968: 'Møbler og inventar i Norge i middelalderen ca. 1100–1600', *Norske møbler i fortid og nåtid* (P. Anker et al.). Bergen, Oslo, Trondheim. Pp. 5–17.

1970: *The art of Scandinavia* 1. With a contribution by Aron Andersson. London, New York, Sydney, Toronto.

1977: 'Om dateringsproblemet i stavkirkeforskningen', *Historisk Tidsskrift*, lvi, 1977, no. 2, pp. 103–42.

Ansgar: see *Quellen des 9. und 11. Jahrhunderts ...*

Antiquarisk Tidsskrift. Det kongelige Nordiske Oldskriftselskab ed. Copenhagen.

Arbman, H. 1937: *Schweden und das karolingische Reich.* Stockholm.

1939: *Birka. Sveriges äldsta Handelsstad.* Stockholm.

1940: *Birka I. Die Gräber.* Stockholm.
1955: *Svear i Österviking.* Stockholm.
1961: *The Vikings.* London.
and Stenberger, M. 1935: *Vikingar i Västerled.* Stockholm.
Arrhenius, B. 1961: 'Vikingatida miniatyrer', *Tor* 1961, pp. 139–64.
1978: 'Ein Amethystanhänger aus Haithabu', *Berichte über die Ausgrabungen in Haithabu* 12 (K. Schietzel ed.). Neumünster. Pp. 9–23.
Arup, E. 1926: *Danmarks Historie.* Copenhagen (repr. 1961).
Atterman, I. 1969: 'Rapport från Bussevikspärren', *Blekingeboken* 47, 1969, pp. 7–28.

Bailey, R. N. 1980: *Viking Age Sculpture in Northern England.* London.
Bantelmann, A. 1975: *Die Frühgeschichtliche Marschensiedlung beim Elisenhof in Eiderstedt. Landschaftsgeschichte und Baubefunde.* Bern-Frankfurt/M.
Bartholin, T. S. 1976: 'Absolut dendrokronologisk datering af de tre brønde fra det ældste Odense', *Fynske Minder* 1976, pp. 33–4.
1978: 'Dendrochronology, wood anatomy and landscape development in South Sweden', *Dendrochronology in Europe. Principles, interpretations and applications to Archaeology and History* (J. Fletcher ed.). National Maritime Museum, Greenwich, Archaeological Series No. 4. BAR International Series 51, 1978, pp. 125–30.
1979: 'Vedanatomi og dendrokronologi i Svendborg', *Naturhistorisk arkæologisk gruppe—Dansk Icom. Svendborgmødet—juni 1978. Skrifter fra Svendborg og Omegns Museum* 3 (H. M. Jansen ed.). Svendborg 1979. Pp. 88–95.
Bartholin, T. S. and Grandt-Nielsen, F. 1974: 'Datering af tre brønde fra det ældste Odense', *Fynske Minder* 1974, pp. 155–67.
Becker, C. J. 1973–4: 'Jernalder-landsbyen i Jylland. Aktuelle problemer omkring dens oprindelse', *Kuml* 1973–4, pp. 294–6.
1975: 'Jyske landsbyer fra vikingetiden', *Kronik* in *Aarhuus Stiftstidende*, 25 June 1975.
Behre, K.-E. 1969: 'Untersuchungen des botanischen Materials der frühmittelalterlichen Siedlung Haithabu (Ausgrabung 1963–1964)', *Berichte über die Ausgrabungen in Haithabu* 2 (K. Schietzel ed.). Neumünster. Pp. 7–55.
Behrend, R. 1970: 'Vandfundne sværd fra middelalderen', *Nationalmuseets Arbejdsmark* 1970, pp. 89–102.
Bencard, M. 1969: 'Grubehuse i Okholm', *Mark og Montre* 1969, pp. 26–36.
1973: 'Ribes vikingetid. En foreløbig redegørelse for udgravningerne 1972/73', *Mark og Montre* 1973, pp. 28–48.
1974a: 'Jagten på Ribe', *Skalk* 1974, no. 2, pp. 7–15.
1974b: 'Ribes ældste udvikling', *Mark og Montre* 1974, pp. 20–7.
1976: 'Ribe zur Zeit der Wikinger', *Haüser und Höfe im Ostseegebiet und im Norden vor 1500. Acta Visbyensia* v. Visby. Pp. 165–72.
1978: *Ribe i 1000 år.* Esbjerg.
Bencard, M. and Wiell, S. 1975: 'Et trefliget spænde fra Ribe', *Mark og Montre* 1975, pp. 37–42.
Bencard, M., with contributions by K. Ambrosiani, L. Bender Jørgensen, H. Brinch Madsen,

I. Nielsen and U. Näsman 1978: 'Wikingerzeitliches Handwerk in Ribe. Eine Übersicht', *Acta Archaeologica* 49, 1978, pp. 113–38.
Bencard, M. and Stief Aistrup, M. 1979: 'Jernankeret fra Ribe', *Nationalmuseets Arbejdsmark* 1979, pp. 156–61.
Bender Jørgensen, L. and Skov, T. 1978: 'Trabjerg. Resultaterne af 5 års udgravninger af en vikingetidsboplads i NV-Jylland', *Holstebro Museum. Arsskrift* 1978, pp. 5–40.
Bendixen, K. 1976: *Danmarks Mønt* (2nd edn.). National Museum Copenhagen.
1977: 'Mønternes funktion i Danmark i perioden c. 1075 til c. 1300 belyst ved skriftlige og numismatiske kildeudsagn', *Fortid og Nutid* XXVII, 1, 1977, pp. 4–21.
1978: 'Møntcirkulation i Danmark fra Vikingetid til Valdemarssønnerne', *Aarbøger for Nordisk Oldkyndighed og Historie* 1978, pp. 155–90.
Berg, G. 1935: *Sledges and wheeled vehicles. Ethnological studies from the view-point of Sweden.* Uppsala.
1955: 'A Tool Chest from the Viking Age. The 'Mästermyr' find in Gotland', *Universitetet i Bergen. Arbok* 1955, pp. 77–83.
Berglund, B. E. 1969: 'Vegetation and human influence in South Scandinavia during Prehistoric time', *Oikos Suppl.* 12, 1969, pp. 9–25.
Bergquist, H. and Lepiksaar, J. 1957: *Animal skeletal remains from Medieval Lund.* Lund.
Biddle, M. 1966: 'A Late Saxon Frieze Sculpture from the Old Minster', *The Antiquaries Journal* XLVI, 1966, pp. 329–32.
1976: 'Towns'. *The Archaeology of Ango-Saxon England* (D. M. Wilson ed.). London. Pp. 99–150.
Binns, A. 1968: 'The navigation of viking ships round the British Isles in Old English and Old Norse sources', *Proceedings of the Fifth Viking Congress. Tórshavn 1965* (B. Niclasen ed.). Tórshavn. Pp. 103–17.
Birkeland, H. 1954: *Nordens historie i middelalderen etter arabiske kilder.* Oslo.
Blackburn, M., Dolley, M., Jonsson, K. 1979: 'Nyt eksemplar af Svend Tveskægs mønt', *Nordisk Numismatisk Unions Medlemsblad* 1979, no. 4, pp. 61–5.
Blindheim, C. 1963: 'Smedgraven fra Bygland i Morgedal', *Viking* XXVI, 1963, pp. 25–80.
1969: 'Kaupangundersøkelsen avsluttet', *Viking* 1969, pp. 5–39.
1976a: 'Kaupang in Skiringssal. I. General Background and the identification of the place', *Häuser und Höfe im Ostseegebiet und im Norden vor 1500. Acta Visbyensia* v, pp. 73–82.
1976b: 'A collection of Celtic (?) bronze objects found at Kaupang (Skiringssal), Vestfold, Norway', *Proceedings of the Seventh Viking Congress. Dublin 1973* (B. Almqvist and D. Greene eds.). Royal Irish Academy. Pp. 9–27.
1978: 'Trade problems in the Viking Age. Some Reflections on Insular Metalwork Found in Norwegian Graves of the Viking Age', *The Vikings. Proceedings of the Symposium of the Faculty of Arts of Uppsala University, 6–9 June 1977* (T. Andersson and K. I. Sandred eds.). Uppsala. Pp. 166–76.
Blindheim, M. ed. 1972: *Sigurds Saga i middelalderens billedkunst.* Oslo.

1973: 'Fra hedensk sagnfigur til kristent forbilde. Sigurdsdiktningen i middelalderens billedkunst', *ICO. Den iconographiske post* 1973, no. 3, pp. 3–28.

Blomqvist, R. 1951: *Lunds historia I. Medeltiden.* Lund.

1974: 'Die älteste Geschichte der Stadt Lund', *Vor- und Frühformen der europäischen Stadt im Mittelalter* 11 (H. Jankuhn et al.). Göttingen. Pp. 128–45.

Blomqvist, R. and Mårtensson, A. W. 1963: *Thulegrävningen 1961.* Lund.

Bonde, N. 1979: 'Trelleborg dateret!', *Nyt fra Nationalmuseet*: December 1979, January and February 1980, no. 5, pp. 11–13.

Boye, V. 1858: 'To Fund af Smedeværktöi fra den sidste hedenske Tid i Danmark', *Annaler for Nordisk Oldkyndighed og Historie* 1858, pp. 191–200.

Brade, C. 1978: 'Knöcherne Kernspaltflöten aus Haithabu', *Berichte über die Ausgrabungen in Haithabu* 12 (K. Schietzel ed.). Neumünster. Pp. 24–35.

Brandt, A. von 1970: 'Netzwerk aus Haithabu', *Berichte über die Ausgrabungen in Haithabu* 4 (K. Schietzel ed.). Neumünster. Pp. 69–73.

Bredsdorff, P. 1973: *Kortlægning og historiske studier. Et værktøj?* Copenhagen.

Brinch Madsen, H. 1976: 'Specialist i spænder', *Skalk* 1976, no. 4, pp. 12–15.

Brooks, N. 1971: 'The development of military obligations in eighth- and ninth-century England', *England before the Conquest* (P. Clemoes and K. Hughes eds.). Cambridge. Pp. 69–84.

Bruce-Mitford, R. 1979: *The Sutton Hoo Ship Burial. A Handbook* (3rd edn.). London.

Brøgger, A. W. and Shetelig, H. 1950: *Vikingskipene, deres forgjengere og efterfølgere.* Oslo. English edition: *The Viking Ships. Their ancestry and evolution.* Oslo 1953 (repr. Oslo 1971).

Brøndsted, J. 1920: 'Nordisk og fremmed Ornamentik i Vikingetiden', *Aarbøger for Nordisk Oldkyndighed og Historie* 1920, pp. 162–282.

1924: *Early English Ornament.* London/Copenhagen.

1934: 'Inedita aus dem dänischen Nationalmuseum. I. Goldarbeiten der Wikingerzeit', *Acta Archaeologica* v, 1934, pp. 179–82.

1936: 'Danish inhumation graves of the Viking Age', *Acta Archaeologica* VII, 1936, pp. 81–228.

1942: 'A frog as a Viking Age burial gift', *Acta Archaeologica* XIII, 1942, pp. 315–18.

1955: 'Thors fiskeri', *Nationalmuseets Arbejdsmark* 1955, pp. 92–104.

1960: *Danmarks Oldtid III. Jernalderen* (2nd edn.). Copenhagen.

Burman Becker, G. 1886: *Helgenskrinene i Skt. Knuds Kirke.* Copenhagen.

Callmer, J. 1973–4: 'Problems related to a gravefind from the outskirts of old Kristiania', *Meddelanden från Lunds Universitets Historiska Museum* 1973–4, pp. 276–90.

1977: *Trade beads and bead trade in Scandinavia ca. 800–1000 A.D.* Lund.

Capelle, T. 1968: *Der Metallschmuck von Haithabu.* Neumünster.

1970: 'Metallschmuck und Gussformen aus Haithabu (Ausgrabung 1963–1964)', *Berichte über die Ausgrabungen in Haithabu* 4 (K.

Schietzel ed.). Neumünster. Pp. 9–23.

Carolingian Chronicles. (Trans. B. W. Scholz and B. Rogers). Ann Arbor 1972.

Cartularium Saxonicum. (W. de Gray Birch ed.). London 1887.

Christensen, A. E. 1938: 'Danmarks Befolkning i Middelalderen', *Nordisk Kultur II. Befolkningen i Middelalderen* (A. Schück ed.). Stockholm, Oslo, Copenhagen. Pp. 1–57.

1966: 'Birka uden frisere', *Handels- og Søfartsmuseets Årbog* 25 (Maritime studies presented to Knud Klem), 1966, pp. 17–38.

1969: *Vikingetidens Danmark. Paa oldhistorisk baggrund.* Copenhagen.

1975: 'The Jelling monuments', *Mediaeval Scandinavia* 8, 1975, pp. 7–20.

1977: 'Tiden 1042–1241', *Danmarks Historie 1. Tiden indtil 1340.* Inge Skovgaard-Petersen, Aksel E. Christensen and Helge Paludan. Copenhagen. Pp. 211–399.

1978: Review of Alex Wittendorff: *Alvej og Kongevej, Historisk Tidsskrift* 78, 1. Copenhagen 1978. Pp. 272–80.

Christensen, Arne E. 1972: 'Scandinavian ships from earliest times to the Vikings', *The History of Seafaring* (G. F. Bass ed.). London. Pp. 159–80.

Christiansen, T. E. 1948: 'En Guldsmede-Matrice fra Vejleby', *Lolland-Falsters Stiftsmuseum. Årsberetning* 1948, pp. 6–12.

1970: 'Træningslejr eller tvangsborg', *Kuml* 1970, pp. 43–63.

1975: 'Bygningen på søndre Jellinghøj', *Kuml* 1975, pp. 163–72.

Christiansen, T. E., Foged, N., Jørgensen, S. and Strand Petersen, K. (at press): *Trelleborg og Pine Mølle.* Copenhagen.

Christie, H., Olsen, O. and Taylor, H. M. 1979: 'The wooden church of St. Andrew at Greensted, Essex', *The Antiquaries Journal* LIX, 1, 1979, pp. 92–112.

Cinthio, H. 1979–80: 'The Löddeköpinge Investigations III. The Early Medieval Cemetery', *Meddelanden från Lunds universitets historiska museum* 1979–80, pp. 112–31.

Collingwood, W. G. 1927: *Northumbrian crosses of the pre-Norman Age.* London.

Colyer, C. 1975: *Lincoln. The archaeology of an historic city.* Lincoln Archaeological Trust.

and Jones, M. J. eds. 1979. 'Excavations at Lincoln. Second Interim Report', *The Antiquaries Journal* LIX:I, 1979, pp. 50–91.

Crumlin-Pedersen, O. 1960: 'Sideroret fra Vorså', *Kuml* 1960, pp. 106–16.

1968: *Træskibet. Fra langskib til fregat.* (Træbranchens Oplysningsråd). Copenhagen. English edition: Crumlin-Pedersen, O. and Finch, R., *From Viking ship to 'Victory'.* London 1977.

1969: 'Das Haithabuschiff', *Berichte über die Ausgrabungen in Haithabu* 3 (K. Schietzel ed.). Neumünster.

1972: 'The Vikings and the Hanseatic merchants: 900–1450', *The History of Seafaring* (G. F. Bass ed.). London. Pp. 181–204.

1972a: 'Kællingen og kløften. Nogle jyske fund af kølsvin og mastefisk fra 800–1200 e. Kr.', *Handels- og Søfartsmuseets Arbog* 1972, pp. 63–80.

1973: 'Helnæs-spærringen', *Fynske Minder* 1973, pp. 29–48.

1975a: 'Viking seamanship questioned', *The Mariner's Mirror* 61, May 1975, pp. 127–31.

1975b: '"Æ Lei" og "Margrethes bro"', *Nordslesvigske Museer* 2, 1975, pp. 9–25.

1977a: *Træskib To. Sømand og købmand.* (Træbranchens Oplysningsråd). Copenhagen.

1977b: 'Some Principles for the Recording and Presentation of Ancient Boat Structures', *Sources and Techniques in Boat Archaeology* (S. McGrail ed.). Oxford. Pp. 163–77.

1978: 'Søvejen til Roskilde', *Historisk årbog for Roskilde amt* 1978, pp. 3–79.

Danmarks Natur 1. Landskabernes opståen (A. Nørrevang and T. J. Meyer eds.). Copenhagen 1967.

Danmarks Kirker, National Museum Copenhagen ed., 1933ff.

Danmarks Riges Breve, ser. 1, vol. 1, 789–1052. (Det danske Sprog- og Litteraturselskab ed.). Copenhagen 1975.

Dietriechson, L. 1892: *De Norske Stavkirker.* Kristiania, Copenhagen (repr. 1972).

Dillmann, F.-X. 1974: 'Bibliographie. Les Vikings dans l'Empire franc', *Revue du Nord* LVI, 1974, pp. 91–9.

Diplomatarium Danicum, ser. 1, vol. 1, 789–1052 (Det danske Sprog- og Litteraturselskab ed., C. A. Christensen and H. Nielsen). Copenhagen 1975—Ser. 1, vol. 2, 1053–1169 (Det danske Sprog- og Litteraturselskab ed., L. Weibull with contributions by N. Skyum-Nielsen). Copenhagen 1963.

Dolley, M. 1965. *Viking Coins of the Danelaw and of Dublin.* British Museum. London.

1978: 'The Anglo-Danish and Anglo-Norse coinages of York', *Viking Age York and the North* (R. A. Hall ed.). CBA Research Report 27, 1978, pp. 26–30.

Dyggve, E. 1942: 'La fouille par le Musée National Danois du Tertre Royal Sud à Jelling en 1941. Rapport préliminaire succinct', *Acta Archaeologica* XIII, 1942, pp. 65–99.

1948: 'The Royal Barrows at Jelling', *Antiquity* 88, 1948, pp. 190–7.

1964: *Mindesmærkerne i Jelling. Form og tydning.* National Museum. Copenhagen.

Eames, P. 1977: *Medieval Furniture.* London.

Eckstein, D. 1977: 'Holzanatomische Untersuchungen an Befunden der frühmittelalterlichen Siedlung Haithabu (Ausgrabung 1966–1969). *Berichte über de Ausgrabungen in Haithabu* 11 (K. Schietzel ed.). Neumünster. Pp. 112–19.

Eckstein, D. and Schietzel, K. 1977: 'Zur dendrokronologischen Gliederung und Datierung der Baubefunde von Haithabu', *Berichte über die Ausgrabungen in Haithabu* 11 (K. Schietzel ed.). Neumünster. Pp. 141–64.

Egils Saga (trans. and ed. C. Fell). London 1975.

Ekman, J. 1973: *Early Mediaeval Lund—the fauna and the landscape.* Lund.

Eldjárn, K. 1953: 'Carved panels from Flatatunga, Iceland', *Acta Archaeologica* XXIV, 1953, pp. 81–101.

1956: *Kuml og Haugfé.* Reykjavik.

Ellehøj, S. 1953: 'Olav Tryggvesons fald og Venderne', *Historisk Tidsskrift* 11, 4. Copenhagen 1953. Pp. 1–55.

Ellmers, D. 1964/5: 'Zum Trinkgeschirr der

Wikingerzeit', Offa 21/2, 1964/5, pp. 21–43.

Encomium Emmae Reginae (A. Campbell ed.). London 1949.

Engelhardt, C. 1881: 'Jernalderens Gravskikke i Jylland', *Aarbøger for Nordisk Oldkyndighed og Historie* 1881, pp. 79–184.

van Es, W. A. 1973: 'Die neuen Dorestad-Grabungen 1967–1972', *Vor- und Frühformen der europäischen Stadt im Mittelalter* 1 (H. Jankuhn *et al.*). Göttingen. Pp. 202–17.

Eskildsen, L. 1979: 'Jordovne', *Skalk* 1979, no. 3, pp. 16–17.

Evison, V. 1967: 'A Sword from the Thames at Wallingford Bridge', *The Archaeological Journal* CXXIV, 1967, pp. 160–89.

Fabritius Buchwald, V. 1976: 'En metallografisk undersøgelse af en vikingetidsøkse fra Sønder Onsild', *Aarbøger for Nordisk Oldkyndighed og Historie* 1976, pp. 96–123.

Fell, C. 1975a: 'Drinks', *Skalk* 1975, no. 6, pp. 3–9.

1975b: 'Old English *Beor', Leeds Studies in English*, N.S. VIII, 1975, pp. 75–95.

Fenger, O. 1972: 'The Danelaw and the Danish Law', *Scandinavian Studies in Law* 16, 1972 (F. Schmidt ed.) pp. 85–96.

Filipowiak, W. 1974: 'Die Entwicklung der Stadt Wolin vom 9. bis zum 12. Jahrhundert', *Vor- und Frühformen der europäischen Stadt im Mittelalter* 11 (H. Jankuhn *et al.*). Göttingen. Pp. 190–208.

Foote, P. 1978: 'Wrecks and Rhymes', *The Vikings. Proceedings of the Symposium of the Faculty of Arts of Uppsala University, 6–9 June 1977* (T. Andersson and K. I. Sandred eds.). Uppsala. Pp. 56–66.

Foote, P. G. and Wilson, D. M. 1970: *The Viking Achievement.* London (2nd edn. 1980).

Friis Johansen, K. 1912: 'Sølvskatten fra Terslev', *Aarbøger for Nordisk Oldkyndighed og Historie* 1912, pp. 189–263.

Fuglesang, see Horn Fuglesang.

Galster, G. 1951: 'Karolingiske Mønter fundne i Danmark', *Nordisk Numismatisk Arsskrift* 1951, pp. 28–40.

1960: 'Knud den Stores og dronning Emmas billeder', *Aarbøger for Nordisk Oldkyndighed og Historie* 1960, pp. 97–117.

1964: *Sylloge of coins of the British Isles*, 4. Royal collection of coins and medals. National Museum Copenhagen, Pt. 1. London.

Geijer, A. 1938: *Birka III. Die Textilfunde aus den Gräbern.* Uppsala.

1972: *Ur textilkonstens historia.* Lund.

Gelling, M. 1978: *Signposts to the Past. Place-Names and the History of England.* London, Melbourne, Toronto.

Glob, P. V. 1951: *Ard og Plov i Nordens Oldtid.* Arhus.

1959: 'Avlsten', *Kuml* 1959, pp. 69–83.

1969a: 'Kong Haralds kumler', *Skalk* 1969, no. 4, pp. 18–27.

1969b: 'Jellings bautasten', *Kuml* 1969, pp. 97–109.

1977: 'Et vikingeskib af bronze og et af guld', *Antikvariske Studier: Tilegnet Knud Thorvildsen.* Copenhagen 1977. Pp. 143–6.

Goldschmidt, A. 1918: *Die Elfenbeinskulpturen* II. Berlin (photographic reprt. Berlin 1970).

Graham-Campbell, J. 1976: 'The Viking-age silver hoards of Ireland', *Proceedings of The Seventh Viking Congress. Dublin 1973* (B. Almqvist and D. Greene eds.). Royal Irish Academy. Pp. 39–74.

1977: 'British Antiquity, 1976–7. Western British, Irish and later Anglo-Saxon', *The Archaeological Journal* 134, 1977, pp. 418–435.

1980: *The Viking World*. New Haven, New York. (This appeared while ch. 11 was being written.)

Graham-Campbell, J. and Kidd, D. 1980: *The Vikings*. British Museum. London.

Grandt-Nielsen, F. 1971: 'Nyt fra Knud den Helliges Odense', *Fynske Minder* 1971, pp. 199–216.

Grenander Nyberg, G. 1977: 'Trampvävstol i vikingatidens Hedeby', *Rig* 60: 2, 1977, pp. 47–8.

Grieg, S. 1928: *Osebergfundet* II (A. W. Brøgger, H. Schetelig eds.). Oslo.

1929: 'Vikingetidens skattefund', *Oslo Universitets Oldsaksamlings Skrifter* 2, 1929, pp. 177–311.

1943: 'Skjoldene i Middelalderen', *Nordisk Kultur XII:B. Vaaben* (B. Thordeman ed.). Stockholm. Pp. 67–89.

1947: *Gjermundbufundet. En høvdingegrav fra 900-årene fra Ringerike*. Oslo.

Græbe, H. and Roesdahl, E. 1977: 'Kirken ved Aggersborg', *Nationalmuseets Arbejdsmark* 1977, pp. 14–26.

Gräslund, A.-S. 1965–6: 'Charonsmynt i vikingatida gravar?', *Tor* 1965–6, pp. 168–97.

1972–3: 'Barn i Birka', *Tor* 1972–3, pp. 161–79.

Grøngård Jeppesen, T. 1977: 'Stedskontinuitet i fynske landsbyer belyst ved hjælp af den arkæologiske metode', *Kontinuitet og bebyggelse* (H. Thrane ed.). Skrifter fra institut for historie og samfundsvidenskab, no. 22. Odense University. Pp. 76–87.

1978a: 'Oldtidsbebyggelse—middelalderbebyggelse. Kontinuitet eller brud?', *Hikuin* 4, 1978, pp. 117–24.

1978b: 'En guldrig—men alligevel fundfattig periode', *Harja* 1978, pp. 5–18.

1979a: *Landsbyens opståen. Indledende studier over middelalderlandsbyernes pladskontinuitet*. Arkæologiske Undersøgelser 1. Skrifter fra Historisk Institut no. 24. Odense University.

1979b: 'Bebyggelsesflytninger på overgangen mellem vikingetid og middelalder', *Fra jernalder til middelalder* (H. Thrane ed.). Skrifter fra Historisk Institut no. 27. Odense University, pp. 99–117.

Grøngård-Jeppesen, T. and Thrane, H. 1978: 'Ebberup-vejen, arkæologi på et vejprojekt', *Fynske Minder* 1978, pp. 17–42.

Gyldendals Tibinds Leksikon: (J. Bang ed.). Copenhagen 1977–8.

Haarnagel, W. 1977: 'Das eisenzeitliche Dorf "Feddersen Wierde"', *Das Dorf der Eisenzeit und des frühen Mittelalters* (H. Jankuhn et al.). Göttingen. Pp. 253–84.

d'Haenens, A. 1967: *Les invasions normandes en Belgique au IXe siècle*. Louvain.

Hald, K. 1965: *Vore stednavne* (2nd edn.). Copenhagen.

1969: *Stednavne og kulturhistorie* (2nd imp.). Copenhagen.

1971: *Personnavne i Danmark I. Oldtiden.* Copenhagen.

1974: *Personnavne i Danmark II. Middelalderen.* Copenhagen.

Hald, M. 1950: *Olddanske Tekstiler*. Copenhagen.

1974: *Primitive Shoes*. Copenhagen.

Hall, R. A. 1976: *The Viking Kingdom of York*. Yorkshire Museum.

ed. 1978: *Viking Age York and the North*. CBA Research Report 27. London.

1979: *Jorvik. Viking Age York*. York.

Hall, R. A., Daniells, M. J. and York, R. N. 1978: *2000 Years of York—the Archaeological Story*. York Archaeological Trust.

Hansen, V. and Nielsen, H. 1977: 'Oldtidens veje og vadesteder belyst ved nye undersøgelser ved Stevns', *Aarbøger for Nordisk Oldkyndighed og Historie* 1977, pp. 72–117.

Hatting, T. 1979: 'Knoglematerialet i Svendborg sammenlignet med andre byer', *Naturhistorisk arkæologisk gruppe — Dansk Icom. Svendborgmødet — juni 1978. Skrifter fra Svendborg og Omegns Museum* 3 (H. Jansen ed.). Svendborg. Pp. 98–117.

Hatz, G. 1970: 'Munus-divinum-Nachahmungen aus Haithabu', *Berichte über die Ausgrabungen in Haithabu* 4 (K. Schietzel ed.). Neumünster. Pp. 24–33.

1974: *Handel und Verkehr zwischen dem Deutschen Reich und Schweden in der späten Wikingerzeit*. Lund.

Hatz, V. 1978: 'Die byzantinischen Einflüsse auf das deutsche Münzwesen des 11. Jahrhunderts', *Zeitschrift für Archäologie* 12:2, 1978, pp. 145–57.

Hauberg, P. 1900: *Myntforhold og Udmyntninger i Danmark indtil 1146*. Copenhagen.

Hauglid, R. 1969: *Norske Stavkirker*. Oslo.

Helbæk, H. 1959: 'Notes on the evolution and history of linum', *Kuml* 1959, pp. 103–29.

1970: 'Da rugen kom til Danmark', *Kuml* 1970, pp. 279–96.

Hellerup Madsen, E. 1977: 'Salt og salthandel i østersøområdet i tidlig middelalder', *Hikuin* 3, 1977, pp. 269–94.

Helmuth, H. 1977: 'Antropologische Untersuchungen an menschlichen Skeletresten der Frühmittelalterlichen Siedlung Haithabu (Ausgrabung 1966–1969)', *Berichte über die Ausgrabungen in Haithabu* 11 (K. Schietzel ed.). Neumünster. Pp. 9–56.

Hencken, H. O. 1933: 'A gaming board of the Viking Age', *Acta Archaeologica* IV, 1933, pp. 85–104.

Herfert, P. 1973: 'Ralswiek. Ein frühgeschichtlicher Seehandelsplatz auf der Insel Rügen', *Greifswald-Stralsunder Jahrbuch* 1972/3, pp. 7–33.

Herrmann, J. ed. 1970: *Die Slawen in Deutschland. Ein Handbuch*. Berlin.

1975: 'Die Ostsee—ein völkerverbindendes Meer im frühen Mittelalter', *Das Altertum*, 1975, pp. 133–42.

1976: *Zwischen Hradschin und Vineta* (2nd edn.). Berlin.

1978: 'Ralswiek auf Rügen—ein Handelsplatz des 9. Jahrhunderts und die Fernhandelsbeziehungen im Ostseegebiet', *Zeitschrift für Archäologie* 12:2, 1978, pp. 163–80.

Herteig, A. E., Lidén, H. E., Blindheim, C. 1975: *Archaeological contributions to the early history of urban communities in Norway*. Oslo.

Hill, D. ed. 1978: *Ethelred the Unready. Papers*

from the *Millenary Conference*. BAR British Series 59.

Hingst, H. and Kersten, K. 1955: 'Die tauchaktion vor Haithabu im Jahre 1953', *Germania* 33, 1955, pp. 265–71.

Hoffmann, M. 1974: *The warp-weighted loom*. Oslo.

Holboe, J. 1927: 'Nytteplanter og ugræs i Osebergfundet', *Osebergfundet* V (A. W. Brøgger, H. Schetelig eds.). Oslo. Pp. 3–78.

Horn Fuglesang, S. 1978: 'Stylistic Groups in late Viking Art', *Anglo-Saxon and Viking Age Sculpture and its Context* (J. Lang ed.). BAR British Series 49. London. Pp. 205–16.

1980: *Some Aspects of the Ringerike Style*. Mediaeval Scandinavia Supplements, 1. Odense.

Hovesen, E. 1968: 'Klæberstenskar fra Djurslands kyst', *Historisk Aarbog fra Randers Amt* 1968, pp. 82–4.

Hundt, H.-J. 1973: 'Zur Verzierungstechnik der beiden wikingerzeitlichen Schwerter aus Bustorf, Kreis Schleswig', *Berichte über die Ausgrabungen in Haithabu* 6 (K. Schietzel ed.). Neumünster. Pp. 90–5.

Hvass, S. 1976: 'Udgravningerne i Vorbasse', *Mark og Montre* 1976, pp. 38–52.

1977a: 'Vikingebebyggelsen i Vorbasse', *Mark og Montre* 1977, pp. 18–29.

1977b: 'Udgravningerne i Vorbasse', *Fra Ribe Amt* 1977, pp. 345–85.

1979a: 'Jernalderlandsbyerne ved Vorbasse', *Nationalmuseets Arbejdsmark* 1979, pp. 105–12.

1979b: 'Jernalderlandsbyerne ved Vorbasse', *Fra Ribe Amt* 1978 (1979), pp. 357–91.

Hübener, W. 1959: *Die Keramik von Haithabu*. Neumünster.

Hägg, I. 1974: *Kvinnodräkten i Birka*. Uppsala.

Hägstad, A. 1964: 'Har At-Tartuschi besøgt Hedeby (Slesvig)?', *Aarbøger for Nordisk Oldkyndighed og Historie* 1964, pp. 82–92.

Hårdh, B. 1976: *Wikingerzeitliche Depotfunde aus Südschweden*. Lund.

1977–8: 'Trade and Money in Scandinavia in the Viking Age', *Meddelanden från Lunds universitets historiska museum* 1977–8, pp. 157–71.

Håstrup, L. 1969: 'Oversigt over kompositionen af danske skattefund ca. 800 – ca. 1150', *Nordisk Numismatisk Unions Medlemsblad* 1969, no. 5, pp. 129–32.

Haasum, S. 1974: *Vikingatidens segling och navigation*. Thesis and papers in North-European Archaeology 4. Stockholm.

Jacob, G. 1927: *Arabische Berichte von Gesandten an germanische Fürstenhöfe aus dem 9. und 10. Jahrhundert*. Quellen zur Deutschen Volkskunde (V. von Geramb *et al.*) 1. Berlin, Leipzig. (German translation with footnotes).

Jacobsen, L. and Moltke, E. 1941–2: *Danmarks Runeindskrifter*. Copenhagen.

Jankuhn, H. 1937: *Die Wehranlagen der Wikingerzeit zwischen Schlei und Treene*. Neumünster.

1943: *Die Ausgrabungen in Haithabu (1937–1939)*. Berlin-Dahlem.

1951: 'Ein Ulfberht-Schwert aus der Elbe bei Hamburg', *Festschrift für Gustav Schwantes* (K. Kersten ed.). Neumünster. Pp. 212–29.

1963: *Haithabu. Ein Handelsplatz der Wikingerzeit* (4th edn.). Neumünster.

1974: 'Zusammenfassende Schlussbemerkungen', *Vor- und Frühformen der europäischen Stadt im Mittelalter II* (H. Jankuhn *et al.*). Göttingen. Pp. 305–22.

1976: *Haithabu. Ein Handelsplatz der Wikingerzeit* (6th extended edn.). Neumünster.

et al. 1973–4: *Vor- und Frühformen der europäischen Stadt im Mittelalter I–II. Proceedings of a Symposium in Rheinhausen, Göttingen 1972*. Göttingen.

Jansen, H. 1974: 'Et middelalderbysamfund tager form', *Fynske Minder* 1974, pp. 168–88.

Janssen, W. 1977: 'Dorf und Dorfformen des 7. bis 12. Jahrhunderts im Lichte neuer Ausgrabungen in Mittel- und Nordeuropa', *Das Dorf der Eisenzeit und des frühen Mittelalters* (H. Jankuhn *et al.*). Göttingen. Pp. 285–356.

Jansson, S. B. F. 1962: *The Runes of Sweden*. Stockholm.

1966: *Swedish Vikings in England. The Evidence of the Rune Stones*. The Dorothea Coke Memorial Lecture in Northern Studies delivered 11 March 1965 at University College London. London.

'Jelling Problems. A discussion', by K. M. Nielsen, N. A. Nielsen, E. Moltke, E. Roesdahl, H. Andersen, O. Olsen. *Mediaeval Scandinavia* 7, 1974, pp. 156–234.

Jensen, G. Fellows 1968: *Scandinavian Personal Names in Lincolnshire and Yorkshire*. Copenhagen.

1972: *Scandinavian Settlement Names in Yorkshire*. Copenhagen.

1975: 'The Vikings in England: a review', *Anglo-Saxon England* 4, 1975, pp. 181–206.

1978: *Scandinavian Settlement Names in the East Midlands*. Copenhagen.

Jensen, J. 1979: *Oldtidens samfund. Tiden indtil år 800. Dansk socialhistorie* 1. Copenhagen.

Jessen, K. 1953–4: 'Plantefund fra vikingetiden i Danmark', *Botanisk tidsskrift* 50, 1953–4, pp. 125–39.

Johansen, E. and Liestøl, A. 1977: 'Jellingsteinen. Steinhogger og Runerister', *Kuml* 1977, pp. 65–84.

Joranson, E. 1924: *The Danegeld in France*. Rock Island.

Jørgensen, B. 1977: 'Stednavne og bebyggelsesarkæologi. Nogle efterræsonneringer', *Kontinuitet og bebyggelse*. (H. Thrane ed.). Skrifter fra institut for historie og samfundsvidenskab no. 22, Odense University, pp. 90–3.

Jørgensen, E. 1908: *Fremmed Indflydelse under den danske Kirkes tidligste Udvikling*. Copenhagen.

Karlson, W. 1928: *Studier i Sveriges Medeltida Möbelkunst*. Lund.

King, A. 1978: 'Gauber high pasture, Ribblehead —an interim report', *Viking Age York and the North* (R. A. Hall ed.). CBA Research Report 27. London. Pp. 21–5.

Kjersgaard, E. 1966: 'Leding og landeværn', *Middelalderstudier. Tilegnede Aksel E. Christensen*. (T. E. Christiansen *et al.*). Copenhagen. Pp. 113–40.

Kjølbye-Biddle, B. and Page, R. I. 1975: 'A Scandinavian rune-stone from Winchester', *The Antiquaries Journal* LV:II, 1975, pp. 389–94.

Klindt-Jensen, O. and Wilson, D. M. 1965:

Vikingetidens kunst. Copenhagen. English edition: see Wilson, D. M. and Klindt-Jensen, O. 1966.

KLNM = *Kulturhistorisk Leksikon for Nordisk Middelalder*, I–XXII. Copenhagen, Helsingfors, Reykjavik, Oslo, Malmö 1956–78 (G. Rona ed.).

Knudsen, G. *et al.* 1940–64; *Danmarks gamle Personnavne* I–II. Copenhagen.

Kock, J. 1975: 'Byarkæologisk topografi i Alborg', *Hikuin* 2, 1975, pp. 187–96.

Kornerup, J. 1875: *Kongehøiene i Jellinge*. Copenhagen.

Kossack, G., Harck, O., Reichstein, J. 1974: 'Zehn Jahre Siedlungsforschung in Archsum auf Sylt', *Bericht der Römisch-Germanischen Kommission* 55/II, 1974, pp. 261–429.

Kousgård Sørensen, J. 1958: *Danske bebyggelsesnavne på -sted*. Copenhagen.

1974: '*Odinkar* og andre navne på *-kar*', *Namn och Bygd* 62, 1974, pp. 108–16.

Krafft, S. 1956: *Pictorial Weavings of the Viking Age*. Oslo.

Krins, H. 1968: *Die frühen Steinkirchen Dänemarks*. Dissertation zur Erlangung der Doktorwürde der Philosophischen Fakultät der Universität Hamburg. Hamburg.

Kristensen, A. K. G. 1975: 'Danelaw institutions and Danish Society in the Viking Age: Sochemanni, liberi homines and Königsfreie', *Mediaeval Scandinavia* 8, 1975, pp. 27–85.

Krogh, K. 1965: 'Det grønne æg', *Skalk* 1965, no. 4, pp. 13–15.

1966: 'Kirken mellem højene', *Skalk* 1966, no. 2, pp. 5–10.

1980a: 'Kongelige smykker?', *Danefæ* (P. V. Glob ed.). National Museum Copenhagen, no. 85.

1980b: 'Jelling', *Nyt fra Nationalmuseet* June, July, August. 1980, no. 7, pp. 20–4.

Krogh, K. and Voss, O. 1960: 'Kirken på vikingens høj', *Skalk*, 1960, no. 4, pp. 9–14.

1961: 'Fra hedenskab til kristendom i Hørning', *Nationalmuseets Arbejdsmark* 1961, pp. 5–34.

Krogh, S. 1969: 'Furreby-hjulet', *Kuml* 1969, pp. 149–64.

Kryger, K. 1976: 'Kirkernes kulører', *Skalk* 1976, no. 3, pp. 4–8.

1977: 'Middelalderens bemalede stenskulptur i Danmark', *Hikuin* 3, 1977, pp. 183–94.

Kulturhistorisk Leksikon for Nordisk Middelalder = *KLNM*.

Körber-Grohne, U. 1977: 'Botanische Untersuchungen des Tauwerks der frühmittelalterlichen Siedlung Haithabu und Hinweise zur Unterscheidung einheimischer Gehölzbaste', *Berichte über die Ausgrabungen in Haithabu* 11 (K. Schietzel ed.). Neumünster. Pp. 64–111.

Kaalund, K. 1913: 'En Islandsk Vejviser for Pilgrimme fra 12. Aarhundrede', *Aarbøger for Nordisk Oldkyndighed og Historie* 1913, pp. 51–105.

la Cour, V. 1951: *Danevirkestudier. En arkæologisk-historisk undersøgelse*. Copenhagen.

1959: 'Havnebondens våben. Nogle kommentarer til Jydske lov III:4', *Våbenhistoriske Arbøger* X, 1959, pp. 16–46.

1961: *Næsholm*. Copenhagen.

1968: 'Kong Gudfreds "vallum". Danevirkes hovedvold eller Kovirke?', *Sønderjyske Årbøger* 1968, pp. 97–118.

Lang, J. T. 1978: 'Anglo-Scandinavian sculpture in Yorkshire', *Viking Age York and the North* (R. A. Hall ed.). CBA Research Report 27. London. Pp. 11–20.

Lang, J. ed. 1978: *Anglo-Saxon and Viking Age Sculpture and its Context*. BAR British Series 49, Oxford.

Lassen, E. 1972: *Dansk Kunsthistorie* I. *Fra runesten til altertavle ca. 900–1500*, Politikens Forlag, Copenhagen.

Laurent, V. 1978: 'Ein byzantinisches Bleisiegel aus Haithabu', *Berichte über die Ausgrabungen in Haithabu* 12 (K. Schietzel ed.). Neumünster. Pp. 36–40.

Lauring, P. 1973: *Vikingerne* (4th edn.). Copenhagen.

Laursen, J. 1960: 'Brandstrup. En ryttergrav fra 10. århundrede', *Kuml* 1960, pp. 90–105.

1970: 'Brandstrup. Nye billeder af et gammelt fund', *Kuml* 1970, pp. 99–107.

Lepiksaar, J. and Heinrich, D. 1977, with a contribution by Radtke, C.: 'Untersuchungen an Fishresten aus der frühmittelalterlichen Siedlung Haithabu', *Berichte über die Ausgrabungen in Haithabu* 10 (K. Schietzel ed.). Neumünster.

Lerche, G. 1968: 'The radiocarbon-dated Danish ploughing implements', *Tools and Tillage* I:1, 1968, pp. 56–60.

1969: 'Kogegruber i New Guineas højland', *Kuml* 1969, pp. 195–209.

1975: 'The radiocarbon-dated implements', *Tools and Tillage* II:4, 1975, pp. 255–56.

1976: 'The spades from Dannevirke and Jelling', *Folk and farm. Essays in Honour of A. T. Lucas* (C. ÓDanachair ed.). Dublin. Pp. 110–26.

Leuner, H. 1970: 'Über die historische Rolle magischer Pflanzen und ihrer Wirkstoffe', *Vorgeschichtliche Heiligtümer und Opferplätze in Mittel- und Nordeuropa* (H. Jankuhn ed.). Göttingen. Pp. 279–96.

Levin Nielsen, E. 1966: *Det ældste Viborg. Nye synspunkter og tolkninger*. Viborg.

1968: 'Pedersstæde i Viborg. Købstadsarkæologiske undersøgelser 1966/7', *Kuml* 1968, pp. 23–81.

1974: 'Stadtentstehung und Thinginstitution. Die wikingerzeitlichen Besiedlungsspuren in der Stadt Viborg (Dänemark) und die Frage der Errichtung des jütischen Zentralthinges', *Vor- und Frühformen der europäischen Stadt im Mittelalter* (H. Jankuhn *et al.*). Göttingen. Pp. 64–81.

1975: 'De byarkæologiske undersøgelser i Viborg', *Arkæologi og Naturvidenskab. Report of the urban archaeology seminar at Odense University 3–4 May 1974* (H. M. Jansen ed.). Skrifter fra institut for historie og samfundsvidenskab. Odense University, pp. 54–62.

1978: *Fra bygd til by*. Viborg.

Lidegård, M. 1977: *Hærvejen i Vejle Amt*. Copenhagen.

Lidén, H.-E. 1969: 'From Pagan Sanctuary to Christian Church. The Excavation of Mære Church in Trøndelag', *Norwegian Archaeological Review* 2, 1969, pp. 3–32. (W. Holmqvist: Comments, pp. 22–4; O. Olsen:

Comments, pp. 25–7; H.-E. Lidén: Reply, pp. 27–32).

Liebgott, N.-K. 1977: 'Keramikfundene fra voldstedet Pedersborg ved Sorø', *Aarbøger for Nordisk Oldkyndighed og Historie* 1977, pp. 118–71.

1978a: *Danske fund af møntdateret keramik ca. 950–1450.* Copenhagen.

1978b: *Keramik fra vikingetid og middelalder.* Copenhagen.

1978c: 'Ornamentalt tilbageblik', *Skalk* 1978, no. 5, pp. 10–15.

1979: 'Telt, hytte, bod. Eksempler på primitive bebyggelsesformer i vikingetid og middelalder', *Strejflys over Danmarks bygningskultur. Festskrift til Harald Langberg* (R. Egevang ed.). Copenhagen. Pp. 9–22.

Liestøl, A. 1951: 'Blodrefill og mål', *Viking* xv, 1951, pp. 71–98.

1953: 'The hanging bowl, a liturgical and domestic vessel', *Acta Archaeologica* xxiv, 1953, pp. 163–70.

1968: 'Correspondence in runes', *Mediaeval Scandinavia* 1, 1968, pp. 17–27.

1971: 'The literate Vikings', *Proceedings of the Sixth Viking Congress, Uppsala 1969* (P. Foote and D. Strömbäck eds.). Uppsala. Pp. 69–78.

1973: 'Runenstäbe aus Haithabu-Hedeby', *Berichte über die Ausgrabungen in Haithabu* 6 (K. Schietzel ed.). Neumünster. Pp. 96–119.

Lindahl, F. 1975: 'Middelalder og renæssance. Orøkorset', *Guld fra Nordvestsjælland* (M. Schou Jørgensen ed.). Holbæk. Pp. 169–81.

Lindquist, I. 1962: 'Två vikingatida gudabeläten', *Kulturen* 1962, pp. 70–8.

Lisse, C. 1974: ' "Gøkstorp qvod nunc Knutstorp dicitur". Landsbynavneskrifter i middelalderen', *Festskrift til Kristian Hald.* Copenhagen. Pp. 117–27.

Loyn, H. 1977: *The Vikings in Britain.* London.

Lund, N. 1967: *De danske vikinger i England. Røvere og bønder.* Copenhagen.

1980: 'Vikingetiden', in N. Lund and K. Hørby, *Samfundet i vikingetid og middelalder 800–1500. Dansk socialhistorie* 2, Copenhagen.

Lund Hansen, U. 1973: *Glas fra danske oldtidsfund.* Copenhagen.

1975: 'Guldhåndværk i Nordens oldtid', *Guld fra Nordvestsjælland* (M. Schou Jørgensen ed.). Holbæk. Pp. 111–60.

MacGregor, A. 1976: 'Bone Skates. A Review of the Evidence', *The Archaeological Journal* 133, 1976, pp. 57–74.

1978: 'Industry and commerce in Anglo-Scandinavian York', *Viking Age York and the North* (R. A. Hall ed.). CBA Research Report 27. London. Pp. 37–57.

Mackeprang, M. 1944: *Vore Landsbykirker* (2nd edn.). Copenhagen.

1948: *Jydske Granitportaler.* Copenhagen.

Madsen, H. J. 1965: 'Sct. Peders sten', *Skalk* 1965, no. 3, pp. 7–10.

1969: 'Om grubehuse', *Mark og Montre* 1969, pp. 19–21.

1970: 'Den frække frø', *Skalk* 1970, no. 2, p. 32.

1972: 'Vikingetidens og middelalderens keramik i Århus', *Kuml* 1972, pp. 123–38.

1975a: *Vikingernes Århus.* Højbjerg.

1975b: 'Uhyre i Århus', *Skalk* 1975, no. 3, pp. 4–8.

1977: *Ansgars byer. Tekster til en udstilling.* Højbjerg.

Malmer, B. 1966: *Nordiska Mynt före år 1000.* Lund.

1974: *King Canute's Coinage in the Northern Countries.* The Dorothea Coke Memorial Lecture in Northern Studies delivered at University College London 30 May 1972. London.

Marcus, G. J. 1953: 'The Navigation of the Norsemen', *The Mariner's Mirror* 39, no. 2, pp. 112–31.

Margeson, S. 1980: 'The Völsung legend in medieval art', *Medieval Iconography and Narrative. Proceedings of the Fourth International Symposium at Odense University 19–20 November 1979* (F. Andersen, E. Nyholm et al.) Odense. Pp. 183–211.

Marseen, O. 1956: 'Oldtidsbrønde', *Kuml* 1956, pp. 68–85.

1959: 'Lindholm Høje', *Kuml* 1959, pp. 53–68.

Marxen, I. and Moltke, E. 1978: 'Jellingmanden. Danmarks ældste figurmaleri', *Nationalmuseets Arbejdmark* 1978, pp. 111–18.

Matthiessen, H. 1930: *Hærvejen.* Copenhagen.

Mertz, E. L. 1924: 'Oversigt over de sen- og postglaciale Niveauforandringer i Danmark', *Danmarks geologiske Undersøgelser*, 2nd ser., 41, 1924.

Moltke, E. 1974: 'The Jelling Monument in the light of the runic inscriptions, in "Jelling Problems. A Discussion"', *Mediaeval Scandinavia* 7, 1974, pp. 183–208.

1976: *Runerne i Danmark og deres oprindelse.* Copenhagen.

Moltke, E. and Lund, N. 1977: 'En debat om runer', *Historie. Jyske Samlinger*, new ser., vol. xii, 1–2, 1977, pp. 191–202.

Morris, C. D. 1977: 'Northumbria and the Viking settlement: The evidence for land-holding', *Archaeologia Aeliana*, 5th ser., vol. V, 1977, pp. 81–103.

1979: 'The Vikings and Irish Monasteries', *Durham University Journal* LXXI:2, 1979, pp. 175–85.

Munksgaard, E. 1968: 'Doodles fra vikingetid', *Skalk* 1968, no. 5, pp. 28–9.

1969: 'To skattefund fra ældre vikingetid. Duesminde og Kærbyholm', *Aarbøger for Nordisk Oldkyndighed og Historie* 1969, pp. 52–62.

1971: 'Det skal han nyde', *Skalk* 1971, no. 6, pp. 4–6.

1974: *Oldtidsdragter.* Copenhagen.

1977: 'En guldhalsring fra Nordvestsjælland', *Fra Holbæk amt* 1977, pp. 6–20.

Museumsmagasinet. Published by Museumstjenesten for Statens Museumsnævn.

Musset, L. 1971: *Les Invasions. Le second assault contre l'Europe Chrétienne (VIIᵉ–XIᵉ Siècles).* Nouvelle Clio 12 bis. Paris.

Müller, S. 1880: 'Dyreornamentikken i Norden', *Aarbøger for Nordisk Oldkyndighed og Historie* 1880, pp. 185–405.

1900a: 'En støbeform til "Thorshamre"', *Aarbøger for Nordisk Oldkyndighed og Historie* 1900, pp. 189–195.

1900b: 'Drikkehornsbeslag fra Oldtidens Slutning', *Aarbøger for Nordisk Oldkyndighed og Historie* 1900, pp. 196–202.

Müller, S. and Neergaard, C. 1903: *Danevirke. Archæologisk undersøgt, beskrevet og tydet.* Copenhagen.

Müller-Wille, M. 1972: 'Zwei wikingerzeitliche Prachtschwerter aus der Umgebung von Haithabu', *Offa* 29, 1972, pp. 50–112.

1973: 'Eisengeräte aus Haithabu (Ausgrabung 1963–1964)', *Berichte über die Ausgrabungen in Haithabu* 6 (K. Schietzel ed.). Neumünster. Pp. 23–37.

1974a: 'Ein Reitergrab der jüngeren Wikingerzeit aus Süderbrarup (Angeln)', *Festgabe Kurt Tackenberg zum 75. Geburtstag.* Bonn. Pp. 175–97.

1974b: 'Das Krummsiel von Elstrup (Alsen)', *Acta Archaeologica* 45, 1974, pp. 144–154.

1976a: 'Das wikingerzeitliche Gräberfeld von Thumby-Bienebek I', *Offa* 36, 1976.

1976b: 'Das Bootkammergrab von Haithabu', *Berichte über die Ausgrabungen in Haithabu* 8 (K. Schietzel ed.). Neumünster.

1977a: 'Krieger und Reiter im Spiegel früh- und hochmittelalterlicher Funde Schleswig-Holsteins', *Offa* 34, 1977, pp. 40–74.

1977b: 'Der frühmittelalterliche Schmied im Spiegel skandinavischer Grabfunde', *Frühmittelalterliche Studien* 11, 1977, pp. 127–201.

1978a: 'Das Schiffsgrab von der Île de Groix (Bretagne)', *Berichte über die Ausgrabungen in Haithabu* 12 (K. Schietzel ed.). Neumünster. Pp. 48–84.

1978b: 'Frühmittelalterliche Prunkgräber im südlichen Skandinavien', *Bonner Jahrbücher* 178, 1978, pp. 633–52.

Møhl, U. 1968: 'Knoglematerialet fra Pedersstræde i Viborg', *Kuml* 1968, pp. 83–92.

Møller, E. 1953: 'Romanske tagkonstruktioner', *Aarbøger for Nordisk Oldkyndighed og Historie* 1953, pp. 136–50.

1963: 'Træbygningskunsten. Fra stenalder til middelalder', *Danmarks bygningskunst. Fra oldtid til nutid* (H. Lund and K. Millec eds.). Copenhagen. Pp. 9–37.

Møller, E. and Olsen, O. 1961: 'Danske trækirker', *Nationalmuseets Arbejdsmark* 1961, pp. 35–58.

Mårtensson, A. W. 1968: 'Aus dem frühmittelalterlichen Lund—ein Stock und eine Spange', *Res Medievales. Ragnar Blomqvist Kal. Mai. MCMLVIII oblata* (A. W. Mårtensson ed.). Lund. Pp. 217–27.

Mårtensson, A. W. ed. 1976: *Uppgrävt förflutet för PKbanken i Lund. En investering i arkeologi.* Lund.

Mårtensson, A. W. and Wahlöö, C. 1970: *Lundafynd. En bilderbok.* Karlshamn.

Nancke-Krogh, S. 1978: 'Søby—en landsby fra vikingetid på Nordsamsø', *Antikvariske Studier* 2, 1978, pp. 81–96.

Naumann, F. K. 1971: 'Metallkundliche Untersuchungen an drei wikingerzeitlichen Zieheisen aus Haithabu', *Berichte über die Ausgrabungen in Haithabu* 5 (K. Schietzel ed.). Neumünster. Pp. 84–99.

Neugebauer, W. 1968: 'Truso und Elbing, ein Beitrag zur Frühgeschichte des Weichelmündungsgebietes', *Studien zur europäischen Vor- und Frühgeschichte* (M. Claus et al.). Neumünster. Pp. 213–234.

Nielsen, I. and Schiørring, O. 1979: 'Roskildes middelalder på kort', *13 bidrag til Roskilde by og egn's historie. Udgivet i anledning af Roskilde Museum's 50 års jubilæum* (F. A. Birkebæk ed.). Roskilde Museum. Pp. 93–110.

Nielsen, K. M. 1974: 'Jelling problems. A discussion', *Mediaeval Scandinavia* 7, 1974, pp. 156–79.

Nielsen, L. C. 1976: 'Omgård—en vestjysk landsby fra vikingetid. En foreløbig redegørelse', *Hardsyssels Årbog* 1976, pp. 37–54.

1977: 'Omgård—en vestjysk landsby fra vikingetid. En redegørelse for de fortsatte undersøgelser 1976', *Hardsyssels Årbog* 1977, pp. 59–84.

Nielsen, S. 1976: 'En vikingetids landsby på Mors', *MIV (Museerne i Viborg amt)* 6, 1976, pp. 52–61.

Nielsen, S. and Noe, P. 1977: 'Karby', *MIV (Museerne i Viborg amt)* 7, 1977, pp. 5–11.

Nielsen, V. 1970: 'Agerlandets historie', *Danmarks Natur.* 8, *Agerlandet* (A. Nørrevang ed.). Copenhagen. Pp. 9–34.

1971: 'Lå vor ældste mølle i Vendsyssel', *Kuml* 1971, pp. 61–72.

Noe, P. 1976: 'Pre-Medieval plough marks in Viborg', *Tools and Tillage* III:1, 1976, pp. 59–64.

Nordqvist, J. 1976: 'Om konserveringen af jerngenstande fra Sdr. Onsild-gravene', *Aarbøger for Nordisk Oldkyndighed og Historie* 1976, pp. 52–6.

Nørlund, P. 1935: 'Bronzegeräte des Mittelalters', *Acta Archaeologica* VI, 1935, pp. 249–60.

1948: *Trelleborg.* Copenhagen.

Ohlhaver, H. 1939: *Der germanische Schmied und sein Werkzeug.* Leipzig.

Ohlsson, T. 1973: 'Vikingatid och medeltid i Löddeköpinge', *Ale* 1973:1, pp. 27–42.

1975–6: 'The Löddeköpinge Investigation I', *Meddelanden från Lunds universitets historiska museum* 1975–6, pp. 59–161.

1977: 'Tidigkristna gravar i Löddeköpinge', *Ale* 1977:4, pp. 1–18.

Ohlsson, T. and Cinthio, H. 1979: 'Löddeköpinge —Kävlingebygdens äldsta centralort', *Kävlingebygden nu och då* 1979, (Kävlinge), pp. 25–65.

Oldeberg, A. 1966: *Metallteknik under vikingatid och medeltid.* Stockholm.

Olsen, M. 1941: *Norges innskrifter med de yngre runer,* I. Oslo.

Olsen, O. 1956: 'Ørslev kirkes døbefont', *Fynske Minder* 1956, pp. 195–202.

1960: 'St. Jørgensbjærg kirke. Arkæologiske undersøgelser i murværk og gulv', *Aarbøger for Nordisk Oldkyndighed og Historie* 1960, pp. 1–71.

1962: 'Trelleborg-problemer. De danske vikingeborge og deres historiske baggrund', *Scandia* 28, 1962, pp. 92–112.

1963: 'Sankt Ibs kirke i Vindebode. Et bidrag til Roskildes ældste historie', *Fra Københavns Amt* 1962 (1963), pp. 61–87.

1966: *Hørg, hov og kirke.* Copenhagen.

1969: 'Die alte Gesellschaft und die neue Kirche', *Acta Visbyensia* III. Visby. Pp. 43–54.

1970: 'Vorchristliche Heiligtümer in Nordeuropa', *Vorgeschichtliche Heiligtümer und Opferplätze in Mittel- und Nordeuropa* (H.

Jahnkuhn ed.). Göttingen. Pp. 259–78.

1972a: 'Die frühen Städte in Dänemark—Forschungsstand', *Kiel Papers '72* (H. Hinz ed.). Kiel. Pp. 72–79.

1972b: 'Sankt Mikkel i Slagelse', *Nationalmuseets Arbejdsmark* 1972, pp. 131–152.

1974: 'The "sanctuary" at Jelling, with some observations on Jelling's significance in the Viking Age', in 'Jelling Problems. A Discussion'. *Mediaeval Scandinavia* 7, 1974, pp. 226–34.

1975a: 'Nogle tanker i anledning af Ribes uventet høje alder', *Fra Ribe Amt* 1975, pp. 225–58.

1975b: 'Viking fortresses in Denmark', *Recent Archaeological Excavations in Europe* (R. Bruce-Mitford ed.). London. Pp. 90–110.

1979: 'Die geometrischen dänischen Wikingerburgen', *Burgen aus Holz und Stein. Colloquium on fortresses at Basel 1977* (M.-L. Heyer-Boscardin ed.). Olten. Pp. 81–94.

Olsen, O. and Crumlin-Pedersen, O. 1967: 'The Skuldelev Ships', *Acta Archaeologica* XXXVIII, 1967, pp. 73–174.

1969: *Fem vikingeskibe fra Roskilde Fjord*. Roskilde. English edition: *Five Viking Ships from Roskilde Fjord*. Copenhagen 1978.

Olsen, O. and Schmidt, H. 1977. With contribution by H. Ødum and excursus by H. Helbæk: *Fyrkat. En jysk vikingeborg. 1. Borgen og bebyggelsen*. Copenhagen.

O'Meadhra, U. 1979: *Early Christian, Viking and Romanesque Art. Motif-pieces from Ireland*. Thesis and Papers in North-European Archaeology, University of Stockholm.

Ó Ríordáin, B. 1971: 'Excavations at High Street and Winetavern Street, Dublin', *Medieval Archaeology* XV, 1971, pp. 73–85.

1976: 'The High Street Excavations', *Proceedings of the Seventh Viking Congress. Dublin 1973* (B. Almqvist and D. Greene eds.). Royal Irish Academy. Pp. 135–40.

de Paor, L. 1976: 'The Viking Towns of Ireland', *Proceedings of the Seventh Viking Congress. Dublin 1973* (B. Almqvist and D. Greene eds.). Royal Irish Academy. Pp. 29–37.

Paulsen, P. 1936: *Der Goldschatz von Hiddensee*. Führer zur Urgeschichte 13. Leipzig.

Petersen, J. 1919: *De Norske Vikingesverd*. Kristiania.

1928: *Vikingetidens Smykker*. Stavanger.

1951: *Vikingetidens Redskaper*. Oslo.

Pleiner, R. *et al.* 1971: 'Untersuchung einer Eisenschlacke aus Haithabu', *Berichte über die Ausgrabungen in Haithabu* 5 (K. Schietzel ed.). Neumünster. Pp. 110–12.

Porsmose Christensen, E. 1977: 'Den stationære landsbys opståen. Overvejelser omkring den fynske bebyggelse på overgangstiden mellem oldtid og middelalder', *Kontinuitet og bebyggelse* (H. Thrane ed.). Skrifter fra institut for historie og samfundsvidenskab no. 22. Odense University. Pp. 66–75.

1979: 'Bebyggelse, kulturlandskab og driftsmåder på overgangen mellem yngre jernalder og ældre middelalder', *Fra jernalder til middelalder* (H. Thrane ed.). Skrifter fra Historisk Institut Odense University no. 27, pp. 118–39.

Proceedings of the Seventh Viking Congress, Dublin 1973 (B. Almqvist and D. Greene eds.). Royal Irish Academy.

Quellen des 9. und 11. Jahrhunderts zur Geschichte der Hamburgischen Kirche und des Reiches. Rimbert Leben Ansgars. Adam von Bremen. Bischofsgeschichte der Hamburger Kirche. Wipo Taten Kaiser Konrad II. Hermann von Reichenau Chronik (W. Trillmich and R. Buchner eds.). Darmstadt 1973. (Latin text and German translation.) The *Life* of Ansgar is also published in *Monumenta Germanicae Historica, Scriptores Rerum Germanicarum*, 55 (G. Waitz ed.). Hanover 1884.

Quellen zur Karolingischen Reichsgechichte I. Die Reichsannalen. Einhard Leben Karls des Grossen. Zwei 'Leben' Ludwigs. Nithard Geschichten (rev. R. Rau). Berlin 1955. (Latin text and German translation.)

Quellen zur Karolingischen Reichgeschichte II. Jahrbücher von St. Bertin. Jahrbücher von St. Vaast. Xantener Jahrbücher (rev. R. Rau). Berlin. (Latin text and German translation.)

Quellen zur Karolingischen Reichsgeschichte III. Jahrbücher von Fulda. Regino Chronik. Notker Taten Karls (rev. R. Rau). Berlin 1960. (Latin text and German translation.)

Rahtz, P. 1976: 'Buildings and rural settlement', *The Archaeology of Anglo-Saxon England* (D. M. Wilson ed.). London. Pp. 49–98.

Ramskou, T. 1950: 'Viking Age Cremation Graves in Denmark', *Acta Archaeologica* XXI, 1950, pp. 137–82.

1953: 'Lindholm Høje. Preliminary report', *Acta Archaeologica* XXIV, 1953, pp. 186–96.

1954: 'Lindholm Høje. En gravplads fra yngre jernalder og en boplads fra tidlig middelalder', *Fra Nationalmuseets Arbejdsmark* 1954, pp. 37–48.

1955: 'Lindholm Høje. Second preliminary report', *Acta Archaeologica* XXVI, 1955, pp. 177–85.

1957a: 'Et landbrug fra 1000-årene på Lindholm Høje', *Fra Nationalmuseets Arbejdsmark* 1957, pp. 83–96.

1957b: 'Lindholm Høje. Third preliminary report', *Acta Archaeologica* XXVIII, 1957, pp. 193–201.

1960a: 'To "naust" ved Harrevig', *Aarbøger for Nordisk Oldkyndighed og Historie* 1960, pp. 168–73.

1960b: *Lindholm Høje*. Nationalmuseets Blå Bøger. Copenhagen.

1962: *Danmarks Historie. 2: Normannertiden 600–1060* (J. Danstrup and H. Kock eds.). Copenhagen.

1963: 'Stil F. En skitse', *Aarbøger for Nordisk Oldkyndighed og Historie* 1963, pp. 100–18.

1963–5: 'Vikingerne ofrede mennesker', *Nationalmuseets Arbejdsmark* 1963–5, pp. 79–86.

1969: *Solstenen*. Copenhagen.

1976: *Lindholm Høje. Gravpladsen*. Copenhagen.

1977: 'Vikingebroen', *Skalk* 1977, no. 1, pp. 3–9.

Rausing, G. 1979: 'Grubehuse', *Skalk* 1979, no. 1, pp. 16–17.

Reallexikon der Germanischen Altertumskunde = *RGA*.

Regteren Altena, H. H. van and Heidinga, H. A. 1977: 'The North Sea region in the Early Medieval period (400–950). *Ex horreo*', *IPP 1951–1976*. Albert Egges van Giffen instituut voor prae- en protohistorie. Amsterdam 1977. Pp. 47–67.

Reichstein, H. and Thiessen, M. 1974: 'Untersuchungen an Tierknochenfunde (1963–1964)', *Berichte über die Ausgrabungen in Haithabu* 7 (K. Schietzel ed.). Neumünster.

Resi, H. G. 1978: 'Skandinavisk handel mot sør og vest i vikingtid', *XV Nordiska Arkeologmötet 1978*. Pt. 4:1.

1979: 'Die Specksteinfunde aus Haithabu', *Berichte über die Ausgrabungen in Haithabu* 14 (K. Schietzel ed.). Neumünster.

RGA = *Reallexikon der Germanischen Altertumskunde*, vol. 1ff., (H. Beck *et al.*). Berlin, New York 1973ff.

Roesdahl, E. 1974: 'The northern mound: burial chamber and grave goods', in 'Jelling Problems. A discussion'. *Mediaeval Scandinavia* 7, 1974, pp. 208–23.

1975: 'A forgotten casket hinge from the burial chamber at Jelling', *Mediaeval Scandinavia* 8, 1975, pp. 21–6.

1976: 'Otte vikingetidsgrave i Sdr. Onsild', *Aarbøger for Nordisk Oldkyndighed og Historie* 1976, pp. 22–51.

1977a. With contribution by Else Østergård and appendix by Peter Wagner: *Fyrkat. En jysk vikingeborg. II. Oldsagerne og gravpladsen.* Copenhagen.

1977b: 'Aggersborg. The Viking settlement and fortress', *Chateau Gaillard* VIII, 1976 (Caen 1977), pp. 269–78.

1977c: 'Borgenes borg', *Skalk* 1977, no. 2, pp. 3–9.

1977d: 'Danmarks ældste relikvieskrin?' *MIV* (*Museerne i Viborg amt*) 7, 1977, pp. 26–33.

1978: 'Vognen og vikingerne', *Skalk* 1978, no. 4, pp. 9–14.

1979: 'Saltede helte', *Skalk* 1979, no. 5, p. 32.

1980: 'Aggersborg in the Viking Age', *Proceedings of the Eighth Viking Congress. Arhus 1977* (H. Bekker Nielsen, P. Foote and O. Olsen eds.). Odense 1981.

at press: Review of Müller-Wille 1976a, in *Zeitschrift für Archäologie des Mittelalters* (probably 1981).

Roesdahl, E., Graham-Campbell, J., Connor, P. and Pearson, K. eds. 1981: *The Vikings in England*. London.

Rosenlund, K. 1976: *Catalogue of subfossil Danish vertebrates. Fishes*. Copenhagen.

Rydberg, O. S. ed. 1877: *Sverges Traktater med främmande Magter* I, 822–1335. Stockholm.

Rønneseth, O. 1968: 'Das Zentrum der ältesten Mühlsteinindustrie in Norwegen', *Studien zur europäischen Vor- und Frühgeschichte* (M. Claus *et al.*). Neumünster. Pp. 241–252.

Sawyer, P. H. 1971: *The Age of the Vikings* (2nd edn.). London.

1978a: *From Roman Britain to Norman England*. London.

1978b: 'Wics, Kings and Vikings', *The Vikings. Proceedings of the Symposium of the Faculty of Arts of Uppsala University 6–9 June, 1977* (T. Andersson and K. I. Sandred eds.). Uppsala. Pp. 23–31.

Saxonis Gesta Danorum I (J. Olrik and H. Ræder eds.). Copenhagen 1931.

Schaefer, U. 1963: *Anthropologische Untersuchung der Skelette von Haithabu*. Neumünster.

Schetelig, H. 1920: *Osebergfundet* III (A. W. Brøgger, Hj. Falk, H. Schetelig eds.).

Kristiania.

Schietzel, K. 1968: 'Zur Frage einer wirtschaftlichen und socialen Gliederung Haithabus', *Studien zur europäischen Vor- und Frühgeschichte* (M. Claus *et al.*). Neumünster. Pp. 253–7.

1969: 'Die archäologischen Befunde der Ausgrabung Haithabu 1963–1964', *Berichte über die Ausgrabungen in Haithabu* 1 (K. Schietzel ed.). Neumünster. Pp. 9–60.

1970: 'Hölzerne Kleinfunde aus Haithabu (Ausgrabung 1963–1964)', *Berichte über die Ausgrabungen in Haithabu* 4 (K. Schietzel ed.). Neumünster. Pp. 77–91.

1974: 'Bemerkungen zur Erforschung der Topographie von Haithabu', *Vor- und Frühformen der europäischen Stadt im Mittelalter* (H. Jankuhn *et al.*). Göttingen. Pp. 30–9.

1975: 'Haithabu. Ein Beiträg zur Entwicklung frühstädtischer Siedlungsformen Nordeuropas', *Ausgrabungen in Deutschland*. Monograph of the Römisch-Germanischen Zentralmuseum 1, pt. III, 1975, pp. 57–71.

Schietzel, K. and Ulbricht, I. 1977: 'Bemerkungen zu Bestattungen und verstreuten Skeletresten der Ausgrabung Haithabu (1963–1969)', *Berichte über die Ausgrabungen in Haithabu* 11 (K. Schietzel ed.). Neumünster. Pp. 57–63.

Schiørring, O. 1978: 'Korset i øksen', *Skalk* 1978, no. 6, pp. 28–29.

Schlabow, K. 1940: 'Textilfunde aus Haithabu', *Offa* 5, 1940, pp. 83–6.

Schledermann, H. 1966: 'Slesvig/Hedebys tilblivelse I', *Sønderjyske Arbøger* 1966, pp. 1–65.

1967: 'Slesvig/Hedebys tilblivelse II', *Sønderjyske Arbøger* 1967, pp. 1–73.

1974: 'Skibe på ruller og i kanaler', *Sønderjyske Arbøger* 1974, pp. 5–33.

Schmidt, H. 1970: 'Vikingernes husformede gravsten', *Nationalmuseets Arbejdsmark* 1970, pp. 13–28.

1973: 'The Trelleborg house reconsidered', *Medieval Archaeology* XVII, 1973, pp. 52–77.

Schoknecht, U. 1977: *Menzlin. Ein frühgeschichtlicher Handelsplatz an der Peene.* Berlin (DDR).

Schou Jørgensen, M. 1975: 'Oldtidsguld', *Guld fra Nordvestsjælland* (M. Schou Jørgensen ed.). Holbæk, pp. 29–110.

1977a: 'Risby-vejene', *Nationalmuseets Arbejdsmark* 1977, pp. 42–51.

1977b: 'Veje af træ', *Antikvariske Studier. Tilegnet Knud Thorvildsen*, 1977, pp. 147–162.

1979: 'En vikingetids bro og vejdæmning over Gudenåen', in 'Mindre meddelelser', *Antikvariske Studier* 3, 1979, pp. 226–7.

Schou Jørgensen, M., Lund Hansen, U., Balslev Jørgensen, J., Hatting, T. and Nielsen, H. 1978: 'Himlingeøje-gravpladsens høje', *Antikvariske Studier* 2, 1978, pp. 47–80.

Schuldt, E. 1975: *Burgen, Brücken und Strassen des frühen Mittelalters in Mecklenburg*. Schwerin.

Schultz, C. G. 1936: 'Hominde og Pæleværket i Vestre Skarholmsrende', *Lolland-Falsters historiske Samfunds Aarbog* XXIV, 1936, pp. 95–114.

1949: 'Aggersborg. Vikingelejren ved Limfjorden', *Fra Nationalmuseets Arbejdsmark* 1949, pp. 91–108.

1952: 'Jellingbægeret—vor ældste kristne Kalk?', *Kuml* 1952, pp. 187–98.

Schwarz-Mackensen, G. 1976: 'Die Knochennadeln von Haithabu', *Berichte über die Ausgrabungen in Haithabu* 9 (K. Schietzel ed.). Neumünster.

1978: 'Thorshämmer aus Haithabu', *Berichte über die Ausgrabungen in Haithabu* 12 (K. Schietzel ed.). Neumünster. Pp. 85–94.

Seehann, G. 1977: 'Pilzfunde aus Haithabu', *Berichte über die Ausgrabungen in Haithabu* 11 (K. Schietzel ed.). Neumünster. Pp. 120–140.

Selling, D. 1955: *Wikingerzeitliche und frühmittelalterliche Keramik in Schweden*. Stockholm.

Shetelig, H. ed. 1940–54: *Viking Antiquities in Great Britain and Ireland* I–VI. Oslo 1940 and 1954.

Skjølsvold, A. 1961: *Klebersteinsindustrien i vikingetiden*. Oslo-Bergen.

Skov, T. 1972–3: 'Vikingetidsbopladsen i Trabjerg', *Holstebro Museum. Arsskrift* 1972–3, pp. 58–66.

1979: 'En vikingetidsbebyggelse i Herrup', *Antikvariske Studier* 3, 1979, pp. 61–8.

Skovgaard-Petersen, I. 1977: 'Oldtid og vikingetid', *Danmarks historie 1. Tiden indtil 1340*. (A. E. Christensen *et al.*). Copenhagen. Pp. 15–209.

Skovmand, R. 1942: De danske Skattefund fra Vikingetiden og den ældste Middelalder indtil omkring 1150, *Aarbøger for Nordisk Oldkyndighed og Historie* 1942.

Skyum-Nielsen, N. 1967: *Vikingerne i Paris. Beretninger fra 9. årh.*—trans. and annotated N. Skyum-Nielsen (2nd rev. edn.). Copenhagen.

1979: Review of *Vikingerne i Franken. Skriftlige kilder fra det 9. århundrede*, trans. Erling Albrechtsen (1976), *Historisk Tidsskrift* 79, Copenhagen 1979, pp. 223–25.

Skaarup, J. 1976. With contributions from Anne Kromann, Lise Bender Jørgensen, Peter Wagner, Rolf Gilberg and Jan Jacobsen: *Stengade II. En langelandsk gravplads med grave fra romersk jernalder og vikingetid.* Rudkøbing.

Statistisk Årbog 1978. Copenhagen.

Steen Jensen, J. 1977: 'Kirkegulvsmønter', *Hikuin* 3, 1977, pp. 295–302.

Steensberg, A. 1943: *Ancient harvesting Implements*. Copenhagen.

1952: *Bondehuse og vandmøller i Danmark gennem 2000 år*. Copenhagen.

1959: 'En skvatmølle i Ljørring', *Kuml* 1959, pp. 130–45.

1973: *Den danske landsby gennem 6000 år*. Copenhagen.

1978: 'The horizontal water mill. A contribution to its early history', *Prace i materiały Muzeum Archeologicznego i Etnograficznego W Łodzi. Seria Archaeologiczna* 25, 1978, pp. 345–56.

Steensberg, A. *et al.* 1968: *Atlas over en del af middelalderlandsbyen Borups agre*. With text volume. Copenhagen.

Steensberg, A. and Østergaard Christensen, J. L. 1974: *Store Valby*. Copenhagen.

Steenstrup, J. 1876: *Normannerne*, I. Copenhagen (photographic repr., Copenhagen 1972).

Steffensen, J. 1953: 'The Physical Anthropology of the Vikings', *The Journal of the Royal Anthropological Institute of Great Britain and Ireland* 83:1, 1953, pp. 86–97.

Stein, F. 1967: *Adelsgräber des achten Jahrhunderts in Deutschland*. Berlin.

Stenberger, M. ed. 1943: *Forntida gårdar i Island*. Copenhagen.

Stenberger, M. 1947 and 1958: *Die Schatzfunde Gotlands der Wikingerzeit* I–II. Stockholm.

1964: *Det forntida Sverige*. Uppsala.

Stenton, Sir F. 1967: *Anglo-Saxon England* (2nd edn.). Oxford 1947 (repr. 1967).

Steuer, H. 1973: 'Gewichte aus Haithabu', *Berichte über die Ausgrabungen in Haithabu* 6 (K. Schietzel ed.). Neumünster. Pp. 9–22.

1974: *Die Südsiedlung von Haithabu. Studien zur frühmittelalterlichen Keramik im Nordseekustbereich und in Schleswig-Holstein.* Neumünster.

1978: 'Geldgeschäfte und Hoheitsrechte im Vergleich zwischen Ostseeländern und islamischer Welt', *Zeitschrift für Archäologie* 12:2, 1978, pp. 255–60.

Stiesdal, H. 1960: 'Kanalen der skærer Samsø over', *Skalk* 1960, no. 4, pp. 6–8.

1964: 'Kanhavekanalen på Samsø', *CN-Post* (Christiani and Nielsen), no. 65, May 1964, pp. 27–30.

1977: 'En middelalderlig gravplads i Stenløse', *Antikvariske Studier. Tilegnet Knud Thorvildsen*, 1977, pp. 203–10.

Stoklund, M. and Moltke, E. 1978: 'Runestenen ved Klejtrup sø', *MIV* (Museerne i Viborg amt) 8, 1978, pp. 56–7.

Stoumann, I. 1977: 'Vikingetidslandsbyen i Sædding', *Mark og Montre* 1977, pp. 30–42.

1978: *De der blev hjemme—En vikingelandsby ved Esbjerg*. Esbjerg (n.d.).

1979: 'Sæddinglandsbyen og et nyt projekt omkring landbyen Hostrup til belysning af vikingetidens bebyggelse i SV-jylland', *Fra jernalder til middelalder* (H. Thrane ed.). Skrifter fra Historisk Institut, Odense University no. 27, pp. 55–62.

Strand Petersen, K. 1975: 'Om Limfjordens postglaciale marine udvikling og niveauforhold, belyst ved mollusk-faunaen og C-14 dateringer', *Danmarks Geologiske Undersøgelser Arbog* 1975, pp. 75–103.

Strömberg, M. 1961: *Untersuchungen zur jüngeren Eisenzeit in Schonen* I–II. Lund.

1964–5: 'Ein Wikingerzeitlicher Kumtbeschlag von Sinclairsholm in Schonen', *Meddelanden från Lunds Universitets historiska museum* 1964–5, pp. 107–31.

1969–70: 'Grubenhäuser in Valleberga', *Meddelanden från Lunds Universitets historiska museum* 1969–70, pp. 192–265.

1978: *En kustby i Ystad, före stadens tilkomst*. Ystad.

Sweet, H. ed. 1883: *King Alfred's Orosius*. Early English Text Society, 79. London.

Søgård, H. 1961: *Det ældste Arhus*. Århus.

Sørensen, C. and E. H. 1978: *Danmark i vikingetiden. Problemer vedrørende den sociale struktur. Historiske kilder*. Copenhagen.

Tauber, H. 1966: 'Danske kulstof-14 dateringer af arkæologiske prøver II', *Aarbøger for Nordisk Oldkyndighed og Historie* 1966, pp. 102–130.

Taylor, H. M. and Taylor, J. 1965: *Anglo-Saxon Architecture*. Cambridge.

The Vikings. Proceedings of the Symposium of the

Faculty of Arts of Uppsala University, 6–9
June 1977 (T. Andersson and K. I. Sandred
eds.). Uppsala 1978.

Thietmar von Merseburg: Chronik. Ausgewählte
Quellen zur deutschen Geschichte des
Mittelalters IX. Freiherr vom Stein-
Gedächtnisausgabe (R. Buchner ed.).
Darmstadt 1970. (Latin text and German
translation.)

Thomsen, N. 1969: 'Grubehuse i Esbjerg', Mark
og Montre 1969, pp. 37–40.

Thomsen, R. 1967: 'Undersøgelse af jernalder-
slagger og jerngenstande fra Hagestad i
Skåne', Kuml 1967, pp. 124–42.

— 1971a: 'Metallografische Untersuchungen an
drei wikingerzeitlichen Eisenäxten aus
Haithabu', Berichte über die Ausgrabungen in
Haithabu 5 (K. Schietzel ed.). Neumünster.
Pp. 30–57.

— 1971b: 'Metallografische Untersuchung einer
wikingerzeitlichen Lanzenspitze aus Haithabu' Berichte über die Ausgrabungen in Haithabu
5 (K. Schietzel ed.). Neumünster. Pp. 58–
83.

— 1971c: 'Metallografische Untersuchungen an
wikingerzeitlichen Eisenbarren aus Haithabu', Berichte über die Ausgrabungen in
Haithabu 5 (K. Schietzel ed.). Neumünster.
Pp. 9–29.

— 1971d: 'Essestein und Ausheizschlacken aus
Haithabu—Zur Technik des wikingerzeitlichen Schmiedens', Berichte über die
Ausgrabungen in Haithabu 5 (K. Schietzel
ed.). Neumünster. Pp. 100–9.

— 1975: Et meget mærkeligt metal. Varde Stålværk.

Thordeman, B. et al. 1939: Armour from the Battle
of Wisby 1361 I. Uppsala.

Thorvildsen, E. 1972: 'Dankirke', Nationalmuseets Arbejdsmark 1972, pp. 47–60.

Thorvildsen, K. 1950: 'En tylvt økser fra vikingetiden', Aarbøger for Nordisk Oldkyndighed og
Historie 1950, pp. 352–8.

— 1957: Ladbyskibet. Copenhagen.

— 1961: 'Den tredie bådgrav', Skalk 1961, no. 1,
pp. 3–7.

Thrane, H. 1978: 'Gipsens arkæologi', Skalk
1978, no. 2, pp. 8–11.

— ed. 1979: Fra jernalder til middelalder. Beretning
fra et symposium 17.–19. maj 1979 afholdt
af Odense Universitet. Skrifter fra Historisk
Institut, Odense University no. 27.

Thun, E. 1962–3: 'Die Wassermühlen, ein
ökonomischer Entwicklungsfaktor der mit-
telalterlichen Städte Schonens', Meddelanden
från Lunds Universitets historiska museum
1962–3, pp. 224–37.

Trap Danmark I–XV (N. Nielsen et al.). Copenhagen 1958–72.

Trimpe Burger, J. A. 1973: 'Oost-Souburg,
Province of Zeeland: a Preliminary Report on
the Excavation of the Site of an Ancient
Fortress (1969–1971)', Berichten van de
R.O.B. 1973, pp. 355–65.

— 1975: 'The geometrical fortress of Oost-
Souburg (Zeeland)', Chateau Gaillard VII,
1974 (Caen 1975), pp. 215–19.

Ulbricht, I. 1978: Die Geweihverarbeitung in
Haithabu. Neumünster.

Ullemeyer, R. 1970: 'Textil- und Lederfunde aus
Haithabu (Ausgrabung 1963–1964)', Berichte
über die Ausgrabungen in Haithabu 4 (K.
Schietzel ed.). Neumünster. Pp. 56–68.

Varangian Problems. Scando-Slavica. Supplement 1. Report on the first international
symposium on 'The Eastern Connections of the
Nordic Peoples in the Viking Period and Early
Middle Ages', Moesgård—University of
Aarhus 7–11 October 1968 (K. Hannestad
et al.). Copenhagen 1970.

Veibæk, O. 1974: Ploven og dens betydning, med
særligt henblik på landsbyorganisationen (Dissertation in history, Copenhagen University,
duplicated 1974).

Vellev, J. 1973: 'Adjunkt Feddersen og vikinge-
graven i Mammen', MIV (Museerne i Viborg
amt) 3, 1973, pp. 44–57.

Vensild, H. 1970: 'Navndrupåsen', Bidrag 1 til
Viborgegnens topografi og historie. Viborg
Stiftsmuseum, pp. 52–70.

Vikingesskibshallens Bådelaug 1980: Nordlands-
båden—analyseret og prøvesejlet af Vikingeskibshallens Bådelaug. Working Papers,
National Museum, Copenhagen 12.

Viking Settlement to Medieval Dublin. Curriculum
Development Unit. Dublin 1978.

Vogel, V. 1974: 'Archäologische Untersuchungen
in der Altstadt von Schleswig', Vor- und
Frühformen der europäischen Stadt im
Mittelalter (H. Jankuhn et al.), Göttingen,
pp. 101–12.

— 1977: 'Die Anfänge des Schleswiger Hafens'
Ausgrabungen in Schleswig. 7.Bericht,
Beiträge zur Schleswiger Stadtgeschichte 22,
1977, pp. 21–8.

von Müller, A. 1970: 'Karneolperlen aus
Haithabu', Berichte über die Ausgrabungen
in Haithabu 4 (K. Schietzel ed.). Neumünster, pp. 53–5.

Vorting, H. C. 1970: 'Flere grubehuse og andet
nyt fra vikingetiden i Esbjerg', Mark og
Montre 1970, pp. 21–7.

— 1972a: 'Gammelby, en vikingetidsbebyggelse i
Esbjerg', Mark og Montre 1972, pp. 20–6.

— 1972b: 'Inden Esbjerg', Skalk 1972, no. 4,
pp. 3–9.

Voss, F., Müller-Wille, M. and Raabe, E.-W.
1973: 'Das Höftland von Langballigau an der
Flensburger Förde. Die Oberflächenformen.
Das jüngereisenzeitliche Gräberfeld. Die
Vegetation der Mündungsniederung', Offa
30, 1973, pp. 60–132.

Voss, O. 1959: 'Bækkemonumentet', Fra Ribe
Amt 1959, pp. 660–70.

de Vries, J. 1923: De Wikingen in de Lage
Landen bij de Zee. Haarlem.

Wagner, P. 1976: 'Ved-bestemmelser fra Sdr.
Onsild-fundet, med forsøg til en kisterekon-
struktion', Aarbøger for Nordisk Oldkyndighed
og Historie 1976, pp. 57–86.

Wahlöö, C. 1976: Keramik 1000–1600 i svenska
fynd. Lund.

Wallace-Hadrill, J. M. 1975: The Vikings in
Francia. The Stenton Lecture 1974. University of Reading.

Warnke, D. 1978: 'Funde und Grabsitten des
Gräberfeldes in den "Schwarzen Bergen" bei
Ralswiek im Rahmen der kulturellen
Beziehungen im Ostseegebiet', Zeitschrift für
Archäologie 12:2, 1978, pp. 275–82.

Waterman, D. M. 1959: 'Late Saxon, Viking and
Early Medieval Finds from York', Archaeologia XCVII, 1959, pp. 59–105.

Wendt, W. 1978: 'Untersuchungen an Skeletresten von Hunden', Berichte über die

Ausgrabungen in Haithabu 13 (K. Schietzel ed.). Neumünster.

White jr., L. 1964: *Medieval Technology and Social Change*. Oxford.

Whitelock, D. ed. 1979 (1955): *English Historical Documents c. 500–1042*. London.

Widukind: *Sachsengeschichte. Quellen zur Geschichte der sächsischen Kaiserzeit* (rev. A. Bauer and R. Rau). Darmstadt 1971. (Latin text and German translation.) *Monumenta Germaniae Historica. Scriptores Rerum Germanicarum* 60. (G. Waitz and K. Kehr eds.). Hanover 1904.

Wilson, D. M. 1955: 'An Irish mounting in the National Museum, Copenhagen', *Acta Archaeologica* XXVI 1955, pp. 163–72.

— 1960a: 'Irsk-britisk import i Lejre', *Nationalmuseets Arbejdsmark* 1960, pp. 36–7.

— 1960b: 'The Fejø Cup', *Acta Archaeologica* XXXI, 1960, pp. 147–73.

— 1964: *Anglo-Saxon ornamental metalwork 700–1100 in The British Museum*. London.

— 1965: 'Some neglected late Anglo-Saxon swords', *Medieval Archaeology* IX, 1965, pp. 32–54.

— 1967: 'The Vikings' relationship with Christianity in Northern England', *Journal of the Archaeological Association*, 3rd ser., vol. XXX, 1967, pp. 37–46.

— 1968: 'Anglo-Saxon carpenters' tools', *Studien zur europäischen Vor- und Frühgeschichte* (M. Claus et al.). Neumünster. Pp. 143–150.

— 1974: 'Men de ligger i London', *Skalk* 1974, no. 5, pp. 3–8.

— 1976a: 'Defence in the Viking Age', *Problems in Economic and Social Archaeology* (G. de G. Sieveking et al.). London. Pp. 439–445.

— 1976b: 'Craft and industry', *The Archaeology of Anglo-Saxon England* (D. M. Wilson ed.). London. Pp. 253–81.

— 1976c: 'The Scandinavians in England', *The Archaeology of Anglo-Saxon England* (D. M. Wilson ed.). London. Pp. 393–403.

— 1976d: 'Scandinavian Settlement in the North and West of The British Isles—an archaeological point-of-view', *Transactions of The Royal Historical Society*, 5th ser., vol. 26, 1976, pp. 95–113.

— 1976e: 'The Borre style in the British Isles', *Minjar og Menntir. Afmælisrit helgad Kristjáni Eldjárn*. Reykjavik. Pp. 502–9.

— 1978a: *Civil and military engineering in Viking Age Scandinavia*. First Paul Johnstone Memorial Lecture. National Maritime Museum (Greenwich).

— 1978b: 'Vikingarna i väst: de ekonomiska aspekternas arkeologiska grundval', *Vid älven. Göteborgs Arkeologiska Museum Arstryck* 1974–8, pp. 85–101.

— 1978c: 'The Dating of Viking Art in England', *Anglo-Saxon and Viking Age Sculpture and its Context* (J. Lang ed.). BAR British Series 49, Oxford, pp. 135–44.

— 1980a: *Economic Aspects of the Vikings in the West—the Archaeological Basis*. Gothenburg University.

— 1980b: 'The Viking adventure', *The Northern World* (D. M. Wilson ed.). London. Pp. 159–82.

Wilson, D. M. and Klindt-Jensen, O. 1966: *Viking Art*. London 1966 (2nd edn. 1980). For Danish ed. see Klindt-Jensen, O. and Wilson, D. M. 1965.

Wittendorf, A. 1973: *Alvej og kongevej. Studier i samfærdselsforhold og vejenes topografi i det 16. og 17. århundrede*. Copenhagen.

Worsaae, I. I. A. 1869: 'Om Mammenfundet', *Aarbøger for Nordisk Oldkyndighed og Historie* 1869, pp. 203–17.

Wulff Andersen, S. 1977a: 'Vikingerne i Lejre', *Historisk årbog fra Roskilde amt* 1977, pp. 11–23.

— 1977b: 'To kilo guld', *Skalk* 1977, no. 3, pp. 4–7.

— 1979: 'Mellem Kongeå og grænse i den sene jernalder. En arkæologisk oversigt', *Fra Nordslesvigske Museer* 6, 1979, pp. 42–52.

Wulff Andersen, S. and Hatting, T. 1978: 'En vikingegrav fra Vestsjælland', *Arbog for historisk Samfund for Sorø amt* 1978, pp. 24–33.

Wåhlin Andersen, V. 1964: 'Skuldelev-skibene i perspektiv', *Skalk* 1964, no. 4, pp. 10–15.

Zachrisson, I. 1960: 'De ovala spännbucklornas tillvirkningssätt', *Tor* 6, 1960, pp. 207–38.

Żak, J. 1963–7: '*Importy*' *skandynawskie na ziemiach zachodniosłowiańskich od IX do XI wieku* 1–3. Poznań 1963, 1967.

— 1970: 'Der westslawische Import in Skandinavien im 9. bis 11. Jahrhundert', *Berichte über den II. Internationalen Kongress für Slawische Archäologie*, 1. Berlin, pp. 25–38.

— 1975: 'Kontakte zwischen Skandinaviern und Westslawen des 9–11. Jahrhunderts n. Chr. im Lichte der archäologischen Quellen', *Offa* 32, 1975, pp. 48–56.

Zettel, H. 1977: *Das Bild der Normannen und der Normanneneinfälle in westfränkischen und angelsächsischen Quellen des 8. bis 11. Jahrhunderts*. Munich.

Zippelius, A. 1969: 'Zur Frage der Dachkonstruktion bei den Holzbauten von Haithabu', *Berichte über die Ausgrabungen in Haithabu* 1 (K. Schietzel ed.). Neumünster. Pp. 61–72.

Ørsnes, M. 1959: 'Det ældste Aalborg', *Skalk* 1959, no. 1, pp. 6–7.

— 1966: *Form og stil i Sydskandinaviens yngre germanske jernalder*. Copenhagen.

— 1968: Review of David M. Wilson and Ole Klindt-Jensen: *Viking Art*, London 1966. *Mediaeval Scandinavia* 1, 1968, Reviews and Notes, pp. 204–213.

Østergård, E. 1976: 'Vikingetidstextiler fra Sdr. Onsild', *Aarbøger for nordisk Oldkyndighed og Historie* 1976, pp. 87–95.

Aaby, B. 1974: 'Cykliske klimavariationer de sidste 7500 år påvist ved undersøgelser af højmoser og marine transgressionsfaser', *Danmarks Geologiske Undersøgelser. Arbog* 1974, pp. 91–104.

Note: Among the books on Vikings published in Spring 1980 and not included in this bibliography, J. Graham-Campbell's *Viking Artefacts. A Select Catalogue* (British Museum, 1980) is particularly relevant to many of the subjects discussed in this book. Klaus Randsborg, in *The Viking Age in Denmark* (London, 1980), gives an account which in some aspects is completely different from the approach of the present work.